READING THE AMERICAN PAST

Selected Historical Documents
Volume I To 1877

READING THE AMERICAN PAST

SECOND EDITION

Selected Historical Documents
Volume I To 1877

MICHAEL P. JOHNSON, EDITOR
Johns Hopkins University

Bedford/St. Martin's ◆ Boston   New York

For Bedford/St. Martin's
Publisher of History: Patricia A. Rossi
Developmental Editor: Louise Townsend
Production Editor: Thomas P. Crehan
Production Supervisor: Maria R. Gonzalez
Marketing Manager: Jenna Bookin Barry
Copyeditor: Barbara Sutton
Indexer: Steve Csipke
Cover Design: Donna Lee Dennison
Cover Art: Painted wooden eagle drum: Fort Ticonderoga Museum
Text Composition: Karla Goethe, Orchard Wind Graphics
Printing and Binding: Haddon Craftsmen, Inc.

President: Charles H. Christensen
Editorial Director: Joan E. Feinberg
Director of Marketing: Karen Melton
Director of Editing, Design, and Production: Marcia Cohen
Managing Editor: Elizabeth Schaaf

Manufactured in the United States of America.

6   5   4   3   2   1
f   e   d   c   b   a

For information, write: Bedford/St. Martin's
75 Arlington Street, Boston MA 02116 (617–399–4000)

ISBN 0–312–39132–3

Acknowledgments

PREFACE FOR INSTRUCTORS

R*eading the American Past* is a collection of compelling firsthand accounts intended to provide depth and breadth to the discussion of important events, ideas, and experiences found in *The American Promise: A History of the United States,* Second Edition — the textbook to which I contribute — and other comprehensive U.S. survey texts. Organized chapter by chapter to parallel *The American Promise,* these sources offer teachers many educational options. Above all, *Reading the American Past* seeks to ignite the sparks of historical imagination that every teacher hopes to see in students' eyes.

Reading a textbook discussion of Columbus's arrival in the New World, for example, gives students basic, up-to-date information that has been collected, sorted out, and synthesized over the past 500 years. But reading the words Columbus wrote in his log shortly after he stepped ashore in the Western Hemisphere recaptures as no textbook can that moment of immense, mutual surprise when fifteenth-century Europeans and the people they called Indians first encountered one another. As every historian knows, primary sources bridge from the present, when they are read, to the past, when they were written. They encourage students to venture across that span connecting present and past and to risk discovering a captivating and unexpected world.

Three basic principles guided my selection of documents. First and foremost, the sources highlight major events and significant perspectives of a given historical era. Second, I chose and edited documents to be accessible, interesting, and often surprising to survey course students. Third, I sought sources that lend themselves to analysis in classroom discussion and writing assignments — documents that vividly portray controversies marking a particular historical moment and that offer multiple avenues of interpretation. To help students read and interpret the sources, consistently user-friendly editorial features appear. These features have been kept brief, providing just enough information to allow students to explore the sources and make their own discoveries. By minimizing editorial interventions, I hope to encourage students to focus on the documents and to become astonished, perplexed, and invigorated by what they read.

This new edition incorporates the insights and suggestions of teachers and students throughout the nation who have used *Reading the American Past*. Guided by their classroom experiences, I worked to include more documents of social and cultural history that capture the viewpoints of ordinary Americans, women and men, Native Americans and newcomers, westerners and easterners, immigrants and minorities, workers and bosses — overall, 25 percent of the documents are new to this edition. To aid students' reading and analysis of the sources, I revised and expanded the questions that accompany each document. New "Questions for Reading and Discussion" point toward key passages in the texts and encourage students to consider both the language of the document and its historical context. Likewise, each chapter concludes with thought-provoking "Comparative Questions" that ask students to consider ways in which the documents comment on one another and disclose the larger historical processes that shaped their era.

FEATURES

A wide variety of perspectives and sources. The documents assembled here provide students with a generous cross-section of the diverse experiences that comprise the American past. The reflections of politicians and thieves, generals and privates, reformers and reprobates can be found here, along with those of the nation's countless ethnic and religious minorities. Classic sources such as John Winthrop's *Arbella* sermon (Volume I, Chapter 3, Document 1), George Kennan's "Long Telegram" (Volume II, Chapter 25, Document 2), and Ronald Reagan's "Evil Empire" speech (Volume II, Chapter 30, Document 1), disclose the perspectives of influential leaders. The no less significant views of common people are revealed by such documents as seventeenth-century witchcraft depositions, the confessions of a slave insurrectionist, and letters from working people to New Dealers. Diaries and court cases convey the immediacy of history as lived experience. Reminiscences and oral histories illuminate the past with memories of participants. Speeches, manifestos, congressional testimony, and White House tape recordings spotlight the ends and means of political power. Essays, addresses, poems, and passages from books offer the considered opinions of cultural leaders, whether captains of industry, novelists, poets, or social critics.

Allows instructors flexibility in the classroom. The selections in *Reading the American Past* allow instructors to choose documents that best serve their teaching needs. Teachers might, for example, ask students to read documents in preparation for lectures, then refer to the assigned selections as they explain, say, Puritanism or the Civil War. An instructor might devote a class to explicating a single source, such as a Mexican account of the Spanish Conquest (Volume I, Chapter 1, Document 4), or Reinhold Niebuhr's probing reflections about the meaning of Christianity in Detroit of the 1920s (Volume II, Chapter 22, Document 2). The documents are ideally suited for provoking discussions in section meetings. Students can be asked to adopt and defend the viewpoint of a given source, to attack it from the perspective of a historical contemporary, to dissect its assumptions and evasions, or to compare and contrast it with other sources. Selections might also be used for brief writing assignments, longer papers, or examinations. The documents open these and many other possibilities for inspiring students to investigate the American past.

An Introduction for Students. A short introduction at the outset of each volume explains the significance of documents for understanding history and outlines basic questions that students should ask themselves in order to decipher any primary source.

Useful chapter apparatus. A brief paragraph begins each chapter, setting the documents in the larger historical context detailed in the corresponding chapter of the textbook. A headnote precedes every document, identifying the source, explaining when it was produced, by whom, and why it presents a revealing point of view. Rather than cluttering documents with numerous explanatory notes, I have assumed that students will—and should—refer to a textbook for basic information about the people and events that appear in the sources.

Questions that help students get the most out of the sources. To guide students toward key passages and central ideas, "Questions for Reading and Discussion" follow each document. They are intended to help students identify fundamental points, analyze what a document means, and think about its larger historical significance. "Comparative Questions" at the end of each chapter ask students to ponder some of the similarities and differences among the chapter's documents, and to consider how the ideas, observations, and viewpoints expressed reveal the major historical developments of the time.

To see more clearly along the many angles of historical vision offered by the documents, students rely on the guidance, insight, and wisdom of their teachers. *Reading the American Past* gives instructors numerous opportunities to entice students to become active collaborators in the study of American history. Ideally, these documents will help persuade students that the American past is neither frozen in time nor entombed in books, but instead shapes their present and prefigures their future. Ideally, they will come to see that they do not simply read American history; they live it.

ACKNOWLEDGMENTS

I am indebted to my coauthors of *The American Promise* — James L. Roark, Patricia Cline Cohen, Sarah Stage, Alan Lawson, and Susan M. Hartmann — for invaluable suggestions of provocative documents. I have also benefited immeasurably from the thoughtful comments of the following historians who have shared their professional insights and their classroom experiences with *Reading the American Past*:

Ben Alexander, Queens College; Mary Ann Barber, University of Pittsburgh, Titusville; Mary Block, Lexington Community College; Holly Brewer, North Carolina State University; Charles Byler, Carroll College; Gareth Canaan, University of Illinois, Chicago; Timothy Dean Draper, Metropolitan Community College, Maplewoods Campus; Rosemary Feurer, Northern Illinois University; Paul Gaffney, Landmark College; Teresa M. Goforth, Lansing Community College; Michael Hutcheson, Landmark College; Lee Irby, University of South Florida; Jeff Janowick, Lansing Community College; Larry Knight, Texas A & M, Kingsville; Ronald H. Kotlik, Canisius College; Brad Lookingbill, Columbia College; Jeffrey McClurken, Mary Washington College; Benjamin Moyer, University of Central Arkansas; David A. Nichols, University of Kentucky; Chris Rasmussen, University of Nevada, Las Vegas; Nancy J. Rosenbloom, Canisius College; Joshua Sanborn, Lafayette College; Mart Stewart, Western Washington University; Kristen Streater, University of Kentucky; Phillip D. Troutman, Mellon Lecturing Fellow, Duke University; Frank Williams, Augusta State University.

Although I have benefited from the advice and support of all of these colleagues, I am nonetheless solely responsible for the final selection of the documents and the edited passages in this anthology.

Many others contributed their energy and creativity to this project. From the outset, Chuck Christensen and Joan Feinberg enthusiastically supported the publication of a collection of American history documents that aspired to the high standards readers have come to expect from Bedford/St. Martin's. Louise Townsend pored over the manuscript, bringing to every page the sympathies of a historian and the balanced judgments of a seasoned editor. Editor Tom Crehan shepherded the book throughout the production process; Barbara Sutton expertly copyedited the manuscript, attentive to the documents' numerous idiosyncracies of spelling and phrasing; and Karla Goethe transformed typescript into book pages. Arrangements that made all of this possible were put in place by Gerry McCauley. Closer to home, Sarah Elizabeth Johnson compiled a small mountain of copies from unwieldy volumes to allow thorough checking and proofreading. And Anne Johnson offered a sympathetic ear and sage advice, lovingly tolerating my repeated seclusion with books and bytes.

INTRODUCTION FOR STUDENTS

Documents allow us to peer into the past and learn what happened and what did not happen — crucial beginning points for understanding how and why the present came to be. It would be convenient if we did not need documents, if we could depend instead on our memory to tell us what happened. Unfortunately, memory is far from perfect, as we are reminded every time we misplace our keys. Not only do we forget things that did happen, but we also remember things that never occurred, such as putting those keys right there on the shelf. Mark Twain once quipped, "When I was younger I could remember anything, whether it happened or not; but my faculties are decaying now, and soon I shall be so [old] I cannot remember any but the things that never happened."

Twain's witticism points to another important property of memory: It changes over time. Every good trial lawyer knows that memory is fragile, volatile, and subject to manipulation by our desires, intentions, and fears. Spin artists routinely perform not just on witness stands and at press conferences but whenever memory is reshaped to serve the needs of the present. Compounding the unreliability of memory are two stubborn realities: Most of the people who might remember something about what happened are dead, their memories erased forever; and no person, no single memory, ever knew all of what there is to know about what happened.

These flaws of memory might cause us to shrug wearily and conclude that it is impossible to determine what happened. But that conclusion would be wrong. Documents make it possible to learn a great deal — although not every last thing — about what really happened. Because they are created by humans, documents are subject to all the frailties of memory, with one vital exception. Documents do not change. Unlike memory, documents freeze words at a moment in time. Ideas, perceptions, emotions, and assumptions expressed in a document allow us to learn now about what happened then. In effect, documents are a kind of bridge from the present to the past. They allow us to cross over and to discover how we got from there to here.

Today you can stand where the audience stood in 1863 to listen to Abraham Lincoln's famous speech at the dedication of the cemetery for the Union soldiers killed at the battle of Gettysburg. Of course you can't hear Lincoln's voice, but you can read his words because the Gettysburg Address exists as a historical document; you can literally read this portion of the American past. The address transports the reader back to that crisp November day more than a century ago, the outcome of the war very much in doubt, when the president and commander-in-chief of more than a million men in blue uniforms explained in a few words his view of the meaning of the war for the nation and the world. Lincoln spoke of the immense sacrifice made by the soldiers at Gettysburg and evoked the nation's highest ideals in words that continue to inspire Americans long after the Civil War was over: "Four score and seven years ago our fathers brought forth on this continent, a new nation, conceived in Liberty, and dedicated to the proposition that all men are created equal. . . . [W]e here highly resolve that these dead shall not have died in vain — that this nation, under God, shall have a new birth of freedom — and that government of the people, by the people, for the people, shall not perish from the earth." Because the Gettysburg Address survives in Lincoln's handwriting, we know not only what Lincoln said, but also what he did not say: for instance, that the thousands of dead soldiers at Gettysburg proved that the price of war was too high and it was time to negotiate a peace settlement. The address captured Lincoln's thoughts at that moment and preserved them, much like a historical snapshot. All documents have this property of stopping time, of indelibly recording the views of somebody in the past.

Documents record far more than the ideas of presidents. They disclose, for instance, Mexicans' views of conquering Spaniards in the sixteenth century, accusations New Englanders made against suspected witches in the seventeenth century, the confessions of slave insurrectionists in the nineteenth century, the reminiscences of Vietnamese immigrants in the twentieth century, and much, much more. These views and many others are recorded by the documents in this collection. They permit you to read the American past from the diversity of perspectives that contributed to the making of America: women and men, workers and bosses, newcomers and natives, slaves and masters, voters and politicians, moderates and radicals, activists and reactionaries, westerners and easterners, northerners and southerners, farmers and urbanites, the famous and the forgotten. These people created historical documents when they stole a spare moment to write a letter or record thoughts in a diary, when they talked to a scribbling friend or stranger, when they appeared in court or made a will, and when they delivered a sermon, gave a speech, or penned a manifesto. Examples of all these kinds of documents are included in *Reading the American Past*. Together, they make it possible for you to learn a great deal about what really happened.

From the almost limitless historical record, I chose documents that clearly and vividly express an important perspective about a major event or a widespread point of view during a certain historical era. I selected documents that are not only revealing but also often surprising, controversial, or troubling. My goal is to bring you face to face with the past through the eyes of the people who lived it.

Reading the American Past is designed specifically to accompany *The American Promise: A History of the United States*. Each chapter in this volume parallels a chapter in *The American Promise*. The documents provide eyewitness accounts that broaden and deepen the textbook narrative. Chapter 15, for example, supplements the textbook discussion of Reconstruction with selections from the 1865 Mississippi Black Code, resolutions of a black convention in Alabama in 1867, testimony of an African-American Republican before the congressional committee investigating the Ku Klux Klan in 1871, and the report of a prominent white Republican about conditions in the South in 1875. As a rule, each chapter contains four documents; occasionally there are more shorter ones or fewer longer ones. To help you read and understand the documents, a brief paragraph at the beginning of each chapter sketches the larger historical context explained in more detail in your textbook; each document is preceded by a headnote that identifies its source, explaining when it was produced, by whom, and why it is revealing; and the questions that follow each selection point you toward key passages and fundamental ideas and ask you to consider both what a document says and what it means.

Making the most of these documents requires reading with care and imagination. Historians are interested in both what a document says and what it suggests about the historical reality that is only partly disclosed by the document itself. A document might be likened to a window through which we may glimpse features of the past. A document challenges us to read and understand the words on the page as a way to look through the window and learn about the larger historical context.

Lincoln's Gettysburg Address, for example, hints that he believed many loyal Americans wondered whether the war was worth the effort, whether all those soldiers, as he said, "have died in vain." Lincoln's words do not explicitly say that many people thought the human tragedy of the war was too great, but that seems to be one of their meanings. His address attempted to answer such doubts by proclaiming the larger meaning of the war and the soldiers' deaths. Behind his public statement of the noble ideals of the Union war effort lie his private perception that many Americans had come to doubt whether the war had any meaning beyond the maiming or death of their loved ones.

To see such unstated historical reality in and through a document, readers must remain alert to exactly what the document says. The first step is to learn something about the era in which the document was written by reading *The American Promise* or another textbook of American history.

The next step is to read the document, keeping in mind three important questions: Who wrote the document? When was it written? Who was the intended audience? To help answer these questions, you will find useful information in the brief headnote and the questions that accompany each document, as well as in the concluding comparative questions that draw attention to similarities and differences among the documents in the chapter. But these editorial features are merely beginning points for your investigation of the documents. You should always take the next step by asking who wrote a document, when, and for what audience.

Obviously, a document expresses the viewpoint of its author. Different people had different views about the same event. At Gettysburg, for example, the Confederacy suffered a painful defeat that weakened their ability to maintain their independence and to defend slavery. If Jefferson Davis, the president of the Confederacy, had delivered a Gettysburg Address, it would have been very different from Lincoln's. Documents also often convey their authors' opinions of the viewpoints of other people, including those who agree with them and those who don't. You should always ask, then: What does a document say about the viewpoint of the author? What does it say about the author's opinion about the views of other people? Does the document suggest the author's point of view was confined to a few people, shared by a substantial minority, or embraced by a great many Americans?

A document conveys valuable information about the time when it was written as well as about the author's point of view. Frequently, a person's point of view changes, making it critical to know exactly when a document was written in order to understand its meaning. When Lincoln delivered the Gettysburg Address, the outcome of the Civil War remained in doubt; seventeen months later, in April 1865, he was certain of northern victory. The address expresses the urgency and uncertainty of the wartime crisis of 1863 rather than the relief and confidence of 1865. As you read every document, you should ask: How does the document reflect the time when it was written? What does it say about the events under way at the time? What does it suggest about how that particular time was perceived by the author and by other people?

In addition to considering who wrote a document and when, one must think about the intended audience. A politician may say one thing in a campaign speech and something quite different in a private letter to a friend. An immigrant might send a rosy account of life in America to family members in the Old Country — one that is at odds with many features of life in the New World. The intended audience shapes the message an author seeks to send. The author's expectations of what the audience wants to hear contribute to what a document says, how it is said, and what is left unsaid. Lincoln knew that his audience at

Gettysburg included thousands of family members mourning the death of loved ones who "gave the last full measure of devotion" on the battlefield; he hoped his remarks would soothe the heartache of the survivors by ennobling the Union and those who died in its defense. To decipher any document, you should always ask: Who is the intended audience? How did the audience shape what the author says? Did consideration of the audience lead the author to emphasize some things and downplay or ignore others? How would the intended audience be likely to read the document? How would people who were not among the intended audience be likely to read it?

The meanings of words, like the viewpoints of individuals, also reflect their historical moment. For the most part, the documents in this collection were written in English; several have been translated into English from Spanish, Portuguese, Latin, German, Swedish, or one of several Native American languages. But even documents originally written in English require you to translate the meaning of English words at the time the document was written into the meaning of English words today. Readers must guard against imputing today's meanings to yesterday's words. When Lincoln said "this nation" in the Gettysburg Address, he referred to the United States in 1863, a vastly different nation from the one founded four score and seven years earlier and from the one that exists today, almost a century and a half later. The word is the same, but the meaning varies greatly.

Although the meaning of many words remains relatively constant, if you are on the lookout for key words whose meanings have changed, you will discover otherwise hidden insights in the documents. You can benefit simply from exercising your historical imagination about the changing meaning of words. To Lincoln, the phrase "all men are created equal" did not have the same meaning that it did for women's rights leaders at the time, or for slaves or slaveowners. You should always pay attention to the words used in a document and ask a final set of questions: How do the words in the document reflect the author, the time, and the intended audience? Would the same words have different meanings to other people at that time? Does the author's choice of words reveal covert assumptions and blindspots along with an overt message?

Historical documents provide readers not only with indelible markers of historical changes that have occurred. They also illuminate the role human beings played in making those changes. Documents instruct us about the achievements and limitations of the past as they inspire and caution us for the future. Documents also instill in us a strong sense of historical humility. Americans in the past were no less good and no more evil, no less right and no more wrong, than we are today. Their ideas, their experiences, and their times were different from ours in many respects. But they made the nation we inhabit. Ideally, the documents in *Reading the American Past* will give you an appreciation of what it took, and will continue to take, to make American history happen.

CONTENTS

Preface for Instructors   *v*

Introduction for Students   *ix*

PROLOGUE: ANCIENT AMERICA BEFORE 1492   1

The Woman Who Fell from the Sky   1
A Seneca Origin Narrative   1

"In the Beginning"   4
Genesis: The Christian Origin Narrative   4

COMPARATIVE QUESTIONS   7

1. EUROPEANS AND THE NEW WORLD, 1492–1600   9

The King of the Congo Writes to the King of Portugal   9
King Afonso Correspondence, 1526   9

Columbus Describes his First Encounter with "Indians"   14
The Diario of Christopher Columbus's First Voyage
to America, 1492–1493   14

A Conquistador Arrives in Mexico, 1519–1520   17
Bernal Díaz del Castillo, *The Conquest of New Spain*, 1632   17

A Mexican Description of the Conquest of Mexico   21
Mexican Accounts of Conquest from the Florentine Codex   21

COMPARATIVE QUESTIONS   26

2. THE SOUTHERN COLONIES IN
THE SEVENTEENTH CENTURY, 1601–1700   27

Opechancanough's 1622 Uprising in Virginia   27
Edward Waterhouse's, *Declaration*, 1622   27

A Yeoman Planter's Tobacco Farm   31
Robert Cole's Inventory, 1661   32

Sex and Race Relations   36
Testimony from Virginia Court Records, 1681   36

Bacon's Rebellion   39
Nathaniel Bacon, *Declaration,* 1676   39

COMPARATIVE QUESTIONS   42

**3. THE NORTHERN COLONIES IN
   THE SEVENTEENTH CENTURY, 1601–1700**   **43**

The *Arbella* Sermon   43
John Winthrop, *"A Model of Christian Charity,"* 1630   44

Observations of New England Indians   48
Roger Williams, *A Key into the Language of America,* 1643   48

Keeping Order in a Puritan Community   52
Suffolk County Court Records, 1671–1673   53

Words of the Bewitched   56
Testimony against Accused Witch Bridget Bishop, 1692   56

COMPARATIVE QUESTIONS   59

**4. COLONIAL AMERICA IN
   THE EIGHTEENTH CENTURY, 1701–1770**   **60**

Confessions of a Thief and Rapist   60
A Boston Broadside, 1768   61

Poor Richard's Advice   64
Benjamin Franklin, *Father Abraham's Speech from
   Poor Richard's Almanac,* 1757   65

A Scottish Immigrant Writes News from America   69
Alexander Thomson, *News from America,* 1774   69

Advertisements for Runaway Slaves   73
South Carolina Gazette and Virginia Gazette, 1737–1745   74

COMPARATIVE QUESTIONS   77

**5. THE BRITISH EMPIRE AND
   THE COLONIAL CRISIS, 1754–1775**   **78**

**An Oration on the Second Anniversary of
   the Boston Massacre**   78
Joseph Warren, *Boston Massacre Oration,* March 5, 1772   79

**A Boston Shoemaker Recalls British Arrogance and
the Boston Tea Party**   82
George R. T. Hewes, *Memoir,* 1834   82

A Loyalist Judge's Catalog of Rebellious Crowds   86
Peter Oliver, *Origin & Progress of the American
Revolution, 1774–1775*   86

**George Washington Concludes That
the Crisis Has Arrived**   89
Letters, 1774   90

COMPARATIVE QUESTIONS   92

6. **THE WAR FOR AMERICA, 1775–1783**   **93**

Thomas Paine Makes the Case for Independence   93
Common Sense, January 1776   94

Letters of John and Abigail Adams   97
Correspondence, 1776   98

A Soldier's Experience of the Revolutionary War   104
Joseph Plumb Martin, *Memoir,* 1830   105

**Joseph Brant Appeals to British Allies to
Keep Promises**   108
Address to British Secretary of State Lord Germain, 1776   109
Message to Governor of Quebec, Frederick Haldimand, 1783   109

COMPARATIVE QUESTIONS   112

7. **BUILDING A REPUBLIC, 1775–1789**   **113**

Benjamin Rush Proposes Republican Education   113
*Thoughts upon the Mode of Education Proper in a
Republic,* 1786   113

Thomas Jefferson on Slavery and Race   117
Notes on the State of Virginia, 1782   117

Making the Case for the Constitution   121
James Madison, *Federalist Number 10,* 1787   121

Mercy Otis Warren Opposes the Constitution   126
Observations on the New Constitution, 1788   127

COMPARATIVE QUESTIONS   131

8. THE NEW NATION TAKES FORM, 1789–1800   132

Why Free Government Has Always Failed   132
William Manning, *The Key of Libberty,* 1798   132

Education for Young Women   135
Molly Wallace and Priscilla Mason, *Valedictory Addresses
    at the Young Ladies Academy of Philadelphia,* 1792, 1793   135

Alexander Hamilton on the Economy   138
Report on the Subject of Manufactures, 1791   139

George Washington's Parting Advice to the Nation   143
"Farewell Address to the People of the United States," 1796   143

COMPARATIVE QUESTIONS   147

9. REPUBLICAN ASCENDANCY, 1800–1824   148

A Jeffersonian Sailmaker's Fourth of July Address   148
Peter Wendover, *Oration,* July 4, 1806   149

Thomas Jefferson's Private and Public Indian Policy   151
Letter to Governor William H. Harrison, February 27, 1803   152
"Address to the Wolf and People of the Mandan Nation,"
    December 30, 1806   153

Meriwether Lewis Describes the Shoshone   155
The Journals of the Lewis and Clark Expedition, 1805   155

Frontier Revival   159
Richard McNemar, *The Kentucky Revival,* 1801   159

COMPARATIVE QUESTIONS   163

10. THE EXPANDING REPUBLIC, 1815–1840   164

Andrew Jackson's Parting Words to the Nation   164
Farewell Address, March 4, 1837   164

Cherokees Debate Removal   168
John Ross, *Answer to Inquiries from a Friend,* 1836   169
Elias Boudinot, *A Reply to John Ross,* 1837   170

Sarah Grimké on the Status of Women   173
Letters on the Equality of the Sexes, 1838   173

Elijah Lovejoy Confronts an Anti-Abolitionist Mob   176
Letter to a Friend, October 3, 1837   176

COMPARATIVE QUESTIONS   180

11. THE FREE NORTH AND WEST, 1840–1860   **181**

The Anxiety of Gain: Henry W. Bellows on Commerce and Morality   181
"The Influence of the Trading Spirit upon the Social and Moral Life of America," 1845   181

"That Woman Is Man's Equal": The Seneca Falls Declaration   185
"Declaration of Sentiments," 1848   185

A Farmer's View of His Wife   188
Eliza Farnham, *"Conversation with a Newly-Wed Westerner,"* 1846   188

Gold Fever   191
Walter Colton, *California Gold Rush Diary,* 1849–1850   191

Comparative Questions   195

12. THE SLAVE SOUTH, 1820–1860   **196**

Plantation Rules   196
Bennet Barrow, *Highland Plantation Journal,* May 1, 1838   196

Nat Turner Explains Why He Became an Insurrectionist   200
The Confessions of Nat Turner, 1831   200

The Pro-Slavery Argument   204
James Henry Hammond, *"Letter to an English Abolitionist,"* 1845   204

A Visit with a Poor White Farmer   208
Frederick Law Olmsted, *The Cotton Kingdom,* 1861   208

Comparative Questions   211

13. THE HOUSE DIVIDED, 1846–1861   **212**

The Kansas-Nebraska Act   212
Abraham Lincoln, *Speech in Peoria, Illinois,* October 16, 1854   212

The Antislavery Constitution   215
Frederick Douglass, *The Constitution of the United States: Is It Pro-Slavery or Anti-Slavery?* 1860   216

The Pro-Slavery Constitution   218
Jefferson Davis, *Speech before the U.S. Senate,* May 1860   218

John Brown: Pottawatomie and Harpers Ferry   220
Confession of James Townsley, December 6, 1879   220
John Brown, *Speech,* November 2, 1859   222

COMPARATIVE QUESTIONS   223

14. THE CRUCIBLE OF WAR, 1861–1865   224

President Lincoln's War Aims   224
Letter to Horace Greeley, August 22, 1862   225
The Emancipation Proclamation, January 1, 1863   225
The Gettysburg Address, November 19, 1863   226

A Former Slave's War Aims   227
Statement from an Anonymous Former Slave,
   New Orleans, 1863   227

**General William T. Sherman Explains the Hard
   Hand of War**   230
Correspondence, 1864   231

War Wounds   238
Walt Whitman, *Specimen Days,* 1862–1863   238

COMPARATIVE QUESTIONS   241

15. RECONSTRUCTION, 1863–1877   242

Black Codes Enacted in the South   242
Mississippi Black Code, November 1865   242

A Black Convention in Alabama   246
*"Address of the Colored Convention to the People
   of Alabama,"* 1867   246

Klan Violence against Blacks   250
Elias Hill, *Testimony before Congressional Committee
   Investigating the Ku Klux Klan,* 1871   250

A Northern Republican's Report on Reconstruction   253
Charles Nordhoff, *The Cotton States,* 1875   253

COMPARATIVE QUESTIONS   256

Index   257

ANCIENT AMERICA
BEFORE 1492

For millennia, human beings have explained who they were and how they came to be with stories, shaped and reshaped in countless tellings. These narratives of human origins differed greatly, but all expressed a sense of the meaning and mystery of human existence. Some of the origin stories told by North American peoples were heard by curious European settlers in the sixteenth and seventeenth centuries. Many others were recorded by professional anthropologists in the nineteenth and twentieth centuries. Those stories, polished and modified over the centuries, are as close as we will ever get to understanding what ancient Americans thought about their origins. The Europeans who encountered ancient Americans had their own notions of human origins created by ancient peoples in Europe, the Middle East, and North Africa. Christianity promoted the creation stories in Genesis, the first book of the Bible. As Christianity spread throughout Europe, there was always debate and contention — among Christians themselves and between Christians and followers of Judaism, Islam, and other ancient faiths. The following excerpts from a Native American origin narrative and the Bible reveal more than contrasting views of the prehistoric origins of the world. They also disclose a great deal about the distinctive worldviews of Native Americans and the Europeans whose encounters did so much to shape American history after 1492.

DOCUMENT 1
A Seneca Origin Narrative

This Seneca story of human origins, created and retold for centuries as part of the Seneca oral tradition, was recorded by Jeremiah Curtin, a white man fluent in the Seneca language. In 1883, 1886, and 1887, Curtin spent many hours talking with Seneca men and women on the Cattaraugus reservation in New York State. The largest of the five tribes of the Iroquois confederacy, the Seneca had inhabited much of central New York in the sixteenth century, but by the mid-seventeenth century they had moved west to Lake Erie and south into Pennsylvania. Curtin recorded this tale in the Seneca language, and it was subsequently translated into English by J. W. B. Hewitt. The story reveals the intimate relationship between human beings and nature found in many other origin narratives.

The Woman Who Fell from the Sky

A long time ago human beings lived high up in what is now called heaven. They had a great and illustrious chief.

It so happened that this chief's daughter was taken very ill with a strange affection. All the people were very anxious as to the outcome of her illness. Every known remedy was tried in an attempt to cure her, but none had any effect.

Near the lodge of this chief stood a great tree, which every year bore corn used for food. One of the friends of the chief had a dream, in which he was advised to tell the chief that in order to cure his daughter he must lay her beside this tree, and that he must have the tree dug up. This advice was carried out to the letter. While the people were at work and the young woman lay there, a young man came along. He was very angry and said: "It is not at all right to destroy this tree. Its fruit is all that we have to live on." With this remark he gave the young woman who lay there ill a shove with his foot, causing her to fall into the hole that had been dug.

Now, that hole opened into this world, which was then all water, on which floated waterfowl of many kinds. There was no land at that time. It came to pass that as these waterfowl saw this young woman falling they shouted, "Let us receive her," whereupon they, at least some of them, joined their bodies together, and the young woman fell on this platform of bodies. When these were wearied they asked, "Who will volunteer to care for this woman?" The great Turtle then took her, and when he got tired of holding her, he in turn asked who would take his place. At last the question arose as to what they should do to provide her with a permanent resting place in this world. Finally it was decided to prepare the earth, on which she would live in the future. To do this it was determined that soil from the bottom of the primal sea should be brought up and placed on the broad, firm carapace of the Turtle, where it would increase in size to such an extent that it would accommodate all the creatures that should be produced thereafter. After much discussion the toad was finally persuaded to dive to the bottom of the waters in search of soil. Bravely making the attempt, he succeeded in bringing up soil from the depths of the sea. This was carefully spread over the carapace of the Turtle, and at once both began to grow in size and depth.

After the young woman recovered from the illness from which she suffered when she was cast down from the upper world, she built herself a shelter, in which she lived quite contentedly. In the course of time she brought forth a girl baby, who grew rapidly in size and intelligence. When the daughter had grown to young womanhood, the mother and she were accustomed to go out to dig wild potatoes. Her mother had said to her that in doing this she must face the West at

*Jeremiah Curtin and J. W. B. Hewitt, "Seneca Fiction, Legends and Myths, Part 1," Report of the Bureau of American Ethnology 32 (1910–11 [1918])

all times. Before long the young daughter gave signs that she was about to be-come a mother. Her mother reproved her, saying that she had violated the injunc-tion not to face the east, as her condition showed that she had faced the wrong way while digging potatoes. It is said that the breath of the West Wind had en-tered her person, causing conception. When the days of her delivery were at hand, she overheard twins within her body in a hot debate as to which should be born first and as to the proper place of exit, one declaring that he was going to emerge through the armpit of his mother, the other saying that he would emerge in the natural way. The first one born, who was of a reddish color, was called Othag-wenda; that is, Flint. The other, who was light in color, was called Djuskaha; that is, the Little Sprout.

The Grandmother of the twins liked Djuskaha and hated the other; so they cast Othagwenda into a hollow tree some distance from the lodge.

The boy that remained in the lodge grew very rapidly, and soon was able to make himself bows and arrows and to go out to hunt in the vicinity. Finally, for several days he returned home without his bow and arrows. At last he was asked why he had to have a new bow and arrows every morning. He replied that there was a young boy in a hollow tree in the neighborhood who used them. The grand-mother inquired where the tree stood, and he told her; whereupon then they went there and brought the other boy home again.

When the boys had grown to man's estate, they decided that it was neces-sary for them to increase the size of their island, so they agreed to start out to-gether, afterward separating to create forests and lakes and other things. They parted as agreed, Othagwenda going westward and Djuskaha eastward. In the course of time, on returning, they met in their shelter or lodge at night, then agree-ing to go the next day to see what each had made. First they went west to see what Othagwenda had made. It was found that he had made the country all rocks and full of ledges, and also a mosquito which was very large. Djuskaha asked the mosquito to run, in order that he might see whether the insect could fight. The mosquito ran, and sticking his bill through a sapling, thereby made it fall, at which Djuskaha said, "That will not be right, for you would kill the people who are about to come." So, seizing him, he rubbed him down in his hands, causing him to become very small; then he blew on the mosquito, whereupon he flew away. He also modified some of the other animals which his brother had made. After returning to their lodge, they agreed to go the next day to see what Djuskaha had fashioned. On visiting the east the next day, they found that Djuskaha had made a large number of animals which were so fat that they could hardly move; that he had made the sugar-maple trees to drop syrup; that he had made the sycamore tree to bear fine fruit; that the rivers were so formed that half the water flowed upstream and the other half downstream. Then the reddish-colored brother, Othagwenda, was greatly displeased with what his brother had made, saying that the people who were about to come would live too easily and be too happy. So he shook violently the various animals — the bears, deer, and turkeys —causing them to become small at once, a characteristic which attached itself to their descendants. He also caused the sugar maple to drop sweetened water only, and the fruit of the sycamore to become small and useless; and lastly he caused the water of the rivers to flow in only one direction, because the original plan would make it too easy for the human beings who were about to come to navi-gate the streams. The inspection of each other's work resulted in a deadly disagreement between the brothers, who finally came to grips and blows, and Othagwenda was killed in the fierce struggle.

QUESTIONS FOR READING AND DISCUSSION

1. According to this narrative how did human beings arrive in the world? What was the significance of the "great tree which every year bore corn used for food" and of the angry young man?
2. Who does the narrative say created the earth, and why? What relationship existed between animals and the earth?
3. According to the narrative, how did human beings reproduce? Why?
4. How did Othagwenda (Flint) and Djuskaha (Little Sprout) differ? Why were those differences important?
5. Who does the narrative identify as God? What difference did it make?

DOCUMENT 2

Genesis: The Christian Origin Narrative

The Bible in use during the fifteenth century was usually written in Latin, which the Christian church adopted as its official language, known only by tiny educated elite — mostly priests and scholars. Because most Europeans could not read, priests tried to teach the doctrines of Christianity orally and with images in paint, glass, or sculpture like those still found in churches today. Although few of the Europeans who first encountered Native Americans in the New World could read Genesis, most of them were familiar with the main features of the biblical story of the origins of the world. The following passage from Genesis is taken from the famous English translation of the Bible authorized by King James I, initially published in 1611 as England's colonizing of the New World was just beginning. It discloses powerful, commonly held views not only about God but also about the relations between men and women and between human beings and the natural world.

"In the Beginning"

In the beginning God created the heaven and the earth. And the earth was without form, and void; and darkness was upon the face of the deep. And the Spirit of God moved upon the face of the waters. And God said, Let there be light: and there was light. And God saw the light, that it was good: and God divided the light from darkness. And God called the light Day, and the darkness he called Night. And the evening and the morning were the first day.

And God said, Let the waters under the heaven be gathered together unto one place, and let the dry land appear; and it was so. And God called the dry land Earth; and the gathering together of the waters called he Seas: and God saw that it was good. And God said, Let the earth bring forth grass, the herb yielding seed, and the fruit tree yielding fruit after his kind, whose seed is in itself, upon the earth: and it was so. And the earth brought forth grass, and herb yielding

---

The Holy Bible, King James Version, Genesis 1–3.

seed after his kind, and the tree yielding fruit, whose seed was in itself, after his kind: and God saw that it was good. And the evening and the morning were the third day.

And God said, Let there be lights in the firmament of the heaven to divide the day from the night; and let them be for signs, and for seasons, and for days, and years: And let them be for lights in the firmament of the heaven to give light upon the earth: and it was so. And God made two great lights; the greater light to rule the day, and the lesser light to rule the night: he made the stars also. And God set them in the firmament of the heaven to give light upon the earth, And to rule over the day and over the night, and to divide the light from the darkness: and God saw that it was good. And the evening and the morning were the fourth day.

And God said, Let the waters bring forth abundantly the moving creature that hath life, and fowl that may fly above the earth in the open firmament of heaven. And God created great whales, and every living creature that moveth, which the waters brought forth abundantly after their kind, and every winged fowl after his kind: and God saw that it was good. And God blessed them, saying, Be fruitful, and multiply, and fill the waters in the seas, and let the fowl multiply in the earth. And the evening and the morning were the fifth day.

And God said, Let the earth bring forth the living creature after his kind, cattle, and creeping thing, and beast of the earth after his kind: and it was so. And God made the beast of the earth after his kind, and cattle after their kind, and every thing that creepeth upon the earth after his kind: and God saw that it was good.

And God said, Let us make man in our image, after our likeness: and let them have dominion over the fish of the seas, and over the fowl of the air, and over the cattle, and over all the earth, and over every creeping thing that creepeth upon the earth. So God created man in his own image, in the image of God created he him; male and female created he them. And God blessed them, and God said unto them, Be fruitful, and multiply, and replenish the earth, and subdue it: and have dominion over the fish of the sea, and over the fowl of the air, and over every living thing that moveth upon the earth.

And God said, Behold, I have given you every herb bearing seed, which is upon the face of all the earth, and every tree, in the which is the fruit of a tree yielding seed; to you it shall be for meat. And to every beast of the earth, and to every fowl of the air, and to every thing that creepeth upon the earth, wherein there is life, I have given every green herb for meat: and it was so. And God saw everything that he had made, and behold, it was very good. And the evening and the morning were the sixth day.

Thus the heavens and the earth were finished, and all the host of them. And on the seventh day God ended his work which he had made; and he rested on the seventh day from all his work which he had made. And God blessed the seventh day, and sanctified it: because that in it he had rested from all his work which God created and made.

These are the generations of the heavens and of the earth when they were created, in the day that the Lord God made the earth and the heavens, And every plant of the field before it was in the earth, and every herb of the field before it grew: for the Lord God had not caused it to rain upon the earth, and there was not a man to till the ground. But there went up a mist from the earth, and watered the whole face of the ground. And the Lord God formed man of the dust of the ground, and breathed into his nostrils the breath of life; and man became a living soul.

And the Lord God planted a garden eastward in Eden; and there he put the man whom he had formed. And out of the ground made the Lord God to grow every tree that is pleasant to the sight, and good for food; the tree of life also in the midst of the garden, and the tree of knowledge of good and evil. And a river went out of Eden to water the garden; . . . And the Lord God took the man, and put him into the garden of Eden to dress it and to keep it. And the Lord God commanded the man, saying, Of every tree of the garden thou mayest freely eat: But of the tree of the knowledge of good and evil, thou shalt not eat of it: for in the day that thou eatest thereof thou shalt surely die.

And the Lord God said, It is not good that the man shall be alone; I will make him an help meet[1] for him. And out of the ground the Lord God formed every beast of the field, and every fowl of the air; and brought them unto Adam to see what he would call them: and whatsoever Adam called every living creature, that was the name thereof. And Adam gave names to all cattle, and to the fowl of the air, and to every beast of the field: but for Adam there was not an help meet for him. And the Lord God caused a deep sleep to fall upon Adam, and he slept: and he took one of his ribs, and closed up the flesh instead thereof; And the rib, which the Lord God had taken from man, made he a woman, and brought her unto the man. And Adam said, This is now bone of my bones, and flesh of my flesh: she shall be called Woman, because she was taken out of Man. Therefore shall a man leave his father and his mother, and shall cleave unto his wife: and they shall be one flesh. And they were both naked, the man and his wife, and were not ashamed.

Now the serpent was more subtil than any beast of the field which the Lord God had made. And he said unto the woman, Yea, hath God said, Ye shall not eat of every tree of the garden? And the woman said unto the serpent, We may eat of the fruit of the trees of the garden: But of the fruit of the tree which is in the midst of the garden, God hath said, Ye shall not eat of it, neither shall ye touch it, lest ye die. And the serpent said unto the woman, Ye shall not surely die: For God doth know that in the day ye eat thereof, then your eyes shall be opened, and ye shall be as gods, knowing good and evil. And when the woman saw that the tree was good for food, and that it was pleasant to the eyes, and a tree to be desired to make one wise, she took of the fruit thereof, and did eat, and gave also unto her husband with her; and he did eat. And the eyes of them both were opened, and they knew that they were naked; and they sewed fig leaves together, and made themselves aprons. And they heard the voice of the Lord God walking in the garden in the cool of the day: and Adam and his wife hid themselves from the presence of the Lord God amongst the trees of the garden. And the Lord God called unto Adam, and said unto him, Where art thou? And he said, I heard thy voice in the garden, and I was afraid, because I was naked; and I hid myself. And he said, Who told thee that thou wast naked? Hast thou eaten of the tree, whereof I commanded thee that thou shouldest not eat? And the man said, The woman whom thou gavest to be with me, she gave me of the tree, and I did eat. And the Lord God said unto the woman, What is this that thou hast done? And the woman

---

[1]**help meet:** Companion, helper; in this case, a wife.

said, The serpent beguiled me, and I did eat. And the Lord God said unto the serpent, Because thou hast done this, thou art cursed above all the cattle, and above every beast of the field; upon thy belly shalt thou go, and dust shalt thou eat all the days of thy life: And I will put enmity between thee and the woman and between thy seed and her seed; it shall bruise thy head, and thou shalt bruise his heel. Unto the woman he said, I will greatly multiply thy sorrow and thy conception; in sorrow thou shalt bring forth children; and thy desire shall be to thy husband, and he shall rule over thee. And unto Adam he said, Because thou has hearkened unto the voice of thy wife, and hast eaten of the tree, of which I commanded thee, saying, Thou shalt not eat of it: cursed is the ground for thy sake; in sorrow shalt thou eat of it all the days of thy life; Thorns also and thistles shall it bring forth to thee; and thou shalt eat the herb of the field; In the sweat of thy face shalt thou eat bread, till thou return unto the ground; for out of it wast thou taken; for dust thou art, and unto dust shalt thou return. And Adam called his wife's name Eve; because she was the mother of all living. Unto Adam also and to his wife did the Lord God make coats of skins, and clothed them.

And the Lord God said, Behold, the man is become as one of us, to know good and evil: and now, lest he put forth his hand, and take also of the tree of life, and eat, and live for ever: Therefore the Lord God sent him forth from the garden of Eden, to till the ground from whence he was taken. So he drove out the man; and he placed at the east of the garden of Eden Cherubims[2], and a flaming sword which turned every way, to keep the way of the tree of life.

QUESTIONS FOR READING AND DISCUSSION

1. According to Genesis, how and why did God create the world?
2. Were plants, animals, and human beings in this account more or less equal in God's eyes?
3. Why did God command human beings to "Be fruitful, and multiply, and replenish the earth, and subdue it: and have dominion . . . over every living thing that moveth upon the earth"?
4. Did God make different demands on men and women? Why?
5. Why did God forbid Adam and Eve to eat from the tree of the knowledge of good and evil? Why did they disobey God? How did God punish them?
6. How might the Genesis account of human origins have influenced Europeans as they encountered peoples in Africa and the New World?

COMPARATIVE QUESTIONS

1. What are the major differences and similarities between these creation myths?
2. Both creation narratives describe a world before humans existed. To what extent were humans a force for good in the world? How did their power compare to that of nature and the creator?
3. What views of women and men do these narratives express? What do they reveal about gender roles and expectations among the Seneca and European Christians?

---

[2]**Cherubims:** Angels.

4. Because both creation narratives originated in oral rather than written stories and neither had a single identifiable author, to what extent can these stories be accepted as expressions of the views of common folk among the Seneca and European Christians?

5. To what extent might such narratives have influenced the behavior of Native Americans and Europeans when they encountered one another?

CHAPTER 1

EUROPEANS AND THE NEW WORLD
1492–1600

D uring the fifteenth and sixteenth centuries, European explorers, traders, and soldiers repeatedly encountered non-Europeans, first in Africa and, beginning in 1492, in the New World. Portuguese mariners venturing down the west coast of Africa inaugurated a thriving trade in African goods, including, most fatefully, slaves. The arrival of Christopher Columbus in the Caribbean launched an unremitting series of encounters between Europeans and Native Americans in the Western Hemisphere. These early encounters around the rim of the Atlantic world informed each group about the other and established patterns that lasted long into the future. The documents that follow illustrate the varied forms of communication exchanged in these encounters between strangers. They reveal the many-layered novelty and complexity of the encounters for all involved.

DOCUMENT 1

The King of the Congo Writes to the King of Portugal

In 1481, a Portuguese explorer happened upon the mouth of the enormous Congo River, and within a decade Portuguese soldiers, traders, and missionaries had made their way inland to Mbanza Congo, the capital of the powerful Kingdom of Congo, establishing a European presence that persisted for centuries. The king of the Congo welcomed the Portuguese intruders who traded European items of all kinds — particularly guns — for such local goods as ivory and, especially, slaves. Portuguese missionaries converted some young Congolese to Christianity, including Mzinga Mbemba Afonso, who became king in 1506 and ruled the Congo for almost forty years. In 1526, concerned about the disastrous consequences of Portuguese trade for both his kingdom and his rule, Afonso wrote King João III of Portugal. Afonso's letters, excerpted here in an English translation of the original Portuguese, are among the very few surviving documents written by an African in the sixteenth century. The letters reveal Afonso's difficult dilemma: how to take advantage of certain features of contact with the Portuguese while avoiding the undesirable — and ultimately destructive — consequences.

King Afonso to King João III
King Afonso Correspondence, 1526

Mbanza Congo, July 6, 1526

My Lord,

On June 26 we heard of the arrival in our harbor of one of Your Highness' ships. This made us truly glad for it had been a long time since any of your ships had docked in our kingdom bringing with it news of Your Highness which, as one would expect, we had often desired to hear. Moreover we are almost entirely lacking wine and flour for the holy sacrifice. . . .

My Lord, Your Highness must know that our kingdom's end is drawing near, so much so that we must find the appropriate remedy to this situation. What causes so much looseness is the fact that the head of your mission and your officers grant merchants the authorization to establish themselves in this kingdom, to open shops and to sell goods, even those [such as guns] which we forbid. They spread them across our kingdoms and provinces in such great amounts that many of our vassals which, until now, obeyed us are beginning to claim their independence. These days they are able to acquire, in larger quantities than us, those very things with which we kept them subdued and satisfied with our vassalage and governance. This causes great loss for God's service as well as for the safety and peace of our kingdoms and ourselves.

We are not even able to measure the extent of this loss because of the merchants constantly taking away our subjects, children of this land, sons of nobles and vassals, even members of our family. Those thieves and remorseless men take them to trade on the country's wealth which they covet. They kidnap them and sell them. This corruption and depravity are so common that our land is entirely deserted. Your Highness must not consider this favorable neither in itself nor for his service. To avoid this abuse this kingdom only needs priests and some people to teach in schools and not goods with the exception of wine and flour for the holy sacrifice. That is why we ask Your Highness to help us and grant us our wish to demand from the heads of your missions that they no longer send goods and merchants here. It is indeed our wish that this kingdom be neither a place of trade nor a place of transit for slaves for the reasons I just explained.

Once again we ask Your Highness to make it so because we do not have any other means of preventing such obvious damages.

May the Lord in His mercy always protect Your Highness and allow you to serve Him. I kiss your hands many times.

Louis Jadin and Mireille Decorato, *Correspondance de Dom Afonso, roi du Congo, 1506–1543* (Brussels: Académie Royale des Sciences d'Outre-Mer, 1974) 154–62; 166–69. English translation by Marianna Dantas.

King Afonso to King João III

Mbanza Congo, August 25, 1526

My Lord,

. . . We often spend five to six months without any mass or sacrament because Your Highness' officers wish it so; this hinders God's service and causes great confusion among our subjects. Some say that Your Highness no longer remembers us or christianity which your father, God bless his soul, had kept for so long in these regions thanks to all the visits he requested, and thanks to his exhortations and encouragement which brought constancy and faith to all and great comfort to us.

Now Your Highness is putting all of this in jeopardy by showing so little interest in us. The [Portuguese ship] pilots' disregard for us is clear when they leave, as they often do, without even waiting for our messages. They pretend to be obeying the orders of Your Highness' officers. When our letters arrive at the harbor they have already left. Then they accuse us of being careless to cover their own errors and to put us in a unfavorable position with regards to Your Highness. Thus they give you an excuse to forget us completely. We beg you not to believe these liars and these men whose sole purpose is to make profit and sell their ill-gotten goods. Through this trade of theirs, they damage and corrupt our kingdom as well as christianity which has been flourishing here for so many years and which cost so much to your ancestors. Yet it is a very precious treasure. The most christian and most catholic kings and princes like Your Highness strive to attract and maintain new peoples into God's service for the increase of the holy catholic faith, to which we all have held on. One can do a lot of damage with so many goods and through such anarchic means. These goods prove themselves so attractive to the simple minded and the ignorant folks that they forget to believe in God in order to believe in them. We must remedy this situation for it is a trick of the devil which could lead to the damnation of all. In addition to this, my Lord, our people fall victim of a monstrous greed which causes them to act like thieves and take their own relatives as well as ours, even christian ones, to trade them and sell them as captives. This corruption is such that our troops are no longer able to put an end to it without frequently conducting numerous and large scale executions[1] among our subjects. This way the innocent will die for the sinner.

It would not be so, my Lord, if Your Highness cared to help us and grant us the favor of sending spiritual medicine, as your father, the King, had done. We cannot do without many priests to celebrate the sacrifice, to conduct preaching, religious education, and confessions. They should visit in pairs all the regions of our kingdom, which is very large and populated. Together with the bishop, our son, we would command them to plant the word of God in the hearts of our subjects. This way, it would remain so deeply engrained that even if they attempted to practice devilish deeds for their damnation the virtue of such remedies would cure them.

My Lord, avoid sending us merchants who engage in vicious trade as well as evil goods. This impedes the salvation of the souls and spoils the good results we had obtained. . . .

---

[1]**Executions:** Punitive war expeditions [Translator's note]

Furthermore, we need three or four good grammarians to complete the instruction of our subjects who have begun their education. We have with us many of your and our subjects who can teach reading and writing, but we need men capable of showing and explaining the truths of the holy faith and of judging on thorny matters, which our other subjects generally cannot do. Yet it is very necessary.

Moreover, my Lord, some churches have already been started. We would need five or six masons and ten carpenters to finish them for the service and praise of God, our Lord. This is mainly about [the church] Our Lady of Victory. We have started it in a very dense forest where, according to pagan customs, kings used to be buried. We have cut down the trees of this forest which was very difficult as much due to the roughness of the terrain as to the important men of our kingdom; we feared that they would not even agree to it. However, they were so prompt to accept it and be helpful that they cut down tall and large trees with their own hands and brought construction stones on their own backs. This indeed seems to be a consequence of the divine grace. . . .

Therefore, we ask Your Highness, for the love of Jesus Christ, to be so good as to help us and grant us all that we have said and all that we have often requested. It is as much for the service of God as it is for yours and everything relies on your conscience; as for us, we cannot do much more than what we continuously do. As far as the remedies that we can provide without external help are concerned, we have done our part. But for what we cannot achieve without Your Highness' help and assistance, we ask you for the cure as one rightfully entitled to it. We should not request this either from the king of Castile, or the king of France, or any other Christian king, and we do not wish to be obliged to them due to the numerous reasons we were given. This duty is not their responsibility particularly due to the little contact they have with this kingdom. This kingdom is as Portuguese and loyal to your service as the one Your Highness rightfully inherited and, moreover, there is no room among us for ingratitude. At this very moment we are aware of the great spiritual and temporal benefits we were granted. These will not be forgotten so as to take more into consideration the flaws of our true mother than the deceitful caresses of a stepmother, even though we all are under the same law and faith. I will say no more for Your Highness is aware of what he can expect from us and it is certain that our kingdoms and provinces will always serve you. . . .

May Our Lord, through his holy mercy, always protect Your Highness and may he bless you with a long life and the strengthening of your royal possessions for his holy service.

King Afonso to King João III

Mbanza Congo, October 18, 1526

My Lord,

Your Highness wrote to have us ask him in our letters everything that we need. He would provide us with everything. The peace and wellbeing of our kingdoms lie, after God, on our life. However we are old already and we have often been affected by various diseases which weaken us to our last resources. The same diseases also strike our sons, relatives and countrymen. Yet in this kingdom we have neither doctors nor surgeons who would know how to administer the appropriate treatment to such infirmities. Also, we have neither pharmacies nor the most efficient medicines. Thus, because we have nothing, many of those who are already educated in the truths of Our Lord Jesus Christ's holy faith die! Most of the inhabitants cure themselves with herbs and various woods or turn to traditional rites. If they survive their faith in those herbs and rites grows and if they die they believe that they are saved which does not favor God's service.

To prevent such damageable erring, since, after God, it is from Your Highness that we receive in our kingdoms all the cures for health, we ask Your Highness to send here two doctors, two pharmacists and one surgeon. Let them come and stay in our kingdoms with all their medicines and tools for we need each of them very much. We shall grant them many favors, because they will be sent by Your Highness; should Your Highness agree to have them work here. We beg Your Highness in urgency to accept to send them to us because this matter is not simply about granting a particular favor but also about serving God for all the reasons we just gave you.

There is, my Lord, yet another great obstacle to the service of God in our kingdoms. Many of our subjects greatly covet the goods which your men bring in our kingdoms from Portugal. To quench this uncontrolled thirst they kidnap many of our free or freed black subjects even nobles, sons of noblemen and even our relatives. They sell them to the white men who are in our kingdom after having delivered their prisoners in secret or during the night in order not to be recognized. As soon as the captives are under the white men's power they are branded. This is how they are found by our guards when they board the ships. The white men then explain that they were bought but they cannot say from whom. Yet it is our duty, as the prisoners claim, to do justice and set them free. To prevent such incidents we have decreed that all white men buying slaves in our kingdoms, however it may happen, should first inform three noblemen and officers of our court to whom I entrusted this control. . . . They will check whether the slaves are not actually free men. If they are found to be slaves nothing will prevent anyone from having them and taking them on board. However, should the opposite be true, the captives will be taken away from the white men. We gave our consent to this favor and these services because of Your Highness' participation in this trade. Indeed we know that it is for your service that these slaves are taken from our kingdoms. If it were not so, we would not agree to it for the reasons we have already given you.

We inform Your Highness of all this so that your subjects will not come to you and say it is otherwise. Indeed they tell Your Highness many lies to keep your mind from remembering the obligations you have towards us and our kingdom for God's service. It seems to us that it would be a great favor if you could let us know through one of your letters what you think of these dispositions.

We kiss Your Highness' hands many times my Lord.

QUESTIONS FOR READING AND DISCUSSION

1. What did Afonso want the Portuguese king to do?
2. Why, according to Afonso, were his "vassals . . . beginning to claim their independence"? What does his statement suggest about his authority over his kingdom and the relations between his people and the Portuguese?
3. According to Afonso, what was wrong with trade with the Portuguese? What special wrongs accompanied the slave trade?

4. Why did the Congolese king believe Christianity was valuable? How did he compare Christianity to common religious beliefs among his people?

5. What meanings are suggested by Afonso's statement that his "kingdom is as Portuguese and loyal to your service as the one Your Highness rightfully inherited"?

6. What hints do these letters contain about why Afonso did not demand an end to the slave trade and insist that the Portuguese leave and never come back?

DOCUMENT 2

Columbus Describes
His First Encounter with "Indians"

Columbus kept a diary or log of his first voyage to the New World. He used the diary to record details of navigation and, once he arrived in the Caribbean, to note the people and places he observed. When Columbus returned to Spain, he presented his diary as a gift to King Ferdinand and Queen Isabella. The monarchs arranged to have a copy made of the diary. The original diary disappeared, but in the 1530s a priest had access to the copy, which he transcribed, summarized, and occasionally quoted. The copy then vanished, but the priest's manuscript has survived. In the quoted passage from the priest's manuscript, excerpted here, Columbus describes his first encounters with indigenous Americans. Columbus's remarks illustrate the understandings and misunderstandings as Europeans and Native Americans "discovered" one another.

The Diario of Christopher Columbus's
First Voyage to America, 1492–1493

Thursday, 11 October. . . . What follows are the very words of the Admiral [Christopher Columbus] in his book about his first voyage to, and discovery of, these Indies. I, he says, in order that they would be friendly to us — because I recognized that they were people who would be better freed [from error] and converted to our Holy Faith by love than by force — to some of them I gave red caps, and glass beads which they put on their chests, and many other things of small value, in which they took so much pleasure and became so much our friends that it was a marvel. Later they came swimming to the ships' launches where we were and brought us parrots and cotton thread in balls and javelins and many other things, and they traded them to us for other things which we gave them, such as small glass beads and bells. In sum, they took everything and gave of what they had very willingly. But it seemed to me that they were a people very poor in everything. All of them go around as naked as their mothers bore them; and the women also, although I did not see more than one quite young girl. And all those that I saw were young people, for none did I see of more than 30 years of age. They are very well formed, with handsome bodies and good faces. Their hair [is] coarse — almost like the tail of a horse — and short. They wear their hair down over their eyebrows except for a little in the back which

Oliver Dunn and James E. Kelley, Jr., eds. and trans., *The Diario of Christopher Columbus's First Voyage to America, 1492–1493,* American Exploration and Traveler Series, vol. 70 (Norman: University of Oklahoma Press, 1989) 65–109.

they wear long and never cut. Some of them paint themselves with black, and they are of the color of the Canarians, neither black nor white; and some of them paint themselves with white, and some of them with red, and some of them with whatever they find. And some of them paint their faces, and some of them the whole body, and some of them only the eyes, and some of them only the nose. They do not carry arms nor are they acquainted with them, because I showed them swords and they took them by the edge and through ignorance cut themselves. They have no iron. Their javelins are shafts without iron and some of them have at the end a fish tooth and others of other things. All of them alike are of good-sized stature and carry themselves well. I saw some who had marks of wounds on their bodies and I made signs to them asking what they were; and they showed me how people from other islands nearby came there and tried to take them, and how they defended themselves; and I believed and believe that they come here from tierra firme to take them captive. They should be good and intelligent servants, for I see that they say very quickly everything that is said to them; and I believe that they would become Christians very easily, for it seemed to me that they had no religion. Our Lord pleasing, at the time of my departure I will take six of them from here to Your Highnesses in order that they may learn to speak. No animal of any kind did I see on this island except parrots. All are the Admiral's words.

Saturday 13   October As soon as it dawned, many of these people came to the beach — all young as I have said, and all of good stature — very handsome people, with hair not curly but straight and coarse, like horsehair; and all of them very wide in the forehead and head, more so than any other race that I have seen so far. And their eyes are very handsome and not small; and none of them are black, but of the color of the Canary Islanders. . . . All alike have straight legs and no belly but are very well formed. They came to the ship with dugouts that are made from the trunk of one tree, like a long boat, and all of one piece, and worked marvelously in the fashion of the land, and so big that in some of them 40 and 45 men came. And others smaller, down to some in which came one man alone. They row with a paddle like that of a baker and go marvelously. And if it capsizes on them they then throw themselves in the water, and they right and empty it with calabashes that they carry. They brought balls of spun cotton and parrots and javelins and other little things that it would be tiresome to write down, and they gave everything for anything that was given to them. I was attentive and labored to find out if there was any gold; and I saw that some of them wore a little piece hung in a hole that they have in their noses. And by signs I was able to understand that, going to the south or rounding the island to the south, there was there a king who had large vessels of it and had very much gold. I strove to get them to go there and later saw that they had no intention of going. I decided to wait until the afternoon of the morrow and then depart for the southwest, for, as many of them showed me, they said there was land to the south and to the southwest and to the northwest and that these people from the northwest came to fight them many times. And so I will go to the southwest to seek gold and precious stones. . . . And these people are very gentle, and because of their desire to have some of our things, and believing that nothing will be given to them without their giving something, and not having anything, they take what they can and then throw themselves into the water to swim. But everything they have they give for anything given to them, for they traded even for pieces of bowls and broken glass cups. . . . And also the gold that they wear hung in their noses originates here; but in order not to lose time I want to go to see if I can find the island of Cipango [Japan]. Now, since night had come, all the Indians went ashore in their dugouts.

Sunday 14 October As soon as it dawned I ordered the ship's boat and the launches of the caravels made ready and went north-northeast along the island in order to see what there was in the other part, which was the eastern part. And also to see the villages, and I soon saw two or three, as well as people, who all came to the beach calling to us and giving thanks to God. Some of them brought us water; others, other things to eat; others, when they saw that I did not care to go ashore, threw themselves into the sea swimming and came to us, and we understood that they were asking us if we had come from the heavens. And one old man got into the ship's boat, and others in loud voices called to all the men and women: Come see the men who came from the heavens. Bring them something to eat and drink. Many men came, and many women, each one with something, giving thanks to God, throwing themselves on the ground; and they raised their hands to heaven, and afterward they called to us in loud voices to come ashore. . . . [T]hese people are very naive about weapons, as Your Highnesses will see from the seven that I caused to be taken in order to carry them away to you and to learn our language and to return them. Except that, whenever Your Highnesses may command, all of them can be taken to Castile or held captive in this same island; because with 50 men all of them could be held in subjection and can be made to do whatever one might wish. . . . I . . . returned to the ship and set sail, and I saw so many islands that I did not know how to decide which one I would go to first. And those men whom I had taken told me by signs that they were so very many that they were numberless. . . .

Tuesday and Wednesday 16 October. . . . I came to a village where I anchored and to which had come that man whom I found mid-sea yesterday in that dugout. He had given so many good reports about us that during the whole night there was no lack of dugouts alongside the ship, to which they brought us water and of what they had. I ordered something given to each one, that is to say ten or twelve little glass beads on a thread, and some brass jingles of the sort that in Castile are worth a maravedi each, and some metal lace-ends, all of which they considered of the greatest excellence. And also I ordered them given food, in order that they might eat when they came to the ship, and molasses. And later . . . I sent the ship's boat to shore for water. And the natives very willingly showed my people where the water was, and they themselves brought the filled barrels to the boat and delighted in pleasing us. This island is exceedingly large and I have decided to sail around it, because according to my understanding, on or near it there is a gold mine. . . . These people are like those of the . . . [other] islands in speech and customs except that these now appear somewhat more civilized and given to commerce and more astute. Because I see that they have brought cotton here to the ship and other little things for which they know better how to bargain payment than the others did. And in this island I even saw cotton cloths made like small cloaks, and the people are more intelligent, and the women wear in front of their bodies a little thing of cotton that scarcely covers their genitals. . . . I do not detect in them any religion and I believe that they would become Christians very quickly because they are of very good understanding. . . .

Monday 22 October All this night and today I stayed waiting [to see] if the king of this place or other persons would bring gold or something else of substance; and there came many of these people, like the others of the other islands, naked and painted, some of them with white, some with red, some with black, and so on in many fashions. They brought javelins and balls of cotton to barter, which they traded here with some sailors for pieces of broken glass cups and for pieces of clay bowls. Some of them were wearing pieces of gold hanging from their noses, and they willingly gave it for a bell of the sort [put] on the foot of a sparrow hawk and for small glass beads; but it is so little that it is nothing. For it is true that any little thing given to them, as well as our coming, they considered great marvels; and they believed that we had come from the heavens.

QUESTIONS FOR READING AND DISCUSSION

1. What features of Native Americans did Columbus notice? How did he believe they compared with Europeans? Why did he conclude that "they were a people very poor in everything"?
2. Why did Columbus think Indians were friendly? Can you detect hints of what the Indians might have thought about Columbus and his men? How did the two groups communicate with each other?
3. What did Indians believe, as far as Columbus could tell? Why did he assume that Indians thought he and his men came from the heavens?
4. If a diary had been kept by one of the Indians who came aboard Columbus's ship, what might it have said about the Europeans?

DOCUMENT 3

A Conquistador Arrives in Mexico, 1519–1520

Bernal Díaz del Castillo, born in Spain in 1492, came to the New World at the age of twenty-two to seek his fortune. After five disappointing years, he joined Hernando Cortés's expedition to Mexico. A battle-hardened conquistador, Díaz participated in all the major events of the Conquest. Afterwards, when he read slanted, inaccurate, or fabricated stories of the Conquest, he decided to write his own eyewitness account. After working on his manuscript for almost thirty years, he sent a copy to the king of Spain in 1575. It lie buried in Spanish archives until it was published in 1632 as The True History of the Conquest of New Spain. *In this selection (translated from Spanish), Díaz describes what he saw when he and the other Spaniards first arrived in Mexico.*

Bernal Díaz del Castillo

The Conquest of New Spain, 1632

Next morning . . . when we saw all those cities and villages built in the water, and other great towns on dry land, and that straight and level causeway leading to Mexico, we were astounded. These great towns and cues [temples] and buildings rising from the water, all made of stone, seemed like an enchanted vi-

Bernal Díaz, *The Conquest of New Spain,* trans. J. M. Cohen (London: Viking Penguin, Penguin Classics, 1963) 214–235.

sion. . . . Indeed, some of our soldiers asked whether it was not all a dream. . . . It was all so wonderful that I do not know how to describe this first glimpse of things never heard of, seen or dreamed of before. . . . I say again that I stood looking at it, and thought that no land like it would ever be discovered in the whole world. . . . But today all that I then saw is overthrown and destroyed; nothing is left standing. . . .

So, with luck on our side, we boldly entered the city of Tenochtitlán or Mexico on 8 November in the year of our Lord 1519. . . .

The great Montezuma was about forty years old, of good height, well proportioned, spare and slight, and not very dark, though of the usual Indian complexion. He did not wear his hair long but just over his ears, and he had a short black beard, well-shaped and thin. His face was rather long and cheerful, he had fine eyes, and in his appearance and manner could express geniality or, when necessary, a serious composure. He was very neat and clean, and took a bath every afternoon. He had many women as his mistresses, the daughters of chieftains, but two legitimate wives who were Caciques [rulers] in their own right, and when he had intercourse with any of them it was so secret that only some of his servants knew of it. He was quite free from sodomy. The clothes he wore one day he did not wear again till three or four days later. He had a guard of two hundred chieftains lodged in rooms beside his own, only some of whom were permitted to speak to him. . . . For each meal his servants prepared him more than thirty dishes cooked in their native style, which they put over small earthenware braziers to prevent them from getting cold. They cooked more than three hundred plates of the food the great Montezuma was going to eat, and more than a thousand more for the guard. I have heard that they used to cook him the flesh of young boys. But as he had such a variety of dishes, made of so many different ingredients, we could not tell whether a dish was of human flesh or anything else, since every day they cooked fowls, turkeys, pheasants, local partridges, quail, tame and wild duck, venison, wild boar, marsh birds, pigeons, hares and rabbits, also many other kinds of birds and beasts native to their country, so numerous that I cannot quickly name them all. . . .

Montezuma had two houses stocked with every sort of weapon; many of them were richly adorned with gold and precious stones. There were shields large and small, and a sort of broadsword, and two-handed swords set with flint blades that cut much better than our swords, and lances longer than ours, with five-foot blades consisting of many knives. Even when these are driven at a buckler or a shield they are not deflected. In fact they cut like razors, and the Indians can shave their heads with them. They had very good bows and arrows, and double and single-pointed javelins as well as their throwingsticks and many slings and round stones shaped by hand, and another sort of shield that can be rolled up when they are not fighting, so that it does not get in the way, but which can be opened when they need it in battle and covers their bodies from head to foot. There was also a great deal of cotton armour richly worked on the outside with different coloured feathers, which they used as devices and distinguishing marks, and they had casques and helmets made of wood and bone which were also highly decorated with feathers on the outside. They had other arms of different kinds . . . and workmen skilled in the manufacture of such things, and stewards who were in charge of these arms.

Let us pass on to the aviary. I cannot possibly enumerate every kind of bird that was in it or describe its characteristics. There was everything from the royal eagle, smaller kinds of eagles, and other large birds, down to multi-coloured little birds, and those from which they take the fine green feathers they use in their feather-work. . . .

I have already described the manner of their sacrifices. They strike open the wretched Indian's chest with flint knives and hastily tear out the palpitating heart which, with the blood, they present to the idols in whose name they have performed the sacrifice. Then they cut off the arms, thighs, and head, eating the arms and thighs at their ceremonial banquets. The head they hang up on a beam, and the body of the sacrificed man is not eaten but given to the beasts of prey. They also had many vipers in this accursed house, and poisonous snakes which have something that sounds like a bell in their tails. These, which are the deadliest snakes of all, they kept in jars and great pottery vessels full of feathers, in which they laid their eggs and reared their young. They were fed on the bodies of sacrificed Indians and the flesh of the dogs that they bred. We know for certain, too, that when they drove us out of Mexico and killed over eight hundred and fifty of our soldiers, they fed those beasts and snakes on their bodies for many days, as I shall relate in due course. These snakes and wild beasts were dedicated to their fierce idols, and kept them company. As for the horrible noise when the lions and tigers roared, and the jackals and foxes howled, and the serpents hissed, it was so appalling that one seemed to be in hell.

I must now speak of the skilled workmen whom Montezuma employed in all the crafts they practised, beginning with the jewellers and workers in silver and gold and various kinds of hollowed objects, which excited the admiration of our great silversmiths at home. . . . There were other skilled craftsmen who worked with precious stones . . . and specialists in feather-work, and very fine painters and carvers. We can form some judgement of what they did then from what we can see of their work today. . . .

Let us go on to the women, the weavers and sempstresses, who made such a huge quantity of fine robes with very elaborate feather designs. . . . In Montezuma's own palaces very fine cloths were woven by those chieftains' daughters whom he kept as mistresses; and the daughters of other dignitaries, who lived in a kind of retirement like nuns in some houses close to the great cue of Huichilobos, wore robes entirely of featherwork. Out of devotion for that god and a female deity who was said to preside over marriage, their fathers would place them in religious retirement until they found husbands. They would then take them out to be married.

Now to speak of the great number of performers whom Montezuma kept to entertain him. There were dancers and stilt-walkers, and some who seemed to fly as they leapt through the air, and men rather like clowns to make him laugh. There was a whole quarter full of these people who had no other occupation. He had as many workmen as he needed, too, stonecutters, masons, and carpenters, to keep his houses in repair.

We must not forget the gardens with their many varieties of flowers and sweet-scented trees planted in order, and their ponds and tanks of fresh water into which a stream flowed at one end and out of which it flowed at the other, and the baths he had there, and the variety of small birds that nested in the branches, and the medicinal and useful herbs that grew there. His gardens were a wonderful sight, and required many gardeners to take care of them. . . .

When we had already been in Mexico for four days, and neither our Captain nor anyone else had left our quarters except to visit these houses and gardens,

Cortés said it would be a good thing to visit the large [market] square of Tlatelolco.
. . . On reaching the market-place, escorted by the many Caciques whom Montezuma had assigned to us, we were astounded at the great number of people
and the quantities of merchandise, and at the orderliness and good arrangements
that prevailed, for we had never seen such a thing before. The chieftains who accompanied us pointed everything out. Every kind of merchandise was kept separate and had its fixed place marked for it.

Let us begin with the dealers in gold, silver, and precious stones, feathers,
cloaks, and embroidered goods, and male and female slaves who are also sold
there. They bring as many slaves to be sold in that market as the Portuguese bring
Negroes from Guinea. Some are brought there attached to long poles by means of
collars round their necks to prevent them from escaping, but others are left loose.
Next there were those who sold coarser cloth, and cotton goods and fabrics made
of twisted thread, and there were chocolate merchants with their chocolate. In
this way you could see every kind of merchandise to be found anywhere in New
Spain, laid out in the same way as goods are laid out in my own district of Medina del Campo, a centre for fairs, where each line of stalls has its own particular
sort. . . . There were sellers of kidney-beans and sage and other vegetables and
herbs in another place, and in yet another they were selling fowls, and birds with
great dewlaps, also rabbits, hares, deer, young ducks, little dogs, and other such
creatures. Then there were the fruiterers; and the women who sold cooked food,
flour and honey cake, and tripe, had their part of the market. Then came pottery
of all kinds, from big water-jars to little jugs, displayed in its own place, also
honey, honey-paste, and other sweets like nougat. Elsewhere they sold timber
too, boards, cradles, beams, blocks, and benches, all in a quarter of their own.

Then there were the sellers of pitch-pine for torches, and other things of that
kind, and I must also mention, with all apologies, that they sold many canoe-loads of human excrement, which they kept in the creeks near the market. This
was for the manufacture of salt and the curing of skins, which they say cannot be
done without it. I know that many gentlemen will laugh at this, but I assure them
it is true. I may add that on all the roads they have shelters made of reeds or straw
or grass so that they can retire when they wish to do so, and purge their bowels
unseen by passersby, and also in order that their excrement shall not be lost.

But why waste so many words on the goods in their great market? If I describe everything in detail I shall never be done. . . . They have a building there
also in which three judges sit, and there are officials like constables who examine
the merchandise. I am forgetting the sellers of salt and the makers of flint knives,
and how they split them off the stone itself, and the fisherwomen and the men
who sell small cakes made from a sort of weed which they get out of the great
lake, which curdles and forms a kind of bread which tastes rather like cheese.
They sell axes too, made of bronze and copper and tin, and gourds and brightly
painted wooden jars.

We went on to the great cue, and as we approached its wide courts, before
leaving the market-place itself, we saw many more merchants who, so I was told,
brought gold to sell in grains, just as they extract it from the mines. This gold is
placed in the thin quills of the large geese of that country, which are so white as
to be transparent. They used to reckon their accounts with one another by the
length and thickness of these little quills, how much so many cloaks or so many
gourds of chocolate or so many slaves were worth, or anything else they were
bartering. . . .

Having examined and considered all that we had seen, we turned back to the great market and the swarm of people buying and selling. The mere murmur of their voices talking was loud enough to be heard more than three miles away. Some of our soldiers who had been in many parts of the world, in Constantinople, in Rome, and all over Italy, said that they had never seen a market so well laid out, so large, so orderly, and so full of people.

QUESTIONS FOR READING AND DISCUSSION

1. How did Mexico compare to Europe, according to Díaz? Did Díaz consider Mexico civilized? Why or why not? What did Díaz think about Mexican practices of human sacrifice?

2. In what ways was Montezuma different from other Mexicans, according to Díaz? Did such differences strike Díaz as bizarre or conventional?

3. Why did Díaz find Mexico astounding, like "an enchanted vision"? To what extent did Mexico differ from what Díaz expected to find? What might have shaped his expectations and in turn his sense of wonder?

4. Since Díaz wrote this description of his entry into Mexico many years after it happened, how reliable is it? How might the passage of time and Díaz's hindsight have distorted his memory of this decisive moment?

DOCUMENT 4

A Mexican Description of the Conquest of Mexico

This remarkable account comes from the Florentine Codex, a massive cultural encyclopedia of the native people of Mexico that was compiled in the mid-sixteenth century under the direction of Bernardino de Sahagún, a Franciscan missionary. Beginning about 1547, Sahagún trained a group of Mexican men to interview prominent elders and to record their words in Nahuatl, their native language. Sahagún's informants had a vivid memory of the conquest of Mexico, which had occurred only a generation earlier. Sahagún published their account, in both Nahuatl and Spanish, in Book 12 of the Codex — the source of the following selection, which was translated from Nahuatl. This account reveals Mexican perspectives on the events of conquest.

Mexican Accounts of Conquest from the Florentine Codex

The Spaniards . . . set out in this direction, about to enter Mexico here. Then they all dressed and equipped themselves for war. They girded themselves, tying their battle gear tightly on themselves and then on their horses. Then they arranged themselves in rows, files, ranks.

James Lockhart, ed. and trans., *We People Here: Nahuatl Accounts of the Conquest of Mexico* (Berkeley and Los Angeles: University of California Press, 1993).

Four horse[men] came ahead, going first, staying ahead, leading. They kept turning about as they went, facing people, looking this way and that, looking sideways, gazing everywhere between the houses, examining things, looking up at the roofs.

Also the dogs, their dogs, came ahead, sniffing at things and constantly panting.

By himself came marching ahead, all alone, the one who bore the standard on his shoulder. He came waving it about, making it spin, tossing it here and there. It came stiffening, rising up like a warrior, twisting and turning.

Following him came those with iron swords. Their iron swords came bare and gleaming. On their shoulders they bore their shields, of wood or leather.

The second contingent and file were horses carrying people, each with his cotton cuirass, his leather shield, his iron lance, and his iron sword hanging down from the horse's neck. They came with bells on, jingling or rattling. The horses, the deer, neighed, there was much neighing, and they would sweat a great deal; water seemed to fall from them. And their flecks of foam splatted on the ground, like soapsuds splatting. As they went they made a beating, throbbing, and hoof-pounding like throwing stones. . . .

The third file were those with iron crossbows, the crossbowmen. As they came, the iron crossbows lay in their arms. They came along testing them out, brandishing them, aiming them. But some carried them on their shoulders, came shouldering the crossbows. Their quivers went hanging at their sides, passed under their armpits, well filled, packed with arrows, with iron bolts. Their cotton upper armor reached to their knees, very thick, firmly sewn, and dense, like stone. And their heads were wrapped in the same cotton armor, and on their heads plumes stood up, parting and spreading.

The fourth file were likewise horse[men]; their outfits were the same as has been said.

The fifth group were those with harquebuses,[1] the harquebusiers, shouldering their harquebuses; some held them [level]. And when they went into the great palace, the residence of the ruler, they repeatedly shot off their harquebuses. They exploded, sputtered, discharged, thundered, disgorged. Smoke spread, it grew dark with smoke, everyplace filled with smoke. The fetid smell made people dizzy and faint.

And last, bringing up the rear, went the war leader, thought to be the ruler and director in battle. . . . Gathered and massed about him, going at his side, accompanying him, enclosing him were his warriors, those with devices, his [aides]. . . .

Then all those from the various altepetl [realms] on the other side of the mountains, the Tlaxcalans[2] [and others] . . . came following behind. They came outfitted for war with their cotton upper armor, shields, and bows, their quivers full and packed with feathered arrows, some barbed, some blunted, some with obsidian points. They went crouching, hitting their mouths with their hands and yelling, singing . . . , whistling, shaking their heads.

---

[1]**harquebuses:** Spaniards' firearms—a small-caliber long gun.

[2]**Tlaxcalans:** A powerful group of Indians hostile to Mexicans and allied with the Spaniards.

Some bore burdens and provisions on their backs; some used [tump lines for] their foreheads, some [bands around] their chests, some carrying frames, some board cages, some deep baskets. Some made bundles, perhaps putting the bundles on their backs. Some dragged the large cannons, which went resting on wooden wheels, making a clamor as they came. . . .

Moteucçoma [Montezuma] went in peace and quiet to meet the Spaniards. . . .

Moteucçoma dressed and prepared himself for a meeting, along with other great rulers and high nobles, his rulers and nobles. Then they went to the meeting. On gourd bases they set out different precious flowers; in the midst of the shield flowers and heart flowers stood popcorn flowers, yellow tobacco flowers, cacao flowers, [made into] wreaths for the head, wreaths to be girded around. And they carried golden necklaces, necklaces with pendants, wide necklaces.

And when Moteucçoma went out to meet them . . . , he gave various things to the war leader, the commander of the warriors; he gave him flowers, he put necklaces on him, he put flower necklaces on him, he girded him with flowers, he put flower wreaths on his head. Then he laid before him the golden necklaces, all the different things for greeting people. He ended by putting some of the necklaces on him.

Then [Cortés] said in reply to Moteucçoma, "Is it not you? Is it not you then? Moteucçoma?"

Moteucçoma said, "Yes, it is me." Thereupon he stood up straight, he stood up with their faces meeting. He bowed down deeply to him. He stretched as far as he could, standing stiffly. Addressing him, he said to him,

"O our lord, be doubly welcomed on your arrival in this land; you have come to satisfy your curiosity about your altepetl of Mexico, you have come to sit on your seat of authority, which I have kept a while for you, where I have been in charge for you, for your agents the [previous] rulers[3] . . . have gone, who for a very short time came to be in charge for you, to govern the altepetl of Mexico. It is after them that your poor vassal [myself] came. Will they come back to the place of their absence? If only one of them could see and behold what has now happened in my time, what I now see after our lords are gone! For I am not just dreaming, not just sleepwalking, not just seeing it in my sleep. I am not just dreaming that I have seen you, have looked upon your face. For a time I have been concerned, looking toward the mysterious place from which you have come, among clouds and mist. It is so that the rulers on departing said that you would come in order to acquaint yourself with your altepetl and sit upon your seat of authority. And now it has come true, you have come. Be doubly welcomed, enter the land, go to enjoy your palace; rest your body. May our lords be arrived in the land."

And when the speech that Moteucçoma directed to [Cortés] . . . had concluded, Marina [an Indian woman who accompanied Cortés and who could speak Nahuatl and Spanish] reported it to him, interpreting it for him. And when [Cortés] . . . had heard what Moteucçoma had said, he spoke to Marina in return, babbling back to them, replying in his babbling tongue,

"Let Moteucçoma be at ease, let him not be afraid, for we greatly esteem him. Now we are truly satisfied to see him in person and hear him, for until now we

---

[3]Evidently, Montezuma and other Mexicans initially believed the Spaniards were ancient Mexican gods who had returned to rule over their empire.

have greatly desired to see him and look upon his face. Well, now we have seen him, we have come to his homeland of Mexico. Bit by bit he will hear what we have to say."

Thereupon [the Spaniards] took [Moteucçoma] by the hand. They came along with him, stroking his hair to show their good feeling. And the Spaniards looked at him, each of them giving him a close look. They would start along walking, then mount, then dismount again in order to see him. . . .

[T]he Spaniards went with Moteucçoma to enter the great palace. . . .

And when they had reached the palace and gone in, immediately they seized Moteucçoma and kept close watch over him, not letting him out of their sight. . . . And when this had happened, then the various guns were fired. It seemed that everything became confused; people went this way and that, scattering and dart-ing about. It was as though everyone's tongue were out, everyone were preoccu-pied, everyone had been taking mushrooms, as though who knows what had been shown to everyone. Fear reigned, as though everyone had swallowed his heart. It was still that way at night; everyone was terrified, taken aback, thunder-struck, stunned.

And when it dawned, everything [the Spaniards] needed was proclaimed: white tortillas, roast turkeys, eggs, fresh water, wood, firewood, charcoal, earthen tubs, polished bowls, waterjars, large clay pitchers, vessels for frying, all kinds of earthenware. Moteucçoma himself ordered it. But when he summoned the noble-men, they would no longer obey him, but grew angry. They no longer performed their duty to him, no longer went to him; no longer was he heeded. But he was not therefore forsaken; he was given all he needed to eat and drink, and water and deer fodder [for the Spaniards].

And when [the Spaniards] were well settled, right away they interrogated Moteucçoma about all the stored treasure of the altepetl, the devices and shields. They greatly prodded him, they eagerly sought gold as a thing of esteem. And then Moteucçoma went along leading the Spaniards. They gathered around him, bunched around him; he went in their midst, leading the way. They went along taking hold of him, grasping him. And when they reached the storehouse . . . then all the shining things were brought out: the quetzal-feather head fan, the de-vices, the shields, the golden disks, the necklaces of the devils, the golden nose crescents, the golden leg bands, the golden arm bands, the golden sheets for the forehead.

Thereupon the gold on the shields and on all the devices was taken off. And when all the gold had been detached, right away they set on fire, set fire to, ig-nited all the different precious things, they all burned. And the Spaniards made the gold into bricks. And they took as much of the green-stone as pleased them; as to the rest of the green-stone, the Tlaxcalans just snatched it up. And [the Spaniards] went everywhere, scratching about in the hiding places, storehouses, places of storage all around. They took everything they saw that pleased them. . . .

[T]he Spaniards killed and annihilated the Mexica who were celebrating the feast of Huitzilopochtli[4] at what they call the . . . [Divine Courtyard, Courtyard of the Gods, temple courtyard].

When things were already going on, when the festivity was being observed and there was dancing and singing, with voices raised in song, the singing was

---

[4]**Huitzilopochtli:** The god of war and the chief god in the Mexican pantheon.

like the noise of waves breaking against the rocks. When it was time, when the moment had come for the Spaniards to do the killing, they came out equipped for battle. They came and closed off each of the places where people went in and out. . . . And when they had closed these exits, they stationed themselves in each, and no one could come out any more.

When this had been done, they went into the temple courtyard to kill people. Those whose assignment it was to do the killing just went on foot, each with his metal sword and his leather shield, some of them iron-studded. Then they surrounded those who were dancing, going among the cylindrical drums. They struck a drummer's arms; both of his hands were severed. Then they struck his neck; his head landed far away. Then they stabbed everyone with iron lances and struck them with iron swords. They stuck some in the belly, and then their entrails came spilling out. They split open the heads of some, they really cut their skulls to pieces, their skulls were cut up into little bits. And some they hit on the shoulders; their bodies broke open and ripped. Some they hacked on the calves, some on the thighs, some on their bellies, and then all their entrails would spill out. And if someone still tried to run it was useless; he just dragged his intestines along. There was a stench as if of sulfur. Those who tried to escape could go nowhere. When anyone tried to go out, at the entryways they struck and stabbed him. . . .

And when it became known [what was happening], everyone cried out, "Mexica warriors, come running, get outfitted with devices, shields, and arrows, hurry, come running, the warriors are dying; they have died, perished, been annihilated, o Mexica warriors!" Thereupon there were war cries, shouting, and beating of hands against lips. The warriors quickly came outfitted, bunched together, carrying arrows and shields. Then the fighting began; they shot at them with barbed darts, spears, and tridents, and they hurled darts with broad obsidian points at them. A cloud of yellow reeds spread over the Spaniards. . . .

[A]t the time the Spaniards left Mexico, there came an illness of pustules of which many local people died; it was called "the great rash" [smallpox].

Before the Spaniards appeared to us, first an epidemic broke out, a sickness of pustules. . . . Large bumps spread on people; some were entirely covered. They spread everywhere, on the face, the head, the chest, etc. [The disease] brought great desolation; a great many died of it. They could no longer walk about, but lay in their dwellings and sleeping places, no longer able to move or stir. They were unable to change position, to stretch out on their sides or face down, or raise their heads. And when they made a motion, they called out loudly. The pustules that covered people caused great desolation; very many people died of them, and many just starved to death; starvation reigned, and no one took care of others any longer.

On some people, the pustules appeared only far apart, and they did not suffer greatly, nor did many of them die of it. But many people's faces were spoiled by it, their faces and noses were made rough. Some lost an eye or were blinded.

This disease of pustules lasted a full sixty days; after sixty days it abated and ended. When people were convalescing and reviving, the pustules disease began to move in the direction of Chalco. And many were disabled or paralyzed by it, but they were not disabled forever. . . . The Mexica warriors were greatly weakened by it.

And when things were in this state, the Spaniards came [back], moving toward us. . . .

And all the common people suffered greatly. There was famine; many died of hunger. They no longer drank good, pure water, but the water they drank was salty. Many people died of it, and because of it many got dysentery and died. Everything was eaten: lizards, swallows, maize straw, grass that grows on salt flats. And they chewed at colorin wood, glue flowers, plaster, leather, and deer-skin, which they roasted, baked, and toasted so that they could eat them, and they ground up medicinal herbs and adobe bricks. There had never been the like of such suffering. The siege was frightening, and great numbers died of hunger. And bit by bit they came pressing us back against the wall, herding us together. . . .

And along every stretch [of road] the Spaniards took things from people by force. They were looking for gold; they cared nothing for green-stone, precious feathers, or turquoise. They looked everywhere with the women, on their ab-domens, under their skirts. And they looked everywhere with the men, under their loincloths and in their mouths. And [the Spaniards] took, picked out the beautiful women, with yellow bodies. And how some women got loose was that they covered their faces with mud and put on ragged blouses and skirts, clothing themselves all in rags. And some men were picked out, those who were strong and in the prime of life, and those who were barely youths, to run errands for them and be their errand boys, called their [priests, acolytes]. Then they burned some of them on the mouth [branded them]; some they branded on the cheeks, some on the mouth.

QUESTIONS FOR READING AND DISCUSSION

1. What did the Mexicans notice about the Spaniards on their entry into Tenochti-tlán? How did their impressions of the Spaniards change, and what happened to change those impressions?
2. Why did Montezuma welcome Cortés, saying "you have come to sit on your seat of authority"?
3. What comparisons did the Mexicans make between themselves and the Spaniards? Did the Mexicans consider the Spaniards civilized? To what extent did the Mexicans perceive the Spaniards as the Spaniards perceived them-selves? By what standards did the Mexicans judge the Spaniards?
4. Since this account was collected a generation after the Conquest, to what ex-tent might post-Conquest Mexican experiences have shaped this narrative?

COMPARATIVE QUESTIONS

1. How did religion influence the perceptions and expectations of the individu-als in these different encounters?
2. How did Columbus's reactions to Native Americans compare with Díaz's? How did the responses of the people Columbus first encountered compare with the reception the Mexicans gave to the conquistadors?
3. What similarities and differences characterized Afonso's relations with the Portuguese and Mexicans' relations with Spaniards?
4. In these encounters between Europeans and non-Europeans, what forms of communication proved most important? How were they learned, and in what ways did they change?
5. What did Europeans and non-Europeans seek from each other, according to these accounts? To what extent did each group gain (or lose) from the encoun-ters, according to these documents?

CHAPTER 2

THE SOUTHERN COLONIES IN THE SEVENTEENTH CENTURY
1601–1700

Native Americans, tobacco planters, servants, and slaves peopled the world of the seventeenth-century southern colonies. Few of these people jotted down their activities, their thoughts, or their longings. Their experiences can nevertheless be glimpsed in public records such as official reports, estate inventories, court testimony, and political announcements. The documents that follow disclose tensions and pleasures of daily life in the seventeenth-century Chesapeake.

DOCUMENT 1
Opechancanough's 1622 Uprising in Virginia

Fifteen years after the settlement of Jamestown in 1607, the coastal Algonqian leader Opechancanough — brother of Powhatan, the chief who first encountered the English settlers — organized a surprise attack against the Virginia colonists. The following account of the attack, written in 1622 by Edward Waterhouse, summarized for members of the London-based Virginia Company the colonists' understanding of what happened and what should be done about it. Waterhouse's Declaration expressed the colonists' sense of betrayal and outrage coupled with justifications for unrestrained hostility toward Native Americans and explanations of how hostility would benefit the colonists and the Virginia Company. To decipher seventeenth-century words that are spelled differently today, try reading passages aloud.

Edward Waterhouse's Declaration, *1622*

A DECLARATION of the state of the Colony and Affaires in VIRGINIA. With a Relation of the barbarous Massacre in the time of peace and League, treacherously executed upon *the English by the native Infidels, 22 March last.* . . .

[T]hat all men may see the unpartiall ingenuity of this Discourse, we freely confesse, that the Countrey is not so good, as the *Natives* are bad, whose barbarous Savagenesse needs more cultivation then the ground it selfe, being more overspread with incivilitie and treachery, then that with Bryers. For the land being tilled and used well by us, deceived not our expectation, but rather exceeded it farre, being so thankfull as to returne an hundred for one. But the *Savages* though never Nation used so kindly upon so small desert, have in stead of that *Harvest* which our paines merited, returned nothing but Bryers and thornes, pricking even to death many of their Benefactors. . . .

[Last November, 1621] the Country [was] setled in a peace (as all men there thought) sure and unviolable, not onely because it was solemnly ratified and sworne, and at the request of the Native King stamped in Brasse, and fixed to one of his Oakes of note, but as being advantagious to both parts; to the Savages as the weaker, under which they were safely sheltred and defended; to us, as being the easiest way then thought to pursue and advance our projects of buildings, plantings, and effecting their conversion by peaceable and fayre meanes. And such was the conceit of firme peace and amitie, as that there was seldome or never a sword worne, and a Peece seldomer, except for a Deere or Fowle. By which assurance of securitie, the Plantations of particular Adventurers and Planters were placed scatteringly and straglingly as a choyce veyne of rich ground invited them, and the further from neighbors held the better. The houses generally set open to the Savages, who were alwaies friendly entertained at the tables of the English, and commonly lodged in their bed-chambers. The old planters (as they thought now come to reape the benefit of their long travels) placed with wonderfull content upon their private dividents, and the planting of particular Hundreds and Colonies pursued with an hopefull alacrity, all our projects . . . in a faire way, and their familarity with the Natives, seeming to open a faire gate for their conversion to Christianitie.

The Country being in this estate, an occasion was ministred of sending to *Opachankano* the King of these Savages, about the middle of *March* last, what time the Messenger returned backe with these words from him, That he held the peace concluded so firme, as the Skie should sooner fall then it dissolve: yea, such was the treacherous dissimulation of that people who then had contrived our destruction, that even two dayes before the Massacre, some of our men were guided thorow the woods by them in safety. . . .

[O]n the Friday morning (the fatal day) the 22 *of March,* as also in the evening, as in other dayes before, they came unarmed into our houses, without Bowes or arrowes, or other weapons, with Deere, Turkies, Fish, Furres, and other provisions, to sell, and trucke with us, for glasse, beades, and other trifles: yea in some places, sate downe at Breakfast with our people at their tables, whom immediately with their owne tooles and weapons, eyther laid downe, or standing in their houses, they basely and barbarously murthered, not sparing eyther age or sexe, man, woman or childe; so sodaine in their cruell execution, that few or none discerned the weapon or blow that brought them to destruction. In which manner they also slew many of our people then at their severall workes and husbandries in the fields, and without their houses, some in planting Corne and Tobacco, some

Susan Myra Kingsbury, ed., *The Records of the Virginia Company of London,* Vol. 3 (Washington D.C.: U.S. Government Printing Office, 1906–1935) 541–64.

in gardening, some in making Bricke, building, sawing, and other kindes of hus-
bandry, they well knowing in what places and quarters each of our men were, in
regard of their daily familiarity, and resort to us for trading and other negotiations, which the more willingly was by us continued and cherished for the desire
we had of effecting that great master-peece of workes, their conversion. And by
this meanes that fatall Friday morning, there fell under the bloudy and barbarous
hands of that perfidious and inhumane people, contrary to all lawes of God and
men, of Nature and Nations, three hundred forty seven men, women, and children, most by their owne weapons; and not being content with taking away life
alone, they fell after againe upon the dead, making as well as they could, a fresh
murder, defacing, dragging, and mangling the dead carkasses into many pieces,
and carying some parts away in derision, with base and bruitish triumph. . . .

[T]he slaughter had beene universall, if God had not put it into the heart of
an Indian belonging to one *Perry,* to disclose it, who living in the house of one
Pace, was urged by another Indian his Brother (who came the night before and
lay with him) to kill *Pace,* (so commanded by their King as he declared) as hee
would kill *Perry:* telling further that by such an houre in the morning a number
would come from divers places to finish the Execution, who failed not at the time:
Perries Indian rose out of his bed and reveales it to *Pace,* that used him as a Sonne:
And thus the rest of the Colony that had warning given them, by this meanes
was saved. Such was (God bee thanked for it) the good fruit of an Infidell converted to Christianity; for though three hundred and more of ours died by many
of these Pagan Infidels, yet thousands of ours were saved by the means of one of
them alone which was made a Christian. . . .

Pace upon this discovery, securing his house, before day rowed over the River
to *James-City* (in that place neere three miles in bredth) and gave notice thereof to
the Governor, by which meanes they were prevented there, and at such other
Plantations as was possible for a timely intelligence to be given; for where they
saw us standing upon our Guard, at the sight of a Peece they all ranne away. In
other places that could have no notice, some Peeces with munition (the use
whereof they know not) were there carried away, and some few Cattell also were
destroyed by them. And as Fame divulgeth (not without probable grounds) their
King hath since caused the most part of the Gunpowder by him surprized, to bee
sowne, to draw therefrom the like increase, as of his Maize or Corne, in Harvest
next. And that it is since discovered, that the last Summer *Opachankano* practised
with a King of the Eastern shore (no well-willer of his) to furnish him with store
of poison (naturally growing in his country) for our destruction, which he absolutely refused, though he sent him great store of Beades, and other presents to
winne him thereunto: which he, with five or sixe of his great men, offered to be
ready to justifie against him. That the true cause of this surprize was most by the
instigation of the Devill, (enemy to their salvation) and the dayly feare that poss-
est them, that in time we by our growing continually upon them, would dispos-
sesse them of this Country, as they had beene formerly of the West Indies by the
Spaniard; produced this bloody act. That never griefe and shame possessed any
people more then themselves, to be thus butchered by so naked and cowardly a
people, who dare not stand the presentment of a staffe in manner of a Peece, nor
an uncharged Peece in the hands of a woman, from which they flye as so many
Hares; much faster then from their tormenting Devill, whom they worship for
feare, though they acknowledge they love him not. . . .

[T]his must needs bee for the good of the Plantation after, and the losse of this blood to make the body more healthfull, as by these reasons may be manifest.

First, Because betraying of innocency never rests unpunished. . . .

Secondly, Because our hands which before were tied with gentlenesse and faire usage, are now set at liberty by the treacherous violence of the Savages, not untying the Knot, but cutting it: So that we, who hitherto have had possession of no more ground then their waste, and our purchase at a valuable consideration to their owne contentment, gained; may now by right of Warre, and law of Nations, invade the Country, and destroy them who sought to destroy us: whereby wee shall enjoy their cultivated places, turning the laborious Mattocke into the victorious Sword (wherein there is more both ease, benefit, and glory) and possessing the fruits of others labours. Now their cleared grounds in all their villages (which are situate in the fruitfullest places of the land) shall be inhabited by us, whereas heretofore the grubbing of woods was the greatest labour.

Thirdly, Because those commodities which the Indians enjoyed as much or rather more than we, shall now also be entirely possessed by us. The Deere and other beasts will be in safety, and infinitly increase, which heretofore not onely in the generall huntings of the King (whereat foure or five hundred Deere were usually slaine) but by each particular Indian were destroied at all times of the yeare, without any difference of Male, Damme, or Young. The like may be said of our owne Swine and Goats, whereof they have used to kill eight in tenne more than the English have done. There will be also a great increase of wild Turkies, and other waighty Fowle, for the Indians never put difference of destroying the Hen, but kill them whether in season or not, whether in breeding time, or sitting on their egges, or having new hatched, it is all one to them: whereby, as also by the orderly using of their fishing Weares, no knowne Country in the world will so plentifully abound in victuall.

Fourthly, Because the way of conquering them is much more easie then of civilizing them by faire meanes, for they are a rude, barbarous, and naked people, scattered in small companies, which are helps to Victorie, but hinderances to Civilitie: Besides that, a conquest may be of many, and at once; but civility is in particular, and slow, the effect of long time, and great industry. Moreover, victorie of them may bee gained many waies; by force, by surprize, by famine in burning their Corne, by destroying and burning their Boats, Canoes, and Houses, by breaking their fishing Weares, by assailing them in their huntings, whereby they get the greatest part of their sustenance in Winter, by pursuing and chasing them with out horses, and blood-Hounds to draw after them, and Mastives to teare them, which take this naked, tanned, deformed Savages, for no other then wild beasts, and are so fierce and fell upon them, that they feare them worse then their old Devill which they worship, supposing them to be a new and worse kinde of Devils then their owne. By these and sundry other wayes, as by driving them (when they flye) upon their enemies, who are round about them, and by animating and abetting their enemies against them, may their ruine or subjection be soone effected. . . .

Fiftly, Because the *Indians*, who before were used as friends, may now most justly be compelled to servitude and drudgery, and supply the roome of men that labour, whereby even the meanest of the Plantation may imploy themselves more entirely in their Arts and Occupations, which are more generous, whilest Savages perform their inferiour workes of digging in mynes, and the like. . . .

Sixtly, This will for ever hereafter make us more [cautelous] and circumspect, as never to bee deceived more by any other treacheries, but will serve for a great instruction to all posteritie there, to teach them that *Trust is the mother of Deceipt,* and . . . Hee that trusts not is not deceived: and make them know that kindnesses are misspent upon rude natures, so long as they continue rude; as also, that Savages and Pagans are above all other for matter of Justice ever to be suspected. Thus upon this Anvile shall wee now beate out to our selves an armour of proofe, which shall for ever after defend us from barbarous Incursions, and from greater dangers that otherwise might happen. . . .

To conclude then, seeing that *Virginia* is most abundantly fruitfull, and that this Massacre must rather be beneficiall to the Plantation then impaire it, let all men take courage, and put to their helping hands, since now the time is most seasonable and advantagious for the reaping of those benefits which the Plantation hath long promised: and for their owne good let them doe it speedily, that so by taking the prioritie of time, they may have also the prioritie of place, in choosing the best Seats of the Country, which now by vanquishing of the Indians, is like to offer a more ample and faire choice of fruitfull habitations, then hitherto our gentlenesse and faire comportment to the Savages could attaine unto. Wherein no doubt but all the favour that may be, shall be shewed to Adventurers and Planters. . . .

QUESTIONS FOR READING AND DISCUSSION

1. Why did the colonists feel betrayed by Opechancanough's attack?
2. How did Opechancanough prepare for the assault? How did the Virginians survive the attack?
3. According to the *Declaration,* how did the attack affect the colonists' attitudes about the Indians and about themselves?
4. Why did Waterhouse believe "conquest" was better than "civility"? Why did he think the "Massacre must . . . be beneficial to the Plantation"?
5. Consider the words Waterhouse used to describe Indians. In what ways did his language reveal his views of Indians and their resistance to "cultivation"?
6. How might the Declaration have been different if Opechacanough had written it?

DOCUMENT 2

A Yeoman Planter's Tobacco Farm

Robert Cole was a prosperous yeoman planter who owned a 300-acre tobacco farm in St. Mary's County, Maryland. The Roman Catholic Cole; his wife, Rebecca; and their children had moved from England to Maryland in 1652 when he was about twenty-five. Cole called himself a "yeoman," and he probably worked in his tobacco fields alongside his servants. Compared to his neighbors, he was wealthier than most, but he had far less land than the wealthiest planters. In 1662, he planned a visit back to England and, given the dangers of the long voyage, he prepared the following inventory of his property. He died in September 1663. His inventory, excerpted here, details the property a tobacco planter needed and valued. It reveals many of the artifacts of daily life among colonists in the seventeenth-century Chesapeake. Because seventeenth-century written English differed

*in spelling, punctuation, and vocabulary from common usages today, the inventory should
be read aloud slowly; listen carefully for its unspoken hints of the meaning and importance of the items listed.*

Robert Cole's Inventory, 1661

March 9th 1661 An Inventory of the cattle belonging to mee Robert Cole and
the markes of them att this time. . . .

Twelve Cowes young and old five Steeres young & old four heifers two
yeares old; Eleaven yeare old calves; one two yeare old heifer of my Sonn Roberts
given by John Thimbleby; one bull att brambley or thereabouts; one black steare
about Bassfoord Mannor. In all thirty & three cattle att home & two from home
which makes 35

The markes of these Cattle are severall. My owne marke is underkeeled[1] on
the Right Eare & overkeeled on the left eare, the Cattle I doe intend for my children hath a Slitt in the left Eare on the underside of the eare.

The marke of my Sonn Roberts heifer is underkeeled on the Right Eare and a
slitte and the left Eare is overkeeled & Slitt.

Some of my cattle are branded in the Horne thus R:C:

The number of my hoggs is uncertaine butt of them that come home I thinke
there is twenty nine of them and four young piggs they bee all underkeeled on
the Right Eare and Overkeeled on the left eare & noe other marke.

My Desire is that all my cattle bee branded in the horne as above & that all
the Calves bee this yeare onely under & overkeeled & noe Slitt att all.

God bless my Stock and send itt to thrive for the good of my poore children. . . .

Four Servants: John Elton Robert Gates John Johnson Isbell Jones

Two tobacco hogsheads full of Salt 28 bushells

Six bushells more of Salt five Iron potts two pair of potthookes two small
Iron Kettles two Skelletts one Copper Kettle 18 gallons [worth] 350 [pounds of to-
bacco]

Two Fryeing panns two pair of bellowes one pair of fire tongs & Shovell

One spitt mortar & pestle bell mettle[2] [worth] 65 [pounds of tobacco]

One Iron pestle one Iron chaine for the Chimney three Small hookes[3]
fiveteene Milktrayes[4] five Cedar tubbs for the Dary one Cedar cheese tubb, one
oaken Milke tubb one Coule & Coule Staffe[5], one powdring tubb[6] one great
Round bowle five payles

Lois Green Carr, Russell R. Menard, and Lorena S. Walsh, *Robert Cole's World:
Agriculture and Society in Early Maryland* (Chapel Hill: University of North Carolina
Press, 1991), 176–82.

[1]**underkeeled:** On the bottom of the ear; overkeeled: on the top of the ear.

[2]**spitt mortar & pestle bell mettle:** A mortar and pestle made of strong bell-metal.

[3]**hookes:** Used to link cooking vessels to the chain and hang them over the fire.

[4]**milk-trayes:** Vessels used to cool milk.

[5]**coule:** A large heavy pot for water, carried suspended from a staff or strong pole
by two men.

[6]**powdring tubb:** A wooden tub for salting or pickling meat.

One Mobby[7] tubb two dozen of trenchers[8] one dozen & halfe of Spoones one Cullender of tinn; three tinn dripping panns; one tinn Funnell; five tinn Candlesticks; two Wyar candlesticks; one pewter bottle; one pepper box of tinn; one pepper grinder; on Straineing Dish

One chafeing dish one tinn Scummer two wooden platters two Sifting trayes one grid Iron, one Iron Ladle, five pewter platters, one pewter bason four pewter porrengers[9]; two small pewter Dishes; five wooden Spoones; three wooden Ladles; two pewter pint potts one pewter quart pott one tinn quart pott one tobacco knife, one charne to charne butter

One Salt box two greate butter potts; five Smaller earthen; one Earthen fryeing pann one three Legged creame Pott earthen one Corne barrell; three thight [i.e., tight] barrells for liquor one thight Ancor[10] tenn Gallons four good small Rundlettss[11] three Meale Sifters of haire one homany Sifter

Three [illegible] Tobacco Hogsheads [worth] 75 [pounds of tobacco]

Four other casque in the Lofts five Joynt Stooles; five Joyner chaires the arme of one is broken, one chaire table, one table and Dresser in the Kitchen; three three Legged Stooles

One Canow none of the best although Shee bee new [worth] 80 [pounds of tobacco]

One warming pann Six pictures in the Hall three Lardge Stone Juggs

One Small pair of Stilliards[12] [worth] 60 [pounds of tobacco]

One Iron bound case with Six bottles pewter Screwes; one earthen pitcher, one earthen Jugg, two gallons of Sweete oyle

One butter tubb [worth] 25 [pounds of tobacco]

Two case of quart bottles; five Specled Dutch potts to drink in nine other like peeces; butt they bee butter potts dishes & porringers

Four paire of Sheetes, one od Sheete, one towell four pillow beares[13] one dyaper[14] tablecloth, two tablecloths Six new napkins, two napkins from my mother two white woomans aprons; one greene Say appron

One white woomans shift [worth] 40 [pounds of tobacco]

One Counterpaine[15] att 80 [pounds of tobacco]

A parcell of child bed Linnen

Two woomans fine Holland Handkecheifes[worth] 50 [pounds of tobacco]

Three Cross cloths[16] [worth] 28 [pounds of tobacco]

---

[7]**mobby:** The juice of peaches and apples, used to make cider and brandy.

[8]**trenchers:** Flat pieces of wood used to hold food to be eaten; the counterpart to modern dinner plates.

[9]**porrengers:** Small shallow basins used for eating porridges, stews, and soups.

[10]**rundlettss:** A keg.

[11]**ancor:** Small casks.

[12]**stilliard:** A portable scale for weighing.

[13]**beares:** Pillow cases.

[14]**dyaper:** A kind of linen.

[15]**counterpaine:** A bed cover.

[16]**cross cloth:** Linen cloth worn across the forehead.

Three fine dressings [worth] 60 [pounds of tobacco]

Two handkecheifes [worth] 30 [pounds of tobacco]

One Holland neckcloth [worth] 30 [pounds of tobacco]

One holland apron [worth] 50 [pounds of tobacco]

One pair of thred gloves one pair of Cotten gloves

One Stometcher[17] [worth] 20 [pounds of tobacco]

One pair of Sheetes for use Left; thirty one yards of Canvas, one pound of Candleweeke[18], one pound more for use left

One pair of woomans bodies[19] [worth] 50 [pounds of tobacco]

Four pair of woomans Shooes; two pair of old woomans Shooes one pair of buckskinn gloves; one pair of woomens new Shooes one pair of woomens woosted Stockins; one pair of woomens yarne Stockins

Three old child's blanketts [worth] 30 [pounds of tobacco]

One Red broad cloth suite [worth] 300 [pounds of tobacco]

One pennistone[20] petticoate [worth] 60 [pounds of tobacco]

One serge wastcoate [worth] 60 [pounds of tobacco]

Four pair of Irish Stockins; one canvas Jackett, Eleaven pair of childrens Stockins; one & 1/2 yards of Flannell for the child, two & 1/2 yards of Red Shag-cloth four & 1/2 yards of penistone; Six & 1/2 yards of penistone: three yards & 3/4 blew linnen four &1/2 yards of course Holland

Eleaven ells[21] of Lockrome[22], four yards of Red Serge, 1/2 pound of pepper, one ounce & 1/2 Saffron, Some nuttmegs cloves & Cynamon two Raysors one pound of Ginger 1/2 pound of Starch use one pound more in the chest nine Shoomakers lasts[23] Joseph hath one of these four Shoomakers Alls a parcell of Greene galume[24] & other laces of two Sorts

A parcell of Linnen in a bundle & one Silver bodkin[25] & one Silver whistle a Curvell[26] 1/2 pound of whited browne thred, four severall sorts of fair thred 3/4 Ib. Red thred, four ounces of Silke one Silke lace Three parcells of Ribbon 2000 of pinns Some tape & Filleten bindeing[27] points; Cotten Ribbon; nine pair of Sissers; pinns & thred needles Sope Soft & hard; Ginger nuttmegg cloves Some, biskett delivered for this years use to Mary with Sugar

One branding Iron R:C: two Ivory Combes for the children one fetherbed boulsters two Pillowes with blanketts two pillowes with blanketts red Rugg two Flock beds with boulsters pillowes two blanketts two greene Rugs one greene Rugg more in the chest [illegible] the Red one before Spoke of

---

[17]**stometcher:** Worn by women across their chest, under the lacing of their bodice.

[18]**candlewicke:** Candlewick.

[19]**woomans bodies:** A bodice was worn by women to cover their upper torso.

[20]**pennistone:** A coarse woolen textile.

[21]**Ell:** A unit of length, about 45 inches.

[22]**lockrome:** A linen fabric.

[23]**shoomakers lasts:** Foot-shaped wooden forms for making shoes.

[24]**galume:** A kind of decorative ribbon.

[25]**bodkin:** A hair ornament used by women.

[26]**curvell:** A toy given to babies for amusement and to help them cut teeth.

[27]**filleten bindeing:** A kind of heavy tape or binding sewn to the edges of fabrics.

My Servants bedding is Sufficient besides the[y] have two white blanketts coverled and Small greene old Rugg

One pair of Cart Wheeles [worth] 200 [pounds of tobacco]

One barrell of Tarr aboute some 18 gallons one grindstone, bramble tooth Saw three Iron Wedges, one pair of small hoopes or Rings for a Mall[28], two hand-sawes one tennent Saw one pair of brass compasses; two hammers, three Axes, five weeding hoes, five hilling hoes

Four Fishing Lines and hookes of all sorts two peeces of new Line reserved one new fishing line reserved

One new strong rope to hould Cattle [worth] 60 [pounds of tobacco]

A parcell of nailes to build a hoghouse & lift the tobacco houses in all by gess 2000 one Coopers Howell[29] & one Spade new a parcell of Coopers timber heading to make twenty hogsheads, Staves for Eight hogsheads one pair of Taylors Sheeres

Three guns lardge & good, or Fowling peeces two Rundletts of Shott in wayght 112 lbs. thirty pound of other Shott for use 12 lbs. powder in a Roundlett that is full

Ten pound of powder in a Rundlett & some in a bottle left for use 2 lbs. two Round bottles of glass, one Carpenters Ads[30], one broad chissell five other chissells 10 quarts of Rumm in bottles for use 8 lbs. of sugar for my childrens use

Goods I carry with mee is in Tobacco [worth] 1900 [pounds]

One gunn to be fixed, one chest . . . one small bed boulster blankett two pair of Stockins two pair of britches two wastcoates one Lardge Coate, one short Coate four Shirts

The Goods above mentioned I doe Vallue them att the price of 18987 [pounds of tobacco] My cattle att the price of 9900 [pounds of tobacco, for a total worth of] 28887 [pounds of tobacco]

One looking glass two tinn pudding panns Several small goods nott here putt Downe.

One trunk & one greate chest one new chest with Linnen in itt in which chest there is 1/2 one pound of asneck or Ratts bane[31], one old chest 3 small chests

I doe Suppose I have left my children Indifferent well Furnished with cloaths till Christmas onely they will want Shooes the which I desire may bee bought for them as soone as they may be gott. . . .

I doe suppose I have left in the house twelve barrells of corne att least and aboute & just 18 Middle peeces of bacon for this years provision.

Most part of these goods before mentioned are about the house & what is nott is in the two biggest chests which are Locked and the Keys are given to Coll Evans or to Capt Gardner.

Two Table cloths & five napkins for the use of my house left with Mary Sheppey.

Seaven bookes in a chest, Six other bookes left out for the children to Read in in the biggest of the bookes in the chest you may find the birth Dayes of my chil-

---

[28]**mall:** A heavy hammer used with wedges to split wood.

[29]**coopers howell:** A special tool used in shaping wood for barrel staves.

[30]**adz:** An axlike tool used to shape wood.

[31]**ratts bane:** Arsenic; used for rat poison.

dren in particular Francis Knott is three yeares older than my Sonn Robert Cole is. Severall small goods not here sett downe.

This Inventory is taken by mee Robert Cole on the 25th Day of Aprill 1662 as Witness my hand. Robt Cole.

QUESTIONS FOR READING AND DISCUSSION

1. Cole's inventory makes it possible to decipher a number of important activities that occurred on his farm. Judging from his possessions, what kinds of things did he, his family, and his servants do in the ordinary course of daily life?
2. What did Cole's inventory suggest about his values, economic and otherwise? What was the significance of assigning monetary value in pounds of tobacco?
3. What did the inventory indicate about Cole's views of his family? What did it suggest about Cole's relationship with his neighbors and his servants?
4. Because Cole was a relatively prosperous planter, how might an inventory for a more typical poorer planter differ from Cole's inventory?

DOCUMENT 3

Sex and Race Relations

Whites and blacks, men and women often worked side by side in the seventeenth-century Chesapeake. Sometimes whites were free and blacks were slaves. Sometimes both whites and blacks were servants who looked forward to their freedom. Sometimes blacks were free, and sometimes they were not even black, but racially mixed mulattos. The court inquiry excerpted here provides conflicting testimony about the behavior of a white woman and slave men in Virginia in August 1681. The testimony reveals the potentially explosive mixture of sexual and racial expectations and stereotypes in the small communities of the southern colonies.

Testimony from Virginia Court Records, 1681

The examination of Katherine Watkins, the wife of Henry Watkins of Henrico County in Virginia had and taken this 13 of September 1681 before us William Byrd and John Farrar two of his Majesties justices of the County aforesaid as followeth. . . .

The said Katherine aforesaid on her Oath and examination deposeth, That on fryday being in the Month of August aboute five weeks since, the said Katherine mett with John Long (a Mulatto belonging to Capt. Thomas Cocke) at or neare the pyney slash betweene the aforesaid Cockes and Henry Watkins house, and at the same tyme and place, the said John threw the said Katherine downe (He starting from behinde a tree) and stopped her Mouth with a handkerchief, and tooke

---

Warren Billings, ed., *The Old Dominion in the Seventeenth Century: A Documentary History of Virginia,* 1606–1689 (Chapel Hill: University of North Carolina Press, 1975), 161–63.

up the said Katherines Coates [petticoats], and putt his yard[1] into her and rav-ished her; Upon which she the said Katherine Cryed out (as she deposeth) and af-terwards (being rescued by another Negroe of the said Cockes named jack White) she departed home, and the said John departed to his Masters likewise, or that way; after which abuse she the said Katherine declares that her husband inclin-able to the quakers[2], and therefore would not prosecute, and she being sicke and her Children likewise, she therefore did not make her complaint before she went to Lt. Col. Farrars (which was yesterday, Morning) and this day in the Morning she went to William Randolphs' and found him not at home, But at night met with the gentlemen justices aforesaid at the house of the aforesaid Cocke in Hen-rico County in Virginia aforesaid before whom she hath made this complaint upon oath. . . .

The deposition of John Aust aged 32 yeares or thereabouts Deposeth,That on fryday being the twelvth of August or thereabouts he came to the house of Mr. Thomas Cocke, and soe went into his Orchard where his servants were a cutting downe weeds, whoe asked the deponent to stay and drinke, soe the deponent stayed and dranke syder with them, and jacke a Mulatto of the said Thomas Cocke went in to draw syder, and he stay'd something long whereupon the deponent followed him, and coming to the doore where the syder was, heard Katherine the wife of Henry Watkins say (Lord) jacke what makes thee refraine our house that you come not oftner, for come when thou wilt thou shalt be as well come as any of My owne Children, and soe she tooke him about the necke and Kissed him, and jacke went out and drawed Syder, and she said jack wilt thou not drinke to me, who sayd yes if you will goe out where our Cupp is, and a little after she came out, where the said Thomas Cockes Negroes were a drinking and there dranke cupp for cupp with them (as others there did) and as she sett Negroe dirke passing by her she tooke up the taile of his shirt (saying) Dirke thou wilt have a good long thing, and soe did several tymes as he past by her; after this she went into the roome where the syder was and then came out againe, and between the two houses she mett Mulatto jacke a going to draw more syder and putt her hand on his codpiece[3], at which he smil'd, and went on his way and drew syder and she came againe into the company but stay'd not long but went out to drinking with two of the said Thomas Cockes Negroes by the garden pale, And a while af-ter she tooke Mingoe one of the said Cocke's Negroes about the Necke and fling on the bedd and Kissed him and putt her hand into his Codpeice, Awhile after Mulatto jacke went into the Fish roome and she followed him, but what they did there this deponent knoweth not for it being near night this deponent left her and the Negroes together, (He thinking her to be much in drinke) and soe this depo-nent went home about one houre by sunn. . . .

The Deposition of William Harding aged about 35 yeares, Deposeth,That he came to the house of Mr. Thomas Cocke to speake with his brother, where he see Katherine the wife of Henry Watkins, and soe spoke to one there and sayd, that the said Henry Watkins wife had been a drinking; And that this deponent see the

---

[1]**yard:** Penis.

[2]**quakers:** That is, a Quaker believer who did not resort to court prosecution.

[3]**codpiece:** The crotch covering in men's trousers.

said Katherine Watkins turne up the taile of Negroe Dirks shirt, and said that he would have a good pricke, whereupon this deponent sayd is that the trick of a quaker, who made him answer, that what hast thou to say to quakers, It being acted on fryday the 12 of August or thereabouts and further saith not. . . .

The Deposition of Mary Winter aged about 22 years. Deposeth,That Mr. Thomas Cocks Negroes and others being in company with them a drinking of syder, Then came in Katherine Watkins the wife of Henry Watkins and went to drinking with them, and tooke Mulatto jack by the hand in the outward roome and ledd him into the inward roome doore and then thrust him in before her and told him she loved him for his Fathers sake for his Father was a very hansome young Man, and afterwards the said Mulattoe went out from her, and then she fetched him into the roome againe and hugged and kist him. And further saith not. . . .

The Deposition of Lambert Tye aged about 26 yeares. Deposeth That being at Worke at Mr. Thomas Cocks on fryday being the twelvth of August or thereabouts, and coming into the house with William Hobson and the rest of Mr. Thomas Cocks servants and others in Company with them to drinke syder, and being a drinking then comes in Katherine Watkins the wife of Henry Watkins having a very high Colour in her face whereupon this deponent asked Humphrey then servant to the said Thomas Cocke; what made his Countrywoman have such a high Colour; whereupon he made this answear; That the [said] Katherine was at Old Humphrey's a drinking and he gave her a Cupp or two that had turned her braines, and soe being a drinking with their company she went into the Chimney (as this deponent thinketh) to light her pipe, and soe made a posture with her body as if she would have gone to danceing, and then afterwards coming into their company againe, she told Mulatto jack, that she loved him for his father's sake, And then having left the Company and she together a drinking, This deponent went home to his owne house, and afterwards coming from home towards the house of the said Thomas Cocke, he mett with the said Katherine Watkins about halfe an houre by sun in the pathway homewards neare to this deponents house. And further saith not. . . .

Humphrey Smith aged 26 yeares, deposeth,That he heard John Aust say (about September last past) what Matter is it what I swore to and likewise the deponent saw Katherine's Mouth (the wife of Henry Watkins) torne and her lipps swell'd, And the handkerchief that she said the Mulatto Stopt her Mouth with very much bloody And the deponent heard the Mulatto confess that he had beene to aske the said Watkins wife forgiveness three tymes, and likewise the Mulatto sayd that Henry Watkins (the last tyme he went) bidd him keepe off his plantation or else he would shoote him and further saith not.

QUESTIONS FOR READING AND DISCUSSION

1. How does Katherine Watkins's testimony differ from that of other witnesses? To what extent does the testimony portray Watkins as the victim or the perpetrator?

2. Who were Katherine Watkins's neighbors, and what did they think of her and her husband? Did they all agree? To what extent did they consider her behavior aberrant?

3. What does the testimony suggest about day-to-day encounters between free people, servants, and slaves? Does the testimony indicate that witnesses were especially concerned that John (or Jack) Long was a "mulatto"? Why did slaves give no testimony?

4. In the end, what did the witnesses seem to believe was at stake in this episode? What kinds of disorder — social, sexual, racial, familial — occurred, according to the testimony? What expectations about order did the witnesses reveal?

DOCUMENT 4

Bacon's Rebellion

In 1676, Nathaniel Bacon led a group of planters, tenants, and servants in battles against Indians along the Virginia frontier. Bacon had arrived in Virginia only two years earlier and carved out a farm on the frontier. Bacon's status as a member of a prominent English family gained him recognition from Virginia's governor, Sir William Berkeley. When Bacon began his private war against Indians, Berkeley — who hoped to keep peace along the frontier — declared the upstart a rebel. Beneath the dispute about Indian policy smouldered hostility between frontier planters and tidewater gentry, between struggling farmers and privileged grandees. That hostility flared into a full-scale rebellion that convulsed Virginia until it was finally suppressed by government authorities in 1677, after Bacon's death and much destruction of life and property. In the following Declaration published in 1676, Bacon detailed his view of the prevailing order in Virginia. Bacon's Declaration disclosed the simmering antagonisms engendered by the inequities among whites, both free people and servants, in the seventeenth-century southern colonies.

Nathaniel Bacon's Declaration, 1676

If vertue be a sin, if Piety be giult, all the Principles of morality goodness and justice be perverted, Wee must confesse That those who are now called Rebells may be in danger of those high imputations, Those loud and severall Bulls[1] would affright Innocents and render the defence of our Brethren and the enquiry into our sad and heavy oppressions, Treason. But if there bee as sure there is, a just God to appeal too, if Religion and justice be a sanctuary here, If to plead the cause of the oppressed, If sincerely to aime at his Majesties Honour and the Publick good without any reservation or by Interest, If to stand in the Gap after soe much blood of our dear Brethren bought and sold, If after the losse of a great

---

Warren Billings, ed., *The Old Dominion in the Seventeenth Century: A Documentary History of Virginia, 1606–1689* (Chapel Hill: University of North Carolina Press, 1975), 277–79.

[1]A reference to the Virginia governor's declaration (or bull) that Bacon and his supporters were rebels.

part of his Majesties Colony deserted and dispeopled, freely with our lives and estates to indeavor to save the remaynders bee Treason God Almighty judge and lett guilty dye, But since wee cannot in our hearts find one single spott of Rebellion or Treason or that wee have in any manner aimed at subverting the setled Government or attempting of the Person of any either magistrate or private man not with standing the severall Reproaches and Threats of some who for sinister ends were disaffected to us and censured our inocent and honest designes, and since all people in all places where wee have yet bin can attest our civill quiet peaseable behaviour farre different from that of Rebellion and tumultuous persons let Trueth be bold and all the world know the real Foundations of pretended giult, Wee appeale to the Country itselfe what and of what nature their Oppressions have bin or by what Caball[2] and mistery the designes of many of those whom wee call great men have bin transacted and caryed on, but let us trace these men in Authority and Favour to whose hands the dispensation of the Countries wealth has been commited; let us observe the sudden Rise of their Estates composed with the Quality in which They first entered this Country Or the Reputation they have held here amongst wise and discerning men, And lett us see wither their extractions and Education have not bin vile, And by what pretence of learning and vertue they could soe soon into Imployments of so great Trust and consequence, let us consider their sudden advancement and let us also consider wither any Publick work for our safety and defence or for the Advancement and propagation of Trade, liberall Arts or sciences is here Extant in any [way] adaquate to our vast chardg, now let us compare these things togit[her] and see what spounges have suckt up the Publique Treasure and wither it hath not bin privately contrived away by unworthy Favourites and juggling Parasites whose tottering Fortunes have bin repaired and supported at the Publique chardg, now if it be so Judg what greater giult can bee then to offer to pry into these and to unriddle the misterious wiles of a powerfull Cabal let all people Judge what can be of more dangerous Import then to suspect the soe long Safe proceedings of Some of our Grandees and wither People may with safety open their Eyes in soe nice a Concerne.

Another main article of our Giult is our open and manifest aversion of all, not onely the Foreign but the protected and Darling Indians, this wee are informed is Rebellion of a deep dye For that both the Governour and Councell are by Colonell Coales Assertion bound to defend the Queen and Appamatocks[3] with their blood Now whereas we doe declare and can prove that they have bin for these Many years enemies to the King and Country, Robbers and Theeves and Invaders of his Majesties' Right and our Interest and Estates, but yet have by persons in Authority bin defended and protected even against His Majesties loyall Subjects and that in soe high a Nature that even the Complaints and oaths of his Majesties Most loyall Subjects in a lawfull Manner proffered by them against those barborous Outlawes have bin by the right honourable Governour rejected and the Delinquents from his presence dismissed not only with pardon and indemnitye but with all incouragement and favour, Their Fire Arms soe destructfull to us and by our lawes prohibited, Commanded to be restored them,

[2]**caball:** Secret plot.
[3]**Appamotocks:** An Indian tribe.

and open Declaration before Witness made That they must have Ammunition although directly contrary to our law, Now what greater giult can be then to oppose and indeavour the destruction of these Honest quiet neighbours of ours.

Another main article of our Giult is our Design not only to ruine and extirpate all Indians in Generall but all Manner of Trade and Commerce with them, judge who can be innocent that strike at this tender Eye of Interest; Since the Right honourable the Governour hath bin pleased by his Commission to warrant this trade who dare oppose it, or opposing it can be innocent, Although Plantations be deserted, the blood of our dear Brethren Spilt, on all Sides our complaints, continually Murder upon Murder renewed upon us, who may or dare think of the generall Subversion of all Mannor of Trade and Commerce with our enemies who can or dare impeach any of [word missing] Traders at the Heades of the Rivers if contrary to the wholesome provision made by lawes for the countries safety, they dare continue their illegall practises and dare asperse the right honourable Governours wisdome and justice soe highly to pretend to have his warrant to break that law which himself made, who dare say That these Men at the Heads of the Rivers buy and sell our blood, and doe still notwithstanding the late Act made to the contrary[4], admit Indians painted and continue to Commerce, although these things can be proved yet who dare bee soe guilty as to doe it.

Another Article of our Guilt is To Assert all those neighbour Indians as well as others to be outlawed, wholly unqualifyed for the benefitt and Protection of the law, For that the law does reciprocally protect and punish, and that all people offending must either in person or Estate make equivalent satisfaction or Restitution according to the manner and merit of the Offences Debts or Trespasses; Now since the Indians cannot according to the tenure and forme of any law to us known be prosecuted, Seised or Complained against, Their Persons being difficulty distinguished or known, Their many nations languages, and their subterfuges such as makes them incapeable to make us Restitution or satisfaction would it not be very giulty to say They have bin unjustly defended and protected these many years.

If it should be said that the very foundation of all these disasters the Grant of the Beaver trade to the Right Honourable Governour[5] was illegall and not granteable by any power here present as being a monopoly, were not this to deserve the name of Rebell and Traytor.

Judge therefore all wise and unprejudiced men who may or can faithfully or truely with an honest heart attempt the country's good, their vindication and libertie without the aspersion of Traitor and Rebell, since as soe doing they must of necessity gall such tender and dear concernes, But to manifest Sincerity and loyalty to the World, and how much wee abhorre those bitter names, may all the world know that we doe unanimously desire to represent our sad and heavy grievances to his most sacred Majesty as our Refuge and Sanctuary, where wee doe well know that all our Causes will be impartially heard and Equall justice administred to all men.

---

[4]Recent legislation prohibited trade with Indians who wore paint, a sign of unreliability, according to Bacon and many other Virginians.

[5]By monopolizing the trade in beaver skins, the governor reaped handsome profits for himself.

QUESTIONS FOR READING AND DISCUSSION

1. According to Bacon, what were the real foundations of the trouble in Virginia? How did he propose "to unriddle the misterious wiles of a powerfull Cabal"?

2. What was Bacon's plan for "the protected and Darling Indians"? Why did he favor such a plan, and why did others oppose it?

3. What did Bacon's statement suggest about the distribution and exercise of political power in the seventeenth-century Chesapeake? What changes in political power did he seek? What principles did he believe should govern colonial society?

4. How might Bacon's arguments have been answered by his opponents, both in the colonial government and among the Indians?

COMPARATIVE QUESTIONS ————————————————————————————

1. To what extent did colonial life, as revealed in the documents, differ from common expectations in England? How did the documents reflect the colonists' adjustment of English ideas and behavior to the realities of life in the southern colonies?

2. Robert Cole's inventory assumed a society governed by legal rules. What assumptions did the other three documents make about the basic rules governing the seventeenth-century southern colonies?

3. How did tobacco influence the experiences of the individuals described by these documents? How did experiences differ according to social rank, gender, race, age, and ethnicity?

4. Each of the documents offers evidence of important concepts of order and disorder. To what extent did the documents suggest broad agreement among free white colonists about the fundamental patterns of order and sources of potential disorder? To what extent did Indians, slaves, and servants share those notions?

CHAPTER 3

THE NORTHERN COLONIES IN THE SEVENTEENTH CENTURY
1601–1700

Puritans and Puritanism made an indelible impression on New England in the seventeenth century. Puritans built churches and towns, distributed land, raised families, passed laws, and rendered verdicts. In all of their activities, Puritans aspired to live according to God's law. At least once a week ministers gave sermons that proclaimed God's way as set forth in the Bible. Although many New Englanders were not church members, those who were governed the society both in principle and in practice. White colonists recognized, however, that most Native Americans adhered neither to Puritanism nor Christianity, providing a durable reminder of the limited scope of religious orthodoxy. The following documents exhibit the Puritans' high standards and illustrate some of the difficulties they had in disciplining themselves and others to live up to those aspirations.

DOCUMENT 1
The Arbella *Sermon*

John Winthrop, Puritan leader of the great migration to New England and first governor of the Massachusetts Bay Colony, delivered perhaps the most famous sermon in American history in 1630 while crossing the Atlantic with his fellow Puritans aboard the Arbella. Although Winthrop was not a minister, Puritan doctrines suffused his sermon. He put into words the Puritans' understanding of their migration to New England — the goals they hoped to achieve and the responsibilities they assumed. The sermon, the source of the following selection, bore the title "A Model of Christian Charity."

John Winthrop
"A Model of Christian Charity," 1630

A Model Hereof

God Almighty in his most holy and wise providence hath so disposed of the condition of mankind, as in all times some must be rich, some poor, some high and eminent in power and dignity, others mean and in subjection.

The Reason Hereof

First, to hold conformity with the rest of his works, being delighted to show forth the glory of his wisdom in the variety and difference of the creatures; and the glory of his power, in ordering all these differences for the preservation and good of the whole; and the glory of his greatness, that as it is the glory of princes to have many officers, so this great king will have many stewards, counting himself more honored in dispensing his gifts to man by man, than if he did it by his own immediate hands.

Secondly, that he might have the more occasion to manifest the work of his spirit: first upon the wicked in moderating and restraining them, so that the rich and mighty should not eat up the poor, nor the poor and despised rise up against their superiors and shake off their yoke; secondly in the regenerate, in exercising his graces in them, as in the great ones, their love, mercy, gentleness, temperance, etc.; in the poor and inferior sort, their faith, patience, obedience, etc.

Thirdly, that every man might have need of other, and from hence they might be all knit more nearly together in the bonds of brotherly affection. From hence it appears plainly that no man is made more honorable than another or more wealthy, etc., out of any particular and singular respect to himself, but for the glory of his creator and the common good of the creature, man. . . . All men being thus (by divine providence) ranked into two sorts, rich and poor, under the first are comprehended all such as are able to live comfortably by their own means duly improved; and all others are poor according to the former distribution.

There are two rules whereby we are to walk one towards another: justice and mercy. . . .

There is likewise a double law by which we are regulated in our conversation one towards another in both the former respects: the law of nature and the law of grace, or the moral law or the law of the gospel. . . . By the first of these laws man as he was enabled so withal [is] commanded to love his neighbor as himself. Upon this ground stands all the precepts of the moral law, which concerns our dealings with men. To apply this to the works of mercy, this law requires two things. First, that every man afford his help to another in every want or distress. Secondly, that he performed this out of the same affection which makes him careful of his own goods, according to that of our Savior. Matthew: "Whatsoever ye would that men should do to you." . . .

This law of the gospel propounds . . . [that] there is a time when a Christian must sell all and give to the poor, as they did in the Apostles' times. There is a time also when a Christian (though they give not all yet) must give beyond their ability. . . . Likewise community of perils calls for extraordinary liberality, and so doth community in some special service for the church. Lastly, when there is no

Alan Heimert and Andrew Delbanco, eds., *The Puritans in America: A Narrative Anthology* (Cambridge, MA.: Harvard University Press, 1985) 82–92.

other means whereby our Christian brother may be relieved in his distress, we must help him beyond our ability, rather than tempt God in putting him upon help by miraculous or extraordinary means. . . . .

Having already set forth the practice of mercy according to the rule of God's law, it will be useful to lay open the grounds of it also, . . . and that is the affection from which this exercise of mercy must arise. The Apostle tells us that this love is the fulfilling of the law. . . . The way to draw men to works of mercy is not by force of argument from the goodness or necessity of the work; for though this course may enforce a rational mind to some present act of mercy, as is frequent in experience, yet it cannot work such a habit in a soul, as shall make it prompt upon all occasions to produce the same effect, but by framing these affections of love in the heart which will as natively bring forth the other, as any cause doth produce effect.

The definition which the scripture gives us of love is this: "Love is the bond of perfection." First, it is a bond or ligament. Secondly, it makes the work perfect. There is no body but consists of parts and that which knits these parts together gives the body its perfection, because it makes each part so contiguous to others as thereby they do mutually participate with each other, both in strength and infirmity, in pleasure and pain. To instance in the most perfect of all bodies: Christ and his church make one body. The several parts of this body, considered apart before they were united, were as disproportionate and as much disordering as so many contrary qualities or elements, but when Christ comes and by his spirit and love knits all these parts to himself and each to other, it is become the most perfect and best proportioned body in the world. . . .

The next consideration is how this love comes to be wrought. Adam in his first estate was a perfect model of mankind in all their generations, and in him this love was perfected in regard of habit. But Adam rent himself from his creator, rent all his posterity also one from another; whence it comes that every man is born with this principle in him, to love and seek himself only, and thus a man continueth till Christ comes and takes possession of the soul and infuseth another principle, love to God and our brother. And this latter having continual supply from Christ, as the head and root by which he is united, gets the predomining in the soul, so by little and little expels the former. . . . [T]his love is the fruit of the new birth, and none can have it but the new creature. Now when this quality is thus formed in the souls of men, it works like the spirit upon the dry bones. . . . It gathers together the scattered bones, or perfect old man Adam, and knits them into one body again in Christ, whereby a man is become again a living soul.

The third consideration is concerning the exercise of this love. . . . We must take in our way that maxim of philosophy . . . , like will to like. . . . This is the cause why the Lord loves the creature, so far as it hath any of his image in it; he loves his elect because they are like himself, he beholds them in his beloved son. So a mother loves her child, because she thoroughly conceives a resemblance of herself in it. Thus it is between the members of Christ. Each discerns, by the work of the spirit, his own image and resemblance in another, and therefore cannot but love him as he loves himself. . . .

So is it in all the labor of love among Christians. The party loving, reaps love again . . . , which the soul covets more than all the wealth in the world. Thirdly, nothing yields more pleasure and content to the soul than when it finds that which it may love fervently, for to love and live beloved is the soul's paradise, both here and in heaven. In the state of wedlock there be many comforts to bear out the troubles of that condition; but let such as have tried the most, say if there be any sweetness in that condition comparable to the exercise of mutual love. . . .

It rests now to make some application of this discourse. . . . Herein are four things to be propounded: first, the persons; secondly, the work; thirdly, the end; fourthly, the means.

First for the persons. We are a company professing ourselves fellow members of Christ, in which respect only though we were absent from each other many miles, and had our imployments as far distant, yet we ought to account ourselves knit together by this bond of love, and live in the exercise of it, if we would have comfort of our being in Christ. . . .

Secondly for the work we have in hand. It is by a mutual consent, through a special overvaluing providence and a more than an ordinary approbation of the churches of Christ, to seek out a place of cohabitation and consortship under a due form of government both civil and ecclesiastical. In such cases as this, the care of the public must oversway all private respects, by which not only conscience but mere civil policy doth bind us. For it is a true rule that particular estates cannot subsist in the ruin of the public.

Thirdly, the end is to improve our lives to do more service to the Lord; the comfort and encrease of the body of Christ whereof we are members; that ourselves and posterity may be the better preserved from the common corruptions of this evil world, to serve the Lord and work out our salvation under the power and purity of his holy ordinances.

Fourthly, for the means whereby this must be effected. They are twofold, a conformity with the work and end we aim at. These we see are extraordinary, therefore we must not content ourselves with usual ordinary means. Whatsoever we did or ought to have done when we lived in England, the same must we do, and more also, where we go. That which the most in their churches maintain as a truth in profession only, we must bring into familiar and constant practice, as in this duty of love. We must love brotherly without dissimulation; we must love one another with a pure heart fervently. We must bear one another's burthens. We must not look only on our own things, but also on the things of our brethren, neither must we think that the Lord will bear with such failings at our hands as he doth from those among whom we have lived; and that for three reasons:

First, in regard of the more near bond of marriage between him and us, wherein he hath taken us to be his after a most strict and peculiar manner, which will make him the more jealous of our love and obedience. So he tells the people of Israel, "You only have I known of all the families of the earth, therefore will I punish you for your transgressions." Secondly, because the Lord will be sanctified in them that come near him. We know that there were many that corrupted the service of the Lord, some setting up altars before his own, others offering both strange fire and strange sacrifices also. . . . Thirdly, when God gives a special commission he looks to have it strictly observed in every article. . . .

Thus stands the cause between God and us. We are entered into covenant with him for this work. We have taken out a commission, the Lord hath given us leave to draw our own articles. We have professed to enterprise these actions, upon these and those ends, we have hereupon besought him of favor and blessing. Now if the Lord shall please to hear us, and bring us in peace to the place we desire, then hath he ratified this covenant and sealed our commission, [and] will expect a strict performance of the articles contained in it. But if we shall neglect the observation of these articles which are the ends we have propounded and, dissembling with our God, shall fall to embrace this present world and prosecute our carnal intentions, seeking great things for ourselves and our posterity, the Lord will surely break out in wrath against us, be revenged of such a perjured people, and make us know the price of the breach of such a covenant.

Now the only way to avoid this shipwreck, and to provide for our posterity, is to follow the counsel of Micah, to do justly, to love mercy, to walk humbly with our God. For this end, we must be knit together in this work as one man. We must entertain each other in brotherly affection, we must be willing to abridge our-selves of our superfluities, for the supply of others' necessities. We must uphold a familiar commerce together in all meekness, gentleness, patience, and liberality. We must delight in each other, make others' conditions our own, rejoice together, mourn together, labor and suffer together, always having before our eyes our commission and community in the work, our community as members of the same body. So shall we keep the unity of the spirit in the bond of peace. The Lord will be our God, and delight to dwell among us as his own people, and will command a blessing upon us in all our ways, so that we shall see much more of his wisdom, power, goodness, and truth, than formerly we have been acquainted with. We shall find that the God of Israel is among us, when ten of us shall be able to resist a thousand of our enemies; when he shall make us a praise and glory that men shall say of succeeding plantations, "the Lord make it like that of New England." For we must consider that we shall be as a city upon a hill. The eyes of all people are upon us, so that if we shall deal falsely with our God in this work we have un-dertaken, and so cause him to withdraw his present help from us, we shall be made a story and a by-word through the world. We shall open the mouths of enemies to speak evil of the ways of God, and all professors for God's sake. We shall shame the faces of many of God's worthy servants, and cause their prayers to be turned into curses upon us till we be consumed out of the good land whither we are ago-ing.

And to shut up this discourse with that exhortation of Moses, that faithful servant of the Lord, in his last farewell to Israel, Deuteronomy 30: Beloved, there is now set before us life and good, death and evil, in that we are commanded this day to love the Lord our God, and to love one another, to walk in his ways and to keep his commandments and his ordinance and his laws, and the articles of our covenant with him, that we may live and be multiplied, and that the Lord our God may bless us in the land whither we go to possess it. But if our hearts shall turn away, so that we will not obey, but shall be seduced, and worship other gods, our pleasures and profits, and serve them; it is propounded unto us this day, we shall surely perish out of the good land whither we pass over this vast sea to pos-sess it.

Therefore let us choose life, that we and our seed may live by obeying his voice and cleaving to him, for he is our life and our prosperity.

QUESTIONS FOR READING AND DISCUSSION

1. What goals did Winthrop set for the migrants to New England? How did Puri-tan faith shape those goals? What was the significance of the "covenant" be-tween God and Puritans?

2. Why, according to Winthrop, was migration to New England important? What was at stake for the migrants, for the new colony, for England, and for Chris-tianity? What did he mean that New England "shall be as a city upon a hill"?

3. Did Winthrop envision a society dedicated to human equality or inequality? How should people demonstrate that "Love is the bond of perfection"?

4. How were Puritans different from other people, according to Winthrop? How did he think they should manifest their distinctive responsibilities? How did he think they should act toward people who were not Puritans or Christians?

DOCUMENT 2

Observations of New England Indians

Puritan minister Roger Williams arrived in Boston in 1631 and preached there, in Salem, and in Plymouth before being banished from Massachusetts in 1635 and taking up residence in what would become Providence, Rhode Island. In both Plymouth and Providence, Williams spent considerable time among Indians. While sailing back to England in 1643, he wrote a dictionary of New England Indian words, including numerous observations — excerpted here — of Indian customs and beliefs. An unusually perceptive observer, Williams noted Native American traits that caught his eye, revealing his Puritan viewpoint as well as the intricacies of the encounters between Indians and English colonists. Most colonists were far less willing than Williams to try to learn Indians' languages or to understand their cultures.

Roger Williams
A Key into the Language of America, 1643

The Natives are of two sorts, (as the English are.) Some more Rude and Clownish, who are not so apt to Salute, but upon *Salutation* resalute lovingly. Others, and the generall, are *sober* and *grave*, and yet chearfull in a meane, and as ready to begin a Salutation as to Resalute, which yet the English generally begin, out of desire to Civilize them. . . . There is a savour of *civility* and *courtesie* even amongst these wild Americans, both amongst *themselves* and towards *strangers*. . . .

Whomsoever commeth in when they are eating, they offer them to eat of that which they have, though but little enough prepar'd for themselves. If any provision of *fish* or *flesh* come in, they make their neighbours partakers with them.

If any stranger come in, they presently give him to eate of what they have; many a time, and at all times of the night (as I have fallen in travell upon their houses) when nothing hath been ready, have themselves and their wives, risen to prepare me some refreshing. . . . It is a strange *truth*, that a man shall generally finde more free entertainment and refreshing amongst these *Barbarians*, then amongst thousands that call themselves *Christians*. . . .

Having no Letter nor Arts, 'tis admirable how quick they are in casting [tallying] up great numbers, with the helpe of graines of Corne, instead of *Europes* pens or counters. . . .

Roger Williams, *A Key into the Language of America* (London: Gregory Dexter, 1643), ed. John J. Teunissen and Evelyn J. Hinz (Detroit: Wayne State University Press, 1973).

Their *affections*, especially to their children, are very strong; so that I have knowne a *Father* take so grievously the losse of his *childe*, that hee hath cut and stob'd himselfe with *griefe* and *rage*.

This extreme *affection*, together with want of *learning*, makes ther children sawcie, bold, and undutifull.

I once came into a *house*, and requested some *water* to drinke; the *father* bid his sonne (of some 8. yeeres of age) to fetch some *water*: the *boy* refused, and would not stir; I told the *father*, that I would correct my *child*, if he should so disobey me, &c. Upon this the *father* took up a sticke, the *boy* another, and flew at his *father*: upon my perswasion, the poore *father* made him smart a little, throw down his stick, and run for *water*, and the *father* confessed the benefit of *correction*, and the evill of their too indugent *affections*. . . .

They are as full of businesse, and as impatient of hinderance (in their kind) as any Merchant in *Europe*. . . .

Whence they call *English-men* Chauquaquock, that is, *Knive-men*, stone formerly being to them in stead of *Knives, Awle-blades, Hatchets* and *Howes*. . . .

It is almost incredible what burthens the poore women carry of *Corne*, of *Fish*, of *Beanes*, of *Mats*, and a childe besides. . . .

Yet some cut their haire round, and some as low and as short as the sober *English*; yet I never saw any so to forget nature it selfe in such excessive length and monstrous fashion, as to the shame of the *English* Nation, I now (with griefe) see my Country-men in *England* are degenerated into. . . .

Mowêsu, & Sukêsu, [their words for] *Blacke*, or *swarfish*. . . . Hence they call a *Blackamore* (themselves are tawnie, by the Sunne and their annoyntings, yet they are borne white:)

Suckáutacone, [their word for] *A cole blacke man*. For, *Sucki* is black, and *Waûtacone*, one that weares clothes, whence *English, Dutch, French, Scotch*, they call *Wautaconâuog*, or *Coatmen*. . . .

Nature knowes no difference between *Europe* and *Americans* in blood, birth, bodies, &c. God having of one blood made all mankind . . . and all by nature being children of wrath. . . .

Their desire of, and delight in newes, is great, as the *Athenians*, and all men, more or lesse; a stranger that can relate newes in their owne language, they will stile him *Manittóo*, a God. . . .

Their manner is upon any tidings to sit round, double or treble, or more, as their numbers be; I have seene neer a thousand in a round, where *English* could not well neere halfe so many have sitten: Every man hath his pipe of their *Tobacco*, and a depe silence they make, and attention give to him that speaketh; and many of them will deliver themselves, either in a relation of news, or in a consultation, with very emphaticall speech and great action, commonly an houre, and sometimes two houres together. . . .

As one answered me when I had discoursed about many points of God, of the creation, of the soule, of the danger of it, and the saving of it, he assented; but when I spake of the rising againe of the body, he cryed out, I shall never believe this. . . .

Canounicus, the old high *Sachim* of the *Nariganset Bay* (a wise and peacable Prince) once in a solemne Oration to my selfe, in a solemne assembly . . . said, I have never suffered any wrong to be offered to the *English* since they landed; nor never will: he often repeated this . . . if the *Englishman* speake true, if hee meane truly, then shall I goe to my grave in peace, and hope that the *English* and my posteritie shall live in love and peace together. I replied, that he had no cause (as I hoped) to question *Englishmans* . . . faithfulnesse, he having had long experience of their friendlinesse and trustinesse. He tooke a sticke, and broke it into ten pieces, and related ten instances (laying downe a sticke to every instance) which gave him cause thus to feare and say; I satisfied him in some presently, and presented the rest to the Governours of the *English*, who, I hope, will be far from giving just cause to have *Barbarians* to question their . . . faithfulnesse. . . .

This question they oft put to me: Why come the *Englishmen* hither? and measuring others by themselves; they say, It is because you want *firing* [lack firewood]: for they, having burnt up the *wood* in one place, (wanting draughts [sleds or conveyances] to bring *wood* to them) they are faine [willing] to follow the *wood*; and so to remove to a fresh new place for the *woods* sake. . . .

I have heard of many *English* lost, and have oft been lost my selfe, and my selfe and others have often been found, and succoured by the *Indians*. . . .

They are joyfull in meeting of any in travell, and will strike fire either with stones or sticks, to take Tobacco, and discourse a little together. . . .

The *Indians* having abundance of these sorts of Foule [ducks] upon their waters, take great pains to kill any of them with their Bow and Arrowes; and are marvellous desirous of our *English* Guns, powder, and shot (though they are wisely and generally denied by the *English*) yet with those which they get from the *French*, and some others (*Dutch* and *English*) they kill abundance of Fowle, being naturally excellent marks-men; and also more hardened to endure the weather, and wading, lying, and creeping on the ground, &c.

I once saw an exercise of training of the *English*, when all the *English* had mist the mark set up to shoot at, an *Indian* with his owne Peece (desiring leave to shoot) onely hit it. . . .

The *Natives* are very exact and punctuall in the bounds of their Lands, belonging to this or that Prince or People, (even to a River, Brooke &c.) And I have knowne them make bargaine and sale amongst themselves for a small piece, or quanitity of Ground: notwithstanding a sinfull opinion amongst many that Christians have right to *Heathens* Lands. . . .

The Women set or plant, weede, and hill, and gather and barne all the corne, and Fruites of the field: Yet sometimes the man himselfe, (either out of love to his Wife, or care for his Children, or being an old man) will help the Woman which (by the custome of the Countrey) they are not bound to.

When a field is to be broken up, they have a very loving sociable speedy way to dispatch it: All the neighbours men and Women forty, fifty, a hundred &c, joyne, and come in to help freely.

With friendly joyning they breake up their fields, build their Forts, hunt the Woods, stop and kill fish in the Rivers, it being true with them as in all the World in the Affaires of Earth or Heaven: By concord little things grow great, by discord the greatest come to nothing. . . .

They have a two-fold nakednesse:

First ordinary and constant, when although they have a Beasts skin, or an English mantle on, yet that covers ordinarily but their hinder parts and all the foreparts from top to toe, (except their secret parts, covered with a little Apron, after the patterne of their and our first Parents) I say all else open and naked.

Their male children goe starke naked, and have no Apron untill they come to ten or twelve yeeres of age; their Female they, in a modest blush cover with a little Apron of an hand breadth from their very birth.

Their second nakednesse is when their men often abroad, and both men and women within doores, leave off their beasts skin, or English cloth, and so (excepting their little Apron) are wholly naked; yet but few of the women but will keepe their skin or cloth (though loose) neare to them ready to gather it up about them.

Custome hath used their minds and bodies to it, and in such a freedom from any wantonesse, that I have never seen that wantonesses amongst them, as, (with griefe) I have heard of in *Europe*. . . .

Our English clothes are so strange unto them, and their bodies inured so to indure the weather, that when (upon gift &c.) some of them have had *English* cloathes, yet in a showre of raine, I have seen them rather expose their skins to the wet then their cloaths, and therefore pull them off, and keep them drie. . . .

While they are amongst the *English* they keep on the *English* apparell, but pull of all, as soone as they come againe into their owne Houses, and Company. . . . He that questions whether God made the World, the Indians will teach him. I must acknowledge I have received in my converse with them many Confirmations of those two great points. . . .

1. That God is.

2. That hee is a rewarder of all them that diligently seek him.

They will generally confesse that God made all: but then in speciall, although they deny not that *English-mans* God made *English* Men, and the Heavens and Earth there! yet their Gods made them, and the Heaven and Earth where they dwell. . . .

But herein is their Misery.

First they branch their God-head into many Gods.

Secondly, attribute it to Creatures. . . .

Even as the Papists [Roman Catholics] have their He and Shee Saint Protectors as St. *George*, St. *Patrick*, St. *Denis*, Virgin *Mary*, &c. . . .

I confesse to have most of these their customes by their owne Relation, for after once being in their Houses and beholding what their Worship was, I durst never bee an eye witnesse, Spectatour, or looker on, least I should have been partaker of Sathans Inventions and Worships. . . .

After I had (as farre as my language would reach) discoursed (upon a time) before the chiefe *Sachim* or *Prince* of the Countrey, with his *Archpriests*, and many others in a full Assembly; and being night, wearied with travell and discourse, I lay downe to rest; and before I slept, I heard this passage:

A[n] . . . Indian (who had heard our discourse) told the *Sachim*. . . . that soules went [not] up to Heaven, or downe to Hell; For, saith he, Our fathers have told us, that our soules goe to the *Southwest*.

The *Sachim* answered, But how doe you know your selfe, that your soules goe to the *Southwest*; did you ever see a soule goe thither?

The Native replyed; when did he (naming my selfe) see a soule goe to Heaven or Hell?

The *Sachim* agine replied: He hath books and writings, and one which God himselfe made, concerning mens soules, and therefore may well know more then wee that have none, but take all upon trust from our forefathers. . . .

I could never discerne that excesse of scandalous sins amongst them, which *Europe* aboundeth with. Drunkennesse and gluttony, generally they know not what sinnes they be; and although they have not so much to restraine them (both in respect of knowledge of God and Lawes of Men) as the *English* have, yet a man shall never heare of such crimes amongst them of robberies, murthers, adulteries, &c as amongst the *English*. . . .

The *Indians* bring downe all their sorts of Furs, which they take in the Countrey, both to the *Indians* and to the *English* for this *Indian Money* [white and black shells of wampum]: this Money the *English, French,* and *Dutch,* trade to the Indians, six hundred miles in severall parts (North and South from *New-England*) for their Furres, and whatsoever they stand in need of from them: as Corne, Venison, &c. . . .

This one fathom of this their stringed money [wampum], now worth of the English but five shillings (sometimes more) some few yeeres since was worth nine, and sometimes ten shillings *per* Fathome: the fall is occasioned by the fall of Beaver in *England*: the Natives are very impatient, when for English commodities they pay so much more of their money, and not understanding the cause of it; and many say the English cheat and deceive them, though I have laboured to make them understand the reason of it. . . .

Who ever deale or trade with them, had need of Wisedom, Patience, and Faithfulnesse in dealing: for they frequently say . . . you lye . . . you deceive me. . . .

O the infinite wisedome of the most holy wise *God*, who hath so advanced *Europe*, above *America*, that there is not a sorry *Howe, Hatchet, Knife*, nor a rag of cloth in all *America*, but what comes over the dreadfull *Atlantick* Ocean from *Europe*: and yet that *Europe* be not proud, nor *America* discouraged. What treasures are hid in some parts of *America*, and in our *New-English* parts, how have foule hands (in smoakie houses) the first handling of those Furres which are after worne upon the hands of Queens and heads of Princes?

QUESTIONS FOR READING AND DISCUSSION

1. What made Indians "barbarians," according to Williams? What standard of comparison did he use, and why?
2. How did Williams think Indians compared to the English? Did Williams believe English colonists mistreated Indians?
3. According to Williams, what did Indians think about English settlers? What did their word for a "cole blacke man" reveal about their notion of racial differences? What did the overheard conversation about the destination of souls reveal about Indian assessments of colonists?
4. In what ways did Williams's religious ideas influence his observations? What did he mean by saying that the source of the Indians' "misery" was that "they branch their God-head into many Gods . . . [and] attribute it to Creatures . . . even as the Papists have their He and Shee Saint Protectors"?
5. If Indians had written observations of Puritans like Williams, what might they have noticed?

DOCUMENT 3

Keeping Order in a Puritan Community

In New England, courts not only considered cases involving murder, assault, and theft. They also shouldered part of the responsibility for maintaining piety and a godly order. The court records of Suffolk County between 1671 and 1673, from which the following

cases have been excerpted, illustrate that New Englanders deviated from the highest aspi-
rations of the Puritan founders and that courts did what they could to curb those devia-
tions. In 1670, Suffolk County had about 10,000 residents, many of them in Boston and
nine neighboring towns.

Suffolk County Court Records, 1671–1673

Peter Egerton & Clemence his wife presented for comitting Fornicacion before Marriage they appeared & acknowledged their Evill in a humble peticion.
The Court Sentencd them to pay five pounds in Money fine to the County & fees
of Court standing comitted till the Sentence be performd.

Upon complaint made against John Tuder of severall incoradgeing speeches
he gave to ye persons in Charlestowne Ferry boat by wch he indeavored to forward ye Escape of one Wheeler who violently (with sword Drawne & pistoll
cockt) ran from ye Constable the Court sentancd him ye sd Tuder to be comitted
to prizon till he finde bonds for his good behavior.

The Court haveing taken into consideracion the many means yt have beene
used with the Church of Brantry & hitherto nothing done to efect as to the ob-
tayning the Ordinances of Christ amongst them, The Court Orders & desiries Mr
Moses Fiske to improve his Labours in preaching the word at Brantry untill the
Church there agree & obtayne suply for the worke of the Ministry or this Court
take further Order.

Alice Thomas being accused of severall shamefull notorious crimes & high
misdemeanors, she put herselfe upon Tryall of a Jury who brought in theire verdict.
     1. That if breaking open warehouses & Vessells in the night & stealing goods
thence bee by Law Burglary then ye sd Alice Thomas is guilty of abetting accessary in Burglary. however that she is guilty of abetting & accessary in Fellonious
Theft in receaving buying & concealing severall goods stol'n out of Thomas
Beards barque [boat] & Mr Hulls & Mr Pincheons warehouses.
     2. That she is guilty of giving frequent secret and unseasonable Entertainmt
in her house to Lewd Lascivious & notorious persons of both Sexes, giving them
oppertunity to commit carnall wickedness, & that by common fame she is a common Baud [prostitute].
     3. That She is guilty of Selling Wine & Strong Waters Wthout Licence.
     4. That She is guilty of Entertaining Servants and Children from theire Mas-
ter's and Parent's Families.
     5. That She is guilty of the profanation of ye Lord's day, by Selling drinke &
entertaining Idle persons & paiing money in a way of Trade upon that day.

The Court vpon due consideration of this Verdict Sentenced her to restore to
Jon Pinchon Junr forty one pounds fifteen shillings and three pence to Thomas

Records of the Suffolk County Court, 1671–1680, *Publications of the Colonial Society of Massachusetts*, vol. 29 (Boston: The Society, 1933) 22–235.

Beard thirteene pounds seaven shillings and eight pence to Capt Jon Hull twelve pounds, all in money being ye proportion of that 3.fold restitution ye Law requireth also to pay fivety pounds fine in money to ye County and fees of Court and prison. Alsoe to bee carried from the prison to ye Gallows, and there stand one hour wth a rope about her necke, one end fastened to ye sd Gallowes, and thence to bee returned to prison. & alsoe to bee carried from the prison to her one house and brought out of the gate or fore-doore strip't to the waste, & there tyed to a Cart's Taile, and soe to be whip't through ye Streete to the prison wth not undr thirty nine Stripes, & there in prison to remaine during the pleasure of this Court.

Robert Marshall being accused by Walter Barefoote for being an Atheist ye Court ordered him ye sd Marshall to bee committed to prison except hee put in bond of two hundred pounds to Appeare at the next Court of Assistance to bee holden at Boston. Accordingly ye sd Robert Marshall in one hundred pounds as principle . . . to ye Treasuror of ye County of Suffolk on condicion that ye sd Marshall shall appear at ye next Court of Assistants to answer what shall bee alledged against him as to his being an Atheist & that . . . in ye meane time bee of good Behavior.

William Carpenter, bound over to this Court to answere for beating his wife, ye Court Sentences him to bee whipt wth fifteen Stripes, & to give in bond for his good behavior paying fees of Court & prison Standing committed till ye Sentence bee performed. . . . Carpenter acknowledged himselfe bound to the Treasuror of ye County of Suffolke in ye Summe of ten pounds upon condicion that he shalbee of good behavior unto all men espetially towards his wife. . . .

Brian Murphey, presented for being a common drunckard, wch hee owned in Court, & also for striking Elinor Shearne that was wth Childe, & other misdemeanors[.] The Court Sentenced him to be whipt wth fifteen Stripes paying fees of Court & prison, Standing committed till the Sentance be performed.

Margarett, the wife of Brian Murphey, presented for common railing & cursing & other misdemeanors, the Court Sentances her to be whipt wth ten Stripes paying fees of Court and prison. Standing committed till the sentence be performed.

William Pollard, presented for taking Eighteen pence for keeping a Horse twenty four hours wth Salt Hey onley, the sd Pollard appeared & alledged hee had take much pains wth the Horse in rubbing him being hot & alsoe that he had other provender, the Court warned him not to exceede in that kinde, & pay fees of Court.

Sarah Carpenter, presented upon strong suspicion of being wth Childe, the Court ordered she should bee Searched by mrs Parker, mrs Williams, & mrs Sands who made return wth Goodwife Tailor a midwife, that she was not wth Childe.

Elizabeth Arnold, convicted of Cursing & Lewd profane Speeches, & other misdemeanors, the Court Sentanced her to pay ten Shillings fine in mony the County & fees of Court & to bee bound to the good behavior. . . .

Ursula the wife of Henry Edwards presented for striking her husband & abusive Carriage & Language the presentment was Owned & she was Sentanced to be whipt wth ten Stripes or pay twenty Shillings fine in money to the County & fees of Court Standing committed till the Sentance bee performed.

Cowesett Indian, convict for his abusive carriage to John Bennett, in comming into his house contrary to his minde & demanding drincke there, throwing Severall Stones at the said John Bennett & pulling him by the haire. The Court Sentanceth him to have his haire cut round close of from his head & to bee whip't wth thirty Stripes, paying fees of Court & prison is discharged, & if hee bee founde in Boston after his discharge hee is to bee taken by the Constable & to bee whipt wth twenty Stripes.

Jonathan Atherton, bound over to this Court for his wounding of an Indian wth his Sword; wch hee owned hee did upon provocacion given him by the Indian. The Court Sentanceth him to defray all the charges about the cure of saide Indian if it bee not already done & disinable him for wearing a Sword during his continuance in this Colony, or till this Court take farther order, & to pay fees of Court.

Jonathan Adams & his wife of Medfielde, presented for absenting themselves from the publique worship of god on the Sabbath dayes, the persons being Summoned & making default in appearance. The Court orders an Attachmt to bee issued forth for them against the next Court.

The Towne of Brantery presented for defect of a Schoolemaster answer was made they were Supplied.

Christopher Mason, convict of getting Mr Rock's Negroe maide Bess with Childe, which hee owned in Court. The Court Sentanceth him to bee whipt with twenty Stripes & to pay fees of Court & prison & to give in bond of twenty pound for the good behaviour till the next Court of this County. . . .

John Veering presented for beeing drunck & abuseing his wife in bad language calling her whore & a reproaching mr Allen & Church members in saying mr Allen was a black hypocriticall Rogue, of all which hee was convict in Court. The Court Sentanceth him to bee whip't with thirty Stripes severely laide on & to stand in the open market place in Boston, exalted upon a Stoole for an houres time on a thursday after Lecture; with a paper fastned to his breast, with this inscription in a lardge character A Prophane & Wicked Slandered & Impious Reviler of a minister of the Gosple & Church-members; & to pay charges of witnesses & Fees of Court standing committed & Upon the peticion of the saide Veering & humble acknowledgment made in open Court The Court reverseth this Sentance & Sentance the saide Veering to pay ten pounds in mony fine to the County & to give in bond for the good behaviour of twenty pounds himselfe & ten pounds apeice two Sureties & to pay the Charge of Witnesses & Fees of Court standing committed.

John Chandler presented for disorder in his house at unseasonable times of night & suffering people to bee singing & fidling at midnight of which hee was convict in Court. The Court Sentanceth him to pay Forty shillings in Mony fine to the County & to pay Charges of Witnesses & Fees of Court & to give bond for his good behaviour of five pounds & fifty shillings apeice two Sureties.

Dr Robert Couch bound over to this Court for making Verses tending to the reproach of the late Govr Richard Bellingham Esqr & of the Ministers: The Court Sentanceth him to give in bond for the good behavior ten pounds himselfe & five pounds apeice two Sureties.

QUESTIONS FOR READING AND DISCUSSION

1. What kinds of disorder did the court consider? To what extent did the court distinguish between speech and other forms of behavior? What did the fines and punishments disclose about the relative importance of different forms of disorder?

2. What values did the court seek to uphold? Did the court judgments reveal different standards for the behavior of men and women?

3. What did the cases indicate about the role of religion in this community? To what extent did the cases reveal both the significance and the limitations of Puritanism?

4. What did the cases demonstrate about structures of authority in Suffolk County society? Why, for example, did the court sentence Alice Thomas "to bee carried from the prison to ye Gallows, and there stand one hour wth a rope about her necke, one end fastened to ye sd Gallowes...& alsoe to bee carried from the prison to her one house and brought out the gate or fore-doore strip't to the waste, & there tyed to a Cart's Taile, and soe to be whip't through ye Streete to the prison wth not undr thirty nine Stripes"?

DOCUMENT 4

Words of the Bewitched

New Englanders believed that witches were capable of using their occult powers to cause bad things to happen to people. Usually, they believed, witches were in league with the devil, who used them as his agents to cause havoc. During the seventeenth century, approximately three hundred New Englanders were accused in court of being witches, about four-fifths of them women. The largest and most famous outbreak of witchcraft accusations occurred at Salem in 1692. The prominent Puritan minister Cotton Mather summarized the testimony against some of the accused witches in his book Wonders of the Invisible World (1692), the source of the following testimony against Bridget Bishop. Bishop was a married, middle-aged woman; both she and her husband were church members. Eight days after her trial, she was executed by hanging.

Testimony against Accused Witch Bridget Bishop, 1692

The trial of Bridget Bishop . . . at the Court of Oyer and Terminer held at Salem, June 2, 1692.

I. She was indicted for bewitching of several persons in the neighborhood, the indictment being drawn up, according to the form in such cases usual. And pleading, not guilty, there were brought in several persons, who had long undergone many kinds of miseries, which were preternaturally inflicted, and generally ascribed unto a horrible witchcraft. There was little occasion to prove the witchcraft; it being evident and notorious to all beholders. Now to fix the witchcraft on the prisoner at the bar, the first thing used was, the testimony of the bewitched; whereof, several testified, that the shape of the prisoner did oftentimes very grievously pinch them, choke them, bite them, and afflict them; urging them to write their names in a book, which the said specter called, ours. One of them did further testify, that it was the shape of this prisoner, with another, which one day took her from her [spinning] wheel, and carrying her to the riverside, threatened there to drown her, if she did not sign to the book mentioned: which yet she refused. Others of them did also testify, that the said shape, did in her threats, brag to them, that she had been the death of sundry persons, then by her named; that she had ridden a man, then likewise named. Another testified, the apparition of ghosts unto the specter of Bishop, crying out, you murdered us! About the truth whereof, there was in the matter of fact, but too much suspicion.

II. It was testified, that at the examination of the prisoner, before the magistrates, the bewitched were extremely tortured. If she did but cast her eyes on them, they were presently struck down; and this in such a manner as there could be no collusion in the business. But upon the touch of her hand upon them, when they lay in their swoons, they would immediately revive; and not upon the touch of anyone else. Moreover, upon some special actions of her body, as the shaking of her head, or the turning of her eyes, they presently and painfully fell into the like postures. . . .

IV. One Deliverance Hobbs, who had confessed her being a witch, was now tormented by the specters, for her confession. And she now testified, that this Bishop, tempted her to sign the book again, and to deny what she had confessed. She affirmed, that it was the shape of this prisoner, which whipped her with iron rods, to compel her thereunto. And she affirmed, that this Bishop was at a general meeting of the witches, in a field at Salem Village and there partook of a diabolical sacrament, in bread and wine then administered!

V. To render it further unquestionable, that the prisoner at the bar, was the person truly charged in this witchcraft, there were produced many evidences of other witchcrafts, by her perpetrated. For instance, John Cook testified, that about five or six years ago, one morning, about sunrise, he was in his chamber, assaulted by the shape of this prisoner: which looked on him, grinned at him, and very much hurt him, with a blow on the side of the head: and that on the same day, about noon, the same shape walked in the room where he was, and an apple strangely flew out of his hand, into the lap of his mother, six or eight foot from him.

VI. Samuel Gray, testified, that about fourteen years ago, he waked on a night, and saw the room where he lay, full of light; and that he then saw plainly a woman between the cradle, and the bedside, which looked upon him. He rose, and it vanished; though he found the doors all fast. Looking out at the entry door, he saw the same woman, in the same garb again; and said, In God's name, what do you come for? He went to bed, and had the same woman again assaulting

Cotton Mather, *Wonders of the Invisible World* (1692), in *Witch-Hunting in Seventeenth-Century New England: A Documentary History, 1638–1692*, ed. David D. Hall (Boston: Northeastern University Press, 1991) 296–301.

him. The child in the cradle gave a great screech, and the woman disappeared. It was long before the child could be quieted; and though it were a very likely thriving child, yet from this time it pined away, and after divers months died in a sad condition. He knew not Bishop, nor her name but when he saw her after this, he knew by her countenance, and apparel, and all circumstances, that it was the apparition of this Bishop, which had thus troubled him.

VII. John Bly and his wife, testified, that he bought a sow of Edward Bishop, the husband of the prisoner; and was to pay the price agreed, unto another person. This prisoner being angry that she was thus hindered from fingering the money, quarrelled with Bly. Soon after which the sow, was taken with strange fits; jumping, leaping, and knocking her head against the fence, she seemed blind and deaf, and would neither eat nor be sucked. Whereupon a neighbor said, she believed the creature was over-looked; and sundry other circumstances concurred, which made the deponents believe that Bishop had bewitched it. . . .

IX. Samuel Shattuck testified, that in the year 1680, this Bridget Bishop, often came to his house upon such frivolous and foolish errands, that they suspected she came indeed with a purpose of mischief. Presently whereupon his eldest child, which was of as promising health and sense, as any child of its age, began to droop exceedingly; and the oftener that Bishop came to the house, the worse grew the child. As the child would be standing at the door, he would be thrown and bruised against the stones, by an invisible hand, and in like sort knock his face against the sides of the house, and bruise it after a miserable manner. Afterwards this Bishop would bring him things to dye, whereof he could not imagine any use; and when she paid him a piece of money, the purse and money were unaccountably conveyed out of a locked box, and never seen more. The child was immediately hereupon taken with terrible fits, whereof his friends thought he would have died: indeed he did almost nothing but cry and sleep for several months together: and at length his understanding was utterly taken away. . . .

XI. William Stacy testified, that receiving money of this Bishop, for work done by him, he was gone but a matter of three rods from her, and looking for his money, found it unaccountably gone from him. Some time after, Bishop asked him whether his father would grind her grist for her? He demanded why? She replied, Because folks count me a witch. He answered, No question, but he will grind it for you. Being then gone about six rods from her, with a small load in his cart, suddenly the off-wheel slumped and sunk down into a hole upon plain ground, so that the deponent, was forced to get help for the recovering of the wheel. But stepping back to look for the hole which might give him this disaster, there was none at all to be found. . . .

XII. To crown all, John Bly, and William Bly, testified, that being employed by Bridget Bishop, to help take down the cellar wall, of the old house, wherein she formerly lived, they did in holes of the said old wall, find several poppets, made up of rags, and hog's bristles, with headless pins in them, the points being outward. Whereof she could now give no account unto the court, that was reasonable or tolerable.

XIII. One thing that made against the prisoner was, her being evidently convicted of gross lying, in the court, several times, while she was making her plea. But besides this, a jury of women, found a preternatural teat upon her body; but upon a second search, within three or four hours, there was no such thing to be seen. There was also an account of other people whom this woman had afflicted.

And there might have been many more, if they had been, inquired for. But there was no need of them.

Questions for Reading and Discussion

1. What made Bishop's witchcraft "evident and notorious to all beholders"? Much of the testimony recalled events that had occurred many years earlier; why had her witchcraft only become "evident and notorious to all beholders" in 1692?

2. In what ways did Bishop act like a witch, according to her accusers? Why did her accusers believe she — rather than an accident of chance — had caused their misfortunes?

3. In what ways did Bishop's gender contribute to the accusations against her? Why were "poppets, made up of rags, and hog's bristles, with headless pins in them" and "a preternatural teat upon her body" considered evidence against her?

4. Judging from the testimony against Bishop, what would protect a person from being accused of witchcraft?

Comparative Questions

1. How did the ideals of the *Arbella* sermon influence the judgments of the Suffolk County Court and the testimony against Bridget Bishop?

2. How did the cases that came before the Suffolk court differ from the accusations made against Bishop? Why, in other words, were the Suffolk offenders not considered witches and why was Bishop not considered guilty of routine misconduct, rather than witchcraft?

3. How did the forms of order and disorder that Williams observed among Indians compare with Puritan ideals in the *Arbella* sermon and the deviations from those ideals in the court cases and witchcraft testimony?

4. Judging from the documents in this chapter, to what extent did Puritan settlers succeed in creating a new England in the northern colonies during the seventeenth century? Do these documents illustrate Puritan successes, failures, or both? How and why? Were the successes or failures the result of Puritanism or in spite of it?

CHAPTER 4

COLONIAL AMERICA IN THE EIGHTEENTH CENTURY
1701–1770

E ighteenth-century colonists lived in a world of change. Older certainties of faith eroded. New patterns of commerce spread. Choices abounded. Where to live? What faith to profess? What kind of work to do? What goods to buy and sell? These and other choices made many colonists think about changing themselves through education, training, discipline, introspection, or religious conversion, among other ways. The documents that follow illustrate the different choices available to slaves, immigrants, and native-born free white colonists. The choices they made helped to create the change they all experienced.

DOCUMENT 1
Confessions of a Thief and Rapist

In New England, executions were occasions for the reaffirmation of community values, particularly when the person to be executed confessed and asked forgiveness. Confessions were sometimes printed as broadsides to warn others of the consequences of crime. In October 1768, a man named Arthur made the following confession about his history as a thief and rapist, which was subsequently circulated as a broadside. Although Arthur was a slave, his confession reveals the world of choices — often wrong choices — that confronted many other working people who were not subjected to the constraints of bondage in eighteenth-century New England.

A Boston Broadside, 1768

The LIFE, and dying SPEECH of ARTHUR, a Negro Man;
Who was Executed at Worcester, October 20th 1768.
For a Rape committed on the Body of one *Deborah Metcalfe*.

I Was born at Taunton, January 15. 1747, in the House of *Richard Godfrey*, Esq; my Mother being his Slave, where I lived fourteen Years; was learned to read and write, and was treated very kindly by my Master; but was so unhappy as often to incur the Displeasure of my Mistress, which caused me then to run away: And this was the beginning of the many notorious Crimes, of which I have been guilty. I went first to Sandwich, where I fell in Company with some Indians, with whom I lived two Months frequently being guilty of Drunkenness and Fornication. . . .

At Sandwich, I stole a Shirt, was detected, and settled the Affair, by paying twenty Shillings. My Character being now known, I thought proper to leave the Place; and accordingly shipped my self on board a Whaling Sloop, with Capt. *Coffin*, of *Nantucket*: We were out eight Months, and then returned to Nantucket, . . . where I tarried six Weeks. In which Time I broke a Store of Mr. Roach's, from which I stole a Quantity of Rum, a pair of Trowsers, a jacket, and some Calicos. — The next Day I got drunk, and by wearing the jacket, was detected, for which Offence I was whip'd fifteen Stripes, and committed to Gaol[1], for the Payment of Cost &c from whence I escaped in half an Hour by breaking the Lock. Being now hardened in my Wickedness, I the next Night broke another Store in the same Place, from which I took several Articles, and then shipped myself on board a Vessel bound to *Swanzey*, where I was discovered, taken on Shoar, and whip'd sixteen Stripes; being then set at Liberty, I returned to *Taunton*, after one Year's Absence, where my Master received me kindly, whom I served three Years: In which Time I followed the Seas, sailing from *Nantucket*, and *Newport*, to divers parts of the *West-Indies*, where I whored and drank, to great Excess. Being now weary of the Seas, on the 27th of October 1764, I came again to live with my Master at *Taunton*, where I behaved well for six Weeks; at the Expiration of which Time, going to Town with some Negroes, I got intoxicated; on returning home went into an House where were several Women only, to whom I offered Indecencies, but was prevented from executing my black Designs, by the coming in of *James Williams*, Esq; upon which I left the House, but was overtaken by him, who with the Assistance of Mr. *Job Smith*, committed me to Taunton Gaol: On the next Day I was tried before the same Mr. *Williams*, and was whip'd thirty-nine Stripes for abusing him, uttering three profane Oaths, and threatning to fire Mr. *Smith's* House. My Master being now determined, by the Advice of his friends, to send me out of the Country. I was sold to — *Hill*, of *Brookfield*, with whom I lived only one Week; was then sold to my last Master, Capt. *Clarke*, of *Rutland* District, where I behaved well for two Months, and was very kindly treated by my Master and Mistress. I then unhappily commenced an Acquaintance with a young Squaw,

---

"Broadside Printed and Sold in Milk Street, Boston, 1768," in *The Rising Glory of America, 1760–1820*, ed. Gordon S. Wood (New York: George Braziller, 1971) 101–05.
    [1]**Gaol:** Jail.

with whom (having stole Six Shillings from one of my Master's Sons) I was advised by other Negroes, to run away, to avoid being taken up. By Advice of my Companion (who like the rest of her Sex, was of a very fruitful Invention) I had recourse to the following Expedient: I dressed in the Habit of a Squaw, and made of my own Cloaths a Pappoose; in this manner we proceeded to *Hadley* undiscover'd, where I was introduced by my Companion, to an Indian Family, where I tarried only one Night, being discover'd in the Morning by one Mr. Shurtless, a Person who had been sent after me; with him I went to *Springfield*, where I met my Master, who took me down to *Middletown* with a Drove of Horses where he sold me to a Dutch Gentleman, whose Name I have since forgot. The very Night after I stole from the Widow *Sherley*, (a Person who kept a public House in that Place) five Pounds; and the next Night, by getting drunk and loosing some of my Money, I was detected and put under the Custody of two Men, for Trial the next Day: From whom I escaped, and went to Farmington, where being advertised, I was immediately taken up by Mr. *John Petterill*, who carried me to my old Master *Clarke's* in *Rutland* District, with whom I spent the Summer, frequently stealing and getting drunk. My Master being now wearied by my repeated Crimes, was determined to part with me: And accordingly we set off for *Boston*, at which Time I took two Dollars from my Master's Desk. On our Way thither, tarrying some Time at Mr. *Fisk's* in *Waltham*; I went with some Negroes to a Husking[2], at Mr. *Thomas Parkes's*, in *Little Cambridge,* where they on the same Night introduced me to a white Woman of that Place: And as our Behaviour was such, as we have both Reason to be ashamed of, I shall for her sake pass over in Silence. On the next Day I went to Boston, was pursued by her Husband, who found me at the Sign of the white Horse, where I left him in Conversation with my Master, who sent me to Little Cambridge with his Team; he again came up with me on *Boston* Neck, where we came to Blows, and coming off Conqueror, put on *for Cambridge.* The next Night I went to another Husking at Mr. *John Denney's*, of that Place; after husking, I went to a Tavern opposite Mr. *Denney's*, and took from a Team there, a Horse, Saddle and Bridle, and rode to Natick, where I met with the Squaw, with whom I formerly made my Tour to *Hadley*, and with her spent the Day; and returning to *Cambridge*, I met my Master, with another Man, in pursuit of me. At our Arrival there, I was sentenced by five Men (to whom the Matter was left) to receive fifteen Stripes, or pay four Dollars; and my Master was so good natur'd, or rather silly, as to pay the Money and let me go with Impunity. . . .

[I] made the best of my way to *Dorchester*, where I stole a Horse, Saddle and Bridle, and proceeded to *Easton*, to pay a Visit to my Parents: who suspecting my Situation, insisted on my returning to my Master, which I promised without either Thoughts or Inclination of performing: For instead of returning to *Boston*, I steered my Course for *Sandwich*. . . . When I got to *Sandwich* I went to an Indian House, where I had been formerly acquainted, and with the Squaws there, spent my Time in a manner which may be easily guessed; but was taken up on Suspicion, by one Mr. *Fish* and by him carried before Col. Otis who on my confessing that I stole the Horse at *Dorchester*, committed me to *Barnstable* Gaol for Trial, from whence I escaped in two Days. I then went to *Southsea*, an Indian Village in *Sandwich* where I tarried six Weeks, spending my Time in drinking and whoreing with the Squaws. By this Time I had got almost naked; and on going to *Falmouth*

---

[2]**Husking:** A gathering of friends and neighbors to husk corn.

with some Indians, went into a Shoemaker's Shop, and from thence stole a pair of Shoes: And from a House in the same Place, I stole a Shirt, and a pair of Trowsers. At Night my Companions getting drunk, I left them; and at a Tavern there, stole a Horse, Saddle and Bridle, on which I returned to the Indian Village, and then let him loose. After tarrying one Week more, I was again taken up and committed to *Barnstable* Gaol, where after laying three Weeks, I was tried and sentenced to receive twenty Stripes; but being unwell, the Man from whom I stole the Horse at *Dorchester*, coming to *Barnstable*, and by paying the Cost, took me out of Gaol, so that I again got off unpunished: With him I lived about three Weeks, and behaved well.

In the mean Time, my Master being sent for, once more took me home, where I had not been three Weeks, before another Negro of my Master's told me that the young Squaw, so often mentioned, was very desirous of seeing me. I one Night, after having stole some Rum from my Master, got pretty handsomely drunk, took one of his Horses, and made the best of my way to her usual Place of Abode; but she not being at home, the Devil put it into my Head to pay a Visit to the Widow *Deborah Metcalfe*, whom I, in a most inhumane manner, ravished: The Particulars of which are so notorious, that it is needless for me here to relate them. The next Morning the unhappy Woman came and acquainted my Master of it, who immediately tyed me, to prevent my running away, and told her (if she was desirous of prosecuting me) to get a Warrant as soon as possible; but she being unwilling to have me hanged, proposed making the Matter up for a proper Consideration, provided my Master would send me out of the Country; to which he agreed, and accordingly set off with me for Albany: But we were overtaken at *Glasgow*, by Mr. *Nathaniel Jennison*, who it seem'd had got a Warrant for me. On our return to *Rutland* District, we stop'd at a Tavern in *Hardwick*, where after I had warmed my self, *Jennison* was Fool enough to bid me put along, and he would overtake me; accordingly I went out of the Door, and seeing his Horse stand handily, what should I do, but mount him, and rode off as fast as I could, leaving *Jennison* to pursue me on Foot. I got home before Bed-time, and took up my Lodging in my Master's Barn for the Night, where I had a Bottle of Cherry-Rum (which I found in Mr. *Jennison's* Baggs) to refresh my self with.

On the next Day, being the 30th of March 1767, was discovered and committed to *Worcester* Gaol, where I continued 'till the 20th of April following; at which Time I broke out with the late celebrated FRASIER, and a young Lad, who was confined for stealing. After which, at *Worcester* we broke into a Barber's Shop, from whence we stole a Quantity of Flour, a Comb, and a Razor: We then set off for *Boston*. At Shrewsbury, we stole a Goose from Mr. *Samuel Jennison*; and from the Widow *Kingsley*, in the same Place, we stole a Kettle, in which we boiled the Goose, in *Westborough* Woods. At *Marlborough*, we broke into a Distill-House, from whence we stole some Cyder Brandy: In the same Town we broke into a Shoe-maker's Shop, and took each of us a pair of Shoes. We like wise broke into Mr. *Ciperon Howe's* House, in the same Place, from whence we stole some Bread, Meat and Rum. At Sudbury, we stole each of us a Shirt, and one pair of Stockings. At *Weston* we stole some Butter from off a Horse. At Waltham we broke into a House belonging to one Mr. Fisk, from whom we took a small Sum of Money, some Chocolate and Rum. At *Watertown* we stole a Brass Kettle from one Mrs. *White* of that Place. My Companions now left me; upon which I went to Mr. *Fish's* in *Waltham*, who knew me. And having heard of my Escape from *Worcester* Gaol, immediately secured me, and with the Assistance of another Man, brought me back again, where on the 17th of September following, I was tryed and found guilty. Upon which, by the Advice of my Counsel, I prayed for the Benefit of the Clergy; which after a Year's Consideration, the Court denied me: And accordingly I was, on the 24th of Sept. last, sentenced to be hanged, which I must confess is but too just a Reward for my many notorious Crimes.

I cannot conclude this my Narrative, without gratefully acknowledging the unwearied Pains that was taken by the Rev. Mr. *Mccarty*, to awaken me to a proper Sense of my miserable and wretched Condition, whose frequent Exhortations, and most fervent Prayers, together with those of the rest of God's People, and my own sincere Endeavours after true Repentance, will I hope prove the Means of my eternal Well-being; which I hope is still the Prayers of every Christian, to whom my unhappy Situation is known.—I earnestly desire that this Recital of my Crimes, and the ignominious Death to which my notorious Wickedness has bro't me, may prove a Warning to all Persons who shall become acquainted therewith. But in a particular Manner, I would solemnly warn those of my own Colour, as they regard their own Souls, to avoid Desertion from their Masters, Drunkenness and Lewdness; which three Crimes was the Source from which have flowed the many Evils and Miseries of my short Life: Short indeed! For I am now at the Age of 21 Years only, just going to launch into a never-ending eternity; not by a natural Death, but to the Dissolution of Soul and Body, so dreadful in itself, are added the Ignominy and Terror of that particular kind of Death, which I am now going to suffer.—I freely acknowledge I have been better teated by Mankind in general, than I deserved: Yet some Injuries I have received, which I now freely forgive. I also humbly ask Forgiveness of all whom I have injured, and desire that they would pray that I may receive the Forgiveness of God, whom I have most of all offended; and on whose Pardon and Grace depends my eternal Happiness or Misery.

QUESTIONS FOR READING AND DISCUSSION

1. What did Arthur's confession reveal about his experiences as a slave? What kinds of work did he do? With whom did he associate? How might his experiences have differed from those of a young, free white man of the era?

2. Why was Arthur able to escape so often? How did his master and his employers treat him? What did they and his parents expect him to do, and why?

3. What did Arthur's confession disclose about relations among slaves, Indians, and whites in eighteenth-century Massachusetts?

4. To what extent might this confession "prove a Warning to all Persons" reading it or hearing it read by others? Might they believe that it revealed more about "those of my own Colour" than about free white people? In what ways did Arthur's confession reinforce community values?

DOCUMENT 2

Poor Richard's Advice

In 1732, Benjamin Franklin began to publish Poor Richard's Almanac, *a calendar packed with astronomical observations, miscellaneous information, and pithy advice about almost everything, all of it written by Franklin under the pseudonym of Richard Saunders. Widely read, the almanac became highly profitable for Franklin, and he continued to publish it every year until 1757. For the last issue, Franklin composed a synthesis of Poor Richard's wisdom in the form of a speech given by an old man. The speech, which follows, describes the temptations faced by eighteenth-century colonists and how they should resist them. The popularity of the almanac suggests that the old man's views were shared by many other colonists.*

Benjamin Franklin

Father Abraham's Speech from Poor Richard's Almanac, *1757*

Courteous Reader,

I have heard that nothing gives an Author so great Pleasure, as to find his Works respectfully quoted by other learned Authors. This Pleasure I have seldom enjoyed. . . . I concluded at length, that the People were the best judges of my Merit; for they buy my Works; and besides, in my Rambles, where I am not personally known, I have frequently heard one or other of my Adages repeated, with, *as Poor Richard says*, at the End on't; this gave me some Satisfaction, as it showed not only that my Instructions were regarded, but discovered likewise some Respect for my Authority; and I own, that to encourage the Practice of remembering and repeating those wise Sentences, I have sometimes *quoted myself* with great Gravity.

Judge then how much I must have been gratified by an Incident I am going to relate to you. I stopt my Horse lately where a great Number of People were collected at a Vendue[1] of Merchant Goods. The Hour of Sale not being come, they were conversing on the Badness of the Times, and one of the Company call'd to a plain clean old Man, with white Locks, *Pray, Father Abraham, what think you of the Times? Won't these heavy Taxes quite ruin the Country? How shall we be ever able to pay them? What would you advise us to?* — Father Abraham stood up, and reply'd, If you'd have my Advice, I'll give it you in short, for a *Word to the Wise is enough*, and *many Words won't fill a Bushel, as Poor Richard says*. They join'd in desiring him to speak his Mind, and gathering round him, he proceeded as follows;

"Friends," says he, "and Neighbours, the Taxes are indeed very heavy, and if those laid on by the Government were the only Ones we had to pay, we might more easily discharge them; but we have many others, and much more grievous to some of us. We are taxed twice as much by our *Idleness*, three times as much by our *Pride*, and four times as much by our *Folly*, and from these Taxes the Commissioners cannot ease or deliver us by allowing an Abatement. However let us hearken to good Advice, and something may be done for us; *God helps them that help themselves, as Poor Richard* says. . . .

It would be thought a hard Government that should tax its People one tenth Part of their *Time*, to be employed in its Service. But *Idleness* taxes many of us much more, if we reckon all that is spent in absolute *Sloth*, or doing of nothing, with that which is spent in idle Employments or Amusements, that amount to nothing. *Sloth*, by bringing on Diseases, absolutely shortens Life. *Sloth, like Rust,*

Poor Richard's Almanac, in Benjamin Franklin, *Writings*, ed. J. A. Leo Lemay (New York: Library of America, 1987) 1294–1303.

[1]**Vendue:** A public auction.

consumes faster than Labour wears, while the used Key is always bright, as *Poor Richard* says. — How much more than is necessary do we spend in Sleep! forgetting that *The sleeping Fox catches no Poultry*, and that *there will be sleeping enough in the Grave*, as *Poor Richard* says. If Time be of all Things the most precious, *wasting Time* must be, as *Poor Richard* says, *the greatest Prodigality*, since, as he elsewhere tells us, *Lost Time is never found again*. . . . Let us then up and be doing, and doing to the Purpose; so by Diligence shall we do more with less Perplexity. *Sloth makes all Things difficult, but Industry all easy*, as *Poor Richard* says; and *He that riseth late, must trot all Day, and shall scarce overtake his Business at Night.* While *Laziness travels so slowly, that Poverty soon overtakes him*, as we read in *Poor Richard*, who adds, *Drive thy Business, let not that drive thee*; and *Early to Bed, and early to rise, makes a Man healthy, wealthy and wise.*

So what signifies *wishing* and *hoping* for better Times. We may make these Times better if we bestir ourselves. *Industry need not wish*, as *Poor Richard* says, and *He that lives upon Hope will die fasting. There are no Gains, without Pains.* . . . And, as *Poor Richard* likewise observes, *He that hath a Trade hath an Estate*, and *He that hath a Calling hath an Office of Profit and Honour*; but then the *Trade* must be worked at, and the *Calling* well followed, or neither the *Estate*, nor the *Office*, will enable us to pay our Taxes. — If we are industrious we shall never starve; for, as *Poor Richard* says, *At the working Man's House Hunger looks in, but dares not enter.* Nor will the Bailiff or the Constable enter, for *Industry pays Debts, while Despair encreaseth them*, says *Poor Richard*. — What though you have found no Treasure, nor has any rich Relation left you a Legacy, *Diligence is the Mother of Good-luck*, as *Poor Richard* says, and *God gives all Things to Industry.* Then *plough deep, while Sluggards sleep, and you shall have Corn to sell and to keep*, says *Poor Dick*. Work while it is called To-day, for you know not how much you may be hindered To-morrow which makes *Poor Richard* say, *One To-day is worth two Tomorrows*; and farther, *Have you somewhat to do To-morrow, do it To-day.* If you were a Servant, would you not be ashamed that a good Master should catch you idle? Are you then your own Master, *be ashamed to catch yourself idle*, as *Poor Dick says.* . . .

Methinks I hear some of you say, *Must a Man afford himself no Leisure?* I will tell thee, my Friend, what *Poor Richard* says, *Employ thy Time well if thou meanest to gain Leisure*; and, *since thou art not sure of a Minute, throw not away an Hour.* Leisure is Time for doing something useful; this Leisure the diligent Man will obtain, but the lazy Man never. . . .

But with our Industry, we must likewise be *steady, settled and careful*, and oversee our own Affairs *with our own Eyes*, and not trust too much to others; for, as *Poor Richard* says,

> *I never saw an oft removed Tree,*
> *Nor yet an oft removed Family,*
> *That throve so well as those that settled be.*

And again, *Three Removes is as bad as a Fire*; and again, *Keep thy Shop, and thy Shop will keep thee*; and again, *If you would have your Business done, go; If not, send.* . . . And again, *The Eye of a Master will do more Work than both his Hands*; and again, *Want of Care does us more Damage than Want of Knowledge*; and again, *Not to oversee Workmen, is to leave them your Purse open.* Trusting too much to others Care is the Ruin of many; for, as the *Almanack* says, *In the Affairs of this World, men are saved, not by Faith, but by the Want of it. . . .* And farther, *If you would have a faithful Servant, and one that you like, serve yourself. . . .*

So much for Industry, my Friends, and Attention to one's own Business; but to these we must add *Frugality*, if we would make our *Industry* more certainly successful. A Man may, if he knows not how to save as he gets, *keep his Nose all his Life to the Grindstone*, and die not worth a *Groat*[2] at last. *A fat Kitchen makes a lean Will*, as Poor Richard says; and,

> *Many Estates are spent in the Getting,*
> *Since Women for Tea forsook Spinning and Knitting,*
> *And Men for Punch forsook Hewing and Splitting.*

If you would be wealthy, says he, in another Almanack, *think of Saving as well as of Getting: The* Indies *have not made* Spain *rich, because her* Outgoes *are greater than her* Incomes. Away then with your expensive Follies, and you will not have so much Cause to complain of hard Times, heavy Taxes, and chargeable Families. . . . And farther, *What maintains one Vice, would bring up two Children.* You may think perhaps, That a *little* Tea, or a *little* Punch now and then, Diet a *little* more costly, Clothes a *little* finer, and a *little* Entertainment now and then, can be no great Matter; but remember what *Poor Richard* says, *Many a Little makes a Mickle*; and farther, *Beware of little Expences; a small Leak will sink a great Ship*; and again, . . . *Fools make Feasts, and wise Men eat them.*

Here you are all got together at this Vendue of *Fineries* and *Knicknacks*. You call them Goods, but if you do not take Care, they will prove Evils to some of you. You expect they will be sold *cheap*, and perhaps they may for less than they cost; but if you have no Occasion for them, they must be dear to you. Remember what *Poor Richard* says, *Buy what thou hast no Need of, and ere long thou shalt sell thy Necessaries.* . . . Many a one, for the Sake of Finery on the Back, have gone with a hungry Belly, and half starved their Families; *Silks and Sattins, Scarlet and Velvets,* as *Poor Richard* says, *put out the Kitchen Fire.* These are not the *Necessaries* of Life; they can scarcely be called the *Conveniencies*, and yet only because they look pretty, how many *want* to *have* them. The *artificial* Wants of Mankind thus become more numerous than the *natural.* . . . By these, and other Extravagancies, the Genteel are reduced to Poverty, and forced to borrow of those whom they formerly despised, but who through *Industry* and *Frugality* have maintained their Standing; in which Case it appears plainly, that a *Ploughman on his Legs is higher than a Gentleman on his Knees*, as *Poor Richard* says. . . . *If you would know the Value of money, go and try to borrow some*; for, *he that goes a borrowing goes a sorrowing*; and indeed so does he that lends to such People, when he goes to get it in again. *Poor Dick* farther advises, and says, *Fond Pride of Dress, is sure a very Curse.* . . . When you have bought one fine Thing you must buy ten more, that your Appearance may be all of a Piece; but *Poor Dick* says, *'Tis easier to suppress the first Desire, than to satisfy all that follow it.* And 'tis as truly Folly for the Poor to ape the Rich, as for the Frog to swell, in order to equal the Ox.

> *Great Estates may venture more,*
> *But little Boats should keep near Shore.*

---

[2]**Groat:** An English coin.

'Tis however a Folly soon punished; for . . . *Pride breakfasted with Plenty, dined with Poverty and supped with Infamy.* And after all, of what Use is this *Pride of Appearance*, for which so much is risked, so much is suffered? It cannot promote Health, or ease Pain; it makes no Increase of Merit in the Person, it creates Envy, it hastens Misfortune. . . . But what Madness must it be to *run in Debt* for these Superfluities! We are offered, by the Terms of this Vendue, *Six Months Credit*; and that perhaps has induced some of us to attend it, because we cannot spare the ready Money, and hope now to be fine without it. But, ah, think what you do when you run in Debt; *You give to another Power over your Liberty.* If you cannot pay at the Time, you will be ashamed to see your Creditor; you will be in Fear when you speak to him; you will make poor pitiful sneaking Excuses, and by Degrees come to lose your Veracity, and sink into base downright lying; for, as *Poor Richard* says . . . *Lying rides upon Debt's Back.* Whereas a freeborn Englishman ought not to be ashamed or afraid to see or speak to any Man living. But Poverty often deprives a Man of all Spirit and Virtue: *'Tis hard for an empty Bag to stand upright,* as *Poor Richard* truly says. What would you think of that Prince, or that Government, who should issue an Edict forbidding you to dress like a Gentleman or a Gentlewoman, on Pain of Imprisonment or Servitude? Would you not say, that you are free, have a Right to dress as you please, and that such an Edict would be a Breach of your Privileges, and such a Government tyrannical? And yet you are about to put yourself under that Tyranny when you run in Debt for such Dress! Your Creditor has Authority at his Pleasure to deprive you of your Liberty, by confining you in Gaol for Life, or to sell you for a Servant, if you should not be able to pay him! When you have got your Bargain, you may, perhaps, think little of Payment; but *Creditors, Poor Richard* tells us, *have better Memories than Debtors.* . . . *The Borrower is a Slave to the Lender, and the Debtor to the Creditor,* disdain the Chain, preserve your Freedom; and maintain your Independency: Be *industrious* and *free*; be *frugal* and *free.* . . .

This Doctrine, my Friends, is *Reason* and *Wisdom*; but after all, do not depend too much upon your own *Industry*, and *Frugality*, and *Prudence*, though excellent Things, for they may all be blasted without the Blessing of Heaven; and therefore ask that Blessing humbly, and be not uncharitable to those that at present seem to want it, but comfort and help them. Remember *Job* suffered, and was afterwards prosperous.

And now to conclude, . . . remember this, *They that won't be counselled, can't be helped,* as *Poor Richard* says: And farther, *That if you will not hear Reason, she'll surely rap your Knuckles.*"

Thus the old Gentleman ended his Harangue. The People heard it, and approved the Doctrine, and immediately practised the contrary, just as if it had been a common Sermon; for the Vendue opened, and they began to buy extravagantly, notwithstanding all his Cautions, and their own Fear of Taxes. . . .

> I am, as ever,
> Thine to serve thee,
> Richard Saunders.

July 7, 1757

QUESTIONS FOR READING AND DISCUSSION

1. According to Father Abraham, what temptations were likely to lead his contemporaries astray, and how could they be resisted?

2. In what ways were idleness, pride, and folly taxes? How would industry, frugality, and reason avoid or minimize such taxes?

3. According to Father Abraham, what were the goals of disciplined behavior? Did people who did not discipline their behavior appropriately have different goals? What, for example, did they think about time, consumption, and debt?

4. After the speech, the people who heard it began "to buy extravagantly"? What does their behavior suggest about the old man's wisdom? To what extent did Father Abraham's advice partake of the ethos of individualism, and to what extent did it critcize that ethos?

5. Many of Father Abraham's maxims are still repeated today. Why? Do you think they are more or less important today than they were in the eighteenth century? Why?

DOCUMENT 3

A Scottish Immigrant Writes News from America

In 1771, Alexander Thomson and his large family left their farm near Glasgow, Scotland, and immigrated to America. In the spring of 1772, Thomson bought a sizable farm near Shippensburg, Pennsylvania. Little over a year later, he described his new home in a letter to a friend in Scotland. Thomson's letter, published in Glasgow in 1774 and excerpted here, contrasted his experiences in Pennsylvania with life in Scotland. His descriptions disclosed both the attractions of immigration and the restraints that kept many from leaving their European homes. Thomson's account also revealed the continuing influence of his Scottish origins.

Alexander Thomson
Letter from America, 1774

In July 1771, I and my wife and twelve of our children went aboard the Friendship in the harbour of Greenock: It was after the middle of that month when we set sail for North-America, and happily we arrived at the city Boston on the tenth of September, all in perfect health.

I believe that some of my neighbours and acquaintance thought it strange, that one of my age [he was forty-nine] should forsake his native country: but I thought I had but too much reason to do as I have done: as I was blessed with a numerous family, (and I have had another child since I left Scotland) I was very desirous to provide for them: All my sons who were able to work were brought up to the business of farming, and it was by their labour that I was assisted to gain any money I have: I therefore endeavoured to have one or two of the eldest of my sons settled in farms at home; and with that view I employed myself for the space of five years, in looking out for such farms as might answer my purpose. I travelled through the country for twenty miles round the place where I lived; but tho' I found plenty of vacant farms, I told you before, and I declare it

Alexander Thomson, *Letter from America* (Glasgow, Scotland, 1774).

again on the word of an honest man, that I could see no farm for which the laird[1] did not ask more than double the rent it was worth; so that if I had meddled with any of them I say well that my sons would never be able to pay the rent, and that in three or four years I would not have had one shilling to rub upon another.

After I had spent so much time and labour to no purpose, I confess that at length I conceived a sort of distaste for the lairds: I imagined that as they knew I had a little money, they wanted to get it from me as fast as they could; and in truth some of my neighbours observed a change in my temper, and alledged that I was turned so obstinate that I would not stay in the country, even though some laird should offer me a farm or two on reasonable terms: and I dare not say they were altogether in the wrong.

As I was going to America not for merchandizing but as a farmer; several of my acquaintance and well-wishers told me that I would save both time and money by landing at New York or Philadelphia, but I had a great curiosity to see Boston, especially as I understood that some of my father's friends had settled there long ago, and some from Paisley very lately. However I stayed at Boston but a few days; for I made all the haste I could to . . . Princeton in West-Jersey. . . .

I had stayed about seven months in the country . . . during which time my family were not idle, but cheerfully applied themselves to such labour as they were employed in by the Planters about Princeton and Philadelphia; by this means it happened that my landing at Boston was not as great a disadvantage as you may think: my stock of money was not much impaired thereby, and my children learned the work of the country; they had never till then worked to any but myself. But I thought nothing of this alteration; when I had been obliged to enter on such an enterprize, I was willing to submit to greater inconveniencies than any I have met with.

It was in April 1772, that I settled on this plantation: It is situate at the distance of 150 miles from Philadelphia, and it is just as far from Fort-pit[2]; it lies in a large and beautiful valley which runs thro' all Pensylvania, Maryland, and Virginia it consists of about 430 acres, and there was a house of two stories high, and office-houses upon it: The house is built of square blocks of wood nocked or indented into one another; it is well plaistered, so that it is warm enough, and I have six convenient rooms in it.

My plantation which I have called Corkerhill, after the name of the farm where my father lived and died, and where I lived so long; My plantation consists wholly of limestone-land, and in general limestone-land is reckoned the best in this country. . . .

Dear Sir, I do assure you I am well pleased with the country, and with my situation in it. I bless God that I came here, and I heartily thank every man who encouraged me and helped me to get the better of that fear which a man is under when he is to venture over so wide a sea, and indeed when, excepting my eldest son, I was to carry along with me all that was dear to me in the world, I could not but be anxious about them; but I was determined in my mind, and providence hath been very favourable to us. We are all at present in good health; and blessed be God, we have always been so since we came into this country. They

---

[1]**Laird:** Wealthy Scottish landowner.
[2]**Fort-pit:** Fort at site of what would become Pittsburgh, Pennsylvania.

say here, that the air and climate of Pensilvania agrees better with European constitutions, than even the air of Europe itself, and I am inclined to think that this is true, from that constant health which my family have enjoyed.

The man from whom I bought this plantation had lived upon it for the space of eleven years, and in all that time he had cleared no more but fifty acres, and I have got other fifty acres cleared since I came to it in April 1772: upon ten acres of which I had a good crop that very season. I and my three sons cleared these fifty acres without any other assistance but that of one man, whom I hired for half a crown a-day of our currency besides his victuals. . . . I gave 300 pounds Sterling for this plantation, and I could sell it already for double that money.

We who are country people used always to think it a great matter, that the gentlemen in Scotland had orchards, we thought this a fine thing; but here, almost every farmer hath a good orchard, and indeed squashes, pimpkins, gourds, cucumbers, melons, and all other garden-stuff grow in the open fields. . . .

Dear Sir, I have said so much about my industry and labour upon the plantation, but I have said it on purpose, because I know that a vile and false report hath been published at home, that it is only lazy persons who come over here. Now you know well, and I need not tell you that the very contrary is true; the lazy are motionless, and like snails abide on the spot where they are, till they either starve, or are compelled by hunger to go a begging: whereas the industrious strive to maintain themselves by their labour without being troublesome to any body, and many of them finding it difficult to live by their labour at home, they are so far from being lazy, that they have activity and spirit to venture over to America: but I pity many of your poor people who are indeed very lazy; and it is impossible but they must be lazy, because they have found by long experience that by all their labour they can make no profit to themselves.

. . . If my dear countrymen knew the beauty and healthiness of the climate, they would not be so afraid to come to North-America. There are a good number of old people just about where I live, some sixty, some seventy, and some eighty years of age. I thought it right to tell you all this, because I know that much pains have been taken to spread abroad a bad opinion of the country and climate, as if it were unhealthy: I will not say why this hath been done, but I suspect it hath taken its rise from some designing men among you, who though they saw many people in great straits, and many next door to starving, have for some views of their own, endeavoured to terrify them from coming here.

In truth, I am sorry to hear of the great distress of farmers and tradesmen in your country. You mention this in your letter, but I have heard much more from some folks I lately met with when I was at Philadelphia; and so far as I understand, the weavers and other tradesmen, as also many farmers are in a far worse condition than they were when I came away in the year 1771, for it seems the tradesmen cannot get employment, and the meal continues to be as dear as it was. If the tradesmen and farmers would come here, they would soon find themselves in a better condition; and there is plenty of room for them all, yea for all the people that are in the three kingdoms [England, Scotland, and Ireland]. And this is the best poor man's country in the world, for the price of provisions is cheap, and the price of labour is dear; and there are many people in Pensilvania and the neighbouring provinces, who had to work here to pay their freight, who have good plantations and are in wealthy circumstances: But this country is chiefly profitable to those farmers who bring along with them one, two, or three hundred pounds; such farmers can afford to eat good pork, beef, or mutton, as often as those who have one, two, or three hundred pounds of yearly rent in Scotland; that is to say, if they have some tolerable skill in farming, and live upon the land they take up here; and I believe there are no farmers in the world who live on so coarse and so poor food as do the generality of farmers in poor Scotland.

With respect to the soil of this province, some parts of it are rich and some poor just as at home: if it is well improved and manured, it will bear good crops just as the land does in other countries: but so far as I have yet seen or heard, the farmers here are really lazy: they make no improvement on their land but just what they do with the plough, in which they are not very expert; many of them do not so much as draw out to the land the dung which is made by their cattle. When I came to this farm there was lying in several heaps at the house all the dung that had been made in the space of eleven years. I was glad to find I had so much ready manure, so I drew it out to the land, and the crops were answerable to my pains and expectations; for I had this year a rich crop of wheat and rye and of Indian corn.

. . . We are in no fear that any harm will be done us by the Indians; I have seen many of them and by all I can learn they are a harmless people, except they be affronted or wronged; I hope we shall never have any bickerings with them. But it would not be a small number of enemies that would terrify us or even those about Fortpit, for besides a well-trained militia we have all guns in our hands. For there is no disarming act or game act[3] as with you. . . . Our young men are at full liberty to shoot all sort of game whenever they please: and by frequent exercise are as good marksmen here as any in the world. . . .

I need not tell you, for you know it already, That we have here no tithes, or general taxes, or poors-rates . . . or such other grievances, as tend to relax the diligence or industry of the farmers. We have the privilege of choosing our ministers, schoolmasters, constables and other parish officers for laying and collecting the necessary assessments; these are chosen by a majority of the votes of the inhabitants. In this neighbourhood if any differences are like to arise about roads and churches, they are amicably adjusted without any law-process. We have no characters hereabout which answers to that of a Scotch justice of peace, which we who came from Scotland look upon as a very great blessing; and there is, I believe no part of the world where justice is more impartially administred, than in the province of Pensylvania in our law-courts the poor are in no danger of being browbeaten and born down by the rich. With respect to our laws they are made by those who are, not nominally only, but really our representatives; for without any bribes or pensions they are chosen by ourselves, and every freeholder has a vote. . . .

I might write to you at large about the religious liberty which is enjoyed in this province in the most extensive manner. We have indeed no religious establishment; but Christians of every denomination, as they choose their own ministers, so they also make provision for them, and so far as I know the several sects live in good friendship with one another. . . .

I want . . . that all my friends and acquaintance should know that I am very happily settled, that all is very well with me, that all my family are cheerful and

---

[3]Laws that prohibited owning firearms and hunting game on open lands.

in good spirits, and that I hope I shall soon provide a comfortable settlement to every one of them who is come up to years. The other reason for my desiring that my letter should be published is, That I hope it may be of some use to my dear countrymen. . . . Perhaps there are many of them who have some thoughts of coming hither, but are hindered by their fears about the climate or the Indians; now if this letter shall help to remove these groundless fears, it will in so far tend to the relief and encouragement of my dear countrymen; and I am sure that no man who knows me will suspect that I have written any thing here but the truth. If tradesmen, or labourers, or farmers design to come over at all, they ought by all means to come immediately, before they be too old or turn so poor, that they will have no money to bring with them, nor even to pay their freight; and the sooner that farmers come over, they will both buy land the cheaper and also have a wider territory, out of which they may make choice of the richest tracts.

The providence of God hath been wonderfully kind to those who have emigrated from your country. For two or three years past, many vessels freighted with emigrants have yearly sailed from the coast of Scotland; and I never knew of any calamity or grievous accident that befel any of these vessels. This is certainly remarkable, it is ground of thankfulness and confidence. But the same providence that preserves your honest people in their way to America, seems to frown upon them while they remain at home. . . .

QUESTIONS FOR READING AND DISCUSSION

1. Why did Thomson leave Scotland? How did Thomson compare himself to other people in Scotland, to other immigrants, and to other Americans?

2. Why, according to Thomson, did Pennsylvania deserve its reputation as "the best poor man's country in the world"? Did Thomson consider himself a poor man? How did he define success?

3. How might Thomson's intended audience have shaped his news? What views among his audience was Thomson trying to dispute?

4. If Thomson's wife or children had written their versions of news from America, how might their accounts have differed from his news, if at all?

DOCUMENT 4

Advertisements for Runaway Slaves

African slaves came to the British North American colonies in unprecedented numbers during the eighteenth century. Because most eighteenth-century slaves could neither read nor write, few documents survive that record their point of view. Advertisements for runaway slaves provide an imperfect but revealing glimpse of specific slaves who defied their masters and mistresses by absconding. Published in local South Carolina and Virginia newspapers, the following advertisements described runaways in sufficient detail for them to be recognized and, masters hoped, recaptured. In addition to listing the characteristics of individual runaways, the advertisements also suggested the conditions of servitude among the many slaves who did not run away.

South Carolina Gazette **and** Virginia Gazette, 1737–1745

South Carolina Gazette, October 29–November 5, 1737

Run away a short squat Negro man, named Stephen, was Patroon[1] of a large Wood Boat, also a lusty strong Angola Negro, flat Nose, and much mark'd with the small Pox, is branded on the Shoulder AD. Whoever takes up these Negroes and carries them to Gaol, or my Plantation in Goose Creek, shall receive 10 £ for the first and 5 £ for the other.

Alexander Vander Dussen

South Carolina Gazette, February 2–9, 1738

Run away from Tho: Wright, about two Years since, a Negro Man named Trampuse, branded on the right Shoulder TW in one, he could not speak English when he went away. If any Person gives any Intelligence of him so that he may be apprehended or discover'd shall receive upon Demand 50£ reward. Also run away in August last, a Negro Man named Paul, who had been one Year in my Plantation near Silk-Hope, he spoke little or no English. Whoever brings him to said Plantation, or can give any Intelligence of him, shall have 10 £ paid upon Demand. Also run away in November last, a Negro Man named Charles, he speaks pretty good English, is an elderly Fellow, is branded TW in one, on the right Shoulder, and has had a large Cut on the Small of his Back, he is supposed to be harboured by the Negroes of Silk-Hope Plantation. Whosoever apprehends him and brings him to my Plantation near Silk-Hope, shall have 5 £. Also run away in January last, from my Plantation near Silk-Hope, two new Negro Men, they speak but little English, they are branded on the right Shoulder TW in one, one of them is named Will, the other Summer. If any Person brings them to said Plantation, shall receive 40 s. reward for each.

Thomas Wright.

South Carolina Gazette, March 9–16, 1738

RUN AWAY from Ferdinando Dart in April last, a Negro Man, named Norcott, he could not speak English when he went away, & in October last, 3 Negro Men, Sambo, Boswine, & Peter; Boswine branded on his Back D. And the 12th Instant, two Negro man, Adam & Strafford, both speak English, stought, able Fellows. Whoever carries them to my Plantation at Pon-Pon, or brings them to me in Charles-Town, shall have 40 s. for each of the two last, and 10 £ for each of the 4 first, from

John Dart.

South Carolina Gazette, March 23–30, 1738

Run away from Benjamin Godin's Plantation, about 3 Weeks since, 3 Angola Negro Men, named Harry, Cyrus and Chatham, they have been in the Country three Years, and speak little English, they are branded BG on the right or left Breast, and are suppos'd to be gone towards Winyaw, Harry having before (about a Year ago) run away and been taken up in that Part of the Country. Also run

---

South Carolina Gazette and *Virginia Gazette*, 1737–45.

[1]**Patroon:** Operator.

away a Mustee Negro Man, named Sam, he is a short thick well made Fellow, and a Gambia Negro Man, named Ned, he speaks English, and is a lusty, tall Fallow, branded as aforesaid. Whoever shall apprehend the said Negroes or any of them, shall receive 10 £ per Head, from

Benj. Godin.

South Carolina Gazette, September 21, 1738
Run away from my Plantation at Goose-Creek, the 10th of Sept. a Negro Boy, named Hector, about 14 Years old, he had on when he went away, a Negro Cloth Jacket dyed Yellow, branded with a Blotch on each Breast, and upon his left Buttock JR. Whosoever brings the said Boy to me at my Plantation, or to Gaol in Charles-Town shall be paid by me the Sum of 40 s. as Witness my Hand,

Ja: Rockford.

South Carolina Gazette, February 1, 1739
Run away from Rebeccah Massey in Charlestown, about 10 Weeks past, a Mustee young Wench, named Ruth, is suppos'd to be gone towards Ponpon or Dorchester; she speaks good English, born in the said Town, and brought up here in a Family; she is of a middle Stature, and her upper fore Teeth are a little rotten. Whoever takes her up, gives her 50 good Lashes, and delivers her to me, shall have 10 £ reward.

Rebeccah Massey.
Robert Chesley.

Virginia Gazette, October 19–26, 1739
RAN away from the Subscriber, living at Capt. Anthony Thornton's Quarter, in Caroline County, a Negro Man; he is a middle-siz'd Fellow, has Three Marks down each Temple, and can't speak a word of English: He had on when he went away, an old Checkt Shirt , and an old pair of Oznabrig Trowsers. Whoever will apprehend the said Slave, so that I may have him again, shall have a Pistole Reward, besides what the Law allows —

John Pearce.

Virginia Gazette, October 26–November 2, 1739
RAN away on the 30th of September last, from the Subscriber, living in Hanover County, Two Negros, viz. A Negro Man, nam'd Roger, born at Angola, a pretty tall, well-set Fellow, about 30 Years Old: He had on, when he went away, a new Oznabrig shirt, and an old Cotton Wastecoat, a Pair of Virginia Cloth Breeches, striped Black and White, and a Pair of Country-made Shoes. The other, a thick square Woman, named Moll, about 18 Years old, Virginia born; is Wife to the above-nam'd Roger, and is very big with Child. She had on, an old Oznabrig Shift, an old cotton Wastecoat and Petticoat. They both speak tolerable good English. Whoever will bring the said Negroes to me, at my House, in Hanover county, shall have a Pistole Reward for each of them, besides what the Law allows.

John Shelton

Virginia Gazette, May 2–9, 1745
RAN away, on the 17th of April last, from the Subscriber in Caroline County, a lusty, tawney Negro Man, nam'd Will; he is hollow-chested, stoops in the Shoulders a little, and is about 30 Years old. Also a small Mulatto Man, nam'd Peter,

aged about 21 Years; well known by the Gentlemen in the Country, for keeping of Horses. He always has a great Quid of Tobacco in his Mouth. He had with him a Pair of Pumps, a Check Shirt, a brown double breasted Coat, and a Felt Hat. Whoever takes up and convoys them, or either of them, to my House in the County aforesaid, shall have a Pistole Reward, for each.

Henry Armistead.

N.B. I desire each Constable to give them 20 Lashes.

And whoever will apprehend the said Servant and Slave, and bring them to me, in St. Mary's County, on Potowmack, or to Major John Waughop, in Northumberland County, Virginia, on Potowmack River, shall have 6 pistoles Reward, and reasonable Charges, paid by Major Waughop, aforesaid, or by me.

Virginia Gazette, May 9–16, 1745
North Carolina, April 24, 1745

RAN away, on the 18th Instant, from the Plantation of the late Col. William Wilson, deceas'd, Two Slaves belonging to the Subscriber, the one a tall Yellow Fellow, named Emanuel, about 6 Feet high, six or seven and Twenty Years of Age; hath a Scar on the outside of his left Thigh, which was cut with an Ax; he had on when he went away, a blue Jacket, an Ozenbrig Shirt and Trousers, and a Worsted Cap; he speaks pretty good English, and calls himself a Portugueze; is by Trade a Cooper, and took with him some Cooper's Tools. The other is a short, thick, well-set Fellow, stoops forward pretty much as he walks; does not speak so plain as the other; had on when he went away an Ozenbrig Pair of Trousers and Shirt, a white Negro Cotton Jacket, and took with him an Axe: They went away in a small Cannoe, and were seen at Capt. Pearson's, on Nuse River, the 18th Inst. and 'tis believ'd are gone towards Virginia. Whoever takes up the said Negros, and brings them to my House on Trent River, North-Carolina, or secures them so that I may have them again, shall have Four Pistoles Reward for each, paid by

Mary Wilson.

Virginia Gazette, May 9–16, 1745

RAN away from the Subscriber's Quarter, on the Robinson River, in Orange County, the following Negro's, viz. Sambo, a small, thin visaged Fellow, about 30 Years of Age, speaks English so as to be understood; had on, when he went away, a Hat, an Oznabrig Shirt, a dark colour'd Coat, with a small Cape to it, lin'd with velvet, and is too long for him, Cotton Jacket and Breaches, a Pair of Yarn stockings, London Fall Shoes and Buckles. Aaron, a tall Fellow, much Pock-fretten, about 35 Years of Age, can't speak English; he took with him a Hat, an Oznabrig Shirt, Cotton Jacket and Breaches, a Pair of Plaid Hose, and Shoes. Berwick, a tall, smooth-faced Fellow, about 20 Years of Age, can't speak English; he took with him a Hat, an Oznabrig Shirt, a fearnothing Coat, Cotton Jacket and Breaches, a Pair of Plaid Hose, and Shoes. They are all new Negro's, and went together; they have not been above 8 Months in the Country. Whoever takes up, and convoys the said Negro's to the aforesaid Quarter, or me, at Fredericksburg, shall have Twenty Shillings Reward for each, besides what the Law allows, and reasonable Charges.

William Hunter.

Virginia Gazette, October 3–10, 1745

RAN away from the Subscriber, living in Hanover, two new Negro Men, imported from Gambia, in the Brig. Ranger, and sold at Newcastle the 5th of September last; they understand no English, and are near 6 Feet high, each; one of them is nam'd Jack, a right Black, with a Scar over the Right Eye-brow; the other a yellow Fellow, with 3 small Strokes on each Side of his Face, like this Mark ( ). They had on, each, a knap'd new Cotton Jacket and Breeches, without either Buttons or Button-holes, a new Oznabrig Shirt, and new Felt Hats. They stole a fine Damask Table-Cloth, 10 qrs. square, 5 Yards and a Half of fine Scot Linen, 3 Yards and a Half of Scots 3 qr. Check, a white Holland Shirt, and a Silk Handkerchief. Whoever takes up the said Negroes, and Goods, and brings them to me, or to Mr. Robert Brown, Merchant, in Newcastle, shall be rewarded, as the law allows.

Margaret Arbuthnott.

QUESTIONS FOR READING AND DISCUSSION

1. How did the advertisers describe Africans? What assumptions did they make about how readers of the ads would recognize the runaways? What do those assumptions suggest about the relationships between whites and blacks, free people and slaves, native-born and African-born people?

2. What did the runaways' names suggest about them and their masters? What evidence suggests how masters treated these runaways?

3. Did the runaways have identifiable skills or traits? Did they have certain characteristics in common?

4. Do the advertisements contain hints about why the runaways absconded? What might have accounted for the lag of time between running away and the placement of the advertisement?

5. What were the differences between the advertisements in South Carolina and in Virginia? How did those differences suggest contrasts in slavery in the two colonies in the eighteenth century?

COMPARATIVE QUESTIONS

1. How did the choices made by Arthur, Thomson, and the runaway slaves compare with those recommended by Father Abraham? What basic values guided the behavior of each?

2. What role does religion play in documents in this chapter? What forms of faith are exhibited in the documents?

3. In what ways do the documents reflect the significance of individualism in the eighteenth-century colonies? What freedoms and constraints did individuals experience?

4. According to the documents, how did relations among people from different racial groups compare with those among people in the same racial group? To what extent do the documents suggest contrasts or similarities between racial relationships in the northern and southern colonies?

5. The documents illustrate many of the ways in which commerce influenced the eighteenth-century colonies. To what extent did commerce introduce change and novelty in the lives of eighteenth-century residents of British North America? In what ways did commerce create conditions of stability and order? To what extent did it foster turmoil and disorder?

CHAPTER 5

THE BRITISH EMPIRE AND THE COLONIAL CRISIS
1754–1775

B ritish policies toward the colonies had the effect of making legally constituted authority seem unjust and illegitimate to many colonists. In such
circumstances, many colonists concluded that it was necessary to point
out injustices and petition for their redress while others resolved to take justice
into their own hands. When existing structures of authority began to crumble,
colonists loyal to the British found themselves judged by crowds who did not
share their notions of law or justice. The following documents disclose the ideas
that animated rebellious colonists and some of the ways they acted on those ideas.

DOCUMENT 1

An Oration on
the Second Anniversary
of the Boston Massacre

*For many years after 1770, Bostonians commemorated the Boston Massacre with an ad-
dress by a leading patriot. This oration by Joseph Warren on March 5, 1772, attacked
British policies and reminded colonists of their duties to themselves and their ancestors.
Warren, a Boston physician and political activist, later served as a militia officer and was
killed at Bunker Hill. His Boston Massacre oration, excerpted here, illustrates the arguments that made sense to many colonists and the passion with which they defended their
beliefs.*

Joseph Warren
Boston Massacre Oration, March 5, 1772

Let us now allow ourselves a few moments to examine the late Acts of the British Parliament for taxing America. Let us with candour judge whether they are constitutionally binding upon us; if they are, in the name of justice let us submit to them, without one murmuring word.

First, I would ask whether the members of the British House of Commons are the democracy of this province? If they are, they are either the people of this province, or are elected by the people of this province to represent them, and have therefore a constitutional right to originate a bill for taxing them; it is most certain they are neither; and therefore nothing done by them can be said to be done by the democratic branch of our constitution. I would next ask, whether the lords, who compose the aristocratic branch of the legislature, are peers of America? I never heard it was . . . so much as pretended, and if they are not, certainly no act of theirs can be said to be the act of the aristocratic branch of our constitution. . . . I do not conceive it to be of the least importance to us by whom our property is taken away, so long as it is taken without our consent; and I am very much at a loss to know by what figure of rhetoric, the inhabitants of this province can be called free subjects, when they are obliged to obey implicitly, such laws as are made for them by men three thousand miles off, whom they know not, and whom they never empowered to act for them, or how they can be said to have property, when a body of men, over whom they have not the least control, and who are not in any way accountable to them, shall oblige them to deliver up any part, or the whole of their substance without even asking their consent; and yet whoever pretends that the late Acts of the British Parliament for taxing America ought to be deemed binding upon us, must admit at once that we are absolute slaves, and have no property of our own; or else that we may be freemen, and at the same time under a necessity of obeying the arbitrary commands of those over whom we have no control or influence, and that we may have property of our own which is entirely at the disposal of another. Such gross absurdities, I believe, will not be relished in this enlightened age: and it can be no matter of wonder that the people quickly perceived, and seriously complained of the inroads which these Acts must unavoidably make upon their liberty, and of the hazard to which their whole property is by them exposed; for, if they may be taxed without their consent, even in the smallest trifle, they may also, without their consent, be deprived of everything they possess, although never so valuable, never so dear. . . . [A]s it was soon found that this taxation could not be supported by reason and argument, it seemed necessary that one act of oppression should be enforced by another, and therefore, contrary to our just rights as possessing, or at least having a just title to possess, all the liberties and immunities of British subjects, a standing army was established among us in time of peace; and evidently for the purpose of . . . enforcement of obedience to acts which, upon fair examination, appeared to be unjust and unconstitutional. . . .

Hezekiah Niles, ed., *Centennial Offering: Republication of the Principles and Acts of the Revolution in America* (New York: A. S. Barres, 1876) 753–59.

That this was the avowed design of stationing an armed force in this town is sufficiently known; and we, my fellow citizens, have seen, we have felt the tragical effects! *The fatal fifth of March, 1770, can never be forgotten.* The horrors of *that dreadful night* are but too deeply impressed on our hearts. Language is too feeble to paint the emotion of our souls, when our streets were stained with the blood of our brethren — when our ears were wounded by the groans of the dying, and our eyes were tormented with the sight of the mangled bodies of the dead.

When our alarmed imagination presented to our view our houses wrapped in flames, our children subjected to the barbarous caprice of the raging soldiery, our beauteous virgins exposed to all the insolence of unbridled passion, our virtuous wives, endeared to us by every tender tie, falling a sacrifice to worse than brutal violence, and perhaps like the famed Lucretia[1], distracted with anguish and despair, ending their wretched lives by their own fair hands. When we beheld the authors of our distress parading in our streets, or drawn up in a regular *battalia*, as though in a hostile city, our hearts beat to arms; we snatched our weapons, almost resolved by one decisive stroke to avenge the death of our slaughtered brethren, and to secure from future danger all that we held most dear: but propitious heaven forbade the bloody carnage and saved the threatened victims of our too keen resentment, not by their discipline, not by their regular array, no, it was royal George's livery that proved their shield — it was that which turned the pointed engines of destruction from their breasts. The thoughts of vengeance were soon buried in our inbred affection to Great Britain, and calm reason dictated a method of removing the troops more mild than an immediate resource to the sword. With united efforts you urged the immediate departure of the troops from the town — you urged it, with a resolution which ensured success — you obtained your wishes, and the removal of the troops was effected without one drop of their blood being shed by the inhabitants. . . .

I do not know one single advantage which can arise to the British nation from our being enslaved. I know not of any gains which can be wrung from us by oppression which they may not obtain from us by our own consent in the smooth channel of commerce. We wish the wealth and prosperity of Britain; we contribute largely to both. . . . The amazing increase of riches to Britain, the great rise of the value of her lands, the flourishing state of her navy, are striking proofs of the advantages derived to her from her commerce with the colonies; and it is our earnest desire that she may still continue to enjoy the same emoluments, until her streets are paved with *American gold*; only, let us have the pleasure of calling it our own whilst it is in our own hands; but this it seems is too great a favour. We are to be governed by the *absolute command of others; our property is to be taken away without our consent.* If we complain, our complaints are treated with contempt; if we assert our rights, that assertion is deemed insolence; if we humbly offer to submit the matter to the impartial decision of reason, the *sword* is judged the most proper argument to silence our murmurs! But this cannot long be the case. Surely the British nation will not suffer the reputation of their justice and their honour to be thus sported away by a capricious ministry; no, they will in a short time open their eyes to their true interest. They nourish in their own breasts

---

[1]**Lucretia:** A virtuous woman of ancient Rome whose suicide, after her rape by the son of King Tarquinius Superbus, led to the expulsion of the Tarquin line of kings and the establishment of the Roman republic.

a noble love of liberty; they hold her dear, and they know that all who have once possessed her charms had rather die than suffer her to be torn from their embraces. They are also sensible that Britain is so deeply interested in the prosperity of the colonies that she must eventually feel every wound given to their freedom; they cannot be ignorant that more dependence may be placed on the affections of a brother than on the forced service of a slave; they must approve your efforts for the preservation of your rights; from a sympathy of soul they must pray for your success. And I doubt not but they will, ere long, exert themselves effectually, to redress your grievances. . . .

You have, my friends and countrymen, frustrated the designs of your enemies by your unanimity and fortitude. It was your union and determined spirit which expelled those troops who polluted your streets with innocent blood. You have appointed this anniversary as a standard memorial of the *bloody consequences of placing an armed force in a populous city*, and of your deliverance from the dangers which then seemed to hang over your heads; and I am confident that you never will betray the least want of spirit when called upon to guard your freedom. None but they who set a just value upon the blessings of liberty are worthy to enjoy her. Your illustrious fathers were her zealous votaries. When the blasting frowns of tyranny drove her from public view they clasped her in their arms, they cherished her in their generous bosoms, they brought her safe over the rough ocean and fixed her seat in this then dreary wilderness; they nursed her infant age with the most tender care; for her sake they patiently bore the severest hardships; for her support they underwent the most rugged toils, in her defence they boldly encountered the most alarming dangers; neither the ravenous beasts that ranged the woods for prey, nor the more furious savages of the wilderness could damp ardour! . . . God prospered their valour, they preserved her brilliancy unsullied; they enjoyed her whilst they lived, and dying, bequeathed the dear inheritance to your care. And as they left you this glorious legacy, they have undoubtedly transmitted to you some portion of their noble spirit, to inspire you with virtue to merit her, and courage to preserve her. You surely cannot, with such examples before your eyes, as every page of the history of this country affords, suffer your liberties to be ravished from you by lawless force, or cajoled away by flattery and fraud.

The voice of your fathers' blood cries to you from the ground, *my sons scorn to be slaves!* In vain we met the frowns of tyrants. In vain we crossed the boisterous ocean, found a new world and prepared it for the happy residence of liberty. In vain we toiled. In vain we fought. We bled in vain, if you, our offspring, want valour to repel the assaults of her invaders! Stain not the glory of your worthy ancestors, but like them resolve never to part with your birthright; be wise in your deliberations, and determined in your exertions for the preservation of your liberties. Follow not the dictates of passion, but enlist yourselves under the sacred banner of reason; use every method in your power to secure your rights; at least prevent the curses of posterity from being heaped upon your memories.

If you, with united zeal and fortitude, oppose the torrent of oppression; if you feel the true fire of patriotism burning in your breasts; if you, from your souls, despise the most gaudy dress that slavery can wear; if you really prefer the lonely cottage (whilst blest with liberty) to gilded palaces surrounded with the ensigns of slavery, you may have the fullest assurance that tyranny, with her whole accursed train, will hide their hideous heads in confusion, shame, and despair. If .

you perform your part, you must have the strongest confidence that the same Almighty Being who protected your pious and venerable forefathers — who enabled them to turn a barren wilderness into a fruitful field, who so often made bare his arm for their salvation, will still be mindful of you, their offspring.

May this Almighty Being graciously preside in all our councils. May he direct us to such measures as he himself shall approve, and be pleased to bless. May we ever be a people favoured of God. May our land be a land of liberty, the seat of virtue, the asylum of the oppressed, a name and a praise in the whole earth, until the last shock of time shall bury the empires of the world in one common undistinguished ruin!

QUESTIONS FOR READING AND DISCUSSION

1. According to Joseph Warren, why were the taxes imposed on the colonies unjust? What did he believe would happen if the colonies submitted to the taxes? How were the colonists threatened with becoming "absolute slaves"?
2. Why was an army stationed in Boston? What dangers did citizens face from such an army?
3. Did Warren believe British policy would change? What did he mean by asserting that the British "cannot be ignorant that more dependence may be placed on the affections of a brother than on the forced service of a slave"? In what ways might British soldiers have criticized Warren's arguments?
4. How should the colonists' history guide them? How did their ancestors preserve liberty?
5. Why do you think Warren feminized the concept of liberty? How would his audience have been likely to respond to his descriptions of liberty?

DOCUMENT 2

A Boston Shoemaker Recalls British Arrogance and the Boston Tea Party

The high-handed arrogance of many British officials rankled many colonists. British assertions of supremacy in face-to-face encounters with colonists seemed to parallel parliamentary assertions of power over the colonies. George R. T. Hewes, a shoemaker in Boston during the 1770s, refused to back down to a haughty custom official and participated in the Boston Tea Party. Many years later, when Hewes was more than ninety years old, he recalled those events in an interview published in 1834. Hewes's narrative illustrates the contagious assertion of colonial rights among many Bostonians in the 1770s.

George R. T. Hewes
Memoir, 1834

One day . . . as I was returning from dinner, I met a man by the name of John Malcom, who was a custom-house officer, and a small boy, pushing his sled along,

---

James Hawkes, *A Retrospect of the Boston Tea-Party with a Memoir of George R.T. Hewes* (New York: S. S. Bliss, 1834) 33–43.

before him and just as I was passing the boy, he said to Malcom, what, sir, did you throw my chips into the snow for, yesterday? Upon which Malcom angrily replied, do you speak to me, you rascal; and, as he raised a cane he had in his hand, aiming it at the head of the boy, I spoke to Malcom, and said to him, you are not about to strike that boy with your cudgel, you may kill him; upon my saying that, he was suddenly diverted from the boy, and turning upon me, says, you d——d rascal, do you presume too, to speak to me? I replied to him, I am no rascal, sir, be it known to you; whereupon he struck me across the head with his cane, and knocked me down, and by the blow cut a hole in my hat two inches in length. At this moment, one Captain Godfry came up, and raising me up, asked who had struck me; Malcom, replied the by standers, while he, for fear of the displeasure of the populace, ran to his house, and shut himself up. The people, many of whom were soon collected around me, advised me to go immediately to Doctor Warren, and get him to dress my wound, which I did without delay; and the doctor, after [he] dressed it, observed to me it can be considered no misfortune that I had a thick skull, for had not yours been very strong, said he, it would have been broke; you have come within a hair's breath of loosing your life. He then advised me to go to Mr. Quincy, a magistrate, and get a warrant, for the purpose of arresting Malcom, which I did, and carried it immediately to a constable, by the name of Justine Hale, and delivered it to him, to serve, but when he came to the house where Malcom was locked up, it was surrounded by such a multitude he could not serve it. The people, however, soon broke open the door, and took Malcom into their custody. They then took him to the place where the massacre was committed, and their flogged him with thirty-nine stripes. After which, they besmeared him thoroughly with tar and feathers; they then whipped him through the town, till they arrived at the gallows, on the neck, where they gave him thirty-nine stripes more, and then, after putting one end of a rope about his neck, and throwing the other end over the gallows, told him to remember that he had come within one of being hanged. They then took him back to the house from whence they had taken him, and discharged him from their custody.

The severity of the flogging they had given him, together, with the cold coat of tar with which they had invested him, had such a benumbing effect upon his health, that it required considerable effort to restore his usual circulation. . . . I shall carry to my grave the scar which the wound Malcom gave me left on my head. . . . [Hewes goes on to describe the Boston Tea Party and its aftermath.]

The tea . . . was contained in three ships, laying near each other, at what was called at that time Griffin's wharf, and were surrounded by armed ships of war; the commanders of which had publicly declared, that if the rebels, as they were pleased to style the Bostonians, should not withdraw their opposition to the landing of the tea before . . . the 17th day of December, 1773, they should on that day force it on shore, under the cover of their cannon's mouth. On the day preceding the seventeenth, there was a meeting of the citizens of the county of Suffolk, convened at one of the churches in Boston, for the purpose of consulting on what measures might be considered, expedient to prevent the landing of the tea, or secure the people from the collection of the duty. At that meeting a committee was appointed to wait on Governor Hutchinson, and request him to inform them whether he would take any measures to satisfy the people on the object of the meeting. To the first application of this committee, the governor told them he would give them a definite answer by five o'clock in the afternoon. At the hour appointed, the committee again repaired to the governor's house, and, on inquiry, found he had gone to his country seat at Milton, a distance of about six miles. When the committee returned and informed the meeting of the absence of the governor, there was a confused murmur among the members, and the meeting was immediately dissolved, many of them crying out, Let every man do his duty, and be true to his country; and there was a general huzza [shout of exclamation] for Griffin's wharf. It was now evening, and I immediately dressed myself in the costume of an Indian, equipped with a small hatchet, which I and my associates denominated the tomahawk, with which, and a club, after having painted my face and hands with coal dust in, the shop of a blacksmith, I repaired to Griffin's wharf, where the ships lay that contained the tea. When I first appeared in the street, after being thus disguised, I fell in with many who were dressed, equipped and painted as I was, and who fell in with me, and marched in order to the place of our destination. When we arrived at the wharf, there were three of our number who assumed an authority to direct our operations, to which we readily submitted. They divided us into three parties, for the purpose of boarding the three ships which contained the tea at the same time. The name of him who commanded the division to which I was assigned, was Leonard Pitt. The names of the other commanders I never knew. We were immediately ordered by the respective commanders to board all the ships at the same time, which we promptly obeyed. The commander of the division to which I belonged, as soon as we were on board the ship, appointed me boatswain, and ordered me to go to the captain and demand of him the keys to the hatches and a dozen candles. I made the demand accordingly, and the captain promptly replied, and delivered the articles; but requested me at the same time to do no damage to the ship or rigging. We then were ordered by our commander to open the hatches, and take out all the chests of tea and throw them overboard, and we immediately proceeded to execute his orders; first cutting and splitting the chests with our tomahawks, so as thoroughly to expose them to the effects of the water. In about three hours from the time we went on board, we had thus broken and thrown overboard every tea chest to be found in the ship; while those in the other ships were disposing of the tea in the same way, at the same time. We were surrounded by British armed ships, but no attempt was made to resist us. We then quietly retired to our several places of residence, without having any conversation with each other, or taking any measures to discover who were our associates. . . . There appeared to be an understanding that each individual should volunteer his services, keep his own secret, and risk the consequences for himself. No disorder took place during that transaction, and it was observed at that time, that the stillest night ensued that Boston had enjoyed for many months.

During the time we were throwing the tea overboard, there were several attempts made by some of the citizens of Boston and its vicinity, to carry off small quantities of it for their family use. To effect that object, they would watch their opportunity to snatch up a handful from the deck, where it became plentifully scattered, and put it into their pockets. One Captain O'Conner, whom I well knew, came on board for that purpose, and when he supposed he was not noticed, filled his pockets, and also the lining of his coat. But I had detected him, and gave information to the captain of what he was doing. We were ordered to take him into custody, and just as he was stepping from the vessel I seized him by the skirt of his coat, and in attempting to pull him back, I tore it off; but springing forward, by a rapid effort, he made his escape. He had however to run a gauntlet through the crowd upon the wharf; each one, as he passed, giving him a kick or a stroke.

The next day, we nailed the skirt of his coat, which I had pulled off, to the whipping post in Charlestown, the place of his residence, with a label upon it, commemorative of the occasion which had thus subjected the proprietor to the popular indignation,

Another attempt was made to save a little tea from the ruins of the cargo, by a tall aged man, who wore a large cocked hat and white wig, which was fashionable at that time. He had slightly slipped a little into his pocket, but being detected, they seized him, and taking his hat and wig from his head, threw them, together with the tea, of which they had emptied his pockets, into the water. In consideration of his advanced age, he was permitted to escape, with now and then a slight kick.

The next morning, after we had cleared the ships of the tea, it was discovered that very considerable quantities of it was floating upon the surface of the water; and to prevent the possibility of any of its being saved for use, a number of small boats were manned by sailors and citizens, who rowed them into those parts of the harbour wherever the tea was visible, and by beating it with oars and paddles, so thoroughly drenched it, as to render its entire destruction inevitable. . . . [Hewes goes on to describe the abuses visited on those who continued to sell tea.]

Mrs. Philips, a tory, . . . would import tea and sell to the tories. To witness the public indignation towards her, . . . a great number of young men in Boston, collected one Saturday evening and employed some menials to besmear her house with substances very offensive to the smell. She discovered what they were doing, and called out to them from her window, You rascals you may plaster, but I will sell tea as much as I please; but the condition in which her house was discovered the next morning, gave such publicity to her name and character, that her gains afterwards in the sale of that article, were acquired at the expense of her peace and the public odium.

There was also a man by the name of Theophalus Lilly, who imported and sold tea; and as a token of contempt and derision, some one nailed a sign upon a post in front of his house, with a hand painted upon it, with a finger pointing to his house, and a notice in writing under it "That is an importer of tea."

QUESTIONS FOR READING AND DISCUSSION

1. What precipitated crowd action against the custom-house officer, John Malcom? What assumptions about the colonists were revealed by Malcom's behavior and by his statement, "Do you presume too, to speak to me"?

2. How and why did Hewes and others destroy the tea? Why did they take care "to do no damage to the ship or rigging"?

3. Hewes and the crowd took action against those who tried to take a little tea for themselves. Why? What values did the crowd see itself upholding?

4. In what ways were the importation and sale of tea comparable to the behavior of Malcom? Why did Hewes and other members of the crowd believe their actions were more just than those of Malcom and the tea sellers?

DOCUMENT 3

A Loyalist Judge's Catalog
of Rebellious Crowds

Colonial crowds enforced their notions of law and justice on supporters of British policy. From the viewpoint of British officials and those loyal to the monarchy, the crowds were composed of rowdy outlaws who terrorized law-abiding citizens and their leaders. Peter Oliver, a wealthy judge in Massachusetts, served as chief justice of the Superior Court when his friend Thomas Hutchinson became governor in 1771. A staunch loyalist, Oliver fled to England and published a history of the American Revolution in 1781. In an appendix, excerpted here, Oliver cataloged some of what he considered outrageous acts of rebellion on the part of his former neighbors in New England. Oliver's appendix illustrates the conflicting notions of hierarchy, authority, and loyalty that separated patriots and Tories.

Peter Oliver

Origin & Progress of the American Revolution, 1774–1775

Exhibiting a few, out of the many, very innocent Frolicks of Rebellion, especially in the Province of *Massachusetts Bay.*

1774 August A Mob in *Berkshire* assembled, & forced the justices of the Court of common Pleas from their Seats on the Bench, and shut up the Court House, preventing any Proceedings at Law. At the same Time driving one of his Majesty's Justices of the Peace from his Dwelling House, so that he was obliged to repair to *Boston* for Protection by the Kings Troops.

At *Taunton* also, about 40 Miles from *Boston*, the Mob attacked the House of *Daniel Leonard* Esqr., one of his Majesty's Justices of the Peace; & a Barrister at Law. They fired Bullets into the House, & obliged him to fly from it to save his Life.

A Colo. *Gilbert*, a Man of Distinction & a firm Loyalist, living at *Freetown*, about 50 Miles from *Boston*, being absent about 20 Miles from his Home, was attacked by a Mob of above an 100 Men, at Midnight. But being a Man of great Bravery & Strength, he, by his single Arm, beat them all off. And on the same Night, & at the same Place, Brigadier *Ruggles*, a distinguished Friend of Government, & for many Years a Member of the general Assembly, was attacked by the same Mob; but by his firm Resolution he routed them all. They, in Revenge, cut his Horses Tail off & painted him all over. The Mob found that Paint was cheaper than Tar and Feathers.

September 1774 The Attorny General, *Mr. Sewall*, living at *Cambridge*, was obliged to repair to *Boston* under the Protection of the King's Troops. His House at Cambridge was attacked by a Mob, his Windows broke, & other Damage done; but

Douglass Adair and John A. Shutz, eds., *Peter Oliver's Origin & Progress of the American Revolution* (Stanford, Calif.: Stanford University Press, 1961) 152–57.

by the Intrepidity of some young Gentlemen of the Family, the Mob were dispersed.

About the same Time *Thomas Oliver* Esqr. the Lieut. Govr. of *Massachusetts Province*, was attacked in his House at *Cambridge*, by a Mob Of 4000 Men; & as he had lately been appointed, by his Majesty, one of the new Council, they forced him to resign that Office; but this Resignation did not pacify the Mob; he was soon forced to fly to *Boston* for Protection. This Mob was not mixed with tag, rag & Bobtail only, Persons of Distinction in the Country were in the Mass, & as the Lieut. Governor was a Man of Distinction, he surely ought to be waited upon by a large Cavalcade & by Persons of Note.

In this Month, also, a Mob of 5000 collécted at *Worcester*, about 50 Miles from *Boston*, a thousand of whom were armed. It being at the Time when the Court of Common Pleas was about sitting, the Mob made a lane, & compelled ye. Judges, Sheriff, & Gentlemen of the Bar, to pass & repass them, Cap in Hand, in the most ignominious Manner; & read their Disavowall of holding Courts under the new Acts of Parliament, no less than Thirty Times in the Procession.

Brigadier *Ruggles's* House at *Hardwicke*, about 70 Miles from *Boston*, was also plundered of his Guns, & one of his fine Horses poisoned.

Colo. *Phips*, the high Sheriff of *Middlesex*, was obliged to promise not to serve any Processes of Courts; & retired to *Boston* for Protection. . . .

Peter Oliver Esqr., a Justice of the Peace at *Middleborough*, was obliged by the Mob to sign an Obligation not to execute his Office under the new Acts. At the same Place, a Mr. Silas Wood, who had signed a Paper to disavow the riotous Proceedings of the Times, was dragged by a Mob of 2[00] or 300 Men about a Mile to a River, in Order to drown him; but one of his Children hanging around him with Cries & Tears, he was induced to recant, though, even then, very reluctantly.

The Mob at *Concord*, about 20 Miles from *Boston*, abused a Deputy Sheriff of *Middlesex*, & compelled him, on Pain of Death, not to execute the Precepts for a new Assembly; they making him pass through a Lane of them, sometimes walking backwards, & sometimes forward, Cap in Hand, & they beating him.

Revd. Mr. *Peters*, of *Hebron* in *Connecticut*, an Episcopalian Clergyman, after having his House broke into by a Mob, & being most barbarously treated in it, was stript of his Canonicals [garments for the clergy], & carried to one of their Liberty Poles, & afterwards drove from his Parish. He had applied to Governor Trumble & to some of the Magistrates, for Redress; but they were as relentless as the Mob; & he was obliged to go to *England* incognito, having been hunted after, to the Danger of his Life....

All the *Plimouth* Protestors against Riots, as also all the military Officers, were compelled by a Mob of 2000 Men collected from that County & the County of *Barnstable* to recant & resign their military Commissions....

A Son of one of the *East India* Companies Agents being at *Plimouth* collecting Debts, a Mob roused him, in the Night, & he was obliged to fly out of the Town; but ye. Midnight favoured his Escape.

December 1774 A *Jesse Dunbar*, of *Hallifax*, in the County of *Plimouth*, an honest Drover, had bought a fat Ox of one of his Majesty's new Council, & carried it to *Plimouth* for sale. The Ox was hung up & skinned. He was just upon quartering it, when the Town's Committee came to the Slaughter House, & finding that the Ox was bought of one of the new Councellors, they ordered it into a Cart, & then put *Dunbar* into the Belly of the Ox and carted him 4 Miles, with a Mob around him, when they made him pay a Dollar after taking three other Cattle & an Horse from him. They then delivered him to another Mob, who carted him 4 Miles further, & forced another Dollar from him. The second Mob delivered him to a third Mob, who abused him by throwing Dirt at him, as also throwing the Offals, in his Face & endeavoring to cover him with it, to the endangering his Life, & after other Abuses, & carrying him 4 Miles further, made him pay another Sum of Mony. They urged the Councellors Lady, at whose House they stopped, to take the Ox; but she being a Lady of a firm Mind refused; upon which they tipped the Cart up & the Ox down into the Highway, & left it to take Care of it self. And in the Month of February following, this same *Dunbar* was selling Provisions at Plimouth, when the Mob seized him, tied him to his Horse's Tail, & in that Manner drove him through Dirt & mire out of the Town, & he falling down, his Horse hurt him.

In November 1774, *David Dunbar* of *Hallifax* aforesaid, being an Ensign in the Militia, a Mob headed by some of the Select Men of the Town, demand[ed] his Colours of him. He refused, saying, that if his commanding Officer demanded them he should obey, otherwise he would not part with them: — upon which they broke into his House by Force & dragged him out. They had prepared a sharp Rail to set him upon; & in resisting them they seized him (by his private parts) & fixed him upon the Rail, & was held on it by his Legs & Arms, & tossed up with Violence & greatly bruised so that he did not recover for some Time. They beat him, & after abusing him about two Hours he was obliged, in Order to save his Life, to give up his Colours. . . .

The Mob Committee, of the County of York, where Sr. *William Pepperells* large Estate lay, ordered that no Person should hire any of his Estates of him, nor buy any Wood of him, nor pay any Debts to *him* that were due to him.

One of the Constables of *Hardwick*, for refusing to pay the Provincial Collection of Taxes which he had gathered, to the new Receiver General of the rebel Government, was confined & bound for 36 Hours, & not suffered to lie in a Bed, & threatened to be sent to *Simsbury* Mines in *Connecticut*. These Mines being converted into a Prison, 50 Feet under Ground, where it is said that many Loyalists have suffered. The Officers Wife being dangerously ill, they suffered him to see her, after he had complied.

The aforementioned Colo. *Gilbert* was so obnoxious for his Attachment to Government, that the Mobs being sometimes afraid to attack him openly, some of them secretly fired Balls at him in the Woods. And as he was driving a Number of Sheep to his Farm, he was attacked by 30 or 40 of them, who robbed him of part of the Flock, but he beat the Mob off. And this same Colo. *Gilbert* was, some Time after, travelling on his Business, when he stopped at an Inn to bait his Horse. Whilst he was in the House, some Person lift up the Saddle from his Horse & put a Piece of a broken Glass Bottle under the Saddle; & when the Colo. mounted, the Pressure run the Glass into the Horses back, which made him frantick. The Horse threw his rider, who was so much hurt as not to recover his Senses 'till he was carried & arrived at his own House, at 3 Miles distance. . . .

February 1775 A Number of Ladies, at *Plimouth*, attempted to divert their selves at the publick Assembly Room; but not being connected with the rebel Faction, the Committee Men met, and the Mob collected who flung Stones & broke the

Windows & Shutters of the Room, endangering the Lives of the Company, who were obliged to break up, & were abused to their Homes.

Soon after this, the Ladies diverted their selves by riding out of Town, but were followed & pelted by the Mob, & abused with the most indecent Language. The Honble. *Israel Williams* Esqr., who was appointed one of his Majesty's new Council, but had refused the Office by Reason of bodily Infirmities, was taken from his House, by a Mob, in the Night, & carried several Miles; then carried home again, after being forced to sign a Paper which they drafted; & a guard set over him to prevent his going from Home.

A Parish Clerk of an Episcopal Church at *East Haddum* in *Connecticut*, a Man of 70 Years of Age, was taken out of his Bed in a Cold Night, & beat against his Hearth by Men who held him by his Arms & Legs. He was then laid across his Horse, without his Cloaths, & drove to a considerable Distance in that naked Condition. His Nephew Dr. *Abner Beebe*, a Physician, complained of the bad Usage of his Uncle, & spoke very freely in Favor of Government; for which he was assaulted by a Mob, stripped naked, & hot Pitch was poured upon him, which blistered his Skin. He was then carried to an Hog Sty & rubbed over with Hogs Dung. They threw the Hog's Dung in his Face, & rammed some of it down his Throat; & in that Condition exposed to a Company of Women. His House was attacked, his Windows broke, when one of his Children was sick, & a Child of his went into Distraction upon this Treatment. His Gristmill was broke, & Persons prevented from grinding at it, & from having any Connections with him.

All the foregoing Transactions were before the Battle of Lexington, when the Rebels say that the War began.

QUESTIONS FOR READING AND DISCUSSION

1. What did Oliver mean by terming these events "very innocent Frolicks of Rebellion"?

2. What forms of punishment and humiliation did crowds use against supporters of the British? Who in particular did they target, according to Oliver? Why?

3. According to Oliver, why was it significant that the "Mob was not mixed with tag, rag & Bobtail only, Persons of Distinction in the Country were in the Mass"? What meanings did he attach to the terms *mob* and *persons of distinction*? What political loyalties were implied by these terms?

4. To what extent did crowd actions interrupt the normal functions of government? For the crowd, what was at stake in these confrontations?

5. What did Oliver believe was wrong with these crowd actions? How might members of the crowds have responded to his claims and assumptions?

DOCUMENT 4

George Washington Concludes That the Crisis Has Arrived

British attempts to divide the colonies against one another failed. British retaliation against Boston engendered support throughout the colonies, including the all-important Virginia. George Washington, writing to a cautious friend, explained why he came to the conclusion that, unfortunately, a crisis had arrived and colonial rights had to be defended. Washington's private letters in the summer of 1774, excerpted here, illustrate the support among leading Virginians for the colonial cause.

Letters, 1774

Williamsburg, June 10, 1774 . . . [After meeting for three weeks, the Virginia Assembly adjourned and] the Members convend themselves at the Raleigh Tavern and enterd into the Inclosd Association which being followed two days after by an Express from Boston accompanied by the Sentiments of some Meetings in our Sister Colonies to the Northwd. the proceedings mentiond in the Inclos'd Papers were had thereupon and a general meeting requested of all the late Representatives in this City on the first of August when it is hopd, and expected that some vigorous (and effectual) measures will be effectually adopted to obtain that justice which is denied to our Petitions and Remonstrances (and Prayers); in short the Ministry may rely on it that Americans will never be tax'd without their own consent that the cause of Boston the despotick Measures in respect to it I mean now is and ever will be considerd as the cause of America (not that we approve their conduct in destroyg. the Tea) and that we shall not suffer ourselves to be sacrificed by piece meals though god only knows what is to become of us, threatned as we are with so many hoverg. evils as hang over us at present; having a cruel and blood thirsty Enemy upon our Backs, the Indians, between whom and our Frontier Inhabitants many Skirmishes have happnd, and with whom a general War is inevitable whilst those from whom we have a right to seek protection are endeavouring by every piece of Art and despotism to fix the Shackles of Slavery upon us.

Mount Vernon, July 20, 1774 . . . The conduct of the Boston people could not justify the rigor of their measures, unless there had been a requisition of payment and refusal of it; nor did that measure require an act to deprive the government of Massachusetts Bay of their charter, or to exempt offenders from trial in the place where offences were committed, as there was not, nor could not be, a single instance produced to manifest the necessity of it. Are not all these things self evident proofs of a fixed and uniform plan to tax us? If we want further proofs, do not all the debates in the House of Commons serve to confirm this? And has not General [Thomas] Gage's conduct since his arrival, (in stopping the address of his Council, and publishing a proclamation more becoming a Turkish bashaw [pasha], than an English governor, declaring it treason to associate in any manner by which the commerce of Great Britain is to be affected,) exhibited an unexampled testimony of the most despotic system of tyranny, that ever was practised in a free government? In short, what further proofs are wanted to satisfy one of the designs of the ministry, than their own acts, which are uniform and plainly tending to the same point, nay, if I mistake not, avowedly to fix the right of taxation? What hope then from petitioning, when they tell us, that now or never is the time to fix the matter? Shall we, after this, whine and cry for relief, when we have al-

John C. Fitzpatrick, ed., *The Writings of George Washington*, vol. 3 (Westport, Conn.: Greenwood Press, 1970) 23–25.

ready tried it in vain? Or shall we supinely sit and see one province after another fall a prey to despotism? If I was in any doubt, as to the right which the Parliament of Great Britain had to tax us without our consent, I should most heartily coincide with you in opinion, that to petition, and petition only, is the proper method to apply for relief; because we should then be asking a favor, and not claiming a right, which, by the law of nature and our constitution, we are, in my opinion, indubitably entitled to. I should even think it criminal to go further than this, under such an idea; but none such I have. I think the Parliament of Great Britain hath no more right to put their hands into my pocket, without my consent, than I have to put my hands into yours for money; and this being already urged to them in a firm, but decent manner, by all the colonies, what reason is there to expect a thing from their justice?

Mount Vernon, August 24, 1774 . . . In truth, persuaded as I am, that you have read all the political pieces, which compose a large share of the [Virginia] Gazette at this time, I should think it, but for your request, a piece of inexcusable arrogance in me, to make the least essay towards a change in your political opinions; for I am sure I have no new lights to throw upon the subject, or any other arguments to offer in support of my own doctrine, than what you have seen; and could only in general add, that an innate spirit of freedom first told me, that the measures, which administration hath for some time been, and now are most violently pursuing, are repugnant to every principle of natural justice; whilst much abler heads than my own hath fully convinced me, that it is not only repugnant to natural right, but subversive of the laws and constitution of Great Britain itself, in the establishment of which some of the best blood in the kingdom hath been spilt. Satisfied, then, that the acts of a British Parliament are no longer governed by the principles of justice, that it is trampling upon the valuable rights of Americans, confirmed to them by charter and constitution they themselves boast of, and convinced beyond the smallest doubt, that these measures are the result of deliberation, and attempted to be carried into execution by the hand of power, is it a time to trifle, or risk our cause upon petitions, which with difficulty obtain access, and afterwards are thrown by with the utmost contempt? Or should we, because heretofore unsuspicious of design, and then unwilling to enter into disputes with the mother country, go on to bear more, and forbear to enumerate our just causes of complaint? For my own part, I shall not undertake to say where the line between Great Britain and the colonies should be drawn; but I am clearly of opinion, that one ought to be drawn, and our rights clearly ascertained. I could wish, I own, that the dispute had been left to posterity to determine, but the crisis is arrived when we must assert our rights, or submit to every imposition, that can be heaped upon us, till custom and use shall make us as tame and abject slaves, as the blacks we rule over with such arbitrary sway.

QUESTIONS FOR READING AND DISCUSSION

1. Why did Washington believe the crisis had arrived, that "the cause of Boston . . . is and ever will be considered the cause of America"?
2. Did Washington agree with everything that patriots had done in Boston? Why or why not?
3. Washington argued that the colonists "must assert our rights" or else become "as tame and abject slaves, as the blacks we rule over with such arbitrary

sway." To what extent did Washington's experiences as a slaveholder impell him toward the rebellion rather than restrain him from joining it?

COMPARATIVE QUESTIONS _____

1. How did Joseph Warren's arguments about colonial grievances compare with those expressed by George Washington and George Hewes?
2. How might Washington, Warren, and Hewes have defended the crowd actions that Peter Oliver criticized?
3. Fundamental assumptions about law, government, and society divided patriots from loyalists. To what extent do the documents in this chapter reveal those divisions? To what extent, if at all, did patriots and loyalists share common assumptions about such basic matters?
4. Do the documents in this chapter suggest that colonists were unified in rebellion? What were the most important sources of unity and of conflict? Do these documents provide evidence of a distinctive American identity among colonists?
5. Judging from the documents in this chapter, why did so many colonists decide to support open and active rebellion against British rule? Why did other colonists decide instead to continue to ally with the British?

CHAPTER 6

THE WAR FOR AMERICA
1775–1783

The Declaration of Independence made crystal clear the momentous stakes of the conflict between the colonies and Great Britain. An independence that seemed impossible, if not unimaginable, to many Americans in 1775 was boldly asserted in 1776 and, after much bloodshed, successfully defended by 1783. Ideas about monarchy and popular government that most British officials and many of their colonial allies considered subversive began to seem sensible to many Americans, and independence became a means to move from promising ideas to practical achievements. The following documents illustrate ideas and experiences that made revolution seem reasonable to many Americans, despite its great risks.

DOCUMENT 1
Thomas Paine Makes the Case for Independence

By the end of 1775, colonial Minutemen had faced royal troops in battle, but the debate about what the colonists should do next continued to rage. Tories believed that the rebellious upstarts should be suppressed. Lukewarm Tories and hesitant patriots still hoped that some basis could be found for reconciliation. Militant rebels believed the time for independence had arrived. Thomas Paine made the case for independence in his compelling pamphlet, Common Sense, published in January 1776. Paine's arguments, excerpted here, rang true to many leading colonists. Yes, they agreed, revolution was now common sense.

Common Sense, *January 1776*

There is something exceedingly ridiculous in the composition of monarchy; it first excludes a man from the means of information, yet empowers him to act in cases where the highest judgment is required. The state of a king shuts him from the world, yet the business of a king requires him to know it thoroughly; wherefore the different parts, unnaturally opposing and destroying each other, prove the whole character to be absurd and useless. . . .

Mankind being originally equals in the order of creation, the equality could only be destroyed by some subsequent circumstance. . . .

But there is . . . [a] distinction for which no truly natural or religious reason can be assigned, and that is, the distinction of men into KINGS and SUBJECTS. Male and female are the distinctions of nature, good and bad the distinctions of heaven; but how a race of men came into the world so exalted above the rest, and distinguished like some new species, is worth inquiring into, and whether they are the means of happiness or of misery to mankind. . . .

As the exalting one man so greatly above the rest cannot be justified on the equal rights of nature, so neither can it be defended on the authority of scripture. . . .

That the Almighty hath . . . entered his protest against monarchial government is true, or the scripture is false. . . . For monarchy in every instance is the Popery of government.

To the evil of monarchy we have added that of hereditary succession. . . . For all men being originally equals, no *one by birth* could have a right to set up his own family in perpetual preference to all others for ever. . . . One of the strongest natural proofs of the folly of hereditary right in kings, is, that nature disapproves it, otherwise she would not so frequently turn it into ridicule by giving mankind an *ass for a lion.* . . .

[C]ould we take off the dark covering of antiquity, and trace [the present lineage of kings] to their first rise, . . . we should find the first of them nothing better than the principal ruffian of some restless gang, whose savage manners or preeminence in subtlety obtained him the title of chief among plunderers. . . .

But it is not so much the absurdity as the evil of hereditary succession which concerns mankind. Did it ensure a race of good and wise men it would have the seal of divine authority, but as it opens a door to the *foolish,* the *wicked,* and the *improper,* it hath in it the nature of oppression. Men who look upon themselves born to reign, and others to obey, soon grow insolent; selected from the rest of mankind their minds are early poisoned by importance; and the world they act in differs so materially from the world at large, that they have but little opportunity of knowing its true interests, and when they succeed to the government are frequently the most ignorant and unfit of any throughout the dominions. . . .

In England a k—— hath little more to do than to make war and give away places; which in plain terms, is to impoverish the nation and set it together by the ears. A pretty business indeed for a man to be allowed eight hundred thousand sterling a year for, and worshipped into the bargain! Of more worth is one honest man to society, and in the sight of God, than all the crowned ruffians that ever lived. . . .

Thomas Paine, *Common Sense* (1776).

THOUGHTS ON THE PRESENT STATE
OF AMERICAN AFFAIRS

In the following pages I offer nothing more than simple facts, plain arguments, and common sense. . . .

Volumes have been written on the subject of the struggle between England and America. Men of all ranks have embarked in the controversy, from different motives, and with various designs; but all have been ineffectual, and the period of debate is closed. Arms, as the last resource, decide the contest; the appeal was the choice of the king, and the continent hath accepted the challenge. . . .

The sun never shined on a cause of greater worth. 'Tis not the affair of a city, a country, a province, or a kingdom, but of a continent — of at least one eighth part of the habitable globe. 'Tis not the concern of a day, a year, or an age; posterity are virtually involved in the contest, and will be more or less affected, even to the end of time, by the proceedings now. Now is the seed time of continental union, faith and honour. . . .

I have heard it asserted by some, that as America hath flourished under her former connection with Great Britain, that the same connection is necessary towards her future happiness, and will always have the same effect. Nothing can be more fallacious than this kind of argument. . . . I answer roundly, that America would have flourished as much, and probably much more, had no European power had any thing to do with her. The commerce by which she hath enriched herself are the necessaries of life, and will always have a market while eating is the custom of Europe. . . .

Alas, we have been long led away by ancient prejudices, and made large sacrifices to superstition. We have boasted the protection of Great Britain, without considering, that her motive was *interest* not attachment; that she did not protect us from our enemies on our account, but from *her enemies* on *her own account*. . . .

But Britain is the parent country, say some. Then the more shame upon her conduct. Even brutes do not devour their young, nor savages make war upon their families. . . . Europe, and not England, is the parent country of America. This new world hath been the asylum for the persecuted lovers of civil and religious liberty from *every part* of Europe. Hither have they fled, not from the tender embraces of the mother, but from the cruelty of the monster; and it is so far true of England, that the same tyranny which drove the first emigrants from home, pursues their descendants still. . . .

I challenge the warmest advocate for reconciliation, to shew, a single advantage that this continent can reap, by being connected with Great Britain. I repeat the challenge, not a single advantage is derived. Our corn will fetch its price in any market in Europe, and our imported goods must be paid for buy them where we will.

But the injuries and disadvantages we sustain by that connection, are without number; and our duty to mankind at large, as well as to ourselves, instruct us to renounce the alliance: Because, any submission to, or dependence on Great Britain, tends directly to involve this continent in European wars and quarrels; and sets us at variance with nations, who would otherwise seek our friendship, and against whom, we have neither anger nor complaint. As Europe is our market for trade, we ought to form no partial connection with any part of it. It is the true interest of America to steer clear of European contentions, which she never can do, while by her dependence on Britain, she is made the make-weight in the scale of British politics.

Europe is too thickly planted with kingdoms to be long at peace, and whenever a war breaks out between England and any foreign power, the trade of America goes to ruin, *because of her connection with Britain.* . . . Every thing that is right or natural pleads for separation. The blood of the slain, the weeping voice of nature cries, 'TIS TIME TO PART. Even the distance at which the Almighty hath placed England and America, is a strong and natural proof, that the authority of the one, over the other, was never the design of Heaven. . . .

Men of passive tempers look somewhat lightly over the offences of Britain, and, still hoping for the best, are apt to call out, *"Come we shall befriends again for all this.".* . . But if you say, you can still pass the violations over, then I ask, Hath your house been burnt? Hath your property been destroyed before your face? Are your wife and children destitute of a bed to lie on, or bread to live on? Have you lost a parent or a child by their hands, and yourself the ruined and wretched survivor? If you have not, then are you not a judge of those who have. But if you have, and can still shake hands with the murderers, then are you unworthy the name of husband, father, friend, or lover, and whatever may be your rank or title in life, you have the heart of a coward, and the spirit of a sycophant. . . .

I mean not to exhibit horror for the purpose of provoking revenge, but to awaken us from fatal and unmanly slumbers, that we may pursue determinately some fixed object. It is not in the power of Britain or of Europe to conquer America, if she did not conquer herself by *delay and timidity.* . . .

It is repugnant to reason, to the universal order of things, to all examples from the former ages, to suppose, that this continent can longer remain subject to any external power. . . . Reconciliation is and was a fallacious dream. Nature hath deserted the connection, and Art cannot supply her place. . . .

Small islands not capable of protecting themselves, are the proper objects for kingdoms to take under their care; but there is something very absurd, in supposing a continent to be perpetually governed by an island. In no instance hath nature made the satellite larger than its primary planet, and as England and America, with respect to each other, reverses the common order of nature, it is evident they belong to different systems: England to Europe, America to itself. . . .

But the most powerful of all arguments, is, that nothing but independence, i.e.[,] a continental form of government, can keep the peace of the continent and preserve it inviolate from civil wars. . . .

If there is any true cause of fear respecting independence, it is because no plan is yet laid down. Men do not see their way out, Wherefore, as an opening into that business, I offer the following hints. . . .

LET the assemblies be annual, with a President only. The representation more equal. Their business wholly domestic, and subject to the authority of a Continental Congress.

Let each colony be divided into six, eight, or ten, convenient districts, each district to send a proper number of delegates to Congress. . . .

[L]et a CONTINENTAL CONFERENCE be held. . . . [L]et their business be to frame a CONTINENTAL CHARTER, or Charter of the United Colonies; (answering to what is called the Magna Charta of England) fixing the number and manner of choosing members of Congress, members of Assembly, with their date of sitting, and drawing the line of business and jurisdiction between them: (Always remembering, that our strength is continental, not provincial:) Securing freedom and property to all men, and above all things the free exercise of religion, according to the dictates of conscience; with such other matter as is necessary for a charter to contain. . . .

But where says some is the King of America? I'll tell you Friend, he reigns above, and doth not make havoc of mankind like the Royal — of Britain. Yet that we may not appear to be defective even in earthly honours, let a day be solemnly set apart for proclaiming the charter; let it be brought forth placed on the divine law, the word of God; let a crown be placed thereon, by which the world may know, that so far as we approve of monarchy, that in America THE LAW IS KING. For as in absolute governments the King is law, so in free countries the law *ought* to be King; and there ought to be no other. But lest any ill use should afterwards arise, let the crown at the conclusion of the ceremony be demolished, and scattered among the people whose right it is.

A government of our own is our natural right: And when a man seriously reflects on the precariousness of human affairs, he will become convinced, that it is infinitely wiser and safer, to form a constitution of our own in a cool deliberate manner, while we have it in our power, than to trust such an interesting event to time and chance. . . . Ye that oppose independence now, ye know not what ye do; ye are opening a door to eternal tyranny, by keeping vacant the seat of government. There are thousands and tens of thousands, who would think it glorious to expel from the continent, that barbarous and hellish power, which hath stirred up the Indians and Negroes to destroy us; the cruelty hath a double guilt, it is dealing brutally by us, and treacherously by them. . . .

O ye that love mankind! Ye that dare oppose, not only the tyranny, but the tyrant, stand forth! Every spot of the old world is over-run with oppression. Freedom hath been hunted round the globe. Asia, and Africa, have long expelled her — Europe regards her like a stranger, and England hath given her warning to depart. O! receive the fugitive, and prepare in time an asylum for mankind.

QUESTIONS FOR READING AND DISCUSSION

1. How did Paine use concepts of equality, reason, and nature to criticize the legitimacy of monarchical government and British control of the colonies?
2. What arguments did Paine give for independence? How were his observations about monarchy connected to his reasons for independence? Why did he propose that law should be "King of America"?
3. Why did he believe that attempts at reconciliation were "a fallacious dream"?
4. Independence, according to Paine, would "expel from the continent, that barbarous and hellish power, which hath stirred up the Indians and Negroes to destroy us" and would create "an asylum for mankind." In what sense would an independent America be an asylum, and for whom?

DOCUMENT 2

Letters of John and Abigail Adams

While the Second Continental Congress deliberated in Philadelphia on the colonial crisis, Massachusetts delegate John Adams maintained a correspondence with his wife, Abigail, who remained at home. A leader in the independence movement, Adams exchanged news, ideas, and concerns with his wife. The following selections from the Adams correspon-

dence illustrates the determination tempered by anxiety that accompanied the fateful passage of the Declaration of Independence.

Correspondence, 1776
John Adams to Abigail Adams

[Philadelphia,] February 18, 1776

My dearest Friend

I sent you from New York a Pamphlet intitled Common Sense, written in Vindication of Doctrines which there is Reason to expect that the further Encroachments of Tyranny and Depredations of Oppression, will soon make the common Faith: unless the cunning Ministry, by proposing Negociations and Terms of Reconciliation, should divert the present Current from its Channell.

Reconciliation if practicable and Peace if attainable, you very well know would be as agreable to my Inclinations and as advantageous to my Interest, as to any Man's. But I see no Prospect, no Probability, no Possibility. And I cannot but despise the Understanding, which sincerely expects an honourable Peace, for its Credulity, and detest the hypocritical Heart, which pretends to expect it, when in Truth it does not. The News Papers here are full of free Speculations, the Tendency of which you will easily discover. The Writers reason from Topicks which have been long in Contemplation, and fully understood by the People at large in New England, but have been attended to in the southern Colonies only by Gentlemen of free Spirits and liberal Minds, who are very few. I shall endeavour to inclose to you as many of the Papers and Pamphlets as I can, as long as I stay here.

The Events of War are uncertain: We cannot insure Success, but We can deserve it.

Write me as often as you can — tell me all the News.

Abigail Adams to John Adams

[Braintree, Mass.,] Saturday Evening March 2 [1776]

. . . I heartily wish every Tory was Extirpated [from] America, they are continually by secret means undermineing and injuring our cause.

I am charmed with the Sentiments of Common Sense; and wonder how an honest Heart, one who wishes the welfare of their country, and the happiness of posterity can hesitate one moment at adopting them; I want to know how those Sentiments are received in Congress? I dare say their would be no difficulty in procuring a vote and instructions from all the Assemblies in New England for independancy. I most sincerely wish that now in the Lucky Minuet it might be done.

I have been kept in a continual state of anxiety and expectation ever since you left me. It has been said to morrow and to morrow for this month, but when the dreadfull to morrow will be I know not—but hark! the House this instant

L. H. Butterfield, ed., Adams Family Correspondence, vols. 1 and 2 (Cambridge, Ma.: Harvard University Press, 1963) 193–202.

shakes with the roar of Cannon.—I have been to the door and find tis a cannonade from our Army, orders I find are come for all the remaining Militia to repair to the Lines a monday night by twelve o clock. No Sleep for me to Night; and if I cannot who have no guilt upon my Soul with regard to this Cause, how shall the misirible wretches who have been the procurers of this Dreadfull Scene and those who are to be the actors, lie down with the load of Guilt upon their Souls.

Sunday Eve March 3

I went to Bed after 12 but got no rest, the Cannon continued firing and my Heart Beat pace with them all night. We have had a pretty quite day, but what to morrow will bring forth God only knows.

Monday Evening

Tolerable quiet to day. The Militia have all musterd with 3 days provision and are all marched by 8 o clock this afternoon tho their notice was no longer than 8 o clock Saturday, and now we have scarcly a Man but our regular guards . . . and the Militia from the more remote towns are call'd in as Sea coast Guards. Can you form to yourself an Idea of our Sensations.

I have just returned from P[enn']s Hill where I have been sitting to hear the amazing roar of cannon and from whence I could see every shell which was thrown. The sound I think is one of the Grandest in Nature and is of the true Species of the Sublime. Tis now an incessant Roar. But O the fatal Ideas which are connected with the sound. How many of our dear country men must fall?

Tuesday Morning

I went to bed about 12 and rose again a little after one. I could no more sleep than if I had been in the ingagement. The ratling of the windows, the jar of the house and the continual roar of 24 pounders, the Bursting of shells give us such Ideas, and realize a scene to us of which we could scarcly form any conception. About Six this morning, there was quiet; I rejoiced in a few hours calm. I hear we got possession of Dorchester Hill Last Night. 4000 thousand men upon it to day — lost but one Man. The Ships are all drawn round the Town.

Sunday Eve March 10

I had scarcly finished these lines when my Ears were again assaulted with the roar of Cannon. I could not write any further. My Hand and heart will tremble, at this domestick fury, and firce civil Strife, which cumber all our parts. Tho,

> Blood and destruction are so much in use
> And Dreadfull objects so familiar,

Yet is not pitty chok'd, nor my Heart grown Callous. I feel for the unhappy wretches who know not where to fly for safety. I feel still more for my Bleading Country men who are hazarding their lives and their Limbs. — A most Terible and incessant Cannonade from half after 8 till Six this morning. I hear we lost four men kill'd and some wounded in attempting to take the Hill nearest the Town call'd Nook Hill. . . .

I have not got all the perticuliars I wish I had but, as I have an opportunity of sending this I shall endeavour to be more perticuliar in my next. . . .

If we have [no] Reinforcements here, I believe we shall be driven from the sea coast, but in what so ever state I am I will endeavour to be therewith content.

Man wants but Little here below
Nor wants that Little long.

You will excuse this very incorrect Letter. You see in what purtubation it has been written and how many times I have left of. Adieu pray write me every opportunity.

John Adams to Abigail Adams

[Philadelphia,] March 19, 1776

. . . [M]y worthy fellow Citizens may be easy about me. I never can forsake what I take to be their Interests. My own have never been considered by me, in Competition with theirs. My Ease, my domestic Happiness, my rural Pleasures, my Little Property, my personal Liberty, my Reputation, my Life, have little Weight and ever had, in my own Estimation, in Comparison of the great Object of my Country. I can say of it with great Sincerity, as Horace says of Virtue — to America only and her Friends a Friend.

You ask, what is thought of Common sense. Sensible Men think there are some Whims, some Sophisms, some artfull Addresses to superstitious Notions, some keen attempts upon the Passions, in this Pamphlet. But all agree there is a great deal of good sense, delivered in a clear, simple, concise and nervous Style.

His Sentiments of the Abilities of America, and of the Difficulty of a Reconciliation with G[reat].B[ritain]. are generally approved. But his Notions, and Plans of Continental Government are not much applauded. Indeed this Writer has a better Hand at pulling down than building.

It has been very generally propagated through the Continent that I wrote this Pamphlet. But altho I could not have written any Thing in so manly and striking a style, I flatter myself I should have made a more respectable Figure as an Architect, if I had undertaken such a Work. This Writer seems to have very inadequate Ideas of what is proper and necessary to be done, in order to form Constitutions for single Colonies, as well as a great Model of Union for the whole.

Your Distresses which you have painted in such lively Colours, I feel in every Line as I read. I dare not write all that I think upon this Occasion. . . .

Abigail Adams to John Adams

Braintree, March 31, 1776

I wish you would ever write me a Letter half as long as I write you; and tell me if you may where your Fleet are gone? What sort of Defence Virginia can make against our common Enemy? Whether it is so situated as to make an able Defence? Are not the Gentery Lords and the common people vassals, are they not like the uncivilized Natives Brittain represents us to be? I hope their Riffel Men who have shewen themselves very savage and even Blood thirsty; are not a specimen of the Generality of the people.

I am willing to allow the Colony great merit for having produced a Washington but they have been shamefully duped by a Dunmore. I have sometimes been ready to think that the passion for Liberty cannot be Eaquelly Strong in the Breasts of those who have been accustomed to deprive their fellow Creatures of theirs. Of this I am certain that it is not founded upon that generous and christian principal of doing to others as we would that others should do unto us. . . .

I feel very differently at the approach of spring to what I did a month ago. We knew not then whether we could plant or sow with safety, whether when we had toild we could reap the fruits of our own industery, whether we could rest in our own Cottages, or whether we should not be driven from the sea coasts to seek shelter in the wilderness, but now we feel as if we might sit under our own vine and eat the good of the land.

Tho we felicitate ourselves, we sympathize with those who are trembling least the Lot of Boston should be theirs. But they cannot be in similar circumstances unless pusilanimity and cowardise should take possession of them. They have time and warning given them to see the Evil and shun it. — I long to hear that you have declared an independancy — and by the way in the new Code of Laws which I suppose it will be necessary for you to make I desire you would Remember the Ladies, and be more generous and favourable to them than your ancestors. Do not put such unlimited power into the hands of the Husbands. Remember all Men would be tyrants if they could. If perticuliar care and attention is not paid to the Laidies we are determined to foment a Rebelion, and will not hold ourselves bound by any Laws in which we have no voice, or Representation.

That your Sex are Naturally Tyrannical is a Truth so thoroughly established as to admit of no dispute, but such of you as wish to be happy willingly give up the harsh title of Master for the more tender and endearing one of Friend. Why then, not put it out of the power of the vicious and the Lawless to use us with cruelty and indignity with impunity. Men of Sense in all Ages abhor those customs which treat us only as the vassals of your Sex. Regard us then as Beings placed by providence under your protection and in immitation of the Supreem Being make use of that power only for our happiness.

Your ever faithful friend.

John Adams to Abigail Adams

[Philadelphia], April 14, 1776

You justly complain of my short Letters, but the critical State of Things and the Multiplicity of Avocations must plead my Excuse. — ask what Sort of Defence Virginia can make. I believe they will make an able Defence. Their Militia and minute Men have been some time employed in training them selves, and they have Nine Battallions of regulars as they call them, maintained among them, under good Officers, at the Continental Expence. They have set up a Number of Manufactories of Fire Arms, which are busily employed. They are tolerably supplied with Powder, and are successfull and assiduous, in making Salt Petre. Their neighbouring Sister or rather Daughter Colony of North Carolina, which is a warlike Colony, and has several Battallions at the Continental Expence, as well as a pretty good Militia, are ready to assist them, and they are in very good Spirits, and seem determined to make a brave Resistance. — The Gentry are very rich, and the common People very poor. This Inequality of Property, gives an Aristocratical Turn to all their Proceedings, and occasions a strong Aversion in their Patricians, to Common Sense. But the Spirit of these Barons, is coming down, and it must submit.

As to Declarations of Independency, be patient. Read our Privateering Laws, and our Commercial Laws. What signifies a Word.

As to your extraordinary Code of Laws, I cannot but laugh. We have been told that our Struggle has loosened the bands of Government every where. That Children and Apprentices were disobedient—that schools and Colledges were grown turbulent — that Indians slighted their Guardians and Negroes grew insolent to their Masters. But your Letter was the first Intimation that another Tribe more numerous and powerfull than all the rest were grown discontented. — This is rather too coarse a Compliment but you are so saucy, I wont blot it out.

Depend upon it, We know better than to repeal our Masculine systems. Altho they are in full Force, you know they are little more than Theory. We dare not exert our Power in its full Latitude. We are obliged to go fair, and softly, and in Practice you know We are the subjects. We have only the Name of Masters, and rather than give up this, which would compleatly subject Us to the Despotism of the Peticoat, I hope General Washington, and all our brave Heroes would fight. I am sure every good Politician would plot, as long as he would against Despotism, Empire, Monarchy, Aristocracy, Oligarchy, or Ochlocracy. — A fine Story indeed. I begin to think the Ministry as deep as they are wicked. After stirring up Tories, Landjobbers, Trimmers, Bigots, Canadians, Indians, Negroes, Hanoverians, Hessians, Russians, Irish Roman Catholicks, Scotch Renegadoes, at last they have stimulated the ladies to demand new Priviledges and threaten to rebell.

John Adams to Abigail Adams

[Philadelphia], May 17, 1776

. . . When I consider the great Events which are passed, and those greater which are rapidly advancing, and that I may have been instrumental of touching some Springs, and turning some small Wheels, which have had and will have such Effects, I feel an Awe upon my Mind, which is not easily described.

G[reat] B[ritain] has at last driven America, to the last Step, a compleat Seperation from her, a total absolute Independence, not only of her Parliament but of her Crown, for such is the Amount of the Resolve of the 15th.

Confederation among ourselves, or Alliances with foreign Nations are not necessary, to a perfect Seperation from Britain. That is effected by extinguishing all Authority, under the Crown, Parliament and Nation as the Resolution for instituting Governments, has done, to all Intents and Purposes. Confederation will be necessary for our internal Concord, and Alliances may be so for our external Defense.

I have Reasons to believe that no Colony, which shall assume a Government under the People, will give it up. There is something very unnatural and odious in a Government 1000 Leagues off. An whole Government of our own Choice, managed by Persons whom We love, revere, and can confide in, has charms in it for which Men will fight. Two young Gentlemen from South Carolina, now in this City, who were in Charlestown when their new Constitution was promulgated, and when their new Governor and Council and Assembly walked out in

Procession, attended by the Guards, Company of Cadetts, Light Horse &c., told me, that they were beheld by the People with Transports and Tears of Joy. The People gazed at them, with a Kind of Rapture. They both told me, that the Reflection that these were Gentlemen whom they all loved, esteemed and revered, Gentlemen of their own Choice, whom they could trust, and whom they could displace if any of them should behave amiss, affected them so that they could not help crying.

They say their People will never give up this Government. . . .

John Adams to Abigail Adams

Philadelphia, July 3, 1776

. . . Yesterday the greatest Question was decided, which ever was debated in America, and a greater perhaps, never was or will be decided among Men. A Resolution was passed without one dissenting Colony "that these united Colonies, are, and of right ought to be free and independent States, and as such, they have, and of Right ought to have full Power to make War, conclude Peace, establish Commerce, and to do all the other Acts and Things, which other States may rightfully do." You will see in a few days a Declaration setting forth the Causes, which have impell'd Us to this mighty Revolution, and the Reasons which will justify it, in the Sight of God and Man. A Plan of Confederation will be taken up in a few days.

When I look back to the Year 1761, and recollect the Argument concerning Writs of Assistance, in the Superiour Court which I have hitherto considered as the Commencement of the Controversy, between Great Britain and America, and run through the whole Period from that Time to this, and recollect the series of political Events, the Chain of Causes and Effects, I am surprized at the Suddenness, as well as Greatness of this Revolution. Britain has been fill'd with Folly, and America with Wisdom, at least this is my Judgment . — Time must determine. It is the Will of Heaven, that the two Countries should be sundered forever. It may be the Will of Heaven that America shall suffer Calamities still more wasting and Distresses yet more dreadfull. If this is to be the Case, it will have this good Effect, at least: it will inspire Us with many Virtues, which We have not, and correct many Errors, Follies, and Vices, which threaten to disturb, dishonour, and destroy Us. The furnace of Affliction produces Refinement, in States as well as Individuals. And the new Governments we are assuming, in every Part, will require a Purification from our Vices, and an Augmentation of our Virtues or they will be no Blessings. The People will have unbounded Power. And the People are extreamly addicted to Corruption and Venality, as well as the Great. — I am not without Apprehensions from this Quarter. But I must submit all my Hopes and Fears, to an overruling Providence, in which, unfashionable as the Faith may be, I firmly believe.

John Adams to Abigail Adams

Philadelphia, July 3d, 1776

. . . [T]he Delay of this Declaration [of Independence] to this Time, has many great Advantages attending it.—The Hopes of Reconciliation, which were fondly entertained by Multitudes of honest and well meaning tho weak and mistaken People, have been gradually and at last totally extinguished. Time has been given for the whole People, maturely to consider the great Question of Independence and to ripen their Judgments, dissipate their Fears, and allure their Hopes, by discussing it in News Papers and Pamphletts, by debating it, in Assemblies, Conventions, Committees of Safety and Inspection, in Town and County Meetings, as well as in private Conversations, so that the whole People in every Colony of the 13, have now adopted it, as their own Act. — This will cement the Union, and avoid those Heats and perhaps Convulsions which might have been occasioned, by such a Declaration Six Months ago.

But the Day is past. The Second Day of July 1776, will be the most memorable Epocha, in the History of America. — I am apt to believe that it will be celebrated, by succeeding Generations, as the great anniversary Festival. It ought to be commemorated, as the Day of Deliverance by solemn Acts of Devotion to God Almighty. It ought to be solemnized with Pomp and Parade, with Shews, Games, Sports, Guns, Bells, Bonfires and Illuminations from one End of this Continent to the other from this Time forward forever more.

You will think me transported with Enthusiasm but I am not. — I am well aware of the Toil and Blood and Treasure, that it will cost Us to maintain this Declaration, and support and defend these States. — Yet through all the Gloom I can see the Rays of ravishing Light and Glory. I can see that the End is more than worth all the Means. And that Posterity will tryumph in that Days Transaction, even altho We should rue it, which I trust in God We shall not.

QUESTIONS FOR READING AND DISCUSSION

1. What did John and Abigail Adams think of Thomas Paine's *Common Sense*? How did they believe it had influenced others? Did their ideas deviate from Paine's in important ways?

2. What did Abigail recommend the new government do in order to "Remember the Ladies"? How did John respond to her suggestions? What did their exchange suggest about the scope and limits of equality among leading supporters of the Revolution?

3. How did the Adamses view southern colonists? What did Abigail mean by asking, "Are not the Gentery Lords and the common people vassals"? How did John respond to her inquiry?

4. Why did John believe that independence would be permanent? What did he anticipate the consequences of independence to be?

DOCUMENT 3

A Soldier's Experience of the Revolutionary War

Soldiers in the Continental Army received notoriously inconsistent support. Few Americans doubted that the success of the American Revolution required effective soldiers. Few also were eager to enlist in the army or to pay the necessary taxes. Joseph Plumb Martin, a sixteen-year-old Massachusetts resident, enlisted in 1776 and served almost continuously for the duration of the war. Martin saw action in many of the war's most important

battles, and by the end he had become disgusted with the nation's treatment of its sol-
diers. Many years later, in 1830, Martin published a memoir of his war experiences —
the only extended account by a common soldier in the Revolution. In the following ex-
cerpt, Martin recalled his enlistment and, six years later, his mustering out.

Joseph Plumb Martin
Memoir, 1830

During the winter of 1775–76, by hearing the conversation and disputes of the good old farmer politicians of the times, I collected pretty correct ideas of the contest between this country and the mother country (as it was then called). I thought I was as warm a patriot as the best of them; the war was waged; we had joined issue, and it would not do to "put the hand to the plough and look back." I felt more anxious than ever, if possible, to be called a defender of my country. . . .

However, the time soon arrived that gratified all my wishes. In the month of June, this year, orders came out for enlisting men for six months from the 25th of this month. The troops were styled new levies; they were to go to New York. And notwithstanding I was told that the British army at that place was reinforced by 15,000 men, it made no alteration in my mind; I did not care if there had been 15 times 15,000, I should have gone just as soon as if there had been but 1,500. I never spent a thought about numbers; the Americans were invincible in my opinion. If anything affected me, it was a stronger desire to see them. . . .

I used frequently to go to the rendezvous, where I saw many of my young associates enlist, had repeated banterings to engage with them, but still when it came "case in hand," I had my misgivings. If I once undertake, thought I, I must stick to it; there will be no receding. Thoughts like these would, at times, almost overset my resolutions.

But . . . I one evening went off with a full determination to enlist at all hazards. When I arrived at the place of rendezvous I found a number of young men of my acquaintance there. The old bantering began — come, if you will enlist I will, says one; you have long been talking about it, says another — come, now is the time. "Thinks I to myself," I will not be laughed into it or out of it, at any rate; I will act my own pleasure after all. But what did I come here for tonight? Why, to enlist; then enlist I will. So seating myself at the table, enlisting orders were immediately presented to me; I took up the pen, loaded it with the fatal charge. . . .Well, thought I, I may as well go through with the business now as not. So I wrote my name fairly upon the indentures. And now I was a soldier, in name at least, if not in practice. . . .

I now bid a final farewell to the service. . . .

When those who engaged to serve during the war enlisted, they were promised a hundred acres of land each, which was to be in their own or the adjoining states. When the country had drained the last drop of service it could screw out of the poor soldiers, they were turned adrift like old worn-out horses,

James Kirby Martin, ed., *Ordinary Courage: The Revolutionary War Adventures of Joseph Plumb Martin* (Saint James, N.Y.: Brandywine Press, 1993) 11–166.

and nothing said about land to pasture them upon. Congress did, indeed, appropriate lands under the denomination of "Soldiers' lands," in Ohio state, or some state, or a future state; but no care was taken that the soldiers should get them. . . . The truth was, none cared for them; the country was served, and faithfully served, and that was all that was deemed necessary. It was, soldiers, look to yourselves, we want no more of you. . . .

They were likewise promised the following articles of clothing per year. One uniform coat, a woolen and a linen waistcoat, four shirts, four pair of shoes, four pair of stockings, a pair of woolen and a pair of linen overalls, a hat or a leather cap, a stock for the neck, a hunting shirt, a pair of shoe buckles, and a blanket. Ample clothing, says the reader; and ample clothing, say I. But what did we ever realize of all this ample store—why, perhaps a coat (we generally did get that) and one or two shirts, the same of shoes and stockings, and, indeed, the same may be said of every other article of clothing—a few dribbled out in a regiment two or three times in a year, never getting a whole suit at a time, and all of the poorest quality; and blankets . . . thin enough to have straws shot through without discommoding the threads. How often have I had to lie whole stormy, cold nights in a wood, on a field, or a bleak hill with such blankets and other clothing like them, with nothing but the canopy of the heavens to cover me. All this too in the heart of winter when a New England farmer, if his cattle had been in my situation, would not have slept a wink from sheer anxiety for them. And if I stepped into a house to warm me when passing, wet to the skin and almost dead with cold, hunger, and fatigue, what scornful looks and hard words have I experienced.

Almost every one has heard of the soldiers of the Revolution being tracked by the blood of their feet on the frozen ground. This is literally true; and the thousandth part of their sufferings has not, nor ever will be told. That the country was young and poor at that time, I am willing to allow; but young people are generally modest, especially females. Now, I think the country (although of the feminine gender, for we say "she" and "her" of it) showed but little modesty at the time alluded to, for she appeared to think her soldiers had no private parts; for on our march from the Valley Forge, through the jerseys, and at the boasted Battle of Monmouth, a fourth part of the troops had not a scrip of anything but their ragged shirt flaps to cover their nakedness, and were obliged to remain so long after. I had picked up a few articles of light clothing during the past winter, while among the Pennsylvania farmers, or I should have been in the same predicament. "Rub and go" was always the Revolutionary soldier's motto. . . .

When we engaged in the service we were promised the following articles for a ration: One pound of good and wholesome fresh or salt beef, or three fourths of a pound of good salt pork, a pound of good flour, soft or hard bread, a quart of salt to every hundred pounds of fresh beef, a quart vinegar to a hundred rations, a gill of rum, brandy, or whiskey per day, some little soap and candies, I have forgot how much, for I had so little of these two articles that I never knew the quantity. And as to the article of vinegar, I do not recollect of ever having any except a spoonful at the famous rice and vinegar thanksgiving in Pennsylvania in the year 1777.

But we never received what was allowed us. Oftentimes have I gone one, two, three, and even four days without a morsel, unless the fields or forests might chance to afford enough to prevent absolute starvation. Often when I have picked the last grain from the bones of my scanty morsel, have I ate the very bones, as much of them as possibly could be eaten, and then have had to perform some hard and fatiguing duty when my stomach has been as craving as it was before I had eaten anything at all. . . . When General Washington told Congress, "The soldiers eat every kind of horse fodder but hay," he might have gone a little farther and told them that they eat considerable hog's fodder and not a trifle of dog's, when they could get it to eat.

We were also promised six dollars and two thirds a month, to be paid us monthly, and how did we fare in this particular? Why, as we did in every other. I received the six dollars and two thirds, till (if I remember rightly) the month of August, 1777, when paying ceased. And what was six dollars and sixty-seven cents of this "Continental currency," as it was called, worth? It was scarcely enough to procure a man a dinner. Government was ashamed to tantalize the soldiers any longer with such trash, and wisely gave it up for its own credit. I received one month's pay in specie while on the march to Virginia, in the year 1781, and except that I never received any pay worth the name while I belonged to the army. Had I been paid as I was promised to be at my engaging in the service, I needed not to have suffered as I did, nor would I have done it; there was enough in the country, and money would have procured it if I had had it. It is provoking to think of it. The country was rigorous in exacting my compliance to my engagements to a punctilio, but equally careless in performing her contracts with me; and why so? One reason was because she had all the power in her own hands, and I had none. Such things ought not to be.

The poor soldiers had hardships enough to endure without having to starve; the least that could be done was to give them something to eat. "The laborer is worthy of his meat" at least, and he ought to have it for his employer's interest, if nothing more. But as I said, there were other hardships to grapple with. How many times have I had to lie down like a dumb animal in the field and bear "the pelting of the pitiless storm," cruel enough in warm weather, but how much more so in the heart of winter. Could I have had the benefit of a little fire, it would have been deemed a luxury. But when snow or rain would fall so heavy that it was impossible to keep a spark of fire alive, to have to weather out a long, wet, cold, tedious night in the depth of winter with scarcely clothes enough to keep one from freezing instantly, how discouraging it must be I leave to my reader to judge.

It is fatiguing, almost beyond belief, to those that never experienced it, to be obliged to march 24 to 48 hours (as very many times I have had to) and often more, night and day without rest or sleep, wishing and hoping that some wood or village I could see ahead might prove a short resting place, when, alas, I came to it almost tired off my legs, it proved no resting place for me. How often have I envied the very swine their happiness, when I have heard them quarreling in their warm dry sties, when I was wet to the skin and wished in vain for that indulgence. And even in dry, warm weather, I have often been so beat out with long and tedious marching that I have fallen asleep while walking the road, and not been sensible of it till I have jostled against someone in the same situation; and when permitted to stop and have the superlative happiness to roll myself in my blanket and drop down on the ground in the bushes, briars, thorns, or thistles, and get an hour or two's sleep, O! how exhilarating.

Fighting the enemy is the great scarecrow to people unacquainted with the duties of an army. To see the fire and smoke, to hear the din of cannon and musketry and the whistling of shot; they cannot bear the sight or hearing of this. They would like the service in an army tolerably well but for the fighting part of it. I never was killed in the army; I never was wounded but once; I never was a prisoner with the enemy; but I have seen many that have undergone all these; and I have many times run the risk of all of them myself. But, reader, believe me, for I tell a solemn truth, that I have felt more anxiety, undergone more fatigue and hardships, suffered more every way, in performing one of those tedious marches than ever I did in fighting the hottest battle I was ever engaged in, with the anticipation of all the other calamities I have mentioned added to it. . . .

It was . . . said at that time that the army was idle, did nothing but lounge about from one station to another, eating the country's bread and wearing her clothing without rendering any essential service. . . .You ought to drive on, said they, you are competent for the business; rid the country at once of her invaders. Poor simple souls! It was very easy for them to build castles in the air, but they had not felt the difficulty of making them stand there. It was easier with them taking whole armies in a warm room and by a good fire than enduring the hardships of one cold winter's night upon a bleak hill without clothing or victuals.

QUESTIONS FOR READING AND DISCUSSION

1. Why did Martin enlist? What ideas were important to him? Why did he have "misgivings" and hesitate for a while?
2. What compensation did he receive for his military service? What food and clothing were promised to him, and what of the promises was supplied?
3. Why, according to Martin, were "poor soldiers . . . turned adrift like old worn-out horses"? Why were the efforts of soldiers not appreciated by other citizens?
4. Given the hardships Martin and other soldiers endured, why did he and others persist? Martin wrote his reminiscences long after the war ended; to what extent might his postwar experiences have shaped his account of his wartime service?

DOCUMENT 4

Joseph Brant Appeals
to British Allies to Keep Promises

In the American Revolution, many Indians allied with the British against the rebellious colonists. In 1776, Joseph Brant, a Mohawk leader, accompanied British colonial officials on a trip to England, where he met the king and queen and delivered an address to the secretary of state, Lord Germain, whom Brant called by the Iroquois name Gorah. Brant asked the British to fulfill the promises that had been made to the Mohawks and other Indians. In the context of the accelerating American Revolution, Brant's address represented an attempt to remind the British that it was in their interest to court Mohawk allies. In 1783, under the Treaty of Paris that ended the Revolution, Britain surrendered to the newly independent states all of the territory east of the Mississippi, from Florida to the Great Lakes, without consulting its Indian allies. Brant wrote the governor of Quebec an impassioned letter asking if it was true that the British had signed the treaty without

considering the claims of their loyal Indian allies. Brant's appeals document Indians' dif-
ficulty in getting European allies to live up to promises made when Indian allies were im-
portant but then neglected when Europeans found it expedient to do so.

Address to British Secretary
of State Lord Germain, 1776

Brother Gorah:

We have cross'd the great Lake and come to this kingdom with our Superintendant Col. Johnson [an official in the British Indian department] from our Confederacy the Six Nations and their Allies, that we might see our Father the Great
King, and joyn in informing him, his Councillors and wise men, of the good intentions of the Indians our bretheren, and of their attachment to His Majesty and
his Government.

Brother: The Disturbances in America give great trouble to all our Nations,
as many strange stories have been told to us by the people in that country. The
Six Nations who alwayes loved the King, sent a number of their Chiefs and Warriors with their Superintendant to Canada last summer, where they engaged their
allies to joyn with them in the defence of that country, and when it was invaded
by the New England people, they alone defeated them.

Brother: In that engagement we had several of our best Warriors killed and
wounded, and the Indians think it very hard they should have been so deceived
by the White people in that country, the enemy returning in great numbers, and
no White people supporting the Indians, they were oblidged to retire to their vi-
lages and sit still. We now Brother hope to see these bad children chastised, and
that we may be enabled to tell the Indians, who have always been faithfull and
ready to assist the King, what His Majesty intends.

Brother: The Mohocks our particular Nation, have on all occasions shewn
their zeal and loyalty to the Great King; yet they have been very badly treated by
his people in that country, the City of Albany laying an unjust claim to the lands
on which our lower Castle is built, as one Klock and others do to those of Conjo-
harrie our Upper Viliage. We have been often assured by our late great friend Sr
William Johnson [the British Indian superintendant who died in 1774] who never
deceived us, and we know he was told so that the King and wise men here would
do us justice; but this notwithstanding all our applications has never been done,
and it makes us very uneasie. We also feel for the distress in which our Bretheren
on the Susquehanna are likely to be involved by a mistake made in the Boundary
we setled in 1768. This also our Superintendant has laid before the King, and we
beg it may be remembered. And also concerning Religion and the want of Ministers of the Church of England, he knows the designs of those bad people and in-
forms us he has laid the same before the King. We have only therefore to request

E. B. O'Callaghan, ed., *Documents Relative to the Colonial History of the State of New
York,* 15 vols. (Albany: Weed, Parsons, 1853–87) 8:670–71; Public Record Office, C.O.
42/44, 133–35, reprinted in Charles M. Johnson, ed., *Valley of the Six Nations* (Toronto:
Champlain Society, 1964) 38–41.

that his Majesty will attend to this matter: it troubles our Nation & they cannot sleep easie in their beds. Indeed it is very hard when we have let the Kings subjects have so much of our lands for so little value, they should want to cheat us in this manner of the small spots we have left for our women and children to live on. We are tired out in making complaints & getting no redress. We therefore hope that the Assurances now given us by the Superintendant may take place, and that he may have it in his power to procure us justice.

Brother: We shall truly report all that we hear from you, to the Six Nations at our return. We are well informed there has been many Indians in this Country who came without any authority, from their own, and gave much trouble. We desire Brother to tell you this is not our case. We are warriors known to all the Nations, and are now here by approbation of many of them, whose sentiments we speak.

Brother: We hope these things will be considered and that the King or his great men will give us such an answer as will make our hearts light and glad before we go, and strengthen our hands, so that we may joyn our Superintendant Col. Johnson in giving satisfaction to all our Nations, when we report to them, on our return; for which purpose we hope soon to be accomodated with a passage

Dictated by the Indians and taken down by
Jo: Chew. Secy

Message to Governor of Quebec, Frederick Haldimand, 1783

Brother Asharekowa and Representatives of the King, the sachems[1] and War Chieftains of the Six United Nations of Indians and their Allies have heard that the King, their Father, has made peace with his children the Bostonians. The Indians distinguish by Bostonians, the Americans in Rebellion, as it first began in Boston, and when they heard of it, they found that they were forgot and no mention made of them in said Peace, wherefore they have now sent me to inform themselves before you of the real truth, whether it is so or not, that they are not partakers of that Peace with the King and the Bostonians.

Brother, listen with great attention to our words, we were greatly alarmed and cast down when we heard that news, and it occasions great discontent and surprise with our People; wherefore tell us the real truth from your heart and we beg that the King will be put in mind by you and recollect what we have been when his people first saw us, and what we have since done for him and his subjects.

Brother, we, the Mohawks, were the first Indian Nation that took you by the hand like friends and brothers, and invited you to live amongst us, treating you with kindness upon your debarkation in small parties. The Oneidas, our neighbors, were equally well disposed towards you and as a mark of our sincerity and love towards you we fastened your ship to a great mountain at Onondaga, the Center of our Confederacy, the rest of the Five Nations approving of it. We were then a great people, conquering all Indian Nations round about us, and you in a

---

[1]**Sachems:** Chiefs.

manner but a handfull, after which you increased by degrees and we continued your friends and allies, joining you from time to time against your enemies, sacrificing numbers of our people and leaving their bones scattered in your enemies country. At last we assisted you in conquering all Canada, and then again, for joining you so firmly and faithfully, you renewed your assuranoes of protecting and defending ourselves, lands and possessions against any encroachment whatsoever, procuring for us the enjoyment of fair and plentiful trade of your people, and sat contented under the shade of the Tree of Peace, tasting the favour and friendship of a great Nation bound to us by Treaty, and able to protect us against all the world.

Brother, you have books and records of our mutual Treaties and Engagements, which will confirm the truth of what I have been telling, and as we are unacquainted with the art of writing, we keep it fresh in our memory by Belts of Wampum deposited in our Council House at Onondaga. We have also received an Ornament for the Head, i.e. a crown, from her late Majesty, Queen Ann, as a token of her mutual and unalterable friendship and alliance with us and our Confederacy. Wherefore, we on our side have maintained an uninterrupted attachment towards you, in confidence and expectation of a Reciprocity, and to establish a Perpetual Friendship and Alliance between us, of which we can give you several instances, to wit, when a few years after the Conquest of Canada, your people in this country thought themselves confined on account of their numbers with regard to a Scarcity of Land, we were applied to for giving up some of ours, and fix a Line or mark between them and Us. We considered upon it, and relinquished a great Territory to the King for the use of his Subjects, for a Trifling consideration, merely as a Confirmation of said Act, and as a proof of our sincere Regard towards them. This happened so late as the year 1768 at Fort Stanwix, and was gratefully Accepted and Ratified by the different Governors and Great men of the respective Colonies on the Sea Side, in presence of our Late Worthy Friend and Superintendent, Sir William Johnson, when we expected a Permanent, Brotherly love and Amity, would be the Consequence, but in vain. The insatiable thirst for Power and the next Object of dissatisfaction to the King's Subjects on the Sea Coast, and they to blind our Eyes, Sent Priests from New England amongst us, whom we took for Messengers of Peace, but we were Surprisingly undeceived when we found soon after, that they came to sow the Seeds of discord among our People, in order to alienate our ancient attachments and Alliance from the King our Father, and join them in Rebellion against him, and when they stood up against him, they first endeavored to ensnare us, the Mohawks, and the Indians of the Six Nations living on the Susquehanna River, and the Oneidas, by which division they imagined the remainder of the Confederacy would soon follow, but to not the Least effect.

About this Sad Period we lost our Greatest Friend, Sir William Johnson, notwithstanding we were unalterably determined to stick to our Ancient Treaties with the Crown of England and when the Rebels attempted to insult the Families and Descendents of our late Superintendent, on whom the management of our affairs devolved, we stuck to them and Protected them as much as in our Power, conducting them to Canada with a determined Resolution inviolably to adhere to our Alliance at the Risque of our Lives Families and Property, the rest of the Six Nations finding the Firmness and Steadiness of us, the Mohawks . . . , followed our Example and espoused the King's cause to this Present Instant.

It is as I tell you, Brother, and would be too tedious to repeat on this Pressing Occasion the many Proofs of Fidelity we have given the King our Father.

Wherefore Brother, I am now Sent in behalf of all the King's Indian Allies to receive a decisive answer from you, and to know whether they are included in the Treaty with the Americans, as faithful Allies should be or not, and whether those Lands which the Great Being above has pointed out for Our Ancestors, and their descendants, and Placed them there from the beginning and where the Bones of our forefathers are laid, is secure to them, or whether the Blood of their Grand Children is to be mingled with their Bones, thro' the means of Our Allies for whom we have often so freely Bled.

QUESTIONS FOR READING AND DISCUSSION

1. What was Brant's message to the British in his statement that "The Disturbances in America give great trouble to all our Nations"? What promises had the British made to the Mohawks? Why had the promises not been kept?

2. Why had the Mohawks "shewn their zeal and loyalty to the Great King"? Did Brant consider the Indians and the British equal partners? How had the Mohawks helped the British, according to Brant?

3. Who were the "Bostonians," and why did Brant think they were important? What were the consequences of the colonists' "insatiable thirst for Power"?

4. Brant affirmed that the British "have books and records of our mutual Treaties and Engagements, which will confirm the truth of what I have been telling, and as we are unacquainted with the art of writing, we keep it fresh in our memory by Belts of Wampum deposited in our Council House." To what extent did these contrasting traditions of communication and record-keeping influence Brant's negotiations and their outcomes?

COMPARATIVE QUESTIONS

1. From the viewpoint of Thomas Paine and Abigail and John Adams, what reasons might account for the treatment of American soldiers described by Joseph Martin? How might Martin have responded to the ideas about popular government expressed by Paine and the Adamses?

2. To what extent did Joseph Brant disagree with ideas expressed by Paine and the Adamses? How might Paine and the Adamses have responded to Brant's alliance with the British?

3. To what extent did the revolutionary experiences documented in this chapter support the ideals of a government of laws advanced in *Common Sense*? To what extent did those experiences provide evidence of a commitment to equality?

4. Judging from the documents in this chapter, to what extent did the achievement of independence fulfill the promises and aspirations of Paine and the Adamses?

CHAPTER 7

BUILDING A REPUBLIC
1775–1789

After the Revolution, Americans no longer had the impetus for unity provided by a common enemy. Divisions among the citizens of the new republic became more pronounced and more noticeable, as individuals and groups sought to realize some of the gains they hoped that independence would bring. In this context of disagreement and — often — of suspicion, proposals were debated for social, educational, and governmental reforms, as well as for new forms of government. The following documents illustrate the context of the debate and the proposals that were made and — in the case of slavery — rejected.

DOCUMENT 1
Benjamin Rush Proposes Republican Education

An enduring republic required properly educated citizens, most thoughtful Americans agreed. But what kind of education was proper? Benjamin Rush, a prominent Philadelphia physician and ardent revolutionary, answered that question in his Thoughts upon the Mode of Education Proper in a Republic, published in 1786. Rush described how education sustained a republic, revealing assumptions about how people learned and how governments depended on the lessons imbibed by their citizens. Rush's Thoughts disclosed many Americans' sense of the fragility of republican government and their optimism that proper education could secure that hard-won legacy of the American Revolution.

Thoughts upon the Mode of Education Proper in a Republic, 1786

The business of education has acquired a new complexion by the independence of our country. The form of government we have assumed has created a new class of duties to every American. It becomes us, therefore, to examine our former habits upon this subject, and in laying the foundations for nurseries of

---

Benjamin Rush, *A Plan for the Establishment of Public Schools and the Diffusion of Knowledge in Pennsylvania; to Which Are Added, Thoughts upon the Mode of Education,*

---

wise and good men, to adapt our modes of teaching to the peculiar form of our government.

The first remark that I shall make upon this subject is that an education in our own is to be preferred to an education in a foreign country. The principle of patriotism stands in need of the reinforcement of *prejudice,* and it is well known that our strongest prejudices in favor of our country are formed in the first one and twenty years of our lives. . . . Passing by . . . the advantages to the community from the early attachment of youth to the laws and constitution of their country, I shall only remark that young men who have trodden the paths of science together, or have joined in the same sports, whether of swimming, skating, fishing, or hunting, generally feel, through life, such ties to each other as add greatly to the obligations of mutual benevolence.

I conceive the education of our youth in this country to be peculiarly necessary in Pennsylvania while our citizens are composed of the natives of so many different kingdoms in Europe. Our schools of learning, by producing one general and uniform system of education, will render the mass of the people more homogeneous and thereby fit them more easily for uniform and peaceable government.

I proceed . . . to inquire what mode of education we shall adopt so as to secure to the state all the advantages that are to be derived from the proper instruction of youth; and here I beg leave to remark that the only foundation for a useful education in a republic is to be laid in RELIGION. Without this, there can be no virtue, and without virtue there can be no liberty, and liberty is the object and life of all republican governments.

Such is my veneration for every religion that reveals the attributes of the Deity, or a future state of rewards and punishments, that I had rather see the opinions of Confucius or Mohammed inculcated upon our youth than see them grow up wholly devoid of a system of religious principles. But the religion I mean to recommend in this place is the religion of JESUS CHRIST.

It is foreign to my purpose to hint at the arguments which establish the truth of the Christian revelation. My only business is to declare that all its doctrines and precepts are calculated to promote the happiness of society and the safety and well-being of civil government. A Christian cannot fail of being a republican. The history of the creation of man and of the relation of our species to each other by birth, which is recorded in the Old Testament, is the best refutation that can be given to the divine right of kings and the strongest argument that can be used in favor of the original and natural equality of all mankind. A Christian, I say again, cannot fail of being a republican, for every precept of the Gospel inculcates those degrees of humility, self-denial, and brotherly kindness which are directly opposed to the pride of monarchy and the pageantry of a court. A Christian cannot fail of being useful to the republic, for his religion teacheth him that no man "liveth to himself." And lastly, a Christian cannot fail of being wholly inoffensive, for his religion teacheth him in all things to do to others what he would wish, in like circumstances, they should do to him. . . .

In order more effectually to secure to our youth the advantages of a religious education, it is necessary to impose upon them the doctrines and discipline of a particular church. Man is naturally an ungovernable animal, and observations on particular societies and countries will teach us that when we add the restraints of ecclesiastical to those of domestic and civil government, we produce in him the highest degrees of order and virtue. . . . Far be it from me to recommend the doctrines or modes of worship of any one denomination of Christians. I only recommend to the persons entrusted with the education of youth to inculcate upon them a strict conformity to that mode of worship which is most agreeable to their consciences or the inclinations of their parents. . . .

NEXT to the duty which young men owe to their Creator, I wish to see a SUPREME REGARD TO THEIR COUNTRY inculcated upon them. . . . Our country includes family, friends, and property, and should be preferred to them all. Let our pupil be taught that he does not belong to himself, but that he is public property. Let him be taught to love his family, but let him be taught at the same time that he must forsake and even forget them when the welfare of his country requires it.

He must watch for the state as if its liberties depended upon his vigilance alone, but he must do this in such a manner as not to defraud his creditors or neglect his family. He must love private life, but he must decline no station, however public or responsible it may be, when called to it by the suffrages of his fellow citizens. He must love popularity, but he must despise it when set in competition with the dictates of his judgment or the real interest of his country. He must love character and have a due sense of injuries, but he must be taught to appeal only to the laws of the state, to defend the one and punish the other. He must love family honor, but he must be taught that neither the rank nor antiquity of his ancestors can command respect without personal merit. He must avoid neutrality in all questions that divide the state, but he must shun the rage and acrimony of party spirit. He must be taught to love his fellow creatures in every part of the world, but he must cherish with a more intense and peculiar affection the citizens of Pennsylvania and of the United States.

I do not wish to see our youth educated with a single prejudice against any nation or country, but we impose a task upon human nature repugnant alike to reason, revelation, and the ordinary dimensions of the human heart when we require him to embrace with equal affection the whole family of mankind. He must be taught to amass wealth, but it must be only to increase his power of contributing to the wants and demands of the state. He must be indulged occasionally in amusements, but he must be taught that study and business should be his principal pursuits in life. Above all he must love life and endeavor to acquire as many of its conveniences as possible by industry and economy, but he must be taught that this life "is not his own" when the safety of his country requires it. . . .

While we inculcate these republican duties upon our pupil, we must not neglect at the same time to inspire him with republican principles. He must be taught that there can be no durable liberty but in a republic and that government, like all other sciences, is of a progressive nature. The chains which have bound this science in Europe are happily unloosed in America. *Here* it is open to investigation and improvement. While philosophy has protected us by its discoveries from a thousand natural evils, government has unhappily followed with an unequal pace. It would be to dishonor human genius only to name the many defects which still exist in the best systems of legislation. We daily see matter of a perishable nature rendered durable by certain chemical operations. In like manner, I conceive that it is possible to analyze and combine power in such a manner as not only to increase the happiness but to promote the duration of republican forms of government far beyond the terms limited for them by history or the common opinions of mankind. . . .

In the education of youth, let the authority of our masters be as *absolute* as possible. The government of schools like the government of private families should be *arbitrary*, that it may not be *severe*. By this mode of education, we prepare our youth for the subordination of laws and thereby qualify them for becoming good citizens of the republic. I am satisfied that the most useful citizens have been formed from those youth who have never known or felt their own wills till they were one and twenty years of age, and I have often thought that society owes a great deal of its order and happiness to the deficiencies of parental government being supplied by those habits of obedience and subordination which are contracted at schools. . . .

From the observations that have been made it is plain that I consider it as possible to convert men into republican machines. This must be done if we expect them to perform their parts properly in the great machine of the government of the state. That republic is sophisticated with monarchy or aristocracy that does not revolve upon the wills of the people, and these must be fitted to each other by means of education before they can be made to produce regularity and unison in government. . . .

Again, let our youth be instructed in all the means of promoting national prosperity and independence, whether they relate to improvements in agriculture, manufactures, or inland navigation. Let him be instructed further in the general principles of legislation, whether they relate to revenue or to the preservation of life, liberty, or property. . . .

But further, considering the nature of our connection with the United States, it will be necessary to make our pupil acquainted with all the prerogatives of the federal government. He must be instructed in the nature and variety of treaties. He must know the difference in the powers and duties of the several species of ambassadors. He must be taught wherein the obligations of individuals and of states are the same and wherein they differ. In short, he must acquire a general knowledge of all those laws and forms which unite the sovereigns of the earth or separate them from each other. . . .

I beg pardon for having delayed so long, to say anything of the separate and peculiar mode of education proper for WOMEN in a republic. I am sensible that they must concur in all our plans of education for young men, or no laws will ever render them effectual. To qualify our women for this purpose, they should not only be instructed in the usual branches of female education but they should be instructed in the principles of liberty and government, and the obligations of patriotism should be inculcated upon them. The opinions and conduct of men are often regulated by the women in the most arduous enterprises of life, and their approbation is frequently the principal reward of the hero's dangers and the patriot's toils. Besides, the *first* impressions upon the minds of children are generally derived from the women. Of how much consequence, therefore, is it in a republic that they should think justly upon the great subjects of liberty and government!

QUESTIONS FOR READING AND DISCUSSION

1. What lessons did Rush believe students must learn in the new American republic? Did he think that young men and women should be taught the same lessons? In what ways would the new republic's schools serve as "nurseries of wise and good men"?

2. Why did Rush believe Christianity was important? In his view, why was it preferable to other religions?

3. How did Rush's plan of education cope with his belief that "man is naturally an ungovernable animal," and why did he propose "to convert men into republican machines"? What were the dangers to republican government that Rush hoped to avoid with his educational plan?

4. How did Rush's assumptions about education and government reflect the legacy of the American Revolution?

DOCUMENT 2

Thomas Jefferson on Slavery and Race

Slavery seemed to many Americans to be inconsistent with the principles of the Revolution. Northern states, where few slaves lived, took the lead in outlawing slavery, but no Southern states abolished slavery. In Notes on the State of Virginia, *written in 1782, Thomas Jefferson explained some of the most important reasons why emancipation never received serious consideration in southern legislatures. Jefferson's explanation, excerpted here, discloses racial views that were widespread among white Americans, North and South.*

Notes on the State of Virginia, 1782

Many of the laws which were in force during the monarchy being relative merely to that form of government, or inculcating principles inconsistent with republicanism, the first assembly which met after the establishment of the commonwealth appointed a committee to revise the whole code, to reduce it into proper form and volume, and report it to the assembly. . . .

The following . . . [is one of] the most remarkable alterations proposed:

To emancipate all slaves born after passing the act. The bill reported by the revisors does not itself contain this proposition; but an amendment containing it was prepared, to be offered to the legislature whenever the bill should be taken up, and further directing, that they should continue with their parents to a certain age, then be brought up, at the public expence, to tillage, arts or sciences, according to their geniusses, till the females should be eighteen, and the males twenty-one years of age, when they should be colonized to such place as the circumstances of the time should render most proper, sending them out with arms, implements of household and of the handicraft arts, feeds, pairs of the useful domestic animals, &c. to declare them a free and independent people, and extend to them our alliance and protection, till they have acquired strength; and to send vessels at the same time to other parts of the world for an equal number of white inhabitants; to induce whom to migrate hither, proper encouragements were to be proposed. It will probably be asked, Why not retain and incorporate the blacks into the state, and thus save the expence of supplying by importation of white settlers, the vacancies they will leave? Deep rooted prejudices entertained by the

Source: Thomas Jefferson, *Notes on the State of Virginia* (1794).

whites; ten thousand recollections, by the blacks, of the injuries they have sustained; new provocations; the real distinctions which nature has made; and many other circumstances, will divide us into parties, and produce convulsions, which will probably never end but in the extermination of the one or the other race. — To these objections, which are political, may be added others, which are physical and moral. The first difference which strikes us is that of colour. Whether the black of the negro resides in the reticular membrane between the skin and scarf-skin, or in the scarf-skin itself; whether it proceeds from the colour of the blood, the colour of the bile, or from that of some other secretion, the difference is fixed in nature, and is as real as if its seat and cause were better known to us. And is this difference of no importance? Is it not the foundation of a greater or less share of beauty in the two races? Are not the fine mixtures of red and white, the expressions of every passion by greater or less suffusions of colour in the one, preferable to that eternal monotony, which reigns in the countenances, that immoveable veil of black which covers all the emotions of the other race? Add to these, flowing hair, a more elegant symmetry of form, their own judgment in favour of the whites, declared by their preference of them, as uniformly as is the preference of the Oranootan for the black women over those of his own species. The circumstance of superior beauty, is thought worthy of attention in the propagation of our horses, dogs, and other domestic animals; why not in that of man? Besides those of colour, figure, and hair, there are other physical distinctions proving a difference of race. They have less hair on the face and body. They secrete less by the kidnies, and more by the glands of the skin, which gives them a very strong and disagreeable odour. This greater degree of transpiration renders them more tolerant of heat, and less so of cold than the whites. . . . They seem to require less sleep. A black after hard labour through the day, will be induced by the slightest amusements to sit up till midnight, or later though knowing he must be out with the first dawn of the morning. They are at least as brave, and more adventuresome. But this may perhaps proceed from a want of forethought, which prevents their seeing a danger till it be present. When present, they do not go through it with more coolness or steadiness than the whites. They are more ardent after their female: but love seems with them to be more an eager desire, than a tender delicate mixture of sentiment and sensation. Their griefs are transient. Those numberless afflictions, which render it doubtful whether heaven has given life to us in mercy or in wrath, are less felt, and sooner forgotten with them. In general, their existence appears to participate more of sensation than reflection. To this must be ascribed their disposition to sleep when abstracted from their diversions, and unemployed in labour. An animal whose body is at rest, and, who does not reflect, must be disposed to sleep of course. Comparing them by their faculties of memory, reason, and imagination, it appears to me that in memory they are equal to the whites; in reason much inferior, as I think one could scarcely be found capable of tracing and comprehending the investigations of Euclid; and that in imagination they are dull, tasteless, and anomalous. It would be unfair to follow them to Africa for this investigation. We will consider them here, on the same stage with the whites, and where the facts are not apocryphal on which a judgement is to be formed. It will be right to make great allowances for the difference of condition, of education, of conversation, of the sphere in which they move. Many millions of them have been brought to, and born in America. Most of them indeed have been confined to tillage, to their own homes, and their own society: yet many have been so situated, that they might have availed themselves of the conversation of their masters; many have been brought up to the handicraft arts, and from that circumstance have always been associated with the whites. Some have been liberally educated, and all have lived in countries where the arts and sciences are cultivated to a considerable degree, and have had before their eyes samples of the best works from abroad. The Indians, with no advantages of this kind, will often carve figures on their pipes not destitute of design and merit. They will crayon out an animal, a plant, or a country, so as to prove the existence of a germ in their minds which only wants cultivation. They astonish you with strokes of the most sublime oratory; such as prove their reason and sentiment strong, their imagination glowing and elevated. But never yet could I find that a black had uttered a thought above the level of plain narration; never see even an elementary trait of painting or sculpture. In music they are more generally gifted than the whites with accurate ears for tune and time, and they have been found capable of imagining a small catch. Whether they will be equal to the composition of a more extensive run of melody, or of complicated harmony, is yet to be proved. Misery is often the parent of the most affecting touches in poetry. — Among the blacks is misery enough, God knows, but no poetry. . . . Their love is ardent, but it kindles the senses only, not the imagination. Religion indeed has produced a Phyllis Whately[1]; but it could not produce a poet. The compositions published under her name are below the dignity of criticism. . . . The improvement of the blacks in body and mind, in the first instance of their mixture with the whites, has been observed by every one, and proves that their inferiority is not the effect merely of their condition of life. . . .

It is not their condition then, but nature, which has produced the distinction. — Whether further observation will or will not verify the conjecture, that nature has been less bountiful to them in the endowments of the head, I believe that in those of the heart she will be found to have done them justice. That disposition to theft with which they have been branded, must be ascribed to their situation, and not to any depravity of the moral sense. The man, in whose favour no laws of property exist, probably feels himself less bound to respect those made in favour of others. When arguing for ourselves, we lay it down as a fundamental, that laws, to be just, must give a reciprocation of right: that, without this, they are mere arbitrary rules of conduct, founded in force, and not in conscience: and it is a problem which I give to the master to solve, whether the religious precepts against the violation of property were not framed for him as well as his slave? And whether the slave may not as justifiably take a little from one, who has taken all from him, as he may slay one would slay him? That a change in the relations in which a man is placed should change his ideas of moral right and wrong, is neither new, nor peculiar to the colour of the blacks. . . .

Notwithstanding these considerations which must weaken their respect for the laws of property, we find among them numerous instances of the most rigid integrity, and as many as among their better instructed masters, of benevolence, gratitude, and unshaken fidelity.—The opinion, that they are inferior in the faculties of reason and imagination, must be hazarded with great diffidence. To justify a general conclusion, requires many observations. . . . [L]et me add too, as a circumstance of great tenderness, where our conclusion would degrade a whole

---

[1]**Phyllis Whately:** Jefferson refers here to Phillis Wheatly (1753?–1784), an African-born poet generally considered the first well-known black writer in America.

race of men from the rank in the scale of beings which their Creator may perhaps have given them. To our reproach it must be said, that though for a century and a half we have had under our eyes the races of black and of red men, they have never yet been viewed by us as subjects of natural history. I advance it therefore as a suspicion only, that the blacks, whether originally a distinct race, or made distinct by time and circumstances, are inferior to the whites in the endowments both of body and mind. It is not against experience to suppose, that different species of the same genus, or varieties of the same species, may possess different qualifications. Will not a lover of natural history then, one who views the gradations in all the races of animals with the eye of philosophy, excuse an effort to keep those in the department of man as distinct as nature has formed them? This unfortunate difference of colour, and perhaps of faculty, is a powerful obstacle to the emancipation of these people. . . .

There must doubtless be an unhappy influence on the manners of our people produced by the existence of slavery among us. The whole commerce between master and slave is a perpetual exercise of the most boisterous passions, the most unremitting despotism on the one part, and degrading submissions on the other. Our children see this, and learn to imitate it; for man is an imitative animal. This quality is the germ of all education in him. From his cradle to his grave he is learning to do what he sees others do. If a parent could find no motive either in his philanthropy or his self-love, for restraining the intemperance of passion towards his slave, it would always be a sufficient one that his child is present. But generally it is not sufficient. The parent storms, the child looks on, catches the lineaments of wrath, puts on the same airs in the circle of smaller slaves, gives a loose to his worst of passions, and thus nursed, educated, and daily exercised in tyranny, cannot but be stamped by it with odious peculiarities. The man must be a prodigy who can retain his manners and morals undepraved by such circumstances. And with what execration should the statesman be loaded, who permitting one half the citizens thus to trample on the rights of the other, transforms those into despots, and these into enemies, destroys the morals of the one part, and the amor patriae of the other. For if a slave can have a country in this world, it must be any other in preference to that in which he is born to live and labour for another: in which he must lock up the faculties of his nature, contribute as far as depends on his individual endeavours to the evanishment of the human race, or entail his own miserable condition on the endless generations proceeding from him. With the morals of the people, their industry also is destroyed. For in a warm climate, no man will labour for himself who can make another labour for him. This is so true, that of the proprietors of slaves a very small proportion indeed are ever seen to labour. And can the liberties of a nation be thought secure when we have removed their only firm basis, a conviction in the minds of the people that these liberties are of the gift of God? That they are not to be violated but with his wrath? Indeed I tremble for my country when I reflect that God is just: that his justice cannot sleep for ever: that considering numbers, nature and natural means only, a revolution of the wheel of fortune, an exchange of situation is among possible events: that it may become probable by supernatural interference! The almighty has no attribute which can take side with us in such a contest. . . . I think a change already perceptible, since the origin of the present revolution. The spirit of the master is abating, that of the slave rising from the dust, his condition mollifying, the way I hope preparing, under the auspices of heaven, for a total emancipation, and that this is disposed, in the order of events, to be with the consent of the masters, rather than by their extirpation.

QUESTIONS FOR READING AND DISCUSSION

1. What were the terms of the emancipation proposal considered by Virginia legislators? Why did the proposal call for colonization?
2. According to Jefferson, what were the differences between the races? Why did he conclude that "It is not their [blacks'] condition, then, but nature, which has produced the distinction"? Did Jefferson believe that blacks were inferior?
3. How did slavery influence masters and other whites? Did slavery have effects on them that Jefferson failed to mention? How did slavery influence slaves, according to Jefferson?
4. Did Jefferson believe that slavery was wrong? Why did he say, "I tremble for my country when I reflect that God is just"? How did he fear slavery would end? How did his hopes for the end of slavery differ from his fears?
5. Reading between the lines of Jefferson's *Notes*, can you detect whether he seemed to believe that his views of slavery and race were typical or unusual as compared with those of other white Americans of the era?

DOCUMENT 3

Making the Case for the Constitution

In the debate on the ratification of the Constitution, Americans argued about how to create a government that defended the achievements of the Revolution without sacrificing its principles. The debate reflected disagreements about the Revolution's achievements and aims. In Federalist Number 10, James Madison explained that the distinctive perils posed by the republican governments instituted during the Revolution were remedied by the proposed federal Constitution. Madison's analysis illustrates the viewpoint of the Constitution's Federalist advocates about the problems and possibilities of American politics.

James Madison
Federalist Number 10, 1787

Among the numerous advantages promised by a well constructed Union, none deserves to be more accurately developed, than its tendency to break and control the violence of faction. The friend of popular governments, never finds himself so much alarmed for their character and fate, as when he contemplates their propensity to this dangerous vice. He will not fail, therefore, to set a due

E. H. Scott. ed., *The Federalist and Other Constitutional Papers,* vol. 1 (Chicago: Scott, Foresman, 1894) 569–74.

value on any plan which, without violating the principles to which he is attached, provides a proper cure for it. The instability, injustice, and confusion introduced into the public councils, have, in truth, been the mortal diseases under which popular governments have everywhere perished; as they continue to be the favorite and fruitful topics from which the adversaries to liberty derive their most precious declamations. The valuable improvements made by the American Constitutions on the popular models, both ancient and modern, cannot certainly be too much admired; but it would be an unwarrantable partiality, to contend that they have as effectually obviated the danger on this side, as was wished and expected. Complaints are everywhere heard from our most considerate and virtuous citizens, equally the friends of public and private faith, and of public and personal liberty, that our governments are too unstable; that the public good is disregarded in the conflicts of rival parties; and that measures are too often decided, not according to the rules of justice, and the rights of the minor party, but by the superior force of an interested and overbearing majority. However anxiously we may wish that these complaints had no foundation, the evidence of known facts will not permit us to deny that they are in some degree true. It will be found, indeed, on a candid review of our situation, that some of the distresses under which we labor, have been erroneously charged on the operations of our governments: but it will be found, at the same time, that other causes will not alone account for many of our heaviest misfortunes; and, particularly, for that prevailing and increasing distrust of public engagements, and alarm for private rights, which were echoed from one end of the continent to the other. These must be chiefly, if not wholly, effects of the unsteadiness and injustice, with which a factious spirit has tainted our public administration;

By a faction, I understand a number of citizens, whether amounting to a majority or minority of the whole, who are united and actuated by some common impulse of passion, or of interest, adverse to the rights of other citizens, or to the permanent and aggregate interests of the community.

There are two methods of curing the mischiefs of faction: The one by removing its causes; the other by controlling its effects.

There are again two methods of removing the causes of faction: The one by destroying the liberty which is essential to its existence; the other, by giving to every citizen the same opinions, the same passions, and the same interests.

It could never be more truly said, than of the first remedy, that it is worse than the disease. Liberty is to faction, what air is to fire, an aliment, without which it instantly expires. But it could not be a less folly to abolish liberty, which is essential to political life, because it nourishes faction, than it would be to wish the annihilation of air, which is essential to animal life, because it imparts to fire its destructive agency.

The second expedient is as impracticable, as the first would be unwise. As long as the reason of man continues fallible, and he is at liberty to exercise it, different opinions will be formed. As long as the connection subsists between his reason and his self-love, his opinions and his passions will have a reciprocal influence on each other; and the former will be the objects to which the latter will attach themselves. The diversity in the faculties of men, from which the rights of property originate, is not less an insuperable obstacle to an uniformity of interests. The protection of these faculties, is the first object of government. From the protection of different and unequal faculties of acquiring property, the possession of different degrees and kinds of property immediately results: and from the influence of these on the sentiments and views of the respective proprietors, ensues a division of the society into different interests and parties.

The latent causes of faction are thus sown in the nature of man; and we see them everywhere brought into different degrees of activity, according to the different circumstances of civil society. A zeal for different opinions concerning religion, concerning government, and many other points, as well of speculation as of practice; an attachment to different leaders, ambitiously contending for preeminence and power; or to persons of other descriptions, whose fortunes have been interesting to the human passions, have, in turn, divided mankind into parties, inflamed them with mutual animosity, and rendered them much more disposed to vex and oppress each other, than to co-operate for their common good. So strong is this propensity of mankind, to fall into mutual animosities, that where no substantial occasion presents itself, the most frivolous and fanciful distinctions have been sufficient to kindle their unfriendly passions, and excite their most violent conflicts. But the most common and durable source of factions, has been the various and unequal distribution of property.—Those who hold and those who are without property, have ever formed distinct interests in society. Those who are creditors, and those who are debtors, fall under a like discrimination. A landed interest, a manufacturing interest, a mercantile interest, a monied interest, with many lesser interests, grow up of necessity in civilized nations, and divide them into different classes, actuated by different sentiments and views. The regulation of these various and interfering interests, forms the principal task of modern legislation, and involves the spirit of party and faction in the necessary and ordinary operations of government.

No man is allowed to be a judge in his own cause; because his interest would certainly bias his judgment, and, not improbably, corrupt his integrity. With equal, nay, with greater reason, a body of men are unfit to be both judges and parties, at the same time; yet, what are many of the most important acts of legislation but so many judicial determinations, not indeed concerning the rights of single persons, but concerning the rights of large bodies of citizens? And what are the different classes of legislators, but advocates and parties to the causes which they determine? Is a law proposed concerning private debts? It is a question to which the creditors are parties on the one side, and the debtors on the other. Justice ought to hold the balance between them. Yet the parties are, and must be, themselves the judges; and the most numerous party, or, in other words, the most powerful faction, must be expected to prevail. Shall domestic manufactures be encouraged, and in what degree, by restrictions on foreign manufactures? are questions which would be differently decided by the landed and the manufacturing classes; and probably by neither with a sole regard to justice and the public good. The apportionment of taxes, on the various descriptions of property, is an act which seems to require the most exact impartiality; yet there is, perhaps, no legislative act in which greater opportunity and temptation are given to a predominant party, to trample on the rules of justice. Every shilling with which they overburden the inferior number, is a shilling saved to their own pockets.

It is in vain to say, that enlightened statesmen will be able to adjust these clashing interests, and render them all subservient to the public good. Enlightened statesmen will not always be at the helm: nor, in many cases, can such an adjustment be made at all, without taking into view indirect and remote considerations, which will rarely prevail over the immediate interest which one party may find in disregarding the rights of another, or the good of the whole.

The inference to which we are brought is, that the causes of faction cannot be removed; and that relief is only to be sought in the means of controlling its effects.

If a faction consists of less than a majority, relief is supplied by the republican principle, which enables the majority to defeat its sinister views, by regular vote. It may clog the administration, it may convulse the society; but it will be unable to execute and mask its violence under the forms of the Constitution. When a majority is included in a faction, the form of popular government, on the other hand, enables it to sacrifice to its ruling passion or interest, both the public good and the rights of other citizens. To secure the public good and private rights against the danger of such a faction, and at the same time to preserve the spirit and the form of popular government, is then the great object to which our inquiries are directed. . . .

By what means is this object attainable? Evidently by one of two only. Either the existence of the same passion or interest in a majority, at the same time, must be prevented; or the majority, having such co-existent passion or interest, must be rendered, by their number and local situation, unable to concert and carry into effect schemes of oppression. If the impulse and the opportunity be suffered to coincide, we well know, that neither moral nor religious motives can be relied on as an adequate control. . . .

From this view of the subject, it may be concluded that a pure democracy, by which I mean a society consisting of a small number of citizens, who assemble and administer the government in person, can admit of no cure for the mischiefs of faction. A common passion or interest will, in almost every case, be felt by a majority of the whole; a communication and concert, results from the form of government itself; and there is nothing to check the inducements to sacrifice the weaker party, or an obnoxious individual. Hence it is, that such democracies have ever been spectacles of turbulence and contention; have ever been found incompatible with personal security, or the rights of property; and have, in general, been as short in their lives, as they have been violent in their deaths. Theoretic politicians, who have patronized this species of government, have erroneously supposed, that by reducing mankind to a perfect equality in their political rights, they would, at the same time, be perfectly equalized and assimilated in their possessions, their opinions, and their passions.

A republic, by which I mean a government in which the scheme of representation takes place, opens a different prospect, and promises the cure for which we are seeking. Let us examine the points in which it varies from pure democracy, and we shall comprehend both the nature of the cure, and the efficacy which it must derive from the union.

The two great points of difference, between a democracy and a republic, are, first, the delegation of the government, in the latter, to a small number of citizens elected by the rest; secondly, the greater number of citizens, and greater sphere of country, over which the latter may be extended.

The effect of the first difference is, on the one hand, to refine and enlarge the public views, by passing them through the medium of a chosen body of citizens, whose wisdom may best discern the true interest of their country, and whose patriotism and love of justice will be least likely to sacrifice it to temporary or partial considerations. Under such a regulation, it may well happen, that the public voice, pronounced by the representatives of the people, will be more consonant to the public good, than if pronounced by the people themselves, convened for the purpose. On the other hand, the effect may be inverted. Men of factious tempers, of local prejudices, or of sinister designs, may by intrigue, by corruption, or by other means, first obtain the suffrages and then betray the interest of the people. The question repeating is whether small or extensive republics are most favorable for the election of proper guardians of the public weal; and it is clearly decided in favor of the latter by two obvious considerations.

In the first place, it is to be remarked, that however small the republic may be, the representatives must be raised to a certain number, in order to guard against the cabals of a few; and that however large it may be, they must be limited to a certain number, in order to guard against the confusion of a multitude. Hence the number of representatives in the two cases not being in proportion to that of the constituents and being proportionably greatest in the small republic, it follows, that if the proportion of fit characters be not less in the large than in the small republic, the former will present a greater option, and consequently a greater probability of a fit choice.

In the next place, as each representative will be chosen by a greater number of citizens in the large than in the small republic, it will be more difficult for unworthy candidates to practice with success the vicious arts, by which elections are too often carried; and the suffrages of the people being more free, will be more likely to centre in men who possess the most attractive merit, and the most diffusive and established characters.

It must be confessed, that in this, as in most other cases, there is a mean, on both sides of which inconveniences will be found to lie. By enlarging too much the number of electors, you render the representative too little acquainted with all their local circumstances and lesser interests; as by reducing it too much, you render him unduly attached to these, and too little fit to comprehend and pursue great and national objects. The Federal Constitution forms, in this respect, a happy combination; the great and aggregate interest being referred to the National — the local and particular, to the State Legislatures.

The other point of difference is, the greater number of citizens and extent of territory, which may be brought within the compass of republican, than of democratic government; and it is this circumstance principally which renders factious combinations less to be dreaded in the former, than in the latter. The smaller the society, the fewer probably will be the distinct parties and interests composing it; the fewer the distinct parties and interests, the more frequently will a majority be found of the same party; and the smaller the number of individuals composing a majority, and the smaller the compass within which they are placed, the more easily will they concert and execute their plans of oppression. Extend the sphere, and you take in a greater variety of parties and interest; you make it less probable that a majority of the whole will have a common motive to invade the rights of other citizens; or if such a common motive exists, it will be more difficult for all who feel it to discover their own strength, and to act in unison with each other. . . .

Hence it clearly appears, that the same advantage, which a republic has over a democracy, in controlling the effects of faction, is enjoyed by a large over a small republic—is enjoyed by the Union over the States composing it. Does this advantage consist in the substitution of representatives, whose enlightened views and virtuous sentiments render them superior to local prejudices, and to schemes of injustice? It will not be denied, that the representation of the Union will be most likely to possess these requisite endowments. Does it consist in the greater security afforded by a greater variety of parties, against the event of any one party being able to outnumber and oppress the rest? In an equal degree does the increased variety of parties, comprised within the Union, increase this security. Does it, in fine, consist in the greater obstacles opposed to the concert and accomplishment of the secret wishes of an unjust and interested majority? Here, again, the extent of the Union gives it the most palpable advantage.

The influence of factious leaders may kindle a flame within their particular States, but will be unable to spread a general conflagration through the other States. A religious sect may degenerate into a political faction in a part of the Confederacy; but the variety of sects dispersed over the entire face of it must secure the national councils against any danger from that source. A rage for paper money, for an abolition of debts, for an equal division of property, or for any other improper or wicked project, will be less apt to pervade the whole body of the Union, than a particular member of it; in the same proportion as such a malady is more likely to taint a particular county or district, than an entire State.

In the extent and proper structure of the Union, therefore, we behold a republican remedy for the diseases most incident to a republican government. And according to the degree of pleasure and pride we feel in being republicans, ought to be our zeal in cherishing the spirit, and supporting the character of, Federalists.

QUESTIONS FOR READING AND DISCUSSION

1. According to Madison, what was a faction? What caused factions? Why did he believe factions to be undesirable?
2. What did he suggest to eliminate the causes of factions? How might the effects of factions be controlled?
3. Why was Madison concerned about "an interested and overbearing majority"? What made a majority dangerous? How would the new Constitution provide checks on majorities?
4. How did a republic differ from a democracy? Which was preferable, according to Madison, and why? Why was a large republic better than a small one?
5. How would the Constitution provide "a republican remedy for the diseases most incident to republican government"? Did Madison believe the Constitution was necessary or simply desirable? Why?
6. To whom might Madison's arguments have most appeal? What audiences did he appear to be addressing?

DOCUMENT 4

Mercy Otis Warren Opposes the Constitution

Opponents of the new Constitution criticized its provisions and its framers, often charging them with subverting the achievements of the American Revolution. The debate in Massachusetts about ratification of the constitution prompted Mercy Otis Warren, a member of a distinguished family of revolutionary leaders who traced their origins back to the Mayflower, *to publish her* Observations on the New Constitution *in 1788 under the pseudonym, "a Columbian Patriot." A brilliant and exceptionally well-educated woman who had been anonymously publishing plays, poems, and essays for fifteen years, Warren argued that the Constitution's framers sought to undermine liberties that Americans had only recently defended from British encroachment. Like other Anti-Federalists, Warren examined specific constitutional provisions to discern Federalists' assumptions about popular government. Her* Observations *disclose Anti-Federalists' deep suspicion of the Constitution, its supporters, and their secret deliberations and hasty plan for ratification.*

Observations on the New Constitution, 1788

Animated with the firmest zeal for the interest of this country, the peace and union of the American States, and the freedom and happiness of a people who have made the most costly sacrifices in the cause of liberty, — who have braved the power of Britain, weathered the convulsions of war, and waded thro' the blood of friends and foes to establish their independence and to support the freedom of the human mind. . . . obliges every one to remonstrate against the strides of ambition, and a wanton lust of domination, and to resist the first approaches of tyranny, which at this day threaten to sweep away the rights for which the brave sons of America have fought with an heroism scarcely paralleled even in ancient republicks. . . . On these shores freedom has planted her standard, [dyed] in the purple tide that flowed from the veins of her martyred heroes; and here every uncorrupted American yet hopes to see it supported by the vigour, the justice, the wisdom and unanimity of the people, in spite of the deep-laid plots, the secret intrigues, or the bold effrontery of those interested and avaricious adventurers for place, who intoxicated with the ideas of distinction and preferment, have prostrated every worthy principle beneath the shrine of ambition. Yet these are the men who tell us republicanism is dwindled into theory — that we are incapable of enjoying our liberties — and that we must have a master. . . . [The] Constitution, which, by the undefined meaning of some parts, and the ambiguities of expression in others, is dangerously adapted to the purposes of an immediate *aristocratic tyranny;* that from the difficulty, if not impracticability of its operation, must soon terminate in the most *uncontrouled despotism.* . . .

And it is with inexpressible anxiety, that many of the best friends to the Union of the States — to the peaceable and equal participation of the rights of nature, and to the glory and dignity of this country, behold the insidious arts, and the strenuous efforts of the partisans of arbitrary power, by their vague definitions of the best established truths, endeavoring to envelope the mind in darkness the concomitant of slavery, and to lock the strong chains of domestic despotism on a country, which by the most glorious and successful struggles is but newly emancipated from the sceptre of foreign dominion. . . .

I will not expatiate long on a Republican *form* of government, founded on the principles of monarchy — a democratick branch with the *features* of aristocracy — and the extravagance of nobility pervading the minds of many of the candidates for office. . . . Some gentlemen with laboured zeal, have spent much time

Mercy Otis Warren, *Observations on the New Constitution, and on the Federal and State Conventions, by a Columbian Patriot* (Boston, 1788).

in urging the necessity of government, from the embarrassments of trade — the want of respectability abroad and confidence in the public engagements at home: — These are obvious truths which no one denies; and there are few who do not unite in the general wish for the restoration of public faith, the revival of commerce, arts, agriculture, and industry, under a lenient, peaceable and energetick government: But the most sagacious advocates for the party have not by fair discussion, and rational argumentation, evinced the necessity of adopting this many-headed monster . . . nor have its friends the courage to denominate it a Monarchy, an Aristocracy, or an Oligarchy, and the favoured bantling[1] must have passed through the short period of its existence without a name, had not Mr. [James]*Wilson*, in the fertility of his genius, suggested the happy epithet of a *Federal Republic.* . . .

[1.] It will be allowed by every one that the fundamental principle of a free government, is the equal representation of a free people. . . . And when society has thus deputed a certain number of their equals to take care of their personal rights, and the interest of the whole community, it must be considered that responsibility is the great security of integrity and honour; and that annual election is the basis of responsibility. . . . [T]he best political writers have supported the principles of annual elections with a precision, that cannot be confuted, though they may be darkened, by the sophistical arguments that have been thrown out with design, to undermine all the barriers of freedom.

2. There is no security in the profered system, either for the rights of conscience, or the liberty of the Press: Despotism usually while it is gaining ground, will suffer men to think, say, or write what they please; but when once established, if it is thought necessary to subserve the purposes of arbitrary power, the most unjust restrictions may take place in the first instance, and an *imprimator*[2] on the Press in the next, may silence the complaints, and forbid the most decent remonstrances of an injured and oppressed people.

3. There are no well defined limits of the Judiciary Powers . . . and as they cannot be comprehended by the clearest capacity, or the most sagacious mind, it would be an Herculean labour to attempt to describe the dangers with which they are replete.

4. The Executive and the Legislative are so dangerously blended as to give just cause of alarm, and every thing relative thereto, is couched in such ambiguous terms — in such vague and indefinite expression, as is a sufficient ground without any other objection, for the reprobation of a system. . . .

5. The abolition of trial by jury in civil causes. . . . [s]hall this inestimable privilege be relinquished in America — either thro' the fear of inquistion for unaccounted thousands of public monies in the hands of some who have been officious in the fabrication of the *consolidated system,* or from the apprehension that some future delinquent possessed of more power than integrity, may be called to a trial by his peers in the hour of investigation?

6. Though it has been said by Mr. *Wilson* and many others, that a Standing-Army is necessary for the dignity and safety of America, yet freedom revolts at the idea, when the . . . Despot, may draw out his dragoons to suppress the mur-

---

[1]**Bantling:** A bratty young child.
[2]**Imprimator:** Official censor.

murs of a few. . . . By the edicts of authority vested in the sovereign power by the proposed constitution, the militia of the country, the bulwark of defence, and the security of national liberty is no longer under the controul of civil authority; but at the rescript of the Monarch, or the aristocracy, they may either be employed to extort the enormous sums that will be necessary to support the civil list — to maintain the regalia of power — and the splendour of the most useless part of the community, or they may be sent into foreign countries for the fulfilment of treaties, stipulated by the President and two thirds of the Senate.

7. Notwithstanding the delusory promise to guarantee a Republican form of government to every State in the Union — If the most discerning eye could discover any meaning at all in the engagement, there are no resources left for the support of internal government, or the liquidation of the debts of the State. Every source of revenue is in the monopoly of Congress. . . .

8. As the new Congress are empowered to determine their own salaries, the requisitions for this purpose may not be very moderate, and the drain for public moneys will probably rise past all calculation. . . .

9. There is no provision for a rotation, nor any thing to prevent the perpetuity of office in the same hands for life; which by a little well timed bribery, will probably be done, to the exclusion of men of the best abilities from their share in the offices of government. — By this neglect we lose the advantages of that check to the overbearing insolence of office, which by rendering him ineligible at certain periods, keeps the mind of man in equilibrio, and teaches him the feelings of the governed, and better qualifies him to govern in his turn.

10. The inhabitants of the United States, are liable to be dragged from the vicinity of their own county, or state, to answer to the litigious or unjust suit of an adversary, on the most distant borders of the Continent; in short the appelate jurisdiction of the Supreme Federal Court, includes an unwarrantable stretch of power over the liberty, life, and property of the subject, through the wide Continent of America.

11. One Representative to thirty thousand inhabitants is a very inadequate representation; and every man who is not lost to all sense of freedom to his country, must reprobate the idea of Congress altering by law, or on any pretence whatever, interfering with any regulations for the time, places, and manner of choosing our own Representatives.

12. If the sovereignty of America is designed to be elective, the circumscribing the votes to only ten electors in this State [Massachusetts], and the same proportion in all the others, is nearly tantamount to the exclusion of the voice of the people in the choice of their first magistrate. It is vesting the choice solely in an aristocratic junto,[3] who may easily combine in each State to place at the head of the Union the most convenient instrument for despotic sway.

13. A Senate chosen for six years will, in most instances, be an appointment for life, as the influence of such a body over the minds of the people will be coequal to the extensive powers with which they are vested, and they will not only forget, but be forgotten by their constituents — a branch of the Supreme Legislature thus set beyond all responsibility is totally repugnant to every principle of a free government.

---

[3]**Junto:** A self-appointed committee or caucus.

14. There is no provision by a bill of rights to guard against the dangerous encroachments of power in too many instances to be named. . . . We are told . . . "that the whole constitution is a declaration of rights" — but mankind must think for themselves, and to many very judicious and discerning characters, the whole constitution with very few exceptions appears to [be a] perversion of the rights of particular states, and of private citizens. — But the gentleman goes on to tell us, "that the primary object is the general government, and that the rights of individuals are only incidentally mentioned, and that there was a clear impropriety in being very particular about them." . . . The rights of individuals ought to be the primary object of all government, and cannot be too securely guarded by the most explicit declarations in their favor. . . .

15. The difficulty, if not impracticability, of exercising the equal and equitable powers of government by a single legislature over an extent of territory that reaches from the Mississippi to the western lakes, and from them to the Atlantic ocean, is an insuperable objection to the adoption of the new system. . . .

16. It is an indisputed fact, that not one legislature in the United States had the most distant idea when they first appointed members for a convention, entirely commercial, or when they afterwards authorised them to consider on some amendments of the Federal union, that they would without any warrant from their constituents, presume on so bold and daring a stride, as ultimately to destroy the state governments, and offer a *consolidated system.* . . .

17. The first appearance of the article which declares the ratification of nine states sufficient for the establishment of the new system, wears the face of dissention, is a subversion of the union of the Confederated States, and tends to the introduction of anarchy and civil convulsions, and may be a means of involving the whole country in blood.

18. The mode in which this constitution is recommended to the people to judge without either the advice of Congress, or the legislatures of the several states, is very reprehensible — it is an attempt to force it upon them before it could be thoroughly understood. . . .

But it is needless to enumerate other instances, in which the proposed constitution appears contradictory to the first principles which ought to govern mankind; and it is equally so to enquire into the motives that induced to so bold a step as the annihilation of the independence and sovereignty of the thirteen distinct states. — They are but too obvious through the whole progress of the business, from the first shutting up the doors of the federal convention and resolving that no member should correspond with gentlemen in the different states on the subject under discussion. . . .

And it is to be feared we shall soon see this country rushing into the extremes of confusion and violence, in consequence of the proceedings of a set of gentlemen, who disregarding the purposes of their appointment, have assumed powers unauthorised by any commission, have unnecessarily rejected the confederation of the United States, and annihilated the sovereignty and independence of the individual governments.

QUESTIONS FOR READING AND DISCUSSION

1. According to Warren, why would the constitution "sweep away" Americans' rights and lead to *"aristocratic tyranny"* or *"uncontrouled despotism"*? Why was the *"Federal Republic"* proposed by the Constitution in reality a "many-headed monster"?

2. In Warren's view, what did the framers of the Constitution perceive as threats? How did they design the Constitution to avoid those threats? In what sense did the Constitution create a *"consolidated system"*?

3. How did Warren disagree with Federalists' diagnosis of threats and their proposals for remedies? What remedies did Warren propose? What constitutional amendments, if any, might have allayed Warren's fears?

4. What assumptions did Warren make about the location and exercise of power?

5. How did Warren's view of the American Revolution influence her critique of the constitution?

COMPARATIVE QUESTIONS

1. What were the principal differences between James Madison's Federalist arguments and Mercy Otis Warren's Anti-Federalist criticisms? To what extent did Madison and Warren agree?

2. Would Benjamin Rush's notions of education appeal equally to Madison, Thomas Jefferson, and Warren? Why or why not? To what extent might education minimize problems caused by factions, majorities, and slavery?

3. How did Jefferson's conclusions about the difficulties of emancipation compare with Madison's views of the dangers of majorities? What minority rights were protected, for example, in Jefferson's Virginia?

4. According to the documents in this chapter, what were the most important qualities for citizens in the new republic? How were those qualities to be created and preserved?

5. What did Rush, Jefferson, Madison, and Warren see as the most important lessons and legacies of the American Revolution?

CHAPTER 8

THE NEW NATION TAKES FORM
1789–1800

The newness of the nation in a long-settled society offered many Americans opportunities for a fresh start, a new departure. Those same opportunities, many other Americans believed, threatened to undermine established institutions, habits, and morals. The 1790s witnessed divisive disputes over just how "new" the new nation should be. Would innovations in government, education, the economy, and politics give shape to recently won liberties or undermine them? The following documents illustrate both the promises and fears of innovation in the new nation.

DOCUMENT 1
Why Free Government Has Always Failed

During the 1790s, many Americans came to believe that the nation was moving backward toward elitism and oligarchy. The free government promised by the Revolution and the Constitution seemed to be subverted by the rule of the few over the many. In his book The Key of Libberty, *published in 1798, William Manning, a self-educated New England farmer, pointed out how elites endangered free government. Manning's remarks, excerpted here, disclosed the profound suspicion many Americans harbored toward those who claimed to be better than their lesser neighbors.*

William Manning
The Key of Libberty, 1798

The reasons why a free government has always failed is from the unreasonable demands and desires of the few. They can't bear to be on a level with their fellow creatures, or submit to the determinations of a legislature where (as they call it) the swinish multitude are fairly represented, but sicken at the idea, and are ever hankering and striving after monarchy or aristocracy where the people have nothing to do in matters of government but to support the few in luxury and idleness.

William Manning, *The Key of Libberty, Shewing the Causes Why a Free Government Has Always Failed,* ed. Samuel Eliot Morison (1922) 231–33.

For these and many other reasons a large majority of those that live without labor are ever opposed to the principles and operation of a free government, and though the whole of them do not amount to one eighth part of the people, yet by their combinations, arts and schemes have always made out to destroy it sooner or later. . . .

Solomon said, train up a child in the way he should go, and when he is old he will not depart from it. And it is as true that if a child is trained up in the way he should not go, when he is old he will keep to it. It is the universal custom and practice of monarchical and despotic government to train up their subjects as much in ignorance as they can in matters of government, and to teach them to reverence and worship great men in office, and to take for truth whatever they say without examining for themselves.

Consequently, whenever revolutions are brought about and free governments established it is by the influence of a few leading men, who, after they have obtained their object (like other men), can never receive compensation and honors enough from the people for their services; and the people being brought up from their youths to reverence and respect such men, they go on old ways and neglect to search and see for themselves and take care of their own interests. Also being naturally very fond of being flattered, they readily hear to measures proposed by great men who, they are convinced, have done them good services. This is the principal ground on which the few work to destroy a free government. . . .

In a free government the few, finding their schemes and views of interest borne down by the many, to gain the power they can't constitutionally obtain, always endeavor to get it by cunning and corruption, conscious at the same time that usurpation, when once begun, the safety of the usurper consists only in grasping the whole. To effect this . . . they . . . unite their plans and schemes by associations, conventions and correspondences with each other. The merchants associate by themselves, the physicians by themselves, the ministers by themselves, the judicial and executive officers are by their professions often called together and know each other's minds, and all literary men and the overgrown rich, that can live without laboring, can spare time for consultation. All being bound together by common interest, which is the strongest bond of union, join in their secret correspondence to counteract the interests of the many and pick their pockets, which is effected only for want of the means of knowledge among them. . . .

Learning is of the greatest importance to the support of a free government, and to prevent this the few are always crying up the advantages of costly colleges, national academies and grammar schools, in order to make places for men to live without work, and so strengthen their party; but are always opposed to cheap schools and women's schools, the only or principal means by which learning is spread among the many. . . .

The doctors have established their medical societies and have both their state and county meetings, by which they have so nearly annihilated quackery of all kinds, that a poor man can't get so great cures of them now for a guinea, as he could fifty years ago of an old squaw for half a pint of rum. The business of a midwife could be performed fifty years ago for half a dollar, and now it costs a poor man five whole ones. . . .

The ministers of the Congregational order and others, for aught I know, have formed themselves into societies and many of them are incorporated and have their state and county meetings which may be of great service or absolutely necessary in their sacred functions. But it is no breach of charity to suppose that they have some political purposes in them; nor do I deny their right to meddle in politics. But . . . instead of preaching about and praying for officers of government as infallible beings, or so perfect that we ought to submit to and praise them for all they do (when in fact they are all our servants and at all times accountable to the people), they ought to teach their hearers to be watchful of men in power, and to guard their own rights and privileges with a jealous eye, and teach them how to do it in a constitutional way.

If their principles forbid this they had better let politics entirely alone, for if they use their great influence to mislead and prejudice their bearers against the true principles of a free government (as many of them have done of late) by praising our executive for making the British treaty, and in short by praising monarchical and despotic government, and running down and blackguarding republican principles and the French nation, they are in fact acting a treasonable and rebellious part and doing all in their power to destroy the government; and their hearers ought not to attend on such teachings. . . . It has been the general practice of all arbitrary governments to prostitute religion to political purposes, and make a handle of this order of men to mislead, flatter, and drive the people by the terrors of the other world into submission to their political schemes and interests. Consequently they ought to be watched and guarded against above all other orders, especially when they preach politics. . . .

No person who is a friend to liberty will be against a large expense in learning, but it ought to be promoted in the cheapest and best manner possible, which in my opinion would be: — For every state to maintain as many colleges in convenient parts thereof as would be attended upon to give the highest degrees of learning, and for every county to keep as many grammar schools or academies in convenient parts thereof as would be attended to by both sexes summer and winter, and no student or scholar to pay anything for tuition, and for the county schools to pay a particular attention to teaching the English language and qualifying its scholars to teach and govern common schools for little children.

And for every town to be obliged to keep as much as six weeks of writing school in the winter and twelve weeks of a woman school in the summer in every part of the town, so that none should be thronged with too many scholars, nor none have too far to travel, and every person be obliged to send his children to school, for the public are as much interested in the learning of one child as another.

If this method of learning was established we should soon have a plenty of school masters and mistresses as cheap as we could hire other labor, and labor and learning would be connected together and lessen the number of those that live without work. Also we should have a plenty of men to fill the highest offices of state for less than half we now give. But instead of this mode of learning the few are always striving to oblige us to maintain great men with great salaries and to maintain grammar schools in every town to teach our children *a b c* all which is only to give employ to gentlemen's sons and make places for men to live without work. For there is no more need of a man's having a knowledge of all the languages to teach a child to read, write and cipher, than there is for a farmer to have the mariner's art to hold plow. . . .

The principal knowledge necessary for a free man to have is obtained by the liberty of the press or public newspapers. But this kind of knowledge is almost ruined of late by the doings of the few. But a few years ago we could have the whole news by one paper in a week, and could put some dependence on what was printed. But the few, being closely combined and determined to destroy our government, find it necessary to destroy the liberty of the press first. To effect this they employ no printers but those that will adhere strictly to their views and interests, and use all the arts and rhetoric hell can invent to blackguard the republican printers and all they print, and strive to make the people believe falsehood for truths and truths for falsehood. And as they have money and leisure they have their papers every day in the week. Consequently the republican printers double their papers, so that a laboring man must now be at the expense of three or four dollars annually and read and study half his time, and then be at a loss to know what is true and what not — thus the few have almost ruined the liberty of the press.

QUESTIONS FOR READING AND DISCUSSION

1. According to Manning, why had free government always failed? Was failure inevitable? Why or why not?

2. How did Manning define "the few"? How did they differ from what he termed "the swinish multitude"? In what ways did the few take advantage of free government? What forms of organization did they have, and why?

3. Why were child-rearing and education important for free government? What kinds of education did Manning favor? What reforms did he recommend?

4. Why did Manning believe that "the principal knowledge necessary for a free man to have is obtained by the liberty of the press or public newspapers"? To what extent had the few undermined the liberty of the press? Why, according to Manning, did freedom of the press strengthen the many against the few?

DOCUMENT 2

Education for Young Women

One index of the liberating influence of revolutionary ideals was the establishment of academies for the education of young women. The Young Ladies Academy of Philadelphia opened in 1787. Its goals were expressed in 1789 by Reverend Sproat, one of its board members. The academy attracted women from all over the nation. The addresses given by prize students Molly Wallace in 1792 and Priscilla Mason in 1793 — excerpted here — suggest that the academy taught more than the knowledge outlined by the Reverend Sproat.

Molly Wallace and Priscilla Mason

Valedictory Addresses at the Young Ladies Academy of Philadephia, 1792, 1793

Rev. Doctor Sproat

The education of youth in the various branches of useful knowledge, appears to be highly important, by the attention paid to it among all nations in a civilized state. Hence we find all polished nations have been peculiarly careful to found and support seminaries of learning, where the rising generation may be

The Rise and Progress of the Young-Ladies' Academy of Philadelphia (1794); reprinted in The Female Experience: An American Documentary, ed. Gerda Lerner (New York: Oxford University Press, 1992) 210–15.

furnished with the best means of instruction, to render them advantageous to themselves, and of public utility in future life. . . . The instruction of female youth, till of late, has not been sufficiently attended to amongst us. . . . The Ladies' Academy, is a new institution in this city. And I cannot but hope, that the plan of female education, now adopted and prosecuted in this excellent seminary, will, merit the approbation and patronage of all who wish well to the learning, virtue and piety of the rising fair of this metropolis. The proficiency these delicate pupils have made, in several branches of useful literature, not only displays the fertility of their blooming geniuses, but reflects honor on the abilities, and praise to the attention of their worthy Preceptor and his assistants in their instruction. Accuracy in orthography, a very necessary part of an early education — reading with propriety their native language — an acquaintance with English grammar — writing a neat and beautiful character — a knowledge of figures, with many of their valuable uses — a general knowledge of the different parts of the terraqueous globe — its divisions, inhabitants, and productions — such knowledge of the planets that compose the solar system, and their periodical motions — together with such a sketch of history, as to remark the rise, progress, declension, and final extinction of the most remarkable states, kingdoms and empires — the virtues which contributed to their greatness, and the vices which were productive of their ruin — these are such valuable branches of literature, as are not only ornamental, but in many respects exceedingly advantageous to the rising generation of the fair sex. Let it suffice to say, that such academical improvements, tend to molify the temper, refine the manners, amuse the fancy, improve the understanding, and strengthen virtue — to lay a foundation for a life of usefulness and happiness here, and if rightly improved, for a blessed immortality hereafter.

Molly Wallace
Valedictory Address, 1792

The silent and solemn attention of a respectable audience, has often, at the beginning of discourses intimidated even veterans in the art of public elocution. What then must my situation be, when my sex, my youth and inexperience all conspire to make me tremble at the task which I have undertaken? But the friendly encouragement, which I behold in almost every countenance, enables me to overcome difficulties, that would otherwise be insurmountable. With some, however, it has been made a question, whether we ought ever to appear in so public a manner. Our natural timidity, the domestic situation to which, by nature and custom we seem destined, are urged as arguments against what I now have undertaken: — Many sarcastical observations have been handed out against female oratory: But to what do they amount? Do they not plainly inform us, that, because we are females, we ought therefore to be deprived of what is perhaps the most effectual means of acquiring a just, natural and graceful delivery? No one will pretend to deny, that we should be taught to read in the best manner. And if to read, why not to speak? . . .

But yet it may be asked, what, has a female character to do with declamation? That she should harangue at the head of an Army, in the Senate, or before a popular Assembly, is not pretended, neither is it requested that she ought to be an adept in the stormy and contentious eloquence of the bar, or in the abstract and subtle reasoning of the Senate; we look not for a female [William] Pitt, Cicero, or Demosthenes. . . .

Why is a boy diligently and carefully taught the Latin, the Greek, or the Hebrew language, in which he will seldom have occasion, either to write or converse? Why is he taught to demonstrate the propositions of Euclid, when during his whole life, he will not perhaps make use of one of them? Are we taught to dance merely for the sake of becoming dancers? No, certainly. These things are commonly studied, more on account of the habits, which the learning of them establishes, than on account of any important advantages which the mere knowledge of them can afford. So a young lady, from the exercise of speaking before a properly selected audience, may acquire some valuable habits, which, otherwise she can obtain from no examples, and that no precept can give. But, this exercise can with propriety be performed only before a select audience: a promiscuous and indiscriminate one, for obvious reasons, would be absolutely unsuitable, and should always be carefully avoided.

Priscilla Mason
Valedictory Address, 1793

Respected and very respectable audience; while your presence inspires our tender minds with fear and anxiety, your countenances promise indulgence, and encourage us to proceed. . . .

A female, young and inexperienced, addressing a promiscuous assembly, is a novelty which requires an apology, as some may suppose. I therefore, with submission, beg leave to offer a few thoughts in vindication of female eloquence. . . .

Is a power of speech, and volubility of expression, one of the talents of the orator? Our sex possess it in an eminent degree.

Do personal attractions give charms to eloquence, and force to the orator's arguments? . . . Do tender passions enable the orator to speak in a moving and forcible manner? . . . In all these respects the female orator stands on equal,—nay, on superior ground. . . .

Granted it is, that a perfect knowledge of the subject is essential to the accomplish'd Orator. But seldom does it happen, that the abstruse sciences, become the subject of eloquence. And, as to that knowledge which is popular and practical . . . who will say that the female mind is incapable?

Our high and mightly Lords (thanks to their arbitrary constitutions) have denied us the means of knowledge, and then reproached us for the want of it. Being the stronger party, they early seized the sceptre and the sword; with these they gave laws to society; they denied women the advantage of a liberal education; forbid them to exercise their talents on those great occasions, which would serve to improve them. They doom'd the sex to servile or frivolous employments, on purpose to degrade their minds, that they themselves might hold unrivall'd, the power and preeminence they had usurped. Happily, a more liberal way of thinking begins to prevail. . . . But supposing now that we possess'd all the talents of the orator, in the highest perfection; where shall we find a theatre for the display of them? The Church, the Bar, and the Senate are shut against us. Who shut them? Man; despotic man, first made us incapable of the duty, and then forbid us the exercise. Let us by suitable education, qualify ourselves for those high departments — they will open before us. They will, did I say? They have done it already. Besides several Churches of less importance, a most numerous and respectable Society, has display'd its impartiality — I had almost said gallentry in this respect. . . . The members of the enlightened and liberal Church . . . look to the soul, and allow all to teach who are capable of it, be they male or female.

But [St.] Paul forbids it! Contemptible little body! The girls laughed at the deformed creature. To be revenged, he declares war against the whole sex: advises men not to marry them; and has the insolence to order them to keep silence in the Church —: afraid, I suppose, that they would say something against celibacy, or ridicule the old bachelor. With respect to the bar, citizens of either sex, have an undoubted right to plead their own cause there. Instances could be given of females being admitted to plead the cause of a friend, a husband, a son; and they have done it with energy and effect. I am assured that there is nothing in our laws or constitutions, to prohibit the licensure of female Attorneys. . . . Heliogabalus, the Roman Emperor of blessed memory, made his grand-mother a Senator of Rome. He also established a senate of women; appointed his mother President; and committed to them the important business of regulating dress and fashions. . . . It would be worthy the wisdom of Congress, to consider whether a similar institution, established at the seat of our Federal Government, would not be a public benefit. . . . Such a Senate, composed of women most noted for wisdom, learning and taste, delegated from every part of the Union, would give dignity, and independence to our manners; uniformity, and even authority to our fashions.

QUESTIONS FOR READING AND DISCUSSION

1. Did Sproat, Wallace, and Mason agree about the ways in which the education of young women should differ from that of young men?

2. Sproat, Wallace, and Mason emphasized "declamation," "oratory," and "the power of speech." Why should women give special attention to public eloquence, according to these individuals?

3. Mason declared that "our high and mighty Lords . . . have denied us the means of knowledge, and then reproached us for the want of it." Why had this happened, according to Mason, and what were the consequences for women?

4. What reforms did Mason propose? Why did she believe a "Senate of women" would be a "public benefit"? How might Sproat or Wallace have responded to Mason's suggestions? How might audiences have reacted?

DOCUMENT 3

Alexander Hamilton on the Economy

No member of George Washington's administration was more important than his brilliant and ambitious secretary of the treasury, Alexander Hamilton. Hamilton had served as Washington's personal secretary and trusted advisor during the Revolution and was a leading proponent of the Constitution and a stronger central government. As secretary of the treasury, Hamilton defined the Federalists' vision of the role of the federal government in the American economy. Encouraging manufacturing was a key feature of that vision, as he explained in his Report on the Subject of Manufactures, submitted to Congress in 1791. The Report, excerpted here, explained how manufacturing strengthened the *agrarian United States both at home and in its relations with foreign powers. Hamilton's Report disclosed fundamental Federalist assumptions about the powers of both the economy and the government.*

Report on the Subject of Manufactures, 1791

The expediency of encouraging manufactures in the United States, which was not long since deemed very questionable, appears at this time to be pretty generally admitted. The embarrassments which have obstructed the progress of our external trade, have led to serious reflections on the necessity of enlarging the sphere of our domestic commerce. The restrictive regulations, which, in foreign markets, abridge the vent of the increasing surplus of our agricultural produce, serve to beget an earnest desire that a more extensive demand for that surplus may be created at home; and the complete success which has rewarded manufacturing enterprise in some valuable branches . . . justify a hope that the obstacles to the growth of this species of industry are less formidable than they were apprehended to be. . . .

[M]anufacturing establishments not only occasion a positive augmentation of the produce and revenue of the society, but . . . they contribute essentially to rendering them greater than they could possibly be without such establishments. . . .

1. As to the division of labor

It has justly been observed, that there is scarcely any thing of greater moment in the economy of a nation than the proper division of labor. The separation of occupations causes each to be carried to a much greater perfection than it could possibly acquire if they were blended. This arises principally from these circumstances:

1st. The greater skill and dexterity naturally resulting from a constant and undivided application to a single object. . . .

2d. The economy of time, by avoiding the loss of it, incident to a frequent transition from one operation to another of a different nature . . . [resulting in] the distractions, hesitations, and reluctances which attend the passage from one kind of business to another.

3d. An extension of the use of machinery. A man occupied on a single object will have it more in his power, and will be more naturally led to exert his imagination, in devising methods to facilitate and abridge labor, than if he were perplexed by a variety of independent and dissimilar operations. Besides this the fabrication of machines, in numerous instances, becoming itself a distinct trade, the artist who follows it has all the advantages which have been enumerated, for improvement in his particular art; and, in both ways, the invention and application of machinery are extended.

And from these causes united, the mere separation of the occupation of the cultivator from that of the artificer, has the effect of augmenting the productive powers of labor, and with them, the total mass of the produce or revenue of a country. In this single view of the subject, therefore, the utility of artificers

Alexander Hamilton, *Report on the Subject of Manufactures* (Washington, D.C., 1791).

or manufacturers, towards producing an increase of productive industry, is apparent.

2. *As to an extension of the use of machinery . . .*

The employment of machinery forms an item of great importance in the general mass of national industry. It is an artificial force brought in aid of the natural force of man; and, to all the purposes of labor, is an increase of hands, an accession of strength, unencumbered too by the expense of maintaining the laborer. May it not, therefore, be fairly inferred, that those occupations which give greatest scope to the use of this auxiliary, contribute most to the general stock of industrious effort, and, in consequence, to the general product of industry?

It shall be taken for granted, and the truth of the position referred to observation, that manufacturing pursuits are susceptible, in a greater degree, of the application of machinery, than those of agriculture. If so, all the difference is lost to a community which, instead of manufacturing for itself, procures the fabrics requisite to its supply from other countries. The substitution of foreign for domestic manufactures is a transfer to foreign nations of the advantages accruing from the employment of machinery, in the modes in which it is capable of being employed with most utility and to the greatest extent.

The cotton-mill, invented in England, within the last twenty years, is a signal illustration of the general proposition which has been just advanced. In consequence of it, all the different processes for spinning cotton are performed by means of machines, which are put in motion by water, and attended chiefly by women and children — and by a smaller number of persons, in the whole, than are requisite in the ordinary mode of spinning. And it is an advantage of great moment, that the operations of this mill continue with convenience during the night as well as through the day. The prodigious effect of such a machine is easily conceived. To this invention is to be attributed, essentially, the immense progress which has been so suddenly made in Great Britain, in the various fabrics of cotton.

3. *As to the additional employment of classes of the community not originally engaged in the particular business*

This is not among the least valuable of the means by which manufacturing institutions contribute to augment the general stock of industry and production. In places where those institutions prevail, besides the persons regularly engaged in them, they afford occasional and extra employment to industrious individuals and families, who are willing to devote the leisure resulting from the intermissions of their ordinary pursuits to collateral labors, as a resource for multiplying their acquisitions or their enjoyments. The husbandman[1] himself experiences a new source of profit and support from the increased industry of his wife and daughters, invited and stimulated by the demands of the neighboring manufactories.

Besides this advantage of occasional employment to classes having different occupations, there is another. . . . This is the employment of persons who would otherwise be idle, and in many cases a burthen on the community, either from

---

[1]**Husbandman:** Farmer.

the bias of temper, habit, infirmity of body, or some other cause, indisposing or disqualifying them for the toils of the country. It is worthy of particular remark that, in general, women and children are rendered more useful, and the latter more early useful, by manufacturing establishments, than they would otherwise be. . . .

4. *As to the promoting of emigration from foreign countries*
    . . . Manufacturers who, listening to the powerful invitations of a better price for their fabrics or their labor, of greater cheapness of provisions and raw materials, of an exemption from the chief part of the taxes, burthens, and restraints which they endure in the Old World, of greater personal independence and consequence, under the operation of a more equal government, and of what is far more precious than mere religious toleration, a perfect equality of religious privileges, would probably flock from Europe to the United States, to pursue their own trades or professions, if they were once made sensible of the advantages they would enjoy. . . .
    If it be true, then, that it is the interest of the United States to open every possible avenue to emigration from abroad, it affords to weighty argument for the encouragement of manufactures. . . .
    Here is perceived an important resource, not only for extending the population, and with it the useful and productive labor of the country, but likewise for the prosecution of manufactures, without deducting from the number of hands which might otherwise be drawn to tillage. . . .

5. *As to the furnishing greater scope for the diversity of talents and dispositions, which discriminate men from each other*
    . . . [T]he results of human exertion may be immensely increased by diversifying its objects. When all the different kinds of industry obtain in a community, each individual can find his proper element, and can call into activity the whole vigor of his nature. And the community is benefited by the services of its respective members, in the manner in which each can serve it with most effect.
    If there be any thing in a remark often to be met with, namely, that there is, in the genius of the people of this country, a peculiar aptitude for mechanic improvements, it would operate as a forcible reason for giving opportunities to the exercise of that species of talent, by the propagation of manufactures.

6. *As to the affording a more ample and various field for enterprise*
    . . . To cherish and stimulate the activity of the human mind, by multiplying the objects of enterprise, is not among the least considerable of the expedients by which the wealth of a nation may be promoted. Even things in themselves not positively advantageous sometimes become so, by their tendency to provoke exertion. Every new scene which is opened to the busy nature of man to rouse and exert itself, is the addition of a new energy to the general stock of effort.
    The spirit of enterprise, useful and prolific as it is, must necessarily be contracted or expanded, in proportion to the simplicity or variety of the occupations and productions which are to be found in a society. It must be less in a nation of mere cultivators, than in a nation of cultivators and merchants; less in a nation of cultivators and merchants, than in a nation of cultivators, artificers, and merchants.

7. As to the creating . . . a more certain and steady demand for the surplus produce of the soil

This . . . is a principal means by which the establishment of manufactures contributes to an augmentation of the produce or revenue of a country, and has an immediate and direct relation to the prosperity of agriculture.

It is evident that the exertions of the husbandman will be steady or fluctuating, vigorous or feeble, in proportion to the steadiness or fluctuation, adequateness or inadequateness, of the markets on which he must depend for the vent of the surplus which may be produced by his labor. . . .

For the purpose of this vent, a domestic market is greatly to be preferred to a foreign one; because it is, in the nature of things, far more to be relied upon. . . .

Considering how fast and how much the progress of new settlements in the United States must increase the surplus produce of the soil, and weighing seriously the tendency of the system which prevails among most of the commercial nations of Europe, . . . there appear strong reasons to regard the foreign demand for that surplus as too uncertain a reliance, and to desire a substitute for it in an extensive domestic market.

To secure such a market there is no other expedient than to promote manufacturing establishments. Manufacturers, who constitute the most numerous class, after the cultivators of land, are for that reason the principal consumers of the surplus of their labor.

This idea of an extensive domestic market for the surplus produce of the soil, is of the first consequence. It is, of all things, that which most effectually conduces to a flourishing state of agriculture. If the effect of manufactories should be to detach a portion of the hands which would otherwise be engaged in tillage, it might possibly cause a smaller quantity of lands to be under cultivation; but, by their tendency to procure a more certain demand for the surplus produce of the soil, they would, at the same time, cause the lands which were in cultivation to be better improved and more productive. And while, by their influence, the condition of each individual farmer would be meliorated, the total mass of agricultural production would probably be increased. . . .

It merits particular observation, that the multiplication of manufactories not only furnishes a market for those articles which have been accustomed to be produced in abundance in a country, but it likewise creates a demand for such as were either unknown or produced in inconsiderable quantities. The bowels as well as the surface of the earth are ransacked for articles which were before neglected. Animals, plants, and minerals acquire a utility and a value which were before unexplored.

QUESTIONS FOR READING AND DISCUSSION

1. In what ways would manufacturing strengthen the United States, according to Hamilton? In his view, how did manufacturing differ from agriculture?
2. In what ways, according to Hamilton, did manufacturing make women and children "more useful"? Why did he think "exertion" was so valuable?
3. How would manufacturing improve the position of the United States in international trade? What was the significance of the "domestic market"? Why would manufacturing stimulate immigration?
4. What assumptions do you think Hamilton was arguing against? What did he believe impeded American manufacturing?

DOCUMENT 4

George Washington's Parting Advice to the Nation

After serving two terms as president, George Washington announced in 1796 that he would not be a candidate for reelection. In a public farewell address published throughout the nation, Washington advised Americans to resist geographic factionalism, partisan divisions, and foreign entanglements in order to preserve their government and thereby their liberty. Washington's unrivaled eminence as the nation's foremost military and political leader gave authority to his advice. Americans referred to his Farewell Address maxims for decades.

"Farewell Address to the People of the United States," 1796

. . . [A] solicitude for your welfare, which cannot end but with my life, and the apprehension of danger, natural to that solicitude, urge me, on an occasion like the present, to offer to your solemn contemplation, and to recommend to your frequent review, some sentiments, which are the result of much reflection, of no inconsiderable observation, and which appear to me all-important to the permanency of your felicity as a People. . . .

Interwoven as is the love of liberty with every ligament of your hearts, no recommendation of mine is necessary to fortify or confirm the attachment.

The unity of Government, which constitutes you one people, is also now dear to you. It is justly so; for it is a main pillar in the edifice of your real independence, the support of your tranquillity at home, your peace abroad; of your safety; of your prosperity; of that very Liberty, which you so highly prize. But as it is easy to foresee, that, from different causes and from different quarters, much pains will be taken, many artifices employed, to weaken in your minds the conviction of this truth; as this is the point in your political fortress against which the batteries of internal and external enemies will be most constantly and actively (though often covertly and insidiously) directed, it is of infinite moment, that you should properly estimate the immense value of your national Union to your collective and individual happiness; that you should cherish a cordial, habitual, and immovable attachment to it; accustoming yourselves to think and speak of it as of the Palladium[1] of your political safety and prosperity; watching for its preservation with jealous anxiety; discountenancing whatever may suggest even a suspicion, that it can in any event be abandoned; and indignantly frowning upon the first dawning of every attempt to alienate any portion of our country from the rest, or to enfeeble the sacred ties which now link together the various parts.

George Washington, "Farewell Address to the People of the United States," *Claypoole's American Daily Advertiser,* September 19, 1796.

[1]**Palladium:** A statute in ancient Troy that was supposed to protect the safety of the city; in general, a safeguard.

For this you have every inducement of sympathy and interest. Citizens, by birth or choice, of a common country, that country has a right to concentrate your affections. The name of AMERICAN, which belongs to you, in your national capacity, must always exalt the just pride of Patriotism, more than any appellation derived from local discriminations. With slight shades of difference, you have the same religion, manners, habits, and political principles. You have in a common cause fought and triumphed together; the Independence and Liberty you possess are the work of joint counsels, and joint efforts, of common dangers, sufferings, and successes.

But these considerations, however powerfully they address themselves to your sensibility, are greatly outweighed by those, which apply more immediately to your interest. Here every portion of our country finds the most commanding motives for carefully guarding and preserving the Union of the whole.

The *North*, in an unrestrained intercourse with the *South*, protected by the equal laws of a common government, finds, in the productions of the latter, great additional resources of maritime and commercial enterprise and precious materials of manufacturing industry. The *South*, in the same intercourse, benefiting by the agency of the *North*, sees its agriculture grow and its commerce expand. . . . The *East*, in a like intercourse with the *West*, already finds, and in the progressive improvement of interior communications by land and water, will more and more find, a valuable vent for the commodities which it brings from abroad, or manufactures at home. The *West* derives from the *East* supplies requisite to its growth and comfort, and, what is perhaps of still greater consequence, it must of necessity owe the *secure* enjoyment of indispensable *outlets* for its own productions to the weight, influence, and the future maritime strength of the Atlantic side of the Union, directed by an indissoluble community of interest as *one nation*. Any other tenure by which the *West* can hold this essential advantage, whether derived from its own separate strength, or from an apostate and unnatural connexion with any foreign power, must be intrinsically precarious.

While, then, every part of our country thus feels an immediate and particular interest in Union, all the parts combined cannot fail to find in the united mass of means and efforts greater strength, greater resource, proportionably greater security from external danger, a less frequent interruption of their peace by foreign nations; and, what is of inestimable value, they must derive from Union an exemption from those broils and wars between themselves, which so frequently afflict neighbouring countries not tied together by the same governments. . . . Hence, likewise, they will avoid the necessity of those overgrown military establishments, which, under any form of government, are inauspicious to liberty, and which are to be regarded as particularly hostile to Republican Liberty. In this sense it is, that your Union ought to be considered as a main prop of your liberty, and that the love of the one ought to endear to you the preservation of the other. . . .

In contemplating the causes, which may disturb our Union, it occurs as matter of serious concern, that any ground should have been furnished for characterizing parties by *Geographical* discriminations, *Northern* and *Southern, Atlantic* and *Western;* whence designing men may endeavour to excite a belief, that there is a real difference of local interests and views. One of the expedients of party to acquire influence, within particular districts, is to misrepresent the opinions and aims of other districts. You cannot shield yourselves too much against the jealousies and heartburnings, which spring from these misrepresentations; they tend to render alien to each other those, who ought to be bound together by fraternal affection. . . .

To the efficacy and permanency of your Union, a Government for the whole is indispensable. . . . Sensible of this momentous truth, you have improved upon your first essay, by the adoption of a Constitution of Government better calculated than your former for an intimate Union, and for the efficacious management of your common concerns. This Government, the offspring of our own choice, uninfluenced and unawed, adopted upon full investigation and mature deliberation, completely free in its principles, in the distribution of its powers, uniting security with energy, and containing within itself a provision for its own amendment, has a just claim to your confidence and your support. Respect for its authority, compliance with its laws, acquiescence in its measures, are duties enjoined by the fundamental maxims of true Liberty. The basis of our political systems is the right of the people to make and to alter their Constitutions of Government. But the Constitution which at any time exists, till changed by an explicit and authentic act of the whole people, is sacredly obligatory upon all. The very idea of the power and the right of the people to establish Government presupposes the duty of every individual to obey the established Government.

All obstructions to the execution of the Laws, all combinations and associations, under whatever plausible character, with the real design to direct, control, counteract, or awe the regular deliberation and action of the constituted authorities, are destructive of this fundamental principle, and of fatal tendency. They serve to organize factions, to give it an artificial and extraordinary force; to put, in the place of the delegated will of the nation, the will of a party, often a small but artful and enterprising minority of the community. . . .

However combinations or associations of the above description may now and then answer popular ends, they are likely, in the course of time and things, to become potent engines, by which cunning, ambitious, and unprincipled men will be enabled to subvert the power of the people, and to usurp for themselves the reins of government; destroying afterwards the very engines, which have lifted them to unjust dominion.

Towards the preservation of your government, and the permanency of your present happy state, it is requisite, not only that you steadily discountenance irregular oppositions to its acknowledged authority, but also that you resist with care the spirit of innovation upon its principles, however specious the pretexts. One method of assault may be to effect, in the forms of the constitution, alterations, which will impair the energy of the system, and thus to undermine what cannot be directly overthrown. . . .

I have already intimated to you the danger of parties in the state, with particular reference to the founding of them on geographical discriminations. Let me now take a more comprehensive view, and warn you in the most solemn manner against the baneful effects of the spirit of party, generally.

This spirit, unfortunately, is inseparable from our nature, having its root in the strongest passions of the human mind. It exists under different shapes in all governments, more or less stifled, controlled, or repressed; but, in those of the popular form, it is seen in its greatest rankness, and is truly their worst enemy.

The alternate domination of one faction over another, sharpened by the spirit of revenge, natural to party dissension, which in different ages and countries has perpetrated the most horrid enormities, is itself a frightful despotism. But this leads at length to a more formal and permanent despotism. The disorders and miseries, which result, gradually incline the minds of men to seek security and repose in the absolute power of an individual; and sooner or later the chief of some prevailing faction, more able or more fortunate than his competitors, turns this disposition to the purposes of his own elevation, on the ruins of Public Liberty. . . .

There is an opinion, that parties in free countries are useful checks upon the administration of the Government, and serve to keep alive the spirit of Liberty. This within certain limits is probably true; and in Governments of a Monarchical cast, Patriotism may look with indulgence, if not with favor, upon the spirit of party. But in those of the popular character, in Governments purely elective, it is a spirit not to be encouraged. From their natural tendency, it is certain there will always be enough to that spirit for every salutary purpose. And, there being constant danger of excess, the effort ought to be, by force of public opinion, to mitigate and assuage it. A fire not to be quenched, it demands a uniform vigilance to prevent its bursting into a flame, lest, instead of warming, it should consume. . . .

Of all the dispositions and habits, which lead to political prosperity, Religion and Morality are indispensable supports. In vain would that man claim the tribute of Patriotism, who should labor to subvert these great pillars of human happiness, these firmest props of the duties of Men and Citizens. . . .

As a very important source of strength and security, cherish public credit. One method of preserving it is, to use it as sparingly as possible; avoiding occasions of expense by cultivating peace, but remembering also that timely disbursements to prepare for danger frequently prevent much greater disbursements to repel it; avoiding likewise the accumulation of debt, not only by shunning occasions of expense, but to vigorous exertions in time of peace to discharge the debts, which unavoidable wars may have occasioned, not ungenerously throwing upon posterity the burthen, which we ourselves ought to bear. The execution of these maxims belongs to your representatives, but it is necessary that public opinion should cooperate. . . . [I]t is essential that you should practically bear in mind, that towards the payment of debts there must be Revenue; that to have Revenue there must be taxes; that no taxes can be devised, which are not more or less inconvenient and unpleasant. . . .

Observe good faith and justice towards all Nations; cultivate peace and harmony with all. . . . In the execution of such a plan, nothing is more essential, than that permanent, inveterate antipathies against particular Nations, and passionate attachments for others, should be excluded. . . . The Nation, which indulges towards another an habitual hatred, or an habitual fondness, is in some degree a slave. It is a slave to its animosity or to its affection, either of which is sufficient to lead it astray from its duty and its interest. . . .

Against the insidious wiles of foreign influence (I conjure you to believe me, fellow-citizens,) the jealousy of a free people ought to be *constantly* awake; since history and experience prove, that foreign influence is one of the most baneful foes of Republican Government. . . .

The great rule of conduct for us, in regard to foreign nations, is, in extending our commercial relations, to have with them as little *political* connexion as possible. So far as we have already formed engagements, let them be fulfilled with perfect good faith. Here let us stop.

Europe has a set of primary interests, which to us have none, or a very remote relation. Hence she must be engaged in frequent controversies, the causes of which are essentially foreign to our concerns. Hence, therefore, it must be unwise in us to implicate ourselves, by artificial ties, in the ordinary vicissitudes of her politics, or the ordinary combinations and collisions of her friendships or enmities.

Our detached and distant situation invites and enables us to pursue a different course. . . . It is our true policy to steer clear of permanent alliances with any portion of the foreign world. . . .

In offering to you, my countrymen, these counsels of an old and affectionate friend, I . . . may even flatter myself, that they may be productive of some partial benefit, some occasional good; that they may now and then recur to moderate the fury of party spirit, to warn against the mischiefs of foreign intrigue, to guard against the impostures of pretended patriotism. . . .

QUESTIONS FOR READING AND DISCUSSION

1. In what ways, according to Washington, was "unity of Government" the "main pillar" of "independence? What experiences, ideas, and beliefs did he believe unified Americans? What did he think undermined unity? How did he describe the Constitution as strengthening unity?

2. Why, according to Washington, were parties more dangerous in a republic than in a monarchy? If "the spirit of party" was, as Washington argued, "inseparable from our nature," how could it be controlled or restrained? Was Washington's advice wholly free of party spirit?

3. Why did Washington believe it was so important "to steer clear of permanent alliances"?

4. Would any Americans have been surprised by Washington's advice or opposed to it? If so, why?

COMPARATIVE QUESTIONS

1. To what extent did William Manning and George Washington agree about the threats to liberty? How might Washington have responded to Manning's fears of the few? How might Manning have replied to Washington's warnings about factions?

2. How did Manning's views of education and its significance compare with those of the Reverend Sproat, Molly Wallace, and Priscilla Mason? Which views would be likely to have appealed to Alexander Hamilton or Washington?

3. Manning was more pessimistic about the fate of the new nation than Hamilton and Washington. What was the source of Manning's pessimism? In contrast, why were Hamilton and Washington more optimistic?

4. Each of the documents in this chapter envisions liberty as a precious source of power. To what extent did the authors of these documents agree about the uses and abuses of liberty's power? As each author looked toward the future, what threats to liberty did he or she see looming on the horizon, and how could these threats be avoided?

CHAPTER 9

REPUBLICAN ASCENDANCY
1800–1824

I n the early republic, Americans continually referred to the ideals of the Revolution to measure the nation's progress, as the following documents illustrate. Signs of unmistakable progress seemed clearest to Jeffersonian
Republicans, who claimed to embody the revolutionary legacy. Politicians were
not the only ones inspired by the Revolution. Farmers moving to the frontier, for
example, claimed the right to pursue happiness on lands inhabited for millennia
by Indians. They gathered in great revival meetings to confess their sins and profess their salvation, but not their dispossession of Indians. Thomas Jefferson and
other leaders seldom hesitated to uphold the rights of white citizens at the expense of Native Americans and African Americans. Few white Americans believed that the inalienable rights inscribed in the Declaration of Independence
extended beyond white men.

DOCUMENT 1
A Jeffersonian Sailmaker's Fourth of July Address

*Fourth of July celebrations featured not just eating, drinking, and fireworks, but also pa-
triotic speeches. Orators invoked the heritage of the American Revolution and surveyed
the nation's achievements made possible by the legacy of freedom and equality. In 1806,
Peter Wendover, a prosperous New York sailmaker and Jeffersonian politician, delivered
an address — excerpted here — to a group of fellow artisans. Wendover's remarks disclosed the pride in the Revolution felt by most Americans and the Jeffersonians' belief
that they were the Revolution's true heirs.*

Peter Wendover
Oration, July 4, 1806

Bretheren, Friends, Fellow Citizens!

When you reflect on the occasion for which we are assembled, and consider for a moment why we have set apart this great anniversary; when you take a view of the scenes that are past, and retrospect to the circumstances which gave rise to our joys; while your hearts beat high with exultation, with me you will exclaim, the subject is highly momentous; the task too important for the Speaker of the Day. . . .

Untaught in the rudiments of language; not versed in the embellishments of diction, or strains of eloquence, I claim your indulgence for a short season, while I presume to remind you that the purpose for which we are collected, is . . . for mutual congratulations that COLUMBIA IS FREE! . . .

Among the various occurrences in which civil society can feel an interest, the EMANCIPATION of a Nation appears to be the greatest; and the annual celebration of such an event is doubtless a duty of public importance. This duty is not only founded on rational principles, but is sanctioned by the oracles of truth. . . .

It would not comport with our present engagements to enter into a detail of the situation of our progenitors who fled from the tyranny of Britain to seek an asylum in this *Western World;* let it be remembered that their love of liberty was rational, and founded on the boasted professions of a nation where it did *not exist.*

Uncontaminated with the vices of the old world, and separated from the scene of pageantry and adulation by the waters of the Atlantic, they fondly imagined that *they* and *their children* would be permitted to cultivate the arts of peace, uninterrupted by the broils of Europe, and undisturbed by the *satellites of power.* Not over solicitous for the exercise of external self-government, and firmly attached to the country from which they had emanated, they were obedient to its sovereign, and respected its laws. Justly appreciating the blessings conferred on them by a bountiful Providence, their hearts glowed in high expectation of *future prosperity* and *long repose.* But, alas! tyranny, ever insatiable, unhallowed ambition, for ever on the rack, not content to wave the sceptre in peaceful sway, the court of Britain seemed to suspect that the benignity of Heaven would lavish its bounties on these favored climes. Well aware that the happiness of the subject would not comport with the views of the monarch, a pretext was sought to curtail our native privileges, and make us submit to terms of the *greatest degradation.* . . .

The Fleets and Armies of England, composed of the slaves of tyrants from home, and purchased vassals from abroad, arrived in splendor, and debarked on our shores, with the instruments of death. Not inured to the tactics of war, untaught in the practice of barbarity, not accustomed to the clang of arms, America trembles; all awake to foreboding fears. All alarmed at the clouds that thicken,

Peter Wendover, National Deliverance: An Oration . . . The Fourth of July, 1806 (1806), reprinted in *Keepers of the Revolution: New Yorkers in the Early Republic,* ed. Paul A. Gilje and Howard B. Rock (Ithaca, N.Y.: Cornell University Press, 1992) 162–69.

Americans collect. The crisis is truly distressing — *Death is a terror,* but *slavery is death.*

Driven by dire necessity to act on the defensive, and conscious of the justice of their cause, the persecuted citizens of Columbia, appealing for protection to the SOVEREIGN of the UNIVERSE, they prepared for the conflict, and met the merciless foe. . . .

The valour of Englishmen is put to the test — Infatuated Britain must humble. Her armies must yield. — For WASHINGTON COMMANDS! . . .

Ye soldiers of liberty, who braved the dangers of the raging battle, on this day of happy triumph we remember your sufferings, we feel for your wrongs! . . .

Having struggled through a long and arduous contest, and obtained a rank among the nations of the earth; it was left for Americans to convince the potentates of Europe, that the end of all *just governments* was the *happiness* of the governed. And finding by experience that a temporary compact could not be productive of permanent advantages, the Genius of America, ever watchful for the interests of posterity, suggested an improvement, exhibiting competent energy, combined with FREE REPRESENTATION and EQUAL RIGHTS. . . .

The same year in which the government of the Union became consolidated, we beheld the commencement of a revolution, *sublime* in its *origin,* but dreadful in its *effects.* The subjects of the French King, having long groaned under the burden of oppression, taking example from the *courage* and *magnanimity of Americans,* burst their chains and nobly contended for the RIGHTS OF MAN.

Alarmed at the enthusiasm of a powerful people, the monarchs of Europe trembled for the consequences; and the peaceful citizens of Columbia, sympathising with the advocates for freedom, feared an entanglement in the general *commotion.* But here we were again permitted to see a happy deliverance — *Peace* was preserved to our favored country, while, with indescribable profusion, all Europe was drenched in human gore. . . .

But, my countrymen, assembled to celebrate the heroism of our citizens, and to recount the blessings of our inheritance, let us remember the high obligations we are under to acknowledge that GOD, who interposed for our country, relieved us from thraldom, and saved us with an omnipotent arm. . . .

Under his propitious care we have been permitted to raise up the fair fabric of EQUAL LAWS, and to cement our dear-bought rights under a CONSTITUTION, founded on the broad basis of *rational liberty;* unalloyed by hereditary absurdity, or regal power; and well calculated to promote the *happiness* of the nation when *sceptres* and *despots* shall lose all their charms!

Let us congratulate our country that, at this day, when the nations of Europe are deluged with war, and held in bondage, we enjoy peace. Governed by laws emanating from the people, and faithfully administered by the wisdom of a JEFFERSON — Excellent citizen — enlightened statesman! In vain shall cruel slander attach the epithet Infidel! Thy FAME shall live in the breasts of *Freemen* — Thy VIRTUES and REPUBLICANISM, shall be celebrated by the world, and with the glories of WASHINGTON, descend to unborn millions; and the tongue of calumny shall confess, that *infidelity* in thee, consists solely in opposing the doctrine, that "A *government by Nobles is the most stupendous fabric of human invention!"*

Let us rejoice that, amidst the profuse blessings of an extensive and fertile country, we enjoy, unawed by tyrants, the sacred right of *elective franchise.* Let us ever recollect, that the preservation of our liberties depend, under *Providence,* on the *purity of legislation,* and the *morality of the people.* Can it ever be contended that *corrupt* measures will produce *pure* effects? Or that men, morally dishonest, may *safely* be trusted with our invaluable rights? Or will even absurdity insist, that citizens, vicious in their practices, are calculated to promote principles of morality, so very essential to public happiness? Let it be indelibly written in our political creed, that PUBLIC LIBERTY and PUBLIC VIRTUE are indissolubly connected — and that where the latter is extinct, the former must expire. Let our children be early and faithfully taught, that acts to be *rightful,* must ever be *just.* That republican principles and true patriotism, can only be promoted by the practice of the *moral virtues* and *conscious integrity.* . . .

Let us ever recollect, that we are accountable for the improvement of our privileges to that GOD who governs the nations, and awards the destinies of men. And remember, that for our advantage he affords us the inestimable blessings of the GOSPEL OF PEACE — the precepts of which, above all others, are eminently calculated to inculcate that excellent maxim, of "doing to others as we wish them to do unto us." These will not fail to promote the best interests of our COUNTRY and the *happiness* of MAN.

QUESTIONS FOR READING AND DISCUSSION

1. According to Wendover, what caused the American Revolution? What lessons did the Revolution teach? How did it influence France?

2. Wendover declared that "the end of all *just governments* was the *happiness* of the *governed.*" How did he define happiness? In what ways did the governed express their happiness? To what extent did the United States embody just government? Who supported unjust government, according to Wendover, and why?

3. Although Wendover emphasized that Jefferson exemplified values embraced by all Americans, how might Jefferson's political opponents have replied to Wendover's statements? Would they have differed principally about Wendover's claims for Jefferson's virtues? Would they have contested Wendover's description of the nation's embodiment of the revolutionary promise of just government?

DOCUMENT 2

Thomas Jefferson's Private and Public Indian Policy

Diplomatic relations with Native Americans were among the new nation's most important activities. A growing population and the rush of settlers to frontier farms pushed to the fore issues of access to Indian lands and subordination of tribal authority to the trade, laws, and customs of white Americans. President Thomas Jefferson outlined his strategy for Indian affairs in 1803 in a private letter to the governor of Indiana Territory, William H. Harrison, excerpted here. In public, Jefferson expressed his Indian policy many times when visiting delegations of Native Americans came to Washington, D.C. Jefferson's address to the Mandans — the source of the next selection — illustrates the public face of American policy.

Letter to Governor William H. Harrison, February 27, 1803

You receive from time to time information and instructions as to our Indian affairs. These communications being for the public records, are restrained always to particular objects and occasions; but this letter being unofficial and private, I may with safety give you a more extensive view of our policy respecting the Indians, that you may the better comprehend the parts dealt out to you in detail through the official channel, and observing the system of which they make a part, conduct yourself in unison with it in cases where you are obliged to act without instruction. Our system is to live in perpetual peace with the Indians, to cultivate an affectionate attachment from them, by everything just and liberal which we can do for them within the bounds of reason, and by giving them effectual protection against wrongs from our own people. The decrease of game rendering their subsistence by hunting insufficient, we wish to draw them to agriculture, to spinning and weaving. The latter branches they take up with great readiness, because they fall to the women, who gain by quitting the labors of the field for those which are exercised within doors. When they withdraw themselves to the culture of a small piece of land, they will perceive how useless to them are their extensive forests, and will be willing to pare them off from time to time in exchange for necessaries for their farms and families. To promote this disposition to exchange lands, which they have to spare and we want, for necessaries, which we have to spare and they want, we shall push our trading uses, and be glad to see the good and influential individuals among them run in debt, because we observe that when these debts get beyond what the individuals can pay, they become willing to lop them off by a cession of lands. At our trading houses, too, we mean to sell so low as merely to repay us cost and charges, so as neither to lessen or enlarge our capital. This is what private traders cannot do, for they must gain; they will consequently retire from the competition, and we shall thus get clear of this pest without giving offence or umbrage to the Indians. In this way our settlements will gradually circumscribe and approach the Indians, and they will in time either incorporate with us as citizens of the United States, or remove beyond the Mississippi. The former is certainly the termination of their history most happy for themselves; but, in the whole course of this, it is essential to cultivate their love. As to their fear, we presume that our strength and their weakness is now so visible that they must see we have only to shut our hand to crush them, and that all our liberalities to them proceed from motives of pure humanity only. Should any tribe be fool-hardy enough to take up the hatchet at any time, the seizing the whole country of that tribe, and driving them across the Mississippi, as the only condition of peace, would be an example to others, and a furtherance of our final consolidation.

Combined with these views, and to be prepared against the occupation of Louisiana by a powerful and enterprising people, it is important that, setting less value on interior extension of purchases from the Indians, we bend our whole views to the purchase and settlement of the country on the Mississippi, from its

The Writings of Thomas Jefferson, vols. 3 and 4, ed. Henry A. Washington (Washington, D.C.: Taylor and Maury, 1853–1854).

mouth to its northern regions, that we may be able to present as strong a front on our western as on our eastern border, and plant on the Mississippi itself the means of its own defence. . . . Of the means, however, of obtaining what we wish, you will be the best judge; and I have given you this view of the system which we suppose will best promote the interests of the Indians and ourselves, and finally consolidate our whole country to one nation only; that you may be enabled the better to adapt your means to the object, for this purpose we have given you a general commission for treating. The crisis is pressing: whatever can now be obtained must be obtained quickly. The occupation of New Orleans, hourly expected, by the French, is already felt like a light breeze by the Indians. You know the sentiments they entertain of that nation; under the hope of their protection they will immediately stiffen against cessions of lands to us. We had better, therefore, do at once what can now be done.

I must repeat that this letter is to be considered as private and friendly, and is not to control any particular instructions which you may receive through official channel. You will also perceive how sacredly it must be kept within your own breast, and especially how improper to be understood by the Indians. For their interests and their tranquillity it is best they should see only the present age of their history.

"Address to the Wolf and People of the Mandan Nation," December 30, 1806

My children, the Wolf and people of the Mandan nation: — I take you by the hand of friendship and give you a hearty welcome to the seat of the government of the United States. The journey which you have taken to visit your fathers on this side of our island is a long one, and your having undertaken it is a proof that you desired to become acquainted with us. . . .

My friends and children, we are descended from the old nations which live beyond the great water, but we and our forefathers have been so long here that we seem like you to have grown out of this land. We consider ourselves no longer of the old nations beyond the great water, but as united in one family with our red brethren here. The French, the English, the Spaniards, have now agreed with us to retire from all the country which you and we hold between Canada and Mexico, and never more to return to it. And remember the words I now speak to you, my children, they are never to return again. We are now your fathers; and you shall not lose by the change. As soon as Spain had agreed to withdraw from all the waters of the Missouri and Mississippi, I felt the desire of becoming acquainted with all my red children beyond the Mississippi, and of uniting them with us as we have those on this side of that river, in the bonds of peace and friendship. I wished to learn what we could do to benefit them by furnishing them the necessaries they want in exchange for their furs and peltries. I therefore sent our beloved man, Captain [Meriwether] Lewis, one of my own family, to go up the Missouri river to get acquainted with all the Indian nations in its neighborhood, to take them by the hand, deliver my talks to them, and to inform us in what way we could be useful to them. Your nation received him kindly, you have taken him by the hand and been friendly to him. My children, I thank you for the services you rendered him, and for your attention to his words. He will now tell us where we should establish trading houses to be convenient to you all, and what we must send to them.

My friends and children, I have now an important advice to give you. I have already told you that you and all the red men are my children, and I wish you to live in peace and friendship with one another as brethren of the same family ought to do. How much better is it for neighbors to help than to hurt one another; how much happier must it make them. If you will cease to make war on one another, if you will live in friendship with all mankind, you can employ all your time in providing food and clothing for yourselves and your families. Your men will not be destroyed in war, and your women and children will lie down to sleep in their cabins without fear of being surprised by their enemies and killed or carried away. Your numbers will be increased instead of diminishing, and you will live in plenty and in quiet. My children, I have given this advice to all your red brethren on this side of the Mississippi; they are following it, they are increasing in their numbers, are learning to clothe and provide for their families as we do. Remember then my advice, my children, carry it home to your people, and tell them that from the day that they have become all of the same family, from the day that we became father to them all, we wish, as a true father should do, that we may all live together as one household, and that before they strike one another, they should go to their father and let him endeavor to make up the quarrel.

My children, you are come from the other side of our great island, from where the sun sets, to see your new friends at the sun rising. . . . I very much desire that you should not stop here, but go . . . and visit our great cities . . . and see how many friends and brothers you have here. . . . I wish you, my children, to see all you can, and to tell your people all you see; because I am sure the more they know of us, the more they will be our hearty friends. . . .

My children, I have long desired to see you; I have now opened my heart to you, let my words sink into your hearts and never be forgotten. If ever lying people or bad spirits should raise up clouds between us, call to mind what I have said, and what you have seen yourselves. Be sure there are some lying spirits between us; let us come together as friends and explain to each other what is misrepresented or misunderstood, the clouds will fly away like morning fog, and the sun of friendship appear and shine forever bright and clear between us.

QUESTIONS FOR READING AND DISCUSSION

1. In his private letter to Harrison, what goals did Jefferson state for the nation's policy toward Indians, and how could they be attained? What impediments did Jefferson foresee to carrying out his policy?
2. From the Indians' perspective, why would being drawn into "agriculture, to spinning and weaving" be appealing? How would such a change alter their ways of life? What alternatives did Indians have?
3. What did Jefferson mean by declaring, "For their own interests and their tranquillity it is best they should see only the present age of their history"?
4. In his address to the Mandan people, how did Jefferson's description of the nation's goals differ from that in his letter to Harrison? Why did Jefferson speak so differently to the Mandans and to Harrison?
5. What was implied by Jefferson's referring to the Indians as "my children"? To what extent was Jefferson's plan an assertion of racial and cultural superiority? Did Jefferson overlook alternatives for relations with Indians?

DOCUMENT 3

Meriwether Lewis Describes the Shoshone

When President Jefferson arranged the Louisiana Purchase in 1803, he did not know pre-cisely what the nation was buying. He had already arranged for a small expedition, com-manded by Meriwether Lewis and William Clark, both soldiers, to make their way up the Missouri River, from its mouth at St. Louis to its headwaters someplace in the mountains of the uncharted interior, and to search out a route to the Pacific Ocean. Jefferson ex-pected Lewis and Clark to be keen-eyed observers not only of the natural environment but also of the Native Americans they encountered along the way. After almost a year and a half of sailing, rowing, pushing, and pulling their heavily loaded boats upstream, they reached the land of the Shoshone, home of their interpreter Sacajawea, near the Continen-tal Divide in present-day Montana. Lewis and Clark desperately needed horses from the Shoshone in order to cross the Rocky Mountains and make their way to the West Coast. While negotiating for the horses and waiting for them to be rounded up, Lewis noted in his journal — excerpted here — Shoshone traits that caught his eye.

The Journals of the Lewis and Clark Expedition, 1805

Friday August 16th 1805.

. . . [T]he young [Shoshone] man . . . had come to inform us that one of the whitemen had killed a deer. in an instant they all gave their horses the whip and I was taken nearly a mile before I could learn what were the tidings; as I was without [s]tirrups and an Indian behind me the jostling was disagreeable I there-fore reigned up my horse and forbid the indian to whip him who had given him the lash . . . for a mile fearing he should loose a part of the feast. the fellow was so uneasy that he left me the horse dismounted and ran on foot at full speed, I am confident a mile. when they arrived where the deer was which was in view of me they dismounted and ran in tumbling over each other like a parcel of fam-ished dogs each seizing and tearing away a part of the intestens which had been previously thrown out by Drewyer [one of Lewis's men] who killed it; the seen was such when I arrived that had I not have had a pretty keen appetite myself I am confident I should not have taisted any part of the venison shortly. each one had a peice of some discription and all eating most ravenously. some were eating the kidnies the melt [spleen] and liver and the blood runing from the corners of their mouths, others were in a similar situation with the paunch and guts but the exuding substance in this case from their lips was of a different discription. one of the last who attacted my attention particularly had been fortunate in his allot-ment or reather active in the division, he had provided himself with about nine feet of the small guts one end of which he was chewing on while with his hands he was squezzing the contents out at the other. I really did not untill now think that human nature ever presented Itself in a shape so nearly allyed to the brute creation. I viewed these poor starved divils with pity and compassion I directed McNeal [another of Lewis's men] to skin the deer and reserved a quarter, the bal-

Gary E. Moulton, ed., *The Journals of the Lewis and Clark Expedition*, vol. 5, July 28–November 1, 1805 (Lincoln: University of Nebraska Press, 1988) 103–59.

lance I gave the Chief to be divided among his people; they devoured the whole of it nearly without cooking. . . . Drewyer . . . killed a second deer; here nearly the same seene was encored. a fire being kindled we cooked and eat and gave the ballance of the two deer to the Indians who eat the whole of them even to the soft parts of the hoofs. . . .

Monday August 19th 1805.

. . . [F]rom what has (already) been said of the Shoshones it will be readily perceived that they live in a wretched stait of poverty. yet notwithstanding their extreem poverty they are not only cheerfull but even gay, fond of gaudy dress and amusements; like most other Indians they are great egotists and frequently boast of heroic acts which they never performed. they are also fond of games of wrisk. they are frank, communicative, fair in dealing, generous with the little they possess, extreemly honest, and by no means beggarly. each individual is his own sovereign master, and acts from the dictates of his own mind; the authority of the Chief being nothing more than mere admonition supported by the influence which the propiety of his own examplery conduct may have acquired him in the minds of the individuals who compose the band. the title of cheif is not heredi-tary . . . in fact every man is a chief, but all have not an equal influence on the minds of the other members of the community, and he who happens to enjoy the greatest share of confidence is the principal Chief. The Shoshonees may be esti-mated at about 100 warriors, and about three times that number of woomen and children. they have more children among them than I expected to have seen among a people who procure subsistence with such difficulty. there are but few very old persons, nor did they appear to treat those with much tenderness or rispect. The man is the sole propryetor of his wives and daughters, and can barter or dispose of either as he thinks proper. a plurality of wives is common among them, but these are not generally sisters as with the Minnetares & Mandans but are purchased of different fathers. The father frequently disposes of his infant daughters in marriage to men who are grown or to men who have sons for whom they think proper to provide wives. the compensation given in such cases usually consists of horses or mules which the father receives at the time of contract and converts to his own uce. the girl remains with her parents untill she is conceived to have obtained the age of puberty which with them is considered to be about the age of 13 or 14 years. the female at this age is surrendered to her sovereign lord and husband agreeably to contract, and with her is frequently restored by the father quite as much as he received in the first instance in payment for his daughter; but this is discretionary with the father. Sah-car-gar-we-ah [Sacajawea] had been thus disposed of before she was taken by the Minnetares, or had ar-rived to the years of puberty. the husband was yet living and with this band. he was more than double her age and had two other wives. he claimed her as his wife but said that as she had had a child by another man, who was Charbono [a French trapper who accompanied Lewis], that he did not want her. They seldom correct their children particularly the boys who soon become masters of their own acts. they give as a reason that it cows and breaks the Sperit of the boy to whip him, and that he never recovers his independence of mind after he is grown. They treat their women but with little rispect, and compel them to perform every species of drudgery. they collect the wild fruits and roots, attend to the horses or assist in that duty cook dreess the skins and make all their apparal, collect wood and make their fires, arrange and form their lodges, and when they travel pack the horses and take charge of all the baggage; in short the man dose little else except attend his horses hunt and fish. the man considers himself degraded if he is compelled to walk any distance, and if he is so unfortunately poor as only to possess two horses he rides the best himself and leavs the woman or women if he has more than one, to transport their baggage and children on the other, and to walk if the horse is unable to carry the additional weight of their persons — the chastity of their women is not held in high estimation, and the husband will for a trifle barter the companion of his bead for a night or longer if he conceives the reward adiquate; tho' they are not so importunate that we should caress their women as the siouxs were and some of their women appear to be held more sacred than in any nation we have seen I have requested the men to give them no cause of jealousy by having connection with their women without their knowledge, which with them strange as it may seem is considered as disgraceful to the husband as clandestine connections of a similar kind are among civilized nations. to prevent this mutual exchange of good officies altogether I know it impossible to effect, particularly on the part of our young men whom some months abstanence have made very polite to those tawney damsels. no evil has yet resulted and I hope will not from these connections. . . . these people are deminutive in stature, thick ankles, crooked legs, thick flat feet and in short but illy formed, at least much more so in general than any nation of Indians I ever saw. their complexion is much that of the Siouxs or darker than the Minnetares mandands or Shawnees. generally both men and women wear their hair in a loos lank flow over the sholders and face. . . . the dress of the men consists of a robe[,] long legings, shirt, tippet and Mockersons, that of the women is also a robe, chemise, and Mockersons; sometimes they make use of short legings. the ornaments of both men and women are very similar, and consist of several species of sea shells, blue and white beads, bras and Iron arm bands, plaited cords of the sweet grass, and collars of leather ornamented with the quills of the porcupine dyed of various colours among which I observed the red, yellow, blue, and black. the ear is purforated in the lower part to receive various ornaments but the nose is not, nor is the ear lasserated or disvigored for this purpose as among many nations. the men never mark their skins by birning, cuting, nor puncturing and introducing a colouring matter as many nations do. there women sometimes puncture a small circle on their forehead nose or cheeks and thus introduce a black matter usually soot and grease which leaves an indelible stand tho' this even is by no means common. their arms offensive and defensive consist in the bow and arrows sheild, some lances, and a weapon called by the Cippeways who formerly used it, the pog-gar'-mag-gon [a weighted war club]. in fishing they employ wairs, gigs, and fishing hooks. the salmon is the principal object of their pursuit. they snair wolves and foxes. I was anxious to learn whether these people had the venerial, and made the enquiry through the intrepreter and his wife; the information was that they sometimes had it but I could not learn their remedy; they most usually die with it's effects. this seems a strong proof that these disorders bothe gonaroehah and Louis venerae are native disorders of America. tho' these people have suffered much by the small pox which is known to be imported and perhaps those other disorders might have been contracted from other indian tribes who by a round of communication might have obtained from the Europeans since it was introduced into that quarter of the globe. but so much detatched on the other had from all communication with the whites that I think it most probable that those disorders are original with them. . . .

August 21st Wednesday 1805.

. . . Those Indians are mild in their disposition appear Sincere in their friend-ship, punctial, and decided. kind with what they have, to Spare. They are exces-sive pore, nothing but horses there Enemies which are noumerous on account of there horses & Defenceless Situation, have Deprived them of tents and all the Small Conveniances of life. . . . The women are held more Sacred among them than any nation we have seen and appear to have an equal Shere in all Conversa-tion, which is not the Case in any othe nation I have Seen. their boeys & Girls are also admited to Speak except in Councils, the women doe all the drugery except fishing and takeing care of the horses, which the men apr. to take upon them-selves. . . .

Friday August 23rd 1805.

. . . The metal which we found in possession of these people consited of a few indifferent knives, a few brass kettles some arm bands of iron and brass, a few buttons, woarn as ornaments in their hair, a spear or two of a foot in length and some iron and brass arrow points which they informed me they obtained in exchange for horses from the Crow or Rocky Mountain Indians on the yellow-stone River. the bridlebits and stirrips they obtained from the Spaniards, tho' these were but few. many of them made use of flint for knives, and with this in-strument, skined the animals they killed, dressed their fish and made their ar-rows; in short they used it for every purpose to which the knife is applyed. . . .

Saturday August 24th 1805.

. . . [T]hese people have many names in the course of their lives, particularly if they become distinguished characters. for it seems that every important event by which they happen to distinguish themselves intitles them to claim another name which is generally scelected by themselves and confirmed by the nation. those distinguishing acts are the killing and scalping an enemy, the killing a white bear, leading a party to war who happen to be successful either in destroying their enemies or robing them of their horses, or individually stealing the horses of an enemy. these are considered acts of equal heroism among them, and that of killing an enemy without scalping him is considered of no importance; in fact the whole honour seems to be founded in the act of scalping, for if a man happens to slay a dozen of his enemies in action and others get the scalps or first lay their hand on the dead person the honor is lost to him who killed them and devolves on those who scalp or first touch them. Among the Shoshones, as well as all the Indians of America, bravery is esteemed the primary virtue; nor can any one be-come eminent among them who has not at some period of his life given proofs of his possessing this virtue. with them there can be no preferment without some ware-like achievement.

QUESTIONS FOR READING AND DISCUSSION

1. The ravenous Shoshone who devoured the deer caused Lewis to write that he "did not untill now think that human nature ever presented Itself in a shape so nearly allyed to the brute creation." How did observing behavior that he considered horrifying shape Lewis's other observations of the Shoshone, if at all? Did Lewis consider the Shoshone subhuman?

2. Lewis admired some qualities of the Shoshone and criticized others. What traits did he mention in his journal? What did he say about relations of gender and power among the Indians? To what extent did he believe the Shoshone were different from white Americans?

3. In what ways had whites already influenced the Shoshone? Did Lewis believe the Shoshone were likely to adopt the ways of white Americans? Why or why not?

4. If the Shoshone had recorded an account of white American behavior based on the activities of Lewis and Clark, what might they have noted? To what extent would such observations have been a reliable guide to typical values and deeds among most white Americans? To what extent were Lewis's observations an accurate account of typical Shoshone ideals and actions?

DOCUMENT 4

Frontier Revival

Egalitarian ideals eroded the appeal of religious doctrines and institutions that emphasized hierarchy, learning, and reason. Especially on the ever-shifting frontier of settlement, many Americans came to believe that religion was something between themselves and God. Churches, ministers, and fine points of theology got in the way of genuine, transforming faith. In the account excerpted here, Richard McNemar, a Presbyterian minister, described the people, ideas, and activities that marked the revivals of the Second Great Awakening in Kentucky at the turn of the century.

Richard McNemar
The Kentucky Revival, 1801

The first extraordinary appearances of the power of God in the late revival, began about the close of the last century, in Logan and Christian counties; on the waters of Casper and Red Rivers. And in the spring of 1801, the same extraordinary work broke out in Mason county, upper part of Kentucky; of which I was an eye witness, and can therefore, with greater confidence, testify what I have heard, seen and felt.

It first began in individuals who had been under deep convictions of sin, and great trouble about their souls, and had fasted and prayed, and diligently searched the scriptures, and had undergone distresses of mind inexpressibly sore, until they had obtained a comfortable hope of salvation. And from seeing and

Richard McNemar, *The Kentucky Revival* (Pittsfield, Ohio: Phinehas Allen, 1808).

feeling the love of Christ, and his willingness to save all that would forsake their sins and turn to God through him; and feeling how freely his love and goodness flowed to them, it kindled their love to other souls, that were lost in their sins; and an ardent desire that they might come and partake of that spiritual light, life, and comfort, which appeared infinite in its nature, and free to all. And under such an overpowering weight of the divine goodness, as tongue could not express, they were constrained to cry out, with tears and trembling, and testify a full and free salvation in Christ, for all that would come; and to warn their fellow-creatures of the danger of continuing in sin; and entreating them in the most tender and affectionate manner, to turn from it; and seek the Lord, in sure and certain hope that he would be found.

Under such exhortations, the people began to be affected in a very strange manner. At first they were taken with an inward throbbing of heart; then with weeping and trembling: from that to crying out, in apparent agony of soul; falling down and swooning away till every appearance of animal life was suspended, and the person appeared to be in a trance. From this state they would recover under different sensations. . . .

And here a new scene was opened, while some trembled like one in a fit of the ague[1]; wept or cried out, lamenting their distance from God, and exposedness to his wrath; others were employed in praying with them, encouraging them to believe on the Son of God — to venture upon his promise — give up their wicked rebellious heart, just as it was; for God to take it away, and give them a heart of flesh; — singing hymns, and giving thanks to God, for the display of his power, without any regard to former rules of order. At this, some were offended and withdrew from the assembly, determined to oppose it, as a work of the wicked one. But all their objections, only tended to open the way for the true nature and spirit of the work to shine out; and encourage the subjects of it, to set out with warmer zeal to promote it. Accordingly a meeting was appointed a few evenings after; to which a crowd of awakened souls flocked, and spent the whole night in singing hymns, praying, and exhorting one another, &c. At this meeting, one man was struck down and lay for about an hour, in the situation above mentioned. This put the matter beyond dispute, that the work was supernatural; and the outcry which it raised against sin, confirmed a number in the belief that it was from above.

From small beginnings, it gradually spread. The news of these strange operations flew about, and attracted many to come and see; who were convinced, not only from seeing and hearing, but feeling; and carried home the testimony, that it was the living work of God. This stirred up others, and brought out still greater multitudes. And these strange exercises still increasing, and having no respect to any stated hours of worship, it was found expedient to encamp on the ground, and continue the meeting day and night. To these encampments the people flocked in hundreds and thousands, on foot, on horseback, and in waggons and other carriages.

At first appearance, those meetings exhibited nothing to the spectator, but a scene of confusion that could scarce be put into human language. They were generally opened with a sermon; near the close of which, there would be an unusual out-cry; some bursting forth into loud ejaculations of prayer, or thanksgiving for

---

[1]**Ague:** Intermittent bouts of fever and chills associated with malaria.

the truth. Others breaking out in emphatical sentences of exhortation. Others flying to their careless friends, with tears of compassion, beseeching them to turn to the Lord. Some struck with terror, and hastening through the croud to make their escape, or pulling away their relations. — Others, trembling, weeping and crying out for the Lord Jesus to have mercy upon them: fainting and swooning away, till every appearance of life was gone, and the extremities of the body assumed the coldness of a dead corpse. — Others surrounding them with melodious songs, or fervent prayers for their happy resurrection, in the love of Christ. — Others collecting into circles around this variegated scene, contending with arguments for and against. And under such appearances, the work would continue for several days and nights together. . . .

The next general camp-meeting was held at Concord, in the county of Bourbon, about the last of May, or beginning of June. The number of people was supposed to be about 4,000, who attended on this occasion. . . . On this occasion, no sex nor color, class nor description, were exempted from the pervading influence of the spirit; even from the age of eight months to sixty years, there were evident subjects of this marvellous operation.

The meeting continued five days and four nights; and after the people generally scattered from the ground, numbers convened in different places and continued the exercise much longer. And even where they were not collected together, these wonderful operations continued among every class of people and in every situation; in their houses and fields, and in their daily employments, falling down and crying out under conviction, or singing and shouting with unspeakable joy, were so common, that the whole country round about, seemed to be leavened with the spirit of the work. . . .

The people among whom the revival began, were generally Calvinists, and altho' they had been long praying in words for the out-pouring of the spirit, and believed that God had *"foreordained whatsoever comes in to pass;"* yet, when it *came to pass* and their prayer was answered, and the spirit began to flow like many waters, from a cloud of witnesses, and souls were convicted of sin and cried for mercy, and found hope and comfort in the news of a Saviour; they rose up and quarreled with the work, because it did not *come to pass* that the subjects of it were willing to adopt their soul stupefying creed. Those who had laboured and travailed to gain some solid hope of salvation, and had ventured their souls upon the covenant of promise, and felt the living zeal of eternal love; could not, dare not preach that salvation was restricted to a certain *definite number;* nor insinuate that any being which God had made, was, by the Creator, laid under the dire necessity of being damned forever. The love of a Saviour constrained them to testify, that one had died for all. This truth, so essential to the first ray of hope in the human breast, was like a dead fly in the ointment of the apothecary, to the Calvinist; hence all this trembling, weeping and groaning under sin, rejoicing in the hope of deliverance and turning from the former practice of it, sent forth a disagreeable savor. Yet these exercises would no doubt, have passed for a good work of God, had they appeared as seals to their doctrine of election, imperfection, and final perseverance. But every thing appeared new, and to claim no relation to the old bed of sand upon which they had been building; and rather than quit the old foundation, they chose to reject, oppose and persecute the truth, accompanied with all that evidence which many of them were obliged to acknowledge was divine. . . .

The first point of doctrine which distinguished the subjects of the revival, was that which respected divine revelation.

The established opinion in the churches had been, that the *Scriptures*, explained according to sound reason and philosophy, was light sufficient; and simply to believe, what we were thus taught, was the highest evidence we could have of the truth of spiritual things. But *these* adopted a very different faith, and taught, as an important truth, that the will of God was made manifest to each individual who honestly sought after it, by an inward light, which shone into the heart. — Hence they received the name of *New-Lights.* . . .

This *new light* first broke out in the Presbyterian church, among those who held the doctrines of Calvin, and therefore it is considered as more immediately contrasted with that system. Those who first embraced it, had also been reputed Calvinists, and belonged to the Presbyterian church, among whom were several persons of distinction in the ministry; of course, the existence of sentiments so very different in the same church, rendered a division unavoidable. . . . This division in sentiment, with its concomitant effects, drew together a vast multitude out of different churches, who formed a general communion, and for a time, acceded to the doctrines, manner of worship, &c. first opened and practised among the *New-Lights*; a brief sketch of which is as follows, viz: that all creeds, confessions, forms of worship, and rules of government invented by men, ought to be laid aside; especially the distinguishing doctrines of Calvin. — That all who received the true light of the spirit in the inner man, and faithfully followed it, would naturally see eye to eye, and understand the things of the spirit alike, without any written tenet or learned expositor. That all who received this true light, would plainly see the purity of God — the depravity of man — the necessity of a new birth, and of a sinless life and conversation to evidence it. — That God was no respecter of persons — willeth the salvation of all souls — has opened a door of salvation, through Christ, for all — will have all invited to enter, and such as refuse to come in, must blame themselves for their own perdition.

As to worship, they allowed each one to worship God agreeably to their own feelings, whatever impression or consciousness of duty they were under; believing the true wisdom, which "lives through all life," to be a safer guide than human forms, which can only affect the outer man: and hence, so wide a door was opened, and such a variety of exercises were exhibited at their public meetings. All distinction of names was laid aside, and it was no matter what any one had been called before, if now he stood in the present light, and felt his heart glow with love to the souls of men; he was welcome to sing, pray, or call sinners to repentance. Neither was there any distinction as to age, sex, color, or any thing of a temporary nature: old and young, male and female, black and white, had equal privilege to minister the light which they received, in whatever way the spirit directed. And it was moreover generally considered, that such as professed to stand in the light and were not actively engaged some way or other, in time of public meeting, were only dead weights upon the cause.

No one, who has not been an eye witness, can possibly paint in their imagination the striking solemnity of those occasions, on which the thousands of Kentuckians were convened in one vast assembly, under the auspicious influence of the above faith. How striking to see hundreds who never saw each other in the face before, moving uniformly into action, without any preconcerted plan, and each, without intruding upon another, taking that part assigned him by a conscious feeling, and in this manner, dividing into bands over a large extent of ground, interspersed with tents and waggons: some uniting their voices in the most melodious songs; others in solemn and affecting accents of prayer: some lamenting with streaming eyes their lost situation, or that of a wicked world; others lying apparently in the cold embraces of death: some instructing the ignorant, directing the doubtful, and urging them in the day of God's visitation, to make sure work for eternity: others, from some eminence, sounding the general trump of a free salvation, and warning sinners to fly from the wrath to come: — the surrounding forest at the same time, vocal with the cries of the distressed, sometimes to the distance of half a mile or a mile in circumference.

How persons, so different in their education, manners and natural dispositions, without any visible commander, could enter upon such a scene, and continue in it for days and nights in perfect harmony, has been one of the greatest wonders that ever the world beheld.

QUESTIONS FOR READING AND DISCUSSION

1. According to McNemar, how did the Kentucky revival begin? What evidence convinced him that it was the work of God? In what ways were the revivals "strange operations"?

2. Who took part in the revivals? Why were some people "offended"? How did the revivals show that "God was no respector of persons"?

3. How did the participants in the revival differ from Calvinists? In what ways did the revivalists' reject "soul stupefying creed"? What significance did McNemar attribute to the term "new light"? From McNemar's perspective, what was wrong with Calvinist doctrines "that salvation was restricted to a certain *definite number*" and that some people were "under the dire necessity of being damned forever"?

4. In what ways did the significance of the revivals reach beyond religious experience? To what extent did the revivals reinforce or transform the ideas and experiences of the people who participated in them?

COMPARATIVE QUESTIONS

1. How did Peter Wendover's and Thomas Jefferson's ideas about America compare with those of the participants in the revivals?

2. To what extent were Jefferson's goals for Native Americans consistent with Meriwether Lewis's observations about the Shoshone? Did Jefferson and Lewis believe that Indians could participate fully and equally in American society? If so, how? If not, why not?

3. To what extent do the documents in this chapter suggest that notions of sin and salvation extended beyond revivals to political ideology as voiced by Wendover and to cultural norms and expectations that informed the writings of Jefferson and Lewis?

4. In what ways do the documents in this chapter provide evidence of the strength of democratic aspirations in the first quarter of the nineteenth century? To what extent did democratic values inform Jeffersonian ideology, relations with Native Americans, and the revivals? What values competed with democracy in each of these areas?

CHAPTER 10

THE EXPANDING REPUBLIC
1815–1840

During the 1820s and 1830s, Americans disagreed over how basic social and economic institutions should be influenced by the ideals of liberty, equality, and democracy. Were corporations and banks to be feared as undemocratic concentrations of power, or were they institutions that fostered economic improvement for all? Were families nurseries of good citizens or prisons to which women were sentenced for life? Should Indian lands be reserved for the use of native tribes or opened to white settlers? If slavery was abolished, how could white supremacy be maintained? The following documents illustrate some of the ways in which Americans grappled with such questions.

DOCUMENT 1
Andrew Jackson's Parting Words to the Nation

As president, Andrew Jackson battled what he considered unconstitutional schemes to expand the powers of the federal government. Determined to defeat the consolidated powers of the monied interests, he championed the many against the few. When Jackson relinquished the presidency to Martin Van Buren in March 1837, he surveyed the political principles that governed Jacksonian Democrats. His farewell address, excerpted here, discloses the suspicion of power felt by many in Jackson's America.

Farewell Address, March 4, 1837

We have now lived almost fifty years under the Constitution framed by the sages and patriots of the Revolution. . . . Our Constitution is no longer a doubtful experiment, and at the end of nearly half a century we find that it has preserved unimpaired the liberties of the people, secured the rights of property, and that

---

James D. Richardson, ed., *A Compilation of the Messages and Papers of the Presidents, 1789–1897* (New York: Bureau of National Literature, 1969) 4: 1512–27.

our country has improved and is flourishing beyond any former example in the history of nations. . . .

In the legislation of Congress also, and in every measure of the general government, justice to every portion of the United States should be faithfully observed. No free government can stand without virtue in the people and a lofty spirit of patriotism, and if the sordid feelings of mere selfishness shall usurp the place which ought to be filled by public spirit, the legislation of Congress will soon be converted into a scramble for personal and sectional advantages. Under our free institutions the citizens of every quarter of our country are capable of attaining a high degree of prosperity and happiness without seeking to profit themselves at the expense of others; and every such attempt must in the end fail to succeed, for the people in every part of the United States are too enlightened not to understand their own rights and interests and to detect and defeat every effort to gain undue advantages over them; and when such designs are discovered it naturally provokes resentments which can not always be easily allayed. Justice — full and ample justice — to every portion of the United States should be the ruling principle of every freeman, and should guide the deliberations of every public body, whether it be state or national.

It is well known that there have always been those amongst us who wish to enlarge the powers of the general government, and experience would seem to indicate that there is a tendency on the part of this government to overstep the boundaries marked out for it by the Constitution. Its legitimate authority is abundantly sufficient for all the purposes for which it was created, and its powers being expressly enumerated, there can be no justification for claiming anything beyond them. Every attempt to exercise power beyond these limits should be promptly and firmly opposed, for one evil example will lead to other measures still more mischievous; and if the principle of constructive powers or supposed advantages or temporary circumstances shall ever be permitted to justify the assumption of a power not given by the Constitution, the general government will before long absorb all the powers of legislation, and you will have in effect but one consolidated government. From the extent of our country, its diversified interests, different pursuits, and different habits, it is too obvious for argument that a single consolidated government would be wholly inadequate to watch over and protect its interests; and every friend of our free institutions should be always prepared to maintain unimpaired and in full vigor the rights and sovereignty of the states and to confine the action of the general government strictly to the sphere of its appropriate duties. . . .

Plain as these principles appear to be, you will yet find there is a constant effort to induce the general government to go beyond the limits of its taxing power and to impose unnecessary burdens upon the people. Many powerful interests are continually at work to procure heavy duties on commerce and to swell the revenue beyond the real necessities of the public service, and the country has already felt the injurious effects of their combined influence. They succeeded in obtaining a tariff of duties bearing most oppressively on the agricultural and laboring classes of society and producing a revenue that could not be usefully employed within the range of the powers conferred upon Congress, and in order to fasten upon the people this unjust and unequal system of taxation extravagant schemes of internal improvement were got up in various quarters to squander the money and to purchase support. Thus one unconstitutional measure was intended to be upheld by another, and the abuse of the power of taxation was to be maintained by usurping the power of expending the money in internal improvements. You can not have forgotten the severe and doubtful struggle through which we passed when the executive department of the government by its veto endeavored to arrest this prodigal scheme of injustice and to bring back the legislation of Congress to the boundaries prescribed by the Constitution. The good sense and practical judgment of the people when the subject was brought before them sustained the course of the Executive, and this plan of unconstitutional expenditures for the purposes of corrupt influence is, I trust, finally overthrown. . . .

But, rely upon it, the design to collect an extravagant revenue and to burden you with taxes beyond the economical wants of the Government is not yet abandoned. The various interests which have combined together to impose a heavy tariff and to produce an overflowing Treasury are too strong and have too much at stake to surrender the contest. The corporations and wealthy individuals who are engaged in large manufacturing establishments desire a high tariff to increase their gains. Designing politicians will support it to conciliate their favor and to obtain the means of profuse expenditure for the purpose of purchasing influence in other quarters; and since the people have decided that the federal government can not be permitted to employ its income in internal improvements, efforts will be made to seduce and mislead the citizens of the several states by holding out to them the deceitful prospects of benefits to be derived from a surplus revenue collected by the general government and annually divided among the states; and if, encouraged by these fallacious hopes, the states should disregard the principles of economy which ought to characterize every republican government, and should indulge in lavish expenditures exceeding their resources, they will before long find themselves oppressed with debts which they are unable to pay, and the temptation will become irresistible to support a high tariff in order to obtain a surplus for distribution. Do not allow yourselves, my fellow-citizens, to be misled on this subject. The federal government can not collect a surplus for such purposes without violating the principles of the Constitution and assuming powers which have not been granted. It is, moreover, a system of injustice, and if persisted in will inevitably lead to corruption, and must end in ruin. The surplus revenue will be drawn from the pockets of the people — from the farmer, the mechanic, and the laboring classes of society; but who will receive it when distributed among the states, where it is to be disposed of by leading state politicians, who have friends to favor and political partisans to gratify? It will certainly not be returned to those who paid it and who have most need of it and are honestly entitled to it. There is but one safe rule, and that is to confine the general government rigidly within the sphere of its appropriate duties. It has no power to raise a revenue or impose taxes except for the purposes enumerated in the Constitution, and if its income is found to exceed these wants it should be forthwith reduced and the burden of the people so far lightened. . . .

Recent events have proved that the paper-money system of this country may be used as an engine to undermine your free institutions, and that those who desire to engross all power in the hands of the few and to govern by corruption or force are aware of its power and prepared to employ it. . . .

But when the charter for the Bank of the United States was obtained from Congress it perfected the schemes of the paper system and gave to its advocates the position they have struggled to obtain from the commencement of the federal government to the present hour. The immense capital and peculiar privileges bestowed upon it enabled it to exercise despotic sway over the other banks in every part of the country. From its superior strength it could seriously injure, if not destroy, the business of any one of them which might incur its resentment; and it openly claimed for itself the power of regulating the currency throughout the United States. In other words, it asserted (and it undoubtedly possessed) the power to make money plenty or scarce at its pleasure, at any time and in any quarter of the Union, by controlling the issues of other banks and permitting an expansion or compelling a general contraction of the circulating medium, according to its own will. . . . The result of the ill-advised legislation which established this great monopoly was to concentrate the whole moneyed power of the Union, with its boundless means of corruption and its numerous dependents, under the direction and command of one acknowledged head, thus organizing this particular interest as one body and securing to it unity and concert of action throughout the United States, and enabling it to bring forward upon any occasion its entire and undivided strength to support or defeat any measure of the government. . . .

The distress and alarm which pervaded and agitated the whole country when the Bank of the United States waged war upon the people in order to compel them to submit to its demands can not yet be forgotten. The ruthless and unsparing temper with which whole cities and communities were oppressed, individuals impoverished and ruined, and a scene of cheerful prosperity suddenly changed into one of gloom and despondency ought to be indelibly impressed on the memory of the people of the United States. . . . No nation but the freemen of the United States could have come out victorious from such a contest; yet, if you had not conquered, the government would have passed from the hands of the many to the hands of the few, and this organized money power from its secret conclave would have dictated the choice of your highest officers and compelled you to make peace or war, as best suited their own wishes. . . .

It is one of the serious evils of our present system of banking that it enables one class of society — and that by no means a numerous one — by its control over the currency, to act injuriously upon the interests of all the others and to exercise more than its just proportion of influence in political affairs. The agricultural, the mechanical, and the laboring classes have little or no share in the direction of the great moneyed corporations, and from their habits and the nature of their pursuits they are incapable of forming extensive combinations to act together with united force. . . .

The planter, the farmer, the mechanic, and the laborer all know that their success depends upon their own industry and economy, and that they must not expect to become suddenly rich by the fruits of their toil. Yet these classes of society form the great body of the people of the United States; they are the bone and sinew of the country — men who love liberty and desire nothing but equal rights and equal laws, and who, moreover, hold the great mass of our national wealth, although it is distributed in moderate amounts among the millions of freemen who possess it. But with overwhelming numbers and wealth on their side they are in constant danger of losing their fair influence in the government, and with difficulty maintain their just rights against the incessant efforts daily made to encroach upon them. . . . [U]nless you become more watchful in your states and check this spirit of monopoly and thirst for exclusive privileges you will in the end find that the most important powers of government have been given or bartered away, and the control over your dearest interests has passed into the hands of these corporations.

The paper-money system and its natural associations — monopoly and exclusive privileges — have already struck their roots too deep in the soil, and it will require all your efforts to check its further growth and to eradicate the evil. The men who profit by the abuses and desire to perpetuate them will continue to besiege the halls of legislation in the general government as well as in the states, and will seek by every artifice to mislead and deceive the public servants. . . .

The progress of the United States under our free and happy institutions has surpassed the most sanguine hopes of the founders of the Republic. Our growth has been rapid beyond all former example in numbers, in wealth, in knowledge, and all the useful arts which contribute to the comforts and convenience of man, and from the earliest ages of history to the present day there never have been thirteen millions of people associated in one political body who enjoyed so much freedom and happiness as the people of these United States. You have no longer any cause to fear danger from abroad; your strength and power are well known throughout the civilized world, as well as the high and gallant bearing of your sons. It is from within, among yourselves — from cupidity, from corruption, from disappointed ambition and inordinate thirst for power — that factions will be formed and liberty endangered. It is against such designs, whatever disguise the actors may assume, that you have especially to guard yourselves. You have the highest of human trusts committed to your care. Providence has showered on this favored land blessings without number, and has chosen you as the guardians of freedom, to preserve it for the benefit of the human race.

QUESTIONS FOR READING AND DISCUSSION

1. What did Jackson cite as the principal dangers to free government? Why were "expressly enumerated" constitutional powers important?

2. How and why had "powerful interests," including "the money power," exercised their influence? In what ways had Jackson dealt with them while he was president?

3. How did Jackson believe freedom could be protected? Why did he expect that the future danger to liberty would be "from within, among yourselves"?

4. To what extent did Jackson envision a future significantly different from the past? What did he identify as the major changes under way in American society? Did he seek largely to restore a golden past or to shape a transformed future?

DOCUMENT 2

Cherokees Debate Removal

President Jackson proudly announced to Congress in 1830 that the "benevolent policy of the government . . . in relation to the removal of the Indians beyond the white settlements is approaching to a conclusion." To the Indians being removed, the policy did not appear benevolent. In 1836, Congress ratified the Treaty of New Echota, which provided that the Cherokees would relinquish all claims to land east of the Mississippi in return for land west of the Mississippi, a large cash payment, and help moving to their new homes. The treaty bitterly divided Cherokees. The largest group, led by the principal chief, John Ross, opposed the treaty and insisted that the Cherokees not give up their lands. A minority group, led by Elias Boudinot, signed the treaty and urged other Cherokees to accept its terms. The following selections from letters by Ross and Boudinot reveal the clashing assessments among Cherokees about the threats they confronted and how best to respond to them.

John Ross
Answer to Inquiries from a Friend, 1836

I wish I could acquiesce in your impression, that a Treaty has been made, by which every difficulty between the Cherokees and the United States has been set at rest; but I must candidly say, that I know of no such Treaty. I do not mean to prophesy any similar troubles to those which have, in other cases, followed the failure to adjust disputed points with Indians; the Cherokees act on a principle preventing apprehensions of that nature — their principle is, "endure and forbear"; but I must distinctly declare to you that I believe, the document [the Treaty of New Echota] signed by unauthorized individuals at Washington, will never be regarded by the Cherokee nation as a Treaty. The delegation appointed by the people to make a Treaty, have protested against that instrument "as deceptive to the world and a fraud upon the Cherokee people." . . .

With your impressions concerning the advantages secured by the subtle instrument in question, you will, no doubt, wonder at this opposition. But it possesses not the advantages you and others imagine; and that is the reason why it has encountered, and ever will encounter opposition. You suppose we are to be removed through it from a home, by circumstances rendered disagreeable and even untenable, to be secured in a better home, where nothing can disturb or dispossess us. *Here is the great mystification.* We are not secured in the new home promised to us. We are exposed to precisely the same miseries, from which, if this measure is enforced, the United States' power professes to relieve us, but does so entirely by the exercise of that power, against our will.

If we really had the security you and others suppose we have, we would not thus complain. . . .

One impression concerning us, is, that though we object to removal, as we are equally averse to becoming citizens of the United States, we ought to be forced to remove; to be tied hand and foot and conveyed to the extreme western frontier, and then turned loose among the wild beasts of the wilderness. Now, the fact is, we never have objected to become citizens of the United States and to conform to her laws; but in the event of conforming to her laws, we have required the protection and privileges of her laws to accompany that conformity on our part. We have asked this repeatedly and repeatedly has it been denied. . . .

In conclusion I would observe, that I still strongly hope we shall find ultimate justice from the good sense of the administration and of the people of the United States. I will not even yet believe that either the one or the other would wrong us with their eyes open. I am persuaded they have erred only in igno-

John Ross, *Letter in Answer to Inquiries from a Friend,* July 2, 1836; Elias Boudinot, *Letters and Other Papers Relating to Cherokee Affairs: Being a Reply to Sundry Publications by John Ross,* 1837, in *The Cherokee Removal: A Brief History with Documents,* ed. Theda Perdue and Michael D. Green (Boston: Bedford Books, 1995) 147–51, 153–59.

rance, and an ignorance forced upon them by the misrepresentation and artifices of the interested. . . . The Cherokees, under any circumstances, have no weapon to use but argument. If that should fail, they must submit, when their time shall come, in silence, but honest argument they cannot think will be forever used in vain. The Cherokee people will always hold themselves ready to respect a *real* treaty and bound to sustain any treaty which they can feel that they are bound to respect. But they are certain not to consider the attempt of a very few persons to sell the country for themselves, as obligatory upon them, and I and all my associates in the regular delegation, still look confidently to the effect of a sense of justice upon the American community, in producing a real settlement of this question, upon equitable terms and with competent authorities. But, on one point, you may be perfectly at rest. Deeply as our people feel, I cannot suppose they will ever be goaded by those feelings to any acts of violence. No, sir. They have been too long inured to suffering without resistance, and they still look to the sympathies and not to the fears, of those who have them in their power. In certain recent discussions in the representative hall at Washington, our enemies made it an objection against me and against others, that we were not Indians, but had *the principles of white men*, and were consequently unworthy of a hearing in the Indian cause. I will own that it has been my pride, as Principal Chief of the Cherokees, to implant in the bosoms of the people, and to cherish in my own, *the principles* of white men! It is to this fact that our white neighbours must ascribe their safety under the smart of the wrongs we have suffered from them. It is in this they may confide for our continued patience. But when I speak of *the principles of white men*, I speak not of such principles as actuate those who talk thus to us, but of those mighty principles to which the United States owes her greatness and her liberty. To principles like these even yet we turn with confidence for redemption from our miseries. When Congress shall be less overwhelmed with business, no doubt, in some way, the matter may be brought to a reconsideration, and when the representatives of the American people have leisure to see how little it will cost them to be just, we are confident they will be true to themselves, in acting with good faith towards us. Be certain that while the Cherokees are endeavouring to obtain a more friendly consideration from the United States, they will not forget to show by their circumspection how well they merit it; and though no doubt there are many who will represent them otherwise, for injurious purposes, I can assure you that the white people have nothing to apprehend, even from our sense of contumely [humiliating insults] and unfairness, unless it be through the perverse and the treacherous manoeuvres of such agents as they themselves may keep among us.

Elias Boudinot
A Reply to John Ross, 1837

"What is to be done?" was a natural inquiry, after we found that all our efforts to obtain redress from the General Government, *on the land of our fathers,* had been of no avail. The first rupture among ourselves was the moment we presumed to answer that question. To a portion of the Cherokee people it early became evident that the interest of their countrymen and the happiness of their posterity, depended upon an entire change of policy. Instead of contending uselessly against superior power, the only course left, was, to yield to circumstances over which they had no control.

In all difficulties of this kind, between the United States and the Cherokees, the only mode of settling them has been by treaties; consequently, when a portion of our people became convinced that no other measures would avail, they became the *advocates of a treaty*, as the only means to extricate the Cherokees from their perplexities; hence they were called *the treaty party*. Those who maintained the old policy, were known as the *anti-treaty party*. At the head of the latter has been Mr. John Ross. . . .

To advocate a treaty was to declare war against the established habits of thinking peculiar to the aborigines. It was to come in contact with settled prejudices — with the deep rooted attachment for the soil of our forefathers. Aside from these natural obstacles, the influence of the chiefs, who were ready to take advantage of the well known feelings of the Cherokees, in reference to their lands, was put in active requisition against us. . . .

It is with sincere regret that I notice you [John Ross] say little or nothing about the moral condition of this people, as affected by present circumstances. I have searched in vain, in all your late communications, for some indication of your sensibility upon this point. . . . Indeed, you seem to have forgotten that your people are a community of moral beings, capable of an elevation to an equal standing with the most civilized and virtuous, or a deterioration to the level of the most degraded, of our race. . . . Can it be possible that you consider the mere pains and privations of the body, and the loss of a paltry sum of money, of a paramount importance to the depression of the mind and the degradation and pollution of the soul? That the difficulties under which they are laboring, originating from the operation of the State laws, and their absorption by a white population, *will* affect them in that light, I need not here stop to argue with you: that they have *already* affected them, is a fact too palpable, too notorious, for us to deny it: that they will *increase* to affect them, in proportion to the delay of applying the remedy, we need only judge from past experience. How, then, can you reconcile your conscience and your sense of what is demanded by the best interest of your people. . . . How can you persist in deluding your people with phantoms, and in your opposition to that which alone is practicable, when you see them dying a moral death?

To be sure, from your account of the condition and circumstances of the Cherokees, the public may form an idea different from what my remarks may seem to convey. When applied to a portion of our people, confined mostly to whites intermarried among us, and the descendants of whites, your account is probably correct . . . but look at the mass, look at the entire population as it now is, and say, can you see any indication of a progressing improvement, anything that can encourage a philanthropist? You know that it is almost a dreary waste. I care not if I am accounted a slanderer of my country's reputation; every observing man in this nation knows that I speak the words of truth and soberness. In the light that I consider my countrymen, not as mere animals, and to judge of their happiness by their condition as such, which, to be sure, is bad enough, but as moral beings, to be affected for better or for worse by moral circumstances, I say their condition is wretched. Look, my dear sir, around you, and see the progress that vice and immorality have already made! see the spread of intemperance, and the wretchedness and misery it has already occasioned! I need not reason with a man of your sense and discernment, and of your observation, to show the debasing character of that vice to our people; you will find an argument in every tippling shop in the country; you will find its cruel effects in the bloody tragedies that are frequently occurring in the frequent convictions and executions for murders, and in the tears and groans of the widows and fatherless, rendered homeless, naked, and hungry, by this vile curse of our race. And has it stopped its cruel ravages with the lower or poorer classes of our people? Are the higher orders, if I may so speak, left untainted? While there are honorable exceptions in all classes . . . it is not to be denied that, as a people, we are making a rapid tendency to a general immorality and debasement. What more evidence do we need, to prove this general tendency, than the slow but sure insinuation of the lower vices into our female population? Oh! it is heart-rending to think of these things, much more to speak of them; but the world *will* know them, the world *does* know them, and we need not try to hide our shame. . . .

If the dark picture which I have here drawn is a true one, and no candid person will say it is an exaggerated one, can we see a brighter prospect ahead? In another country, and under other circumstances, there is a *better* prospect. Removal, then, is the only remedy, the only *practicable* remedy. By it there *may be* finally a renovation; our people *may* rise from their very ashes, to become prosperous and happy, and a credit to our race. Such has been and is now my opinion, and under such a settled opinion I have acted in all this affair. My language has been; "fly for your lives"; it is now the same. I would say to my countrymen, you among the rest, fly from the moral pestilence that will finally destroy our nation.

What is the prospect in reference to *your* plan of relief, if you are understood at all to have any plan? It is dark and gloomy beyond description. Subject the Cherokees to the laws of the States in their present condition? It matters not how favorable those laws may be, instead of remedying the evil you would only rivet the chains and fasten the manacles of their servitude and degradation. The final destiny of our race, under such circumstances, is too revolting to think of. Its course must be downward, until it finally becomes extinct or is merged in another race, more ignoble and more detested. Take my word for it, it is the sure consummation, if you succeed in preventing the removal of your people. The time will come when there will be only here and there those who can be called upon to sign a protest, or to vote against a treaty for their removal; when the few remnants of our once happy and improving nation will be viewed by posterity with curious and gazing interest, as relics of a brave and noble race. Are our people destined to such a catastrophe? Are we to run the race of all our brethren who have gone before us, and of whom hardly any thing is known but their name, and, perhaps, only here and there a solitary being, waking, "as a ghost over the ashes of his fathers," to remind a stranger that such a race *once* existed? May God preserve us from such a destiny.

QUESTIONS FOR READING AND DISCUSSION

1. For Ross, what did the principle "endure and forbear" suggest the Cherokee should do? In what sense did Ross believe argument was a "weapon"?
2. What was Ross's view of the *principles of white men*"? How did they differ from the principles of Cherokees?
3. According to Boudinot, why was removal "the only course left"? Why was "the moral condition" of the Cherokees an inducement for removal?

4. According to Boudinot, what would be the result of following Ross's plan and not leaving ancestral lands in the East?

5. How did Ross and Boudinot differ in their views of whites and of state and federal governments? How did they differ in their views of Cherokees? What did each see as the most important sources of security and safety?

DOCUMENT 3

Sarah Grimké on the Status of Women

The ideals of liberty and equality appealed strongly to many American women. Those ideals confronted the strength of male supremacy and of widespread assumptions about the proper domestic role for women. Sarah Grimké took a leading role in attacking the unjust subordination of women in American life. The daughter of a wealthy slaveholder in Charleston, South Carolina, Grimké found slavery repugnant and moved to Philadelphia, where she became a Quaker and a leader for women's rights and abolition. Grimké's Letters on the Equality of the Sexes and the Condition of Women, *published in 1838 and excerpted here, reveal her criticisms of the prevailing inequality of the sexes.*

Letters on the Equality of the Sexes, 1838

During the early part of my life, my lot was cast among the butterflies of the *fashionable* world; and of this class of women, I am constrained to say, both from experience and observation, that their education is miserably deficient; that they are taught to regard marriage as the one thing needful, the only avenue to distinction; hence to attract the notice and win the attentions of men, by their external charms, is the chief business of fashionable girls. They seldom think that men will be allured by intellectual acquirements, because they find, that where any mental superiority exists, a woman is generally shunned and regarded as stepping out of her "appropriate sphere," which, in their view, is to dress, to dance, and to set out to the best possible advantage her person, to read the novels which inundate the press, and which do more to destroy her character as a rational creature, than any thing else. Fashionable women regard themselves, and are regarded by men, as pretty toys or as mere instruments of pleasure; and the vacuity of mind, the heartlessness, the frivolity which is the necessary result of this false and debasing estimate of women, can only be fully understood by those who have mingled in the folly and wickedness of fashionable life; and who have been called from such pursuits by the voice of the Lord Jesus, inviting their weary and heavy laden souls to come unto Him and learn of Him, that they may find something worthy of their immortal spirit, and their intellectual powers; that they may learn the high and holy purposes of their creation, and consecrate themselves unto the service of God; and not, as is now the case, to the pleasure of man.

There is another and much more numerous class in this country, who are withdrawn by education or circumstances from the circle of fashionable amuse-

Sarah Grimké, *Letters on the Equality of the Sexes and the Condition of Women* (Boston: I, Knapp, 1838).

ments, but who are brought up with the dangerous and absurd idea, that marriage is a kind of preferment; and that to be able to keep their husband's house, and render his situation comfortable, is the end of her being. Much that she does and says and thinks is done in reference to this situation; and to be married is too often held up to the view of girls as the sine qua non of human happiness and human existence. For this purpose more than for any other, I verily believe the majority of girls are trained. This is demonstrated by the imperfect education which is bestowed upon them, and the little pains taken to cultivate their minds, after they leave school by the little time allowed them for reading, and by the idea being constantly inculcated, that although all household concerns should be attended to with scrupulous punctuality at particular seasons, the improvement of their intellectual capacities, is only a secondary consideration, and may serve as an occupation to fill up the odds and ends of time. In most families, it is considered a matter of far more consequence to call a girl off from making a pie, or a pudding, than to interrupt her whilst engaged in her studies. This mode of training necessarily exalts, in their view, the animal above the intellectual and spiritual nature, and teaches women to regard themselves as a kind of machinery, necessary to keep the domestic engine in order, but of little value as the *intelligent* companions of men.

Let no one think, from these remarks, that I regard a knowledge of housewifery as beneath the acquisition of women. Far from it: I believe that a complete knowledge of household affairs is an indispensable requisite in a woman's education, — that by the mistress of a family, whether married or single, doing her duty thoroughly and *understandingly*, the happiness of the family is increased to an incalculable degree, as well as a vast amount of time and money saved. All I complain of is, that our education consists so almost exclusively in culinary and other manual operations. I do long to see the time, when it will no longer be necessary for women to expend so many precious hours in furnishing "a well spread table," but that their husbands will forgo some of their accustomed indulgences in this way, and encourage their wives to devote some portion of their time to mental cultivation, even at the expense of having to dine sometimes on baked potatoes, or bread and butter. . . .

There is another way in which the general opinion, that women are inferior to men, is manifested, that bears with tremendous effect on the laboring class, and indeed on almost all who are obliged to earn a subsistence, whether it be by mental or physical exertion — I allude to the disproportionate value set on the time and labor of men and of women. A man who is engaged in teaching, can always, I believe, command a higher price for tuition than a woman — even when he teaches the same branches, and is not in any respect superior to the woman. This I know is the case in boarding and other schools with which I have been acquainted, and it is so in every occupation in which the sexes engage indiscriminately. As for example, in tailoring, a man has twice, or three times as much for making a waistcoat or pantaloons as a woman, although the work done by each may be equally good. In those employments which are peculiar to women, their time is estimated at only half the value of that of men. A woman who goes out to wash, works as hard in proportion as a wood sawyer, or a coal heaver, but she is not generally able to make more than half as much by a day's work. The low remuneration which women receive for their work, has claimed the attention of a few philanthropists, and I hope it will continue to do so until some remedy is applied for this enormous evil. . . . All these things evince the low estimation in which woman is held. There is yet another and more disastrous consequence aris-ing from this unscriptural notion — women being educated, from earliest child-hood, to regard themselves as inferior creatures, have not that self-respect which conscious equality would engender, and hence when their virtue is assailed, they yield to temptation with facility, under the idea that it rather exalts than debases them, to be connected with a superior being.

There is another class of women in this country, to whom I cannot refer, with-out feelings of the deepest shame and sorrow. I allude to our female slaves. Our southern cities are whelmed beneath a tide of pollution; the virtue of female slaves is wholly at the mercy of irresponsible tyrants, and women are bought and sold in our slave markets, to gratify the brutal lust of those who bear the name of Christians. In our slave States, if amid all her degradation, and ignorance, a woman desires to preserve her virtue unsullied, she is either bribed or whipped into compliance, or if she dares resist her seducer, her life by the laws of some of the slave States may be, and has actually been sacrificed to the fury of disap-pointed passion. Where such laws do not exist, the power which is necessarily vested in the master over his property, leaves the defenceless slave entirely at his mercy, and the sufferings of some females on this account, both physical and mental, are intense. . . . But even if any laws existed in the United States, as in Athens formerly, for the protection of female slaves, they would be null and void, because the evidence of a colored person is not admitted against a white, in any of our Courts of Justice in the slave States. . . .

Nor does the colored woman suffer alone: the moral purity of the white woman is deeply contaminated. In the daily habit of seeing the virtue of her en-slaved sister sacrificed without hesitancy or remorse, she looks upon the crimes of seduction and illicit intercourse without horror, and although not personally involved in the guilt, she loses that value for innocence in her own, as well as the other sex, which is one of the strongest safeguards to virtue. She lives in habitual intercourse with men, whom she knows to be polluted by licentiousness, and of-ten is she compelled to witness in her own domestic circle, those disgusting and heart-sickening jealousies and strafes which disgraced and distracted the family of Abraham. In addition to all this, the female slaves suffer every species of degra-dation and cruelty, which the most wanton barbarity can inflict; they are inde-cently divested of their clothing, sometimes tied up and severely whipped, sometimes prostrated on the earth, while their naked bodies are torn by the scor-pion lash. . . .

Can any American woman look at these scenes of shocking licentiousness and cruelty, and fold her hands in apathy, and say, "I have nothing to do with slavery"? *She cannot and be guiltless.*

QUESTIONS FOR READING AND DISCUSSION

1. According to Grimké, what were the deficiencies of "the butterflies of the *fash-ionable* world"?

2. Why were "women being educated, from earliest childhood, to regard them-selves as inferior creatures"? In what ways did this sense of inferiority affect women? How should women be educated, according to Grimké? Why did she believe that a "knowledge of housewifery" was "an indispensable requisite in a woman's education"?

3. What were the particular oppressions of slave women? What meanings did Grimké attach to the term *enslaved sister*? Why was "the moral purity of the white woman . . . deeply contaminated" by slavery?

4. How did Grimké propose to promote the equality of the sexes?

DOCUMENT 4

Elijah Lovejoy Confronts an Anti-Abolitionist Mob

Vigilante violence occurred frequently in Jacksonian America. Targets of vigilantes were usually individuals who were perceived as violating prevailing community values. Abolitionist speakers often faced hostile mobs. Elijah Lovejoy published an abolitionist newspaper in St. Louis, Missouri (Missouri was a slave state), before attacks on his printing establishment drove him across the Mississippi River to Alton, Illinois (Illinois was a free state). In October 1837, Lovejoy wrote a letter to a friend — excerpted here — recounting what had happened when he spoke in a neighboring town. Barely a month after this letter was written, Lovejoy was murdered in Alton.

Letter to a Friend, October 3, 1837

On Sabbath, I preached for the Rev. Mr. Campbell, the Presbyterian minister of St. Charles, [Illinois,] with whom I had formerly been acquainted. . . . I preached in the morning, and at night. After the audience was dismissed at night, and when all had left the house but Mr. Campbell, his brother-in-law, Mr. Copes, and myself, a young man came in, and passing by me, slipped the following note into my hand:

> Mr. Lovejoy,
>   Be watchful as you come from church to-night.
> A Friend

I showed the note to the two brethren present; and Mr. Campbell invited me to go home with him in consequence. I declined, however, and in company with him and Mr. Copes walked home, but a short distance, to my mother-in-law's. Brother Campbell went in with me, and Mr. C. passed on. This was about nine o'clock, and a very dark night. We received no molestation on our way, and the whole matter had passed my mind. Brother C. and I had sat conversing for nearly an hour. . . .

About ten o'clock, as Mr. Campbell and myself were conversing, I heard a knocking at the foot of the stairs. I took a candle, and opening the door of the room in which I sat, to learn the cause, I found that the knocking had called up Mrs. Lovejoy and her mother, who had enquired what was wanted. The answer was, "We want to see Mr. Lovejoy, is he in." To this I answered myself, "Yes, I am

---

Joseph Lovejoy and Owen Lovejoy, eds., *Memoir of Elijah Parish Lovejoy Who Was Murdered in the Defense of Liberty of the Press* (New York: J. S. Taylor, 1838).

here." They immediately rushed up to the portico, and two of them coming into the room laid hold of me. These two individuals, the name of one was Littler, formerly from Virginia, the other called himself a Mississippian, but his name I have not learned, though it is known in St. Charles. I asked them what they wanted of me. "We want you down stairs, d——n you," was the reply. They accordingly commenced attempting to pull me out of the house. And not succeeding immediately, one of them, Littler, began to beat me with his fists. By this time, Mrs. L. had come into the room. In doing so she had to make her way through the mob on the portico, who attempted to hinder her from coming, by rudely pushing her back, and one "chivalrous" southerner actually drew his dirk upon her. Her only reply was to strike him in the face with her hand, and then rushing past him, she flew to where I was, and throwing her arms around me, boldly faced the mobites, with a fortitude and self-devotion which none but a women and a WIFE ever displayed. While they were attempting with oaths and curses to drag me from the room, she was smiting them in the face with her hands, or clinging to me to aid in resisting their efforts, and telling them that they must first take her before they should have her husband. Her energetic measures, seconded by those of her mother and sister, induced the assailants to let me go and leave the room.

As soon as they were gone, Mrs. L.'s powers of endurance failed her, and she fainted. I carried her into another room and laid her on the bed. So soon as she recovered from her fainting, she relapsed into hysterical fits, moaning and shrieking, and calling upon my name, alternately. Mrs. L.'s health is at all times extremely delicate, and at present peculiarly so, she being some months advanced in pregnancy. Her situation at this time was truly alarming and distressing. To add to the perplexities of the moment, I had our sick child in my arms, taken up from the floor where it had been left by its grandmother, in the hurry and alarm of the first onset of the mob. The poor little sufferer, as if conscious of danger from the cries of its mother, clung to me in silence. In this condition, and while I was endeavouring to calm Mrs. L.'s dreadfully excited mind, the mob returned to the charge, breaking into the room, and rushing up to the bed-side, again attempting to force me from the house. The brutal wretches were totally indifferent to her heart-rending cries and shrieks — she was too far exhausted to move; and I suppose they would have succeeded in forcing me out, had not my friend William M. Campbell, Esq. at this juncture come in, and with undaunted boldness, assisted me in freeing myself from their clutches. Mr. Campbell is a southerner, and a slaveholder; but he is a MAN, and he will please accept my grateful thanks for his aid so promptly and so opportunely rendered; others aided in forcing the mob from the room, so that the house was now clear a second time.

They did not, however, leave the yard of the house, which was full of drunken wretches, uttering the most awful and soul-chilling oaths and imprecations, and swearing they would have me at all hazards. I could hear the epithets, "The infernal scoundrel, the d——d amalgamating Abolitionist, we'll have his heart out yet," &c. &c. They were armed with pistols and dirks, and one pistol was discharged, whether at any person or not, I did not know. The fellow from Mississippi seemed the most bent on my destruction. He did not appear at all drunken, but both in words and actions manifested the most fiendish malignity of feeling and purpose. He was telling a story of the mobites [members of mobs], which, whether true or false, (I know not,) was just calculated to madden them. His story was, that his wife had lately been violated by a negro. And this he said was all owing to me, who had instigated the negro to do the deed. He was a ruined man, he said, had just as leif die as not; but before he died he "would have my blood."

The mob now rushed up the stairs a third time, and one of them, a David Knott, of St. Charles, came in with a note signed "A citizen of St. Charles.". . . It was short, . . . requiring me to leave the town the next day at ten o'clock, in the morning. I told Mr. K. I presumed he expected no answer to such a note. He said he did not, and immediately left the room. As soon as he got out, they set up a yell, as if so many demons had just broken loose from hell. I had insulted them, it seems, by not returning an answer to their note. My friends now came round me, entreating me to send them a written answer. This I at first declined, but yielding to their urgent advice, I took my pencil and wrote as follows:

> I have already taken my passage in this stage, to leave to-morrow morning, at least by nine o'clock.
> *Elijah P. Lovejoy*

This was carried out and read to them, and at first, after some pretty violent altercation among themselves, seemed to pacify them. They went away, as I supposed finally. But after having visited the grog-shop, they returned with augmented fury and violence. My friends in the house, of whom by the way, there were not many, now became thoroughly alarmed. They joined in advising me to leave the house, and make my escape, should an opportunity occur. This I at first absolutely declined doing. I did so on the principle I had adopted, of never either seeking or avoiding danger in the way of duty. . . . I was at length, however, compelled by the united entreaties of them all, and especially of my wife, to consent to do so, should opportunity offer. Accordingly, when the efforts of those below had diverted the attention of the mob for a few moments, I left the house and went away unperceived. . . .

It was now about midnight. Through the good hand of my God upon me, I got away unperceived. I walked about a mile to my friend, Maj. Sibley's residence. Having called him up and informed him of my condition, he kindly furnished me with a horse; and having rested myself on the sofa an hour or two, for I was much exhausted, I rode to Mr. Watson's, another friend, where I arrived about day-break, four miles from town. Here Mrs. L., though exhausted and utterly unfit to leave her bed, joined me in the morning, and we came home, reaching Alton about noon, meeting with no let or hindrance, though Mrs. L. was constantly alarmed with apprehensions of pursuit from St. Charles.

On our arrival in Alton, as we were going to our house, almost the first person we met in the street, was one of the very individuals who had first broken into the house at St. Charles. Mrs. L. instantly recognized him, and at once became greatly alarmed. There was the more reason for fear, inasmuch as the mob in St. Charles had repeatedly declared their determination to pursue me, and to have my life, and one of them, the fellow from Mississippi, boasted that he was chasing me about, and that he had assisted to destroy my press in Alton. . . .

Upon these facts being made known to my friends, they deemed it advisable that our house should be guarded on Monday night. Indeed, this was necessary to quiet Mrs. L.'s fears. Though completely exhausted, as may well be supposed, from the scenes of the night before, she could not rest. The mob haunted her excited imagination, causing her continually to start from her moments of fitful slumber, with cries of alarm. This continued all the afternoon and evening of Monday, and I began to entertain serious apprehensions of the consequences. As soon, however, as our friends, to the number of ten arrived with arms in their hands, her fears subsided, and she sank into a comparatively silent sleep, which continued through most of the night. It is now Tuesday night. I am writing by the bedside of Mrs. L., whose excitement and fears have measurably returned with the darkness. She is constantly starting at every sound, while her mind is full of the horrible scenes through which she has so lately passed. What the final result will be for her I know not, but hope for the best. We have no one with us tonight, except the members of our own family. A loaded musket is standing at my bed-side, while my two brothers, in an adjoining room, have three others, together with pistols, cartridges, &c. And this is the way we live in the city of Alton! I have had inexpressible reluctance to resort to this method of defence. But dear-bought experience has taught me that there is at present no safety for me, and no defence in this place, either in the laws or the protecting aegis of public sentiment. I feel that I do not walk the streets in safety, and every night when I lie down, it is with the deep settled conviction, that there are those near me and around me, who seek my life. I have resisted this conviction as long as I could, but it has been forced upon me. Even were I safe from my enemies in Alton, my proximity to Missouri exposes me to attack from that state. And now that it is known that I am to receive no protection here, the way is open for them to do with me what they please. Accordingly a party of them from St. Louis came up and assisted in de-stroying my press, the first time. This was well known. They came armed and stationed themselves behind a wall for the purpose of firing upon any one who might attempt to defend the office. Yet who of this city has rebuked this daring outrage on the part of citizens of our state and city, upon the rights and person of the citizens of another state and city? No one. I mean there has been no public ex-pression of opinion on the subject. Our two political papers have been silent, or if speaking at all, have thrown the blame on me rather than on any one else. And if you go through the streets of Alton, or into stores and shops, where you hear one condemning these outrages upon me, you will find five approving them. This is true, both of professor and non-professor. I have no doubts that four-fifths of the inhabitants of this city are glad that my press has been destroyed by a mob, both once and again. They hate mobs, it is true, but they hate Abolitionism a great deal more. Whether creditable to them or not, this is the state of public sentiment among our citizens.

QUESTIONS FOR READING AND DISCUSSION

1. How and why did the St. Charles mob threaten Lovejoy? What was the signif-icance of the epithet "d——d amalgamating Abolitionist"? What did citizens who were not members of the mob think of Lovejoy?

2. Who protected Lovejoy? How and why? Why did public officials fail to pro-tect him?

3. Lovejoy concluded that the citizens of Alton "hate mobs . . . but they hate Abo-litionism a great deal more." Why did hate for abolitionism outweigh hate for mobs? What values underlay these hatreds? In what ways did Lovejoy chal-lenge those values?

COMPARATIVE QUESTIONS

1. How did the vision of the future expressed by John Ross and Elias Boudinot compare with that of Andrew Jackson? To what extent did their concepts of justice differ?

2. How did Jackson's opposition to the concentration of power compare with Sarah Grimké's criticisms of the inequality of the sexes? To what extent would Jackson have agreed with Grimké and vice versa?

3. The Cherokees, Grimké, and Elijah Lovejoy confronted powerful, widespread, and hostile attitudes and interests. What methods did they plan to use to change attitudes and overcome opposing interests? What were the principal ideas that both aided and hindered their efforts?

4. Judging from the documents in this chapter, how did the experiences of the federal government, Cherokees, women, and abolitionists reflect the achievements and limitations of democracy and equality during the 1820s and 1830s?

CHAPTER 11

THE FREE NORTH AND WEST
1840–1860

Americans in the 1840s and 1850s celebrated freedom, democracy, and opportunity. Whether clearing land for a farm, moving west to start over, opening a store, or working in a factory, many Americans took advantage of what Abraham Lincoln and others called the free labor system. Free labor unleashed human potential, its proponents claimed, and made possible the era's impressive economic growth and geographic expansion. The achievements of free labor came at a price, others pointed out in the following documents. Competition and accumulation stunted human growth. Women, blacks, and others were excluded from enjoying the virtues of free labor. Both the shortcomings and the strengths of free labor were magnified in the frenzy of the California gold rush.

DOCUMENT 1
The Anxiety of Gain:
Henry W. Bellows on Commerce and Morality

The opportunities that the free-labor system offered to striving, disciplined, frugal Americans had far more than economic consequences. Henry W. Bellows, a prominent Unitarian minister in New York City, criticized the personal and moral effects of Americans' desire to get ahead, to do better, to take care of business. In an article published in a Whig journal in 1845, Bellows analyzed a dark side of the free-labor system that its proponents usually ignored.

"The Influence of the Trading Spirit upon the Social and Moral Life of America," 1845

All strangers who come among us remark the excessive anxiety written in the American countenance. The widespread comfort, the facilities for livelihood, the spontaneous and cheap lands, the high price of labor, are equally observed,

---

Henry W. Bellows, "The Influence of the Trading Spirit upon the Social and Moral Life of America," in *The American Review: A Whig Journal of Politics, Literature, Art, and Science* (1845).

and render it difficult to account for these lines of painful thoughtfulness. It is not poverty, nor tyranny, nor overcompetition which produces this anxiety; that is clear. It is the concentration of the faculties upon an object, which in its very nature is unattainable — the perpetual improvement of the outward condition. There are no bounds among us to the restless desire to be better off; and this is the ambition of all classes of society. We are not prepared to allow that wealth is more valued in America than elsewhere, but in other countries the successful pursuit of it is necessarily confined to a few, while here it is open to all. No man in America is contented to be poor, or expects to continue so. There are here no established limits within which the hopes of any class of society must be confined, as in other countries. There is consequently no condition of hopes realized, in other words, of contentment. In other lands, if children can maintain the station and enjoy the means, however moderate, of their father, they are happy. Not so with us. This is not the spirit of our institutions. Nor will it long be otherwise in other countries. That equality, that breaking down of artificial barriers which has produced this universal ambition and restless activity in America, is destined to prevail throughout the earth. But because we are in advance of the world in the great political principle, and are now experiencing some of its first effects, let us not mistake these for the desirable fruits of freedom. Commerce is to become the universal pursuit of men. It is to be the first result of freedom, of popular institutions everywhere. Indeed, every land not steeped in tyranny is now feeling this impulse. But while trade is destined to free and employ the masses, it is also destined to destroy for the time much of the beauty and happiness of every land. This has been the result in our own country. We are free. It is a glorious thing that we have no serfs, with the large and unfortunate exception of our slaves — no artificial distinctions — no acknowledged superiority of blood — no station which merit may not fill — no rounds in the social ladder to which the humblest may not aspire. But the excitement, the commercial activity, the restlessness, to which this state of things has given birth, is far from being a desirable or a natural condition. It is natural to the circumstances, but not natural to the human soul. It is good and hopeful to the interests of the race, but destructive to the happiness, and dangerous to the virtue of the generation exposed to it.

Those unaccustomed, by reading or travel, to other states of society, are probably not aware how very peculiar our manner of life here is. The laboriousness of Americans is beyond all comparison, should we except the starving operatives of English factories. . . . Nay, we are all, no matter what our occupations, more or less, and all greatly, sufferers from the excessive stimulus under which every thing is done. We are all worn out with thought that does not develop our thinking faculties in a right direction, and with feeling expended upon poor and low objects. There is no profession that does not feel it. The lawyer must confine himself to his office, without vacation, to adjust a business which never sleeps or relaxes. The physician must labor day and night to repair bodies, never well from over-exertion, over-excitement, and over-indulgence. The minister must stimulate himself to supply the cravings of diseased moral appetites, and to arouse the attention of men deafened by the noise, and dizzy with the whirl in which they constantly live.

We call our country a happy country; happy, indeed, in being the home of noble political institutions, the abode of freedom; but very far from being happy in possessing a cheerful, light-hearted, and joyous people. Our agricultural regions even are infected with the same anxious spirit of gain. If ever the curse of labor was upon the race, it is upon us; nor is it simply now "by the sweat of thy brow thou shalt earn thy bread." Labor for a livelihood is dignified. But we labor for bread, and labor for pride, and labor for pleasure. A man's life with us does consist of the abundance of the things which he possesseth. To get, and to have the reputation of possessing, is the ruling passion. To it are bent all the energies of nine-tenths of our population. Is it that our people are so much more miserly and earth-born than any other? No, not by any constitutional baseness; but circumstances have necessarily given this direction to the American mind. In the hard soil of our common mother, New England — the poverty of our ancestors — their early thrift and industry — the want of other distinctions than those of property — the frown of the Puritans upon all pleasures; these circumstances combined, directed our energies from the first into the single channel of trade. And in that they have run till they have gained a tremendous head, and threaten to convert our whole people into mere money-changers and producers. Honor belongs to our fathers, who in times of great necessity met the demand for a most painful industry with such manly and unflinching hearts. But what was their hard necessity we are perpetuating as our willing servitude! what they bore as evil we seek as good. . . .

It is said that we are not a happy people. And it is true; for we most unwisely neglect all those free fountains of happiness which Providence has opened for all its children. Blessed beyond any people with the means of living, supplied to an unparalleled extent with the comforts and luxuries of life, our American homes are sombre and cheerless abodes. There is even in the air of comfort which their well-furnished apartments wear something uncomfortable. They are the habitations of those who do not live at home. They are wanting in a social and cheerful aspect. They seem fitted more to be admired than to be enjoyed. The best part of the house is for the occasional use of strangers, and not to be occupied by those who might, day by day, enjoy it, which is but one proof among many that we love to appear comfortable rather than to be so. Thus miserable pride bangs like a millstone about our hospitality. . . . We are ashamed of any thing but affluence, and when we cannot make an appearance, or furnish entertainments as showy as the richest, we will do nothing. Thus does pride close our doors. . . .

It is rare . . . to find a virtuous American past middle life, who does not regard amusements of all sorts either as childish or immoral; who possesses any acquaintance with or taste for the arts, except it be a natural and rude taste for music; or who reads any thing except newspapers, and only the political or commercial columns of those. It is the want of tastes for other things than business which gives an anxious and unhappy turn to our minds. It cannot be many years before the madness of devoting the whole day to the toils of the countinghouse will be acknowledged; before the claim of body and mind to relaxation and cheerful, exhilarating amusement will be seen. We consider the common suspicion which is felt of amusements among thoughtful people to be one of the most serious evils to which our community is exposed. . . . Children are without the protection of their parents in their enjoyments. And thus, too, is originated one of the greatest curses of our social state — the great want of intimacy and confidence between children and their parents, especially between fathers and sons.

Overt sins are more rare here than elsewhere. As far as morality is restrictive in its nature, it has accomplished a great work in America. The vices or sins which are reducible to statute, or known by name, are generally restrained. We have a large class of persons of extraordinary propriety and faultlessness of life. Our view of morals has a tendency to increase this class. Our pursuits are favorable to it. The love of gain is one of the most sober of all desires. The seriousness of a miser surpasses the gravity of a devotee. Did not every commercial city draw a large body of strangers to it, and attract many reckless and vicious persons, it would wear a very solemn aspect. The pleasure-seeking, the gay, the disorderly, are never the trading population. Large commercial cities tend to great orderliness and decency of manners and morals. But they also tend to very low and barren views of moral excellence. And the American spirit of our own day illustrates this. Our moral sense operates only in one direction. Our virtues are the virtues of merchants, and not of men. We run all to honesty, and mercantile honesty. We do not cultivate the graces of humanity. We have more conscience than heart, and more propriety than either. The fear of evil consequences is more influential than the love of goodness. There is nothing hearty, gushing, eloquent, in the national virtue. You do not see goodness leaking out from the full vessel at every motion it feels. Our goodness is formal, deliberate, premeditated. The upright man is not benevolent, and the just man is not generous. The good man is not cheerful. The religious man is not agreeable. In other words, our morals are partial, and therefore barren. It is not generally understood how great scrupulousness of character may be united with great selfishness, and how, along with a substantial virtue, there may exist the most melancholy deficiencies. This seems to be very common with us, and to be the natural result of our engrossing pursuits. Every one minds his own business, to the extreme peril of his own soul. . . . Our social condition makes us wary, suspicious, slow to commit ourselves too far in interest for others. The shyness of the tradesman communicates itself to the manners of the visitor; we learn to live within ourselves; we grow unsocial, unfraternal in feeling; and the sensibility, the affection, the cordiality, the forth-putting graces of a warm and virtuous heart, die of disuse. For our part, we are ready to say, let us have more faults and more virtues; more weaknesses and more grace; less punctilio, and more affluence of heart. Let us be less dignified and more cordial; less sanctimonious and more unselfish; less thriving and more cheerful; less toilsome and more social.

We want, as a people, a rounder character. Our humanity is pinched; our tastes are not generous. The domestic and social virtues languish. . . . Children grow up unknown to their parents. The mature despise their own youth, and have no sympathy with the romance, the buoyancy, the gayety of their children. Enterprise is our only enthusiasm. We grow to be ashamed of our best affections. We are afraid to acknowledge that we derive enjoyment from trifles, and make apologies for being amused with any thing. Thus is the beautiful field of life burnt over, and all its spontaneous flowers and fruitage destroyed; a few towering trunks alone redeeming the landscape.

QUESTIONS FOR READING AND DISCUSSION

1. According to Bellows, what were the sources of the "anxious spirit of gain"?
2. Why was there no contentment in America? Why did comfort and morality coexist with narrowness and barrenness? To what extent did ideals of equality produce discontent?
3. What remedies did Bellows propose? Why would those remedies work?

4. Bellows analyzed the costs of Americans' pursuit of happiness. What standards did he use to measure those costs? What alternative standards of happiness did he value?
5. Do you think most Americans would have agreed with Bellows? Why or why not?

DOCUMENT 2

"That Woman Is Man's Equal": The Seneca Falls Declaration

Women did not share the opportunities that the free-labor system made available to white men. In 1848, more than 150 women and 30 men met at Seneca Falls, New York, to protest the male supremacy that prevailed throughout America. This first women's-rights convention adopted the "Declaration of Sentiments," reprinted here, drafted by Elizabeth Cady Stanton. Born in 1815 in a small town in New York, Stanton received a good education and, with her husband, Henry B. Stanton, was an active abolitionist. Stanton's Seneca Falls Declaration appealed to widely shared American ideals in order to demonstrate that drastic changes were necessary if those ideals were to have much meaning for women.

"Declaration of Sentiments," 1848

When, in the course of human events, it becomes necessary for one portion of the family of man to assume among the people of the earth a position different from that which they have hitherto occupied, but one to which the laws of nature and of nature's God entitle them, a decent respect to the opinions of mankind requires that they should declare the causes that impel them to such a course.

We hold these truths to be self-evident: that all men and women are created equal; that they are endowed by their Creator with certain inalienable rights; that among these are life, liberty, and the pursuit of happiness; that to secure these rights governments are instituted, deriving their just powers from the consent of the governed. Whenever any form of government becomes destructive of these ends, it is the right of those who suffer from it to refuse allegiance to it, and to insist upon the institution of a new government, laying its foundations on such principles, and organizing its powers in such form, as to them shall seem most likely to effect their safety and happiness. Prudence, indeed, will dictate that governments long established should not be changed for light and transient causes; and accordingly all experience hath shown that mankind are more disposed to suffer, while evils are sufferable, than to right themselves by abolishing the forms to which they were accustomed. But when a long train of abuses and usurpations, pursuing invariably the same object evinces a design to reduce them under absolute despotism, it is their duty to throw off such government, and to provide new guards for their future security. Such has been the patient sufferance of the

Susan B. Anthony, Elizabeth Cady Stanton, and Matilda Joslyn Gage, eds., *History of Woman Suffrage* (Rochester, N.Y.: S. B. Anthony, 1889).

women under this government, and such is now the necessity which constrains them to demand the equal station to which they are entitled.

The history of mankind is a history of repeated injuries and usurpations on the part of man toward woman, having in direct object the establishment of an absolute tyranny over her. To prove this, let facts be submitted to a candid world.

He has never permitted her to exercise her inalienable right to the elective franchise. He has compelled her to submit to laws, in the formation of which she had no voice. He has withheld from her rights which are given to the most ignorant and degraded men — both natives and foreigners.

Having deprived her of this first right of a citizen, the elective franchise, thereby leaving her without representation in the halls of legislation, he has opposed her on all sides.

He has made her, if married, in the eye of the law, civilly dead.

He has taken from her all right in property, even to the wages she earns.

He has made her, morally, an irresponsible being, as she can commit many crimes with impunity, provided they be done in the presence of her husband. In the covenant of marriage, she is compelled to promise obedience to her husband, he becoming, to all intents and purposes, her master — the law giving him power to deprive her of her liberty, and to administer chastisement.

He has so framed the laws of divorce, as to what shall be the proper causes, and in case of separation, to whom the guardianship of the children shall be given, as to be wholly regardless of the happiness of women — the law, in all cases, going upon a false supposition of the supremacy of man, and giving all power into his hands.

After depriving her of all rights as a married woman, if single, and the owner of property, he has taxed her to support a government which recognizes her only when her property can be made profitable to it.

He has monopolized nearly all the profitable employments, and from those she is permitted to follow, she receives but a scanty remuneration. He closes against her all the avenues to wealth and distinction which he considers most honorable to himself. As a teacher of theology, medicine, or law, she is not known.

He has denied her the facilities for obtaining a thorough education, all colleges being closed against her.

He allows her in Church, as well as State, but in a subordinate position, claiming Apostolic authority for her exclusion from the ministry, and, with some exceptions, from any public participation in the affairs of the Church.

He has created a false public sentiment by giving to the world a different code of morals for men and women, by which moral delinquencies which exclude women from society, are not only tolerated, but deemed of little account in man.

He has usurped the prerogative of Jehovah himself, claiming it as his right to assign for her a sphere of action, when that belongs to her conscience and to her God.

He has endeavored, in every way that he could, to destroy her confidence in her own powers, to lessen her self-respect, and to make her willing to lead a dependent and abject life.

Now, in view of this entire disfranchisement of one-half the people of this country, their social and religious degradation — in view of the unjust laws above mentioned, and because women do feel themselves aggrieved, oppressed, and fraudulently deprived of their most sacred rights, we insist that they have immediate admission to all the rights and privileges which belong to them as citizens of the United States.

In entering upon the great work before us, we anticipate no small amount of misconception, misrepresentation, and ridicule; but we shall use every instrumentality within our power to effect our object. We shall employ agents, circulate tracts, petition the State and National legislatures, and endeavor to enlist the pulpit and the press in our behalf. We hope this Convention will be followed by a series of Conventions embracing every part of the country.

RESOLUTIONS

WHEREAS, The great precept of nature is conceded to be, that "man shall pursue his own true and substantial happiness." [William] Blackstone in his *Commentaries* remarks, that this law of Nature being coequal with mankind, and dictated by God himself, is of course superior in obligation to any other. It is binding over all the globe, in all countries and at all times; no human laws are of any validity if contrary to this, and such of them as are valid, derive all their force, and all their validity, and all their authority, mediately and immediately, from this original; therefore,

Resolved, That such laws as conflict, in any way, with the true and substantial happiness of woman, are contrary to the great precept of nature and of no validity, for this is "superior in obligation to any other."

Resolved, That all laws which prevent woman from occupying such a station in society as her conscience shall dictate, or which place her in a position inferior to that of man, are contrary to the great precept of nature, and therefore of no force or authority.

Resolved, That woman is man's equal — was intended to be so by the Creator, and the highest good of the race demands that she should be recognized as such.

Resolved, That the women of this country ought to be enlightened in regard to the laws under which they live, that they may no longer publish their degradation by declaring themselves satisfied with their present position, nor their ignorance, by asserting that they have all the rights they want.

Resolved, That inasmuch as man, while claiming for himself intellectual superiority, does accord to woman moral superiority, it is pre-eminently his duty to encourage her to speak and teach, as she has an opportunity, in all religious assemblies.

Resolved, That the same amount of virtue, delicacy, and refinement of behavior that is required of woman in the social state, should also be required of man, and the same transgressions should be visited with equal severity on both man and woman.

Resolved, That the objection of indelicacy and impropriety, which is so often brought against woman when she addresses a public audience, comes with a very ill-grace from those who encourage, by their attendance, her appearance on the stage, in the concert, or in feats of the circus.

Resolved, That woman has too long rested satisfied in the circumscribed limits which corrupt customs and a perverted application of the Scriptures have marked out for her, and that it is time she should move in the enlarged sphere which her great Creator has assigned her.

Resolved, That it is the duty of the women of this country to secure to themselves their sacred right to the elective franchise.

Resolved, That the equality of human rights results necessarily from the fact of the identity of the race in capabilities and responsibilities.

Resolved, therefore, That, being invested by the Creator with the same capabilities, and the same consciousness of responsibility for their exercise, it is demonstrably the right and duty of woman, equally with man, to promote every righteous cause by every righteous means; and especially in regard to the great subjects of morals and religion, it is self-evidently her right to participate with her brother in teaching them, both in private and in public, by writing and by speaking, by any instrumentalities proper to be used, and in any assemblies proper to be held; and this being a self-evident truth growing out of the divinely implanted principles of human nature, any custom or authority adverse to it, whether modern or wearing the hoary sanction of antiquity, is to be regarded as a self-evident falsehood, and at war with mankind.

QUESTIONS FOR READING AND DISCUSSION

1. Why do you think that the writers of the Seneca Falls Declaration used the Declaration of Independence as their model?
2. In what ways did men exercise "an absolute tyranny" over women? Why?
3. In what sense were married women "civilly dead" in the eyes of the law? Why was suffrage important for women?
4. What changes did the Seneca Falls Declaration propose? What methods might bring about those changes?
5. How might opponents of the declaration have responded to these arguments? How would the assumptions of opponents be likely to differ from those of the declaration?

DOCUMENT 3

A Farmer's View of His Wife

Widespread assumptions about the proper relations between husband and wife emerged from a conversation Eliza Farnham had with a newly married farmer on an Illinois river-boat. Born in New York, Farnham described her conversation in Life in Prairie Land *(1846), a book about her experiences in Illinois in the late 1830s, shortly after her marriage. Farnham's account of the conversation disclosed her own views as well as those of the farmer.*

Eliza Farnham
"Conversation with a Newly-Wed Westerner," 1846

The strange character of the feeling manifested by [the] husband, made me very desirous of drawing him into an expression of it in words before he left us, and as their landing-place would probably be reached on the third morning, I availed myself of a chance meeting . . . to engage him in conversation. A few

---

Eliza Farnham, *Life in Prairie Land* (New York: Harper and Brothers, 1846).

words about the height of the water, the timber, and the prairies, served the purpose.

"You are going to become a prairie farmer?" I said.

"No, I've been one afore, I've got a farm up the river hyur that I've *crapped* twice a'ready; there's a good cabin on it, and it's about as good a place, I reckon, as can be found in these diggins."

"Then you built a cage," I said, "and went back for your bird to put in it?"

He looked at me, and his face underwent a contortion, of which words will convey but a faint idea. It was a mingled expression of pride and contempt, faintly disguised by a smile that was intended to hide them.

"Why, I don't know what you Yankees call a bird," he replied, "but I call her a woman. I shouldn't make much account of havin a bird in my cabin, but a good, stout woman I should calculate was worth somethin. She can pay her way, and do a handsome thing besides, helpin me on the farm."

Think of that, ye belles and fair-handed maidens! How was my sentiment rebuked!

"Well, we'll call her a woman, which is, in truth, much the more rational appellation. You intend to make her useful as well as ornamental to your home?"

"Why, yes; I calculate 'taint of much account to have a woman if she ain't of no use. I lived up hyur two year, and had to have another man's woman do all my washin and mendin and so on, and at last I got tired o' totin my plunder back and forth, and thought I might as well get a woman of my own. There's a heap of things beside these, that she'll do better than I can, I reckon; every man ought to have a woman to do his cookin and such like, 'kase it's easier for them than it is for us. They take to it kind o' naturally."

I could scarcely believe that there was no more human vein in the animal, and determined to sound him a little deeper.

"And this bride of yours is the one, I suppose, that you thought of all the while you were making your farm and building your cabin? You have, I dare say, made a little garden, or set out a tree, or done something of the kind to please her alone?"

"No, I never allowed to get a woman till I found my neighbors went ahead of me with 'em, and then I should a got one right thar, but there wasn't any stout ones in our settlement, and it takes so long to make up to a *stranger*, that I allowed I mought as well go back and see the old folks, and git somebody that I know'd thar to come with me."

"And had you no choice made among your acquaintances? was there no one person of whom you thought more than another?" said I.

"Yas, there was a gal I used to know that was stouter and bigger than this one. I should a got her if I could, but she'd got married and gone off over the *Mississippi*, somewhar."

The cold-hearted fellow! it was a perfectly business matter with him.

"Did you select this one solely on account of her size?" said I.

"Why, pretty much," he replied; "I reckon women are some like horses and oxen, the biggest can do the most work, and that's what I want one for."

"And is that all?" I asked, more disgusted at every word. "Do you care nothing about a pleasant face to meet you when you go home from the field, or a soft voice to speak kind words when you are sick, or a gentle friend to converse with you in your leisure hours?"

"Why, as to that," he said. "I reckon a woman ain't none the worse for talk because she's stout and able to work. I calculate she'll mind her own business pretty much, and if she does she won't talk a great deal to me; that ain't what I got her for."

"But suppose when you get home she should be unhappy, and want to see her parents and other friends?"

"Why I don't allow she will; I didn't get her for that. . . . I shall give her enough to eat and wear, and I don't calculate she'll be very *daunsey* if she gets that; if she is she'll git *shet* of it after a while."

My indignation increased at every word.

"But you brought her away from her home to be treated as a human being, not as an animal or machine. Marriage is a moral contract, not a mere bargain of business. The parties promise to study each other's happiness, and endeavor to promote it. You could not marry a woman as you could buy a washing machine, though you might want her for the same purpose. If you take the machine there is no moral obligation incurred, except to pay for it. If you take the woman, there is. Before you entered into this contract I could have shown you a machine that would have answered your purpose admirably. It would have washed and ironed all your clothes, and when done, stood in some out-of-the-way corner till it was wanted again. You would have been under no obligation, not even to feed and clothe it, as you now are. It would have been the better bargain, would it not?"

"Why that would be according to what it cost in the fust place; but it would-n't be justly the same thing as havin a wife, I reckon, even if it was give to you."

"No, certainly not; it would free you from many obligations that you are un-der to a wife" (it was the first time, by the way, he had used the word), "and leave you to pursue your own pleasure without seeing any sorrowful or sour faces about you."

"Oh, I calculate sour faces won't be of much account to me. If a woman'll mind her business, she may look as thunderin as a live airthquake, I shan't mind it. . . . I reckon the Yankees may do as they like about them things, and I shall do jist the same. I don't think a woman's of much account anyhow, if she can't help herself a little and me too. If the Yankee women was *raised up like the women* here *aar*, they'd cost a heap less and be worth more."

I turned away, saying that I trusted his wife would agree with him in these opinions, or they might lead to some unpleasant differences.

"Oh, as to that," said he, "I reckon her pinions won't go fur anyhow; she'll think pretty much as I do, or not at all."

QUESTIONS FOR READING AND DISCUSSION

1. Why did the farmer want a wife? What traits did he seek in a wife?
2. What did Farnham mean by saying to the farmer, "you built a cage . . . and went back for your bird to put in it"? How did Farnham's views about wives differ from the farmer's?
3. Did Farnham and the farmer disagree on all points?
4. Farnham stated that she "trusted his [the farmer's] wife would agree with him in these opinions." Why did Farnham think the farmer's wife would agree with him rather than with her? What did Farnham's observations suggest about her own perceptions of what women believed about themselves and why?

DOCUMENT 4

Gold Fever

California gold epitomized the wealth and success that seemed just beyond the grasp of many Americans during the 1840s and 1850s. The gold rush offered opportunities for gain that years of ordinary toil could never supply. Gold was there for the taking, for the dissolute hustler as well as the upright practitioner of free-labor values. Or so it seemed. Walter Colton kept a diary as the gold fever struck Monterey, California, in the summer of 1849. Born in Vermont in 1797, Colton became a minister and served as a chaplain in the U.S. Navy. Shortly after Americans seized Monterey for the United States in 1846, Colton was appointed alcalde of the city, an office that combined duties of mayor and judge. When rumors of gold reached Monterey, Colton witnessed the contagion of gold fever and charted the spread of the epidemic in his diary, excerpted here.

Walter Colton
California Gold Rush Diary, 1849–1850

Monday, May 29 [1849]. Our town was startled out of its quiet dreams to-day, by the announcement that gold had been discovered on the American Fork. The men wondered and talked, and the women too; but neither believed. . . .

Monday, June 5. Another report reached us this morning from the American Fork. The rumor ran, that several workmen, while excavating for a millrace, had thrown up little shining scales of a yellow ore, that proved to be gold; that an old Sonoranian, who had spent his life in gold mines, pronounced it the genuine thing. Still the public incredulity remained, save here and there a glimmer of faith. . . .

Tuesday, June 6. Being troubled with the golden dream . . . , I determined to put an end to the suspense, and dispatched a messenger this morning to the American Fork. He will have to ride, going and returning, some four hundred miles, but his report will be reliable. We shall then know whether this gold is a fact or a fiction. . . .

Tuesday, June 20. My messenger sent to the mines, has returned with specimens of the gold; he dismounted in a sea of upturned faces. As he drew forth the yellow lumps from his pockets, and passed them around among the eager crowd, the doubts, which had lingered till now, fled. All admitted they were gold, except one old man, who still persisted they were some Yankee invention, got up to reconcile the people to the change of flag. The excitement produced was intense; and many were soon busy in their hasty preparations for a departure to the mines. The family who had kept house for me caught the moving infection. Husband and wife were both packing up; the blacksmith dropped his hammer, the carpenter his plane, the mason his trowel, the farmer his sickle, the baker his loaf, and the tapster his bottle. All were off for the mines, some on horses, some on carts,

---

Walter Colton, *Three Years in California* (1850; Temecula, Calif.: Reprint Services Corp., 1992) 242–375.

and some on crutches, and one went in a litter. An American woman, who had recently established a boarding-house here, pulled up stakes, and was off before her lodgers had even time to pay their bills. Debtors ran, of course. I have only a community of women left, and a gang of prisoners, with here and there a soldier, who will give his captain the slip at the first chance. I don't blame the fellow a whit; seven dollars a month, while others are making two or three hundred a day! [T]hat is too much for human nature to stand. . . .

Tuesday, July 18. Another bag of gold from the mines, and another spasm in the community. It was brought down by a sailor from Yuba river, and contains a hundred and thirty-six ounces. It is the most beautiful gold that has appeared in the market. . . . My carpenters, at work on the school-house, on seeing it, threw down their saws and planes, shouldered their picks, and are off for the Yuba. Three seamen ran from the Warren, forfeiting their four years' pay; and a whole platoon of soldiers from the fort left only their colors behind. . . .

Thursday, Aug. 16. Four citizens of Monterey are just in from the gold mines on Feather River, where they worked in company with three others. They employed about thirty wild Indians, who are attached to the rancho owned by one of the party. They worked precisely seven weeks and three days, and have divided seventy-six thousand eight hundred and forty-four dollars — nearly eleven thousand dollars to each. . . . [L]et me introduce a man, well known to me, who has worked on the Yuba river sixty-four days, and brought back, as the result of his individual labor, five thousand three hundred and fifty-six dollars. . . . [L]et me introduce another townsman, who has worked on the North Fork fifty-seven days, and brought back four thousand five hundred and thirty-four dollars. . . . Is not this enough to make a man throw down his leger and shoulder a pick? . . .

Tuesday, Aug. 28. The gold mines have upset all social and domestic arrangements in Monterey; the master has become his own servant, and the servant his own lord. The millionaire is obliged to groom his own horse, and roll his wheelbarrow; and the hidalgo — in whose veins flows the blood of all the Cortes—to clean his own boots! Here is lady L——, who has lived here seventeen years, the pride and ornament of the place, with a broomstick in her jewelled hand! And here is lady B—— with her daughter — all the way from "old Virginia," where they graced society with their varied accomplishments — now floating between the parlor and kitchen, and as much at home in the one as the other! And here is lady S——, whose cattle are on a thousand hills, lifting, like Rachel of old, her bucket of water from the deep well! And here is lady M. L——, whose honeymoon is still full of soft seraphic light, unhouseling a potatoe, and hunting the hen that laid the last egg. And here am I, who have been a man of some note in my day, loafing on the hospitality of the good citizens, and grateful for a meal, though in an Indian's wigwam. Why, is not this enough to make one wish the gold mines were in the earth's flaming centre, from which they sprung? . . .

Saturday, Sept. 16 . . . All distinctions indicative of means have vanished; the only capital required is muscle and an honest purpose. I met a man to-day from the mines in patched buckskins, rough as a badger from his hole, who had fifteen thousand dollars in yellow dust, swung at his back. . . . And there is more where this came from. His rights in the great domain are equal to yours, and his prospects of getting it out vastly better. With these advantages, he bends the knee to no man, but strides along in his buckskins, a lord of earth by a higher prescriptive privilege than what emanates from the partiality of kings. . . . Clear out of the way with your crests, and crowns, and pedigree trees, and let this democrat pass. . . .

Wednesday, Oct. 18. We are camped in the centre of the gold mines, in the heart of the richest deposits which have been found, and where there are many hundred at work. I have taken some pains to ascertain the average per man that is got out; it must be less than half an ounce per day. It might be more were there any stability among the diggers; but half their time is consumed in what they call prospecting; that is, looking up new deposits. An idle rumor, or more surmise, will carry them off in this direction or that, when perhaps they gathered nothing for their weariness and toil. . . . I have never met with one who had the strength of purpose to resist these roving temptations. . . .

Thursday, Oct. 19. All the gold-diggers through the entire encampment, were shaken out of their slumbers this morning by a report that a solid pocket of gold had been discovered in a bend of the Stanislaus. In half an hour a motley multitude, covered with crowbars, pickaxes, spades, rifles, and washbowls, went streaming over the hills in the direction of the new deposits. You would have thought some fortress was to be stormed, or some citadel sapped. . . . The most curious feature in this business is, that out of a regiment of gold-hunters, where the utmost apparent confusion prevails, the absence of two men should be noticed. But the motions of every man are watched. Even when he gathers up his traps, takes formal leave, and is professedly bound home, he is tracked for leagues. No disguise can avail him; the most successful war-stratagem would fail here. . . .

Thursday, Nov. 2. Quite a sensation was produced among the gold-diggers this morning by the arrival of a wagon from Stockton, freighted with provisions and a barrel of liquor. The former had been getting scarce, and the latter had long since entirely given out. The prices of the first importation were — flour, two dollars a pound; sugar and coffee, four dollars; and the liquor, which was nothing more nor less than New England rum, was twenty dollars the quart. But few had bottles: every species of retainer was resorted to; some took their quart cups, some their coffee-pots, and others their sauce-pans; while one fellow, who had neither, offered ten dollars to let him suck with a straw from the bung. All were soon in every variety of excitement, from prattling exhilaration, to roaring inebriety. Some shouted, some danced, and some wrestled: a son of Erin poured out his soul on the beauties of the Emerald isle; a German sung the songs of his father-land; a Yankee apostrophized the mines, which swelled in the hills around; an Englishman challenged all the bears in the mountain glens to mortal combat; and a Spaniard, posted aloft on a beetling crag, addressed the universe. . . .

Wednesday, Nov. 8. Some fifty thousand persons are drifting up and down these slopes of the great Sierra, of every hue, language, and clime, tumultuous and confused as a flock of wild geese taking wing at the crack of a gun, or autumnal leaves strown on the atmospheric tides by the breath of the whirlwind. All are in quest of gold; and, with eyes dilated to the circle of the moon, rush this way and that, as some new discovery, or fictitious tale of success may suggest. Some are with tents, and some without; some have provisions, and some are on their last ration; some are carrying crowbars; some pickaxes and spades; some wash-bowls and cradles; some hammers and drills, and powder enough to blow up the rock of Gibraltar. . . . Such a mixed and motley crowd — such a restless, roving, rummaging, ragged multitude, never before roared in the rookeries of man. . . . Each great camping-ground is denoted by the ruins of shovels and shanties, the bleaching bones of the dead, disinhumed by the wolf, and the skeleton of the culprit, still swinging in the wind, from the limb of a tree, overshadowed by the raven. . . .

Monday, May 14 [1850]. Much has been said of the amounts of gold taken from the mines by Sonoranians, Chilians, and Peruvians, and carried out of the country. As a general fact, this apprehension and alarm is without any sound basis. Not one pound of gold in ten, gathered by these foreigners, is shipped off to their credit: it is spent in the country for provisions, clothing, and in the hazards of the gaming table. It falls into the hands of those who command the avenues of commerce, and ultimately reaches our own mints. I have been in a camp of five hundred Sonoranians, who had not gold enough to buy a month's provisions — all had gone, through their improvident habits, to the capacious pockets of the Americans. To drive them out of California, or interdict their operations, is to abstract that amount of labor from the mines, and curtail proportionably the proceeds. If gold, slumbering in the river banks and mountains of California, be more valuable to us than when stamped into eagles and incorporated into our national currency, then drive out the Sonoranians: but if you would have it here and not there, let those diggers alone. When gold shall begin to fail, or require capital and machinery, you will want these hardy men to quarry the rocks and feed your stampers; and when you shall plunge into the Cinnabar mountains, you will want them to sink your shafts and kindle fires under your great quicksilver retorts. They will become the hewers of wood and drawers of water to American capital and enterprise. But if you want to perform this drudgery yourself, drive out the Sonoranians, and upset that cherished system of political economy founded in a spirit of wisdom and national justice. . . .

Wednesday, June 20. The causes which exclude slavery from California lie within a nut-shell. All here are diggers, and free white diggers wont dig with slaves. They know they must dig themselves: they have come out here for that purpose, and they wont degrade their calling by associating it with slave-labor: self-preservation is the first law of nature. They have nothing to do with slavery in the abstract, or as it exists in other communities; not one in ten cares a button for its abolition, nor the Wilmot proviso either: all they look at is their own position; they must themselves swing the pick, and they wont swing it by the side of negro slaves. That is their feeling, their determination, and the upshot of the whole business. An army of half a million, backed by the resources of the United States, could not shake their purpose. Of all men with whom I have ever met, the most firm, resolute, and indomitable, are the emigrants into California. They feel that they have got into a new world, where they have a right to shape and settle things in their own way. No mandate, unless it comes like a thunder-bolt straight out of heaven, is regarded. . . . They walk over hills treasured with the precious ores; they dwell by streams paved with gold; while every mountain around soars into the heaven. . . . All these belong to them; they walk in their midst; they feel their presence and power, and partake of their grandeur. Think you that such men will consent to swing the pick by the side of slaves? Never! While the stream owns its source, or the mountain its base. You may call it pride, or what you will, but *there* it is — deep as the foundations of our nature, and unchangeable as the laws of its divine Author.

QUESTIONS FOR READING AND DISCUSSION

1. According to Colton, how and why did gold fever upset social and domestic arrangements in Monterrey? What did he mean by stating, "All distinctions indicative of means have vanished; the only capital required is muscle and an honest purpose"?
2. How did gold fever influence white miners' attitudes toward other racial and ethnic groups? Why, according to Colton, did miners favor excluding slavery from California?
3. To what extent did the gold rush exemplify the operation of the free-labor system?
4. Was California during the gold rush atypical of American society east of the Mississippi during the 1840s and 1850s? Why or why not?

COMPARATIVE QUESTIONS

1. How do Henry Bellows's views of the temptations and anxieties of material success compare with the gold rush scenes witnessed by Walter Colton?
2. In what ways are the views of men in the Seneca Falls Declaration comparable to those of Bellows and the prairie farmer interviewed by Eliza Farnham?
3. The prairie farmer, Farnham, and the authors of the Seneca Falls Declaration asserted convictions about what women's rights were in fact and what they should be. What assumptions, if any, did these commentators share? What differences did they express? What arguments might appeal most strongly to the farmer's wife? What might influence her or her husband to reconsider their opinions?
4. Each of the documents in this chapter provides evidence of the achievements and limitations freedom offered Americans in the 1840s and 1850s. To what extent do the documents suggest that the problems of American society could be overcome by expanding freedom?

CHAPTER 12

THE SLAVE SOUTH
1820–1860

B y the 1850s, white southerners often claimed that cotton was king. The southern states produced millions of pounds of cotton, but they also grew huge quantities of tobacco, rice, and sugar. Slaves provided most of the labor for these valuable crops, as well as doing a wide variety of other chores, ranging from cleaning house and minding children to building houses, sailing boats, and even managing the labor of other slaves. In most ways, slavery was king in the South. The following documents disclose the distinctive tensions that slavery generated among white and black southerners and between the South and the North.

DOCUMENT 1
Plantation Rules

Masters made the rules on their plantations. The rules defined in general terms what the master expected slaves to do and not to do. Rules differed greatly from master to master, and, as circumstances required, they had to be changed. In most cases, masters communicated their rules in face-to-face encounters with their slaves. Some masters recorded their rules for their own reference or the use of an overseer or stranger. Bennet Barrow, the owner of nearly 200 slaves on his cotton plantation in Louisiana, noted his plantation rules in his diary on May 1, 1838, the source of the following selection. Barrow's rules illustrate not only his specific concerns but also the underlying question that every master confronted: How best to get slaves to do what their masters wanted?

Bennet Barrow
Highland Plantation Journal, May 1, 1838

No negro shall leave the place at any time without my permission, or in my absence that of the Driver the driver in that case being responsible, for the cause of such absence, which ought never to be omitted to be enquired into —

Edwin Adams Davis, ed., *Plantation Life in the Florida Parishes of Louisiana, 1836–1846, as Reflected in the Diary of Bennet H. Barrow* (New York: AMS Press, 1943).

The Driver should never leave the plantation, unless on business of the plantation

No negro shall be allowed to marry out of the plantation

No negro shall be allowed to sell anything without my express permission I have ever maintained the doctrine that my negroes have no time Whatever, that they are always liable to my call without questioning for a moment the propriety of it, I adhere to this on the grounds of expediency and right. The verry security of the plantation requires that a general and uniform control over the people of it should be exercised. Who are to protect the plantation from the intrusions of ill designed persons When evry body is a broad? Who can tell the moment When a plantation might be threatened with destruction from Fire — could the flames be arrested if the negroes are scattered throughout the neighborhood, seeking their amusement. Are these not duties of great importance, and in which evry negro himself is deeply interested to render this part of the rule justly applicable, however, it would be necessary that such a settled arrangement should exist on the plantation as to make it unnecessary for a negro to leave it. . . . You must, therefore make him as comfortable at Home as possible, affording him What is essentially necessary for his happiness — you must provide for him Your self and by that means creat in him a habit of perfect dependence on you—Allow it ounce to be understood by a negro that he is to provide for himself, and you that moment give him an undeniable claim on you for a portion of his time to make this provision, and should you from necessity, or any other cause, encroach upon his time — disappointment and discontent are seriously felt — if I employ a labourer to perform a certain quantum of work per day and I agree to pay him, a certain amount for the performance of said work When he had accomplished it I of course have no further claim on him for his time or services — but how different is it with a slave — Who can calculate the exact profit or expence of a slave one year with another, if I furnish my negro with evry necessary of life, without the least care on his part — if I support him in sickness, however long it may be, and pay all his expenses, though he does nothing — if I maintain him in his old age, when he is incapable of rendering either himself or myself any service, am I not entitled to an exclusive right to his time good feelings, and a sense of propriety would all ways prevent unnecessary employment on the Sabbath, and policy would check any exaction of excessive labor in common. . . . I never give a negro a Pass to go from home without he first states particularly where he wishes to go, and assigns a cause for his desiring to be absent. if he offers a good reason, I never refuse, but otherwise, I never grant him a Pass, and feel satisfied that no practice is more prejudicial to the community, and to the negros themselves, than that of giving them general Passes to go Where they please I am so opposed to this plan that I never permit any negro to remain on my plantation, whose Pass does not authorize him expressly to come to it — Some think that after a negro has done his work it is an act of oppression to confine him to the plantation, when he might be strolling about the neighborhood for his amusement and recreation — this is certainly a mistaken humanity. Habit is evry thing — The negro who is accustomed to remain constantly at Home, is just as satisfied with the society on the plantation as that which he would find elsewhere, and the verry restrictions laid upon him being equally imposed on others, he does not feel them, for society is kept at Home for them. . . . No rule that I have stated is of more importance than that relating to negroes marrying out of the plantation it seems to me, from What observations I have made it is utterly impossible to have any method, or regularity when the men and women are permitted to take wives and husbands indiscriminately off the plantation, negroes are verry much desposed to pursue a course of this kind, and without being able to assign any good reason, though the motive can be readily perceived, and is a strong one with them, but one that tend not in the Least to the benefit of the Master, or their ultimate good. the inconveniences that at once strikes one as arising out of such a practice are these —

First — in allowing the men to marry out of the plantation, you give them an uncontrolable right to be frequently absent

2d — Wherever their wives live, there they consider their homes, consequently they are indifferent to the interest of the plantation to which they actually belong —

3d — it creates a feeling of independance, from being, of right, out of the control of the masters for a time —

4th — They are repeatedly exposed to temptation from meeting and associating with negroes from different directions, and with various habits & vices —

5th — Where there are several women on a plantation, they may have husbands from different plantations belonging to different persons. These men posess different habits are acustomed to different treatment, and have different privileges, so your plantation every day becomes a rendeezvous of a medly of characters. Negroes who have the privilege of a monthly Passes to go where they please, and at any hour that they say they have finished their work, to leave their Master's plan'tn come into yours about midday, When your negroes are at work, and the Driver engaged, they either take possession of houses their wives live — and go to sleep or stroll about in perfect idleness — feeling themselves accessible to every thing. What an example to those at work at the time — can any circumstance be more Intrusive of good order and contentment

Sixthly — When a man and his wife belong to different persons, they are liable to be separated from each other, as well as their children, whether by caprice of either of the parties, or When there is a sale of property — this keeps up an unsettled state of things, and gives rise to repeated new connections. . . . I prefer giving them money of Christmas to their making any thing, thereby creating an interest with you and yours. . . . I furnish my negroes regularly with their full share of allowance weakly. 4 pound & 5 pound of meat to evry thing that goes in the field—2 pound over 4 years 1 1/2 between 15 months and 4 years old — Clear good meat — I give them cloths twice a year, two suits — one pair shoes for winter evry third year a blanket. . . . I supply them with tobacco if a negro is suffered to sell any thing he chooses without any inquiry being made, a spirit of trafficing at once is created. to carry this on, both means and time are necessary, neither of which is he of right possessed. A negro would not be content to sell only What he raises or makes either corn (should he be permitted) or poultry, or the like, but he would sell part of his allowance allso, and would be tempted to commit robberies to obtain things to sell. Besides, he would never go through his work carefully, particularly When other engagements more interesting and pleasing are constantly passing through his mind, but would be apt to slight his work That the general conduct of master has a verry considerable influence on the character and habits of his slave, will be readily admitted. When a master is uniform in his own habits & conduct, his slaves know his wishes, and What they are to expect if they act in opposition to, or conformity with them, therefore, the more order and contentment Exist.

A plantation might be considered as a piece of machinery, to operate success-fully, all of its parts should be uniform and exact, and the impelling force regular and steady; and the master, if he pretended at all to attend to his business, should be their impelling force, if a master exhibits no extraordinary interest in the pro-ceedings on his plantation, it is hardly to be expected that any other feelings but apathy, and perfect indifference could exist with his negroes, and it would be un-reasonable for him . . . to expect attention and exaction from those, Who have no other interest than to avoid the displeasure of their master. in the different de-partments on the plantation as much destinction and separation are kept up as possible with a view to create responsibility — The Driver has a directed charge of every thing, but there are subordinate persons, who take the more immediate care of the different departments. For instance, I make one persons answerable for my stock. Horses cattle hogs, &c. another the plantation untensials &c. one the sick — one the poultry. another providing for and taking care of the children whose parents are in the field &c. As good a plan as could be adopted, to estab-lish security and good order on the plantation is that of constituting a watch at night, consisting of two or more men. they are answerable for all trespasses com-mited during their watch, unless they produce the offender. or give immediate alarm. When the protection of a plantation is left to the negroes generally, you at once percieve the truth of the maxim that what is evry one's business, is no one's business. but when a regular watch is Established, Each in turn performs his tour of duty, so that the most careless is at times, made to be observant and watch-ful — the very act of organizing a watch bespeaks a care and attention on the part of a master, Which has the due influence on the negro —

Most of the above rules "in fact with the exception of the last" I have adopted since 1833. And with success — get your negroes ounce disciplined and planting is a pleasure — A Hell without it never have an Overseer — Every negro to come up Sunday after their allowance Clean & head well combed — it gives pride to every one, the fact of master feeling proud of them, When clean &c.

Never allow any man to talk to your negroes, nothing more injurious.

QUESTIONS FOR READING AND DISCUSSION

1. Barrow wrote that he considered it a matter of "expediency and right" that his slaves "have no time Whatever, that they are always liable to my call without questioning for a moment the propriety of it." In what ways did this rule in-fluence Barrow's slaves and Barrow himself? Did Barrow's slaves have any free time?

2. Why did Barrow prohibit his slaves from marrying slaves belonging to an-other master and from selling chickens or corn?

3. What did he believe motivated his slaves? How did he try to influence their motivation? Why did he believe it so important to "furnish my negro with evry necessary of life"?

4. Does the diary offer hints about the degree to which Barrow's slaves followed his rules? Does it provide evidence that his slaves had rules of their own, in conflict with his? If Barrow's slaves had commented on his rules, what might they have said about them to one another?

DOCUMENT 2

Nat Turner Explains Why
He Became an Insurrectionist

In August 1831, Nat Turner led a slave insurrection in Southampton, Virginia, not far from the small town of Jerusalem. A learned and deeply religious man, Turner, accompanied by a small band of fellow rebels, killed fifty-five whites, more than half of them children, before they themselves were captured and executed by local whites. Turner's insurrection electrified the nation. To white southerners, it demonstrated the necessity of unrelenting vigilance and unyielding control over slaves. To many people in the free states, it demonstrated slaves' unquenchable desire for freedom and desperate willingness to kill to get it. When Turner was captured, Thomas Gray, a white lawyer from Virginia, interviewed him in his cell shortly before his execution. Gray quickly published Turner's Confessions, *which was read avidly throughout the country. This text must be examined with care to attempt to sift what Turner said and believed — as well as what he may have left unsaid — from what Gray wrote. This selection contains Turner's account of how and why he became an insurrectionist. It discloses Turner's belief in miraculous, supernatural omens that impelled his actions and provides revealing glimpses of slaves' relationships with one another and with their white owners.*

The Confessions of Nat Turner, 1831

You have asked me to give a history of the motives which induced me to undertake the late insurrection, as you call it — To do so I must go back to the days of my infancy, and even before I was born. I was thirty-one years of age the 2nd of October last, and born the property of Benj. Turner, of this county. In my childhood a circumstance occurred which made an indelible impression on my mind, and laid the ground work of that enthusiasm, which has terminated so fatally to many, both white and black, and for which I am about to atone at the gallows. It is here necessary to relate this circumstance — trifling as it may seem, it was the commencement of that belief which has grown with time, and even now, sir, in this dungeon, helpless and forsaken as I am, I cannot divest myself of. Being at play with other children, when three or four years old, I was telling them something, which my mother overhearing, said it had happened before I was born — I stuck to my story, however, and related some things which went, in her opinion, to confirm it — others being called on were greatly astonished, knowing that these things had happened, and caused them to say in my hearing, I surely would be a prophet, as the Lord had shewn me things that had happened before my birth. And my father and mother strengthened me in this my first impression, saying in my presence, I was intended for some great purpose, which they had always thought from certain marks on my head and breast. . . . My grandmother,

---

The Confessions of Nat Turner, the Leader of the Late Insurrection in Southampton, Va. As Fully and Voluntarily Made to Thomas R. Gray, in the Prison Where He Was Confined . . . (Baltimore, 1831).

who was very religious, and to whom I was much attached—my master, who belonged to the church, and other religious persons who visited the house, and whom I often saw at prayers, noticing the singularity of my manners, I suppose, and my uncommon intelligence for a child, remarked I had too much sense to be raised, and if I was, I would never be of any service to any one as a slave — To a mind like mine, restless, inquisitive and observant of every thing that was passing, it is easy to suppose that religion was the subject to which it would be directed, and although this subject principally occupied my thoughts — there was nothing that I saw or heard of to which my attention was not directed — The manner in which I learned to read and write, not only had great influence on my own mind, as I acquired it with the most perfect ease, so much so, that I have no recollection whatever of learning the alphabet — but to the astonishment of the family, one day, when a book was shewn to me to keep me from crying, I began spelling the names of different objects — this was a source of wonder to all in the neighborhood, particularly the blacks — and this learning was constantly improved at all opportunities — when I got large enough to go to work, while employed, I was reflecting on many things that would present themselves to my imagination, and whenever an opportunity occurred of looking at a book, when the school children were getting their lessons, I would find many things that the fertility of my own imagination had depicted to me before; all my time, not devoted to my master's service, was spent either in prayer, or in making experiments in casting different things in moulds made of earth, in attempting to make paper, gun-powder, and many other experiments, that although I could not perfect, yet convinced me of its practicability if I had the means. I was not addicted to stealing in my youth, nor have ever been — Yet such was the confidence of the negroes in the neighborhood, even at this early period of my life, in my superior judgment, that they would often carry me with them when they were going on any roguery, to plan for them. Growing up among them, with this confidence in my superior judgment, and when this, in their opinions, was perfected by Divine inspiration, from the circumstances already alluded to in my infancy, and which belief was ever afterwards zealously inculcated by the austerity of my life and manners, which became the subject of remark by white and black. — Having soon discovered to be great, I must appear so, and therefore studiously avoided mixing in society, and wrapped myself in mystery, devoting my time to fasting and prayer — by this time, having arrived to man's estate, and hearing the scriptures commented on at meetings, I was struck with that particular passage which says: "Seek ye the kingdom of Heaven and all things shall be added unto you." I reflected much on this passage, and prayed daily for light on this subject — As I was praying one day at my plough, the spirit spoke to me, saying "Seek ye the kingdom of Heaven and all things shall be added unto you." *Question* — what do you mean by the Spirit. *Ans.* The Spirit that spoke to the prophets in former days — and I was greatly astonished, and for two years prayed continually, whenever my duty would permit — and then again I had the same revelation, which fully confirmed me in the impression that I was ordained for some great purpose in the hands of the Almighty. Several years rolled round, in which many events occurred to strengthen me in this my belief. At this time I reverted in my mind to the remarks made of me in my childhood, and the things that had been shewn me — and as it had been said of me in my childhood by those by whom I had been taught to pray, both white and black, and in whom I had the greatest confidence, that I had too much sense to be raised, and if I was, I would never be of any use to any one as a slave. Now finding I had arrived to man's estate, and was a slave, and these revelations being made known to me, I began to direct my attention to this great object, to fulfill the purpose for which, by this time, I felt assured I was intended. Knowing the influence I had obtained over the minds of my fellow servants, (not by the means of conjuring and such like tricks — for to them I always spoke of such things with contempt) but by the communion of the Spirit whose revelations I often communicated to them, and they believed and said my wisdom came from God. I now began to prepare them for my purpose, by telling them something was about to happen that would terminate in fulfilling the great promise that had been made to me — About this time I was placed under an over-seer, from whom I ranaway — and after remaining in the woods thirty days, I returned, to the astonishment of the negroes on the plantation, who thought I had made my escape to some other part of the country, as my father had done before. But the reason of my return was, that the Spirit appeared to me and said I had my wishes directed to the things of this world, and not to the kingdom of Heaven, and that I should return to the service of my earthly master — "For he who knoweth his Master's will, and doeth it not, shall be beaten with many stripes, and thus have I chastened you." And the negroes found fault, and murmured against me, saying that if they had my sense they would not serve any master in the world. And about this time I had a vision — and I saw white spirits and black spirits engaged in battle, and the sun was darkened — the thunder rolled in the Heavens, and blood flowed in streams — and I heard a voice saying, "Such is your luck, such you are called to see, and let it come rough or smooth, you must surely bare it." I now withdrew myself as much as my situation would permit, from the intercourse of my fellow servants, for the avowed purpose of serving the Spirit more fully — and it appeared to me, and reminded me of the things it had already shown me, and that it would then reveal to me the knowledge of the elements, the revolution of the planets, the operation of tides, and changes of the seasons. After this revelation in the year of 1825, and the knowledge of the elements being made known to me, I sought more than ever to obtain true holiness before the great day of judgment should appear, and then I began to receive the true knowledge of faith. And from the first steps of righteousness until the last, was I made perfect; and the Holy Ghost was with me, and said, "Behold me as I stand in the Heavens" — and I looked and saw the forms of men in different attitudes — and there were lights in the sky to which the children of darkness gave other names than what they really were — for they were the lights of the Savior's hands, stretched forth from east to west, even as they were extended on the cross on Calvary for the redemption of sinners. And I wondered greatly at these miracles, and prayed to be informed of a certainty of the meaning thereof — and shortly afterwards, while laboring in the field, I discovered drops of blood on the corn as though it were dew from heaven — and I communicated it to many, both white and black, in the neighborhood — and I then found on the leaves in the woods hieroglyphic characters, and numbers, with the forms of men in different attitudes, portrayed in blood, and representing the figures I had seen before in the heavens. And now the Holy Ghost had revealed itself to me, and made plain the miracles it had shown me — For as the blood of Christ had been shed on this earth, and had ascended to heaven for the salvation of sinners, and was now returning to earth again in the form of dew — and as the leaves on the trees bore the impression of the figures I had seen in the heavens, it was plain to me that the Savior was about to lay down the yoke he had borne for the sins of men, and the great day of judgment was at hand. About this time I told these things to a white man, (Etheldred T. Brantley) on whom it had a wonderful effect — and he ceased from his wickedness, and was attacked immediately with a cutaneous eruption, and blood oozed from the pores of his skin, and after praying and fasting nine days, he was healed, and the Spirit appeared to me again, and said, as the Savior had been baptised so should we be also — and when the white people would not let us be baptised by the church, we went down into the water together, in the sight of many who reviled us, and were baptised by the Spirit — After this I rejoiced greatly, and gave thanks to God. And on the 12th of May, 1828, I heard a loud noise in the heavens, and the Spirit instantly appeared to me and said the Serpent was loosened, and Christ had laid down the yoke he had borne for the sins of men, and that I should take it on and fight against the Serpent, for the time was fast approaching when the first should be last and the last should be first. *Ques.* Do you not find yourself mistaken now? *Ans.* Was not Christ crucified? And by signs in the heavens that it would make known to me when I should commence the great work — and until the first sign appeared, I should conceal it from the knowledge of men — And on the appearance of the sign, (the eclipse of the sun last February) I should arise and prepare myself, and slay my enemies with their own weapons. And immediately on the sign appearing in the heavens, the seal was removed from my lips, and I communicated the great work laid out for me to do, to four in whom I had the greatest confidence, (Henry, Hark, Nelson, and Sam) — It was intended by us to have begun the work of death on the 4th July last — Many were the plans formed and rejected by us, and it affected my mind to such a degree, that I fell sick, and the time passed without our coming to any determination how to commence — Still forming new schemes and rejecting them, when the sign appeared again, which determined me not to wait longer.

Since the commencement of 1830, I had been living with Mr. Joseph Travis, who was to me a kind master, and placed the greatest confidence in me; in fact, I had no cause to complain of his treatment to me. On Saturday evening, the 20th of August, it was agreed between Henry, Hark and myself to prepare a dinner the next day for the men we expected, and then to concert a plan, as we had not yet determined on any. Hark, on the following morning, brought a pig, and Henry brandy, and being joined by Sam, Nelson, Will and Jack, they prepared in the woods a dinner, where, about three o'clock, I joined them.

Q. Why were you so backward in joining them?

A. The same reason that had caused me not to mix with them for years before.

I saluted them on coming up, and asked Will how came he there, he answered, his life was worth no more than others, and his liberty as dear to him. I asked him if he thought to obtain it? He said he would, or lose his life. This was enough to put him in full confidence. Jack, I knew, was only a tool in the hands of Hark, it was quickly agreed we should commence at home (Mr. J. Travis') on that night, and until we had armed and equipped ourselves, and gathered sufficient force, neither age nor sex was to be spared, (which was invariably adhered to). We remained at the feast, until about two hours in the night, when we went to the house and found Austin; they all went to the cider press and drank, except myself. On returning to the house, Hark went to the door with an axe, for the purpose of breaking it open, as we knew we were strong enough to murder the family, if they were awakened by the noise; but reflecting that it might create an alarm in the neighborhood, we determined to enter the house secretly, and murder them whilst sleeping. . . .

QUESTIONS FOR READING AND DISCUSSION

1. According to Turner's *Confessions,* in what ways did he consider himself "great," set apart from other slaves? How did he receive confirmation of his special qualities?
2. What did his family and friends think about him? Why did some find fault and murmur against him? What did Turner mean by the question "Was not Christ crucified?"
3. Because Turner's owner, Joseph Travis, was "a kind master," why did Turner and the other insurrectionists begin by killing him and his family?
4. How might the fact that Turner made his *Confessions* to a white man while in jail awaiting execution have influenced what he said? How might Gray have shaped Turner's testimony? If one assumes, for the sake of argument, that Gray wrote exactly what Turner said, do you think Turner gave an accurate account of his beliefs and motives? Why or why not?
5. To what extent does this excerpt from Turner's *Confessions* document the significance of religion among slaves? Can one distinguish the relative significance of Christianity as compared with other religious beliefs? To what degree did religious beliefs encourage or discourage insurrection among slaves?

DOCUMENT 3
The Pro-Slavery Argument

Slaveholders passionately defended slavery from attacks by abolitionists. Their pro-slavery arguments not only responded to criticisms of slaveholders but also indicted the character and values of free society. James Henry Hammond, the author of the following letter addressed to an English abolitionist, was a prominent South Carolina planter and politician. Owner of a large plantation and scores of slaves, Hammond had served a term in Congress and had been governor of his state when he wrote this letter, which first appeared in a Columbia, South Carolina, newspaper in 1845.

James Henry Hammond
"Letter to an English Abolitionist," 1845

You will say that man cannot hold *property in man.* The answer is, that he can and actually does hold property in his fellow all the world over, in a variety of *forms, and has always done so.* . . .

If you were to ask me whether I am an advocate of Slavery in the abstract, I should probably answer, that I am not, according to my understanding of the question. I do not like to deal in abstractions. It seldom leads to any useful ends. There are few universal truths. I do not now remember any single moral truth

James Henry Hammond, "Letter to an English Abolitionist" (Columbia, S.C.: Allen, McCarter and Co., 1845).

universally acknowledged. . . . Justice itself is impalpable as an abstraction, and abstract liberty the merest phantasy that ever amused the imagination. This world was made for man, and man for the world as it is. We ourselves, our relations with one another and with all matter, are real, not ideal. I might say that I am no more in favor of Slavery in the abstract, than I am of poverty, disease, deformity, idiocy, or any other inequality in the condition of the human family; that I love perfection, and think I should enjoy a millennium such as God has promised. But what would that amount to? A pledge that I would join you to set about eradicating those apparently inevitable evils of our nature, in equalizing the condition of all mankind, consummating the perfection of our race, and introducing the millennium? By no means. To effect these things, belongs exclusively to a higher power. And it would be well for us to leave the Almighty to perfect his own works and fulfil his own covenants. Especially, as the history of the past shows how entirely futile all human efforts have proved, when made for the purpose of aiding Him in carrying out even his revealed designs, and how invariably he has accomplished them by unconscious instruments, and in the face of human expectation. Nay more, that every attempt which has been made by fallible man to extort from the world obedience to his "abstract" notions of right and wrong, has been invariably attended with calamities dire, and extended just in proportion to the breadth and vigor of the movement. On Slavery in the abstract, then, it would not be amiss to have as little as possible to say. Let us contemplate it as it is. And thus contemplating it, the first question we have to ask ourselves is, whether it is contrary to the will of God, as revealed to us in his Holy Scriptures — the only certain means given us to ascertain his will. If it is, then Slavery is a sin. And I admit at once that every man is bound to set his face against it, and to emancipate his slaves, should he hold any.

Let us open these Holy Scriptures. . . . You cannot deny that God especially authorized his chosen people to purchase "bondmen forever" from the heathen, as recorded in the twenty-fifth chapter of Leviticus, and that they are there designated by the very Hebrew word used in the tenth commandment. Nor can you deny that a "BONDMAN FOREVER" is a "SLAVE"; yet you endeavor to hang an argument of immortal consequence upon the wretched subterfuge, that the precise word "slave" is notrto be found in the translation of the Bible. As if the translators were canonical expounders of the Holy Scriptures, and *their words,* not God's *meaning,* must be regarded as his revelation. . . .

It is impossible, therefore, to suppose that Slavery is contrary to the will of God. It is equally absurd to say that American Slavery differs in form or principle from that of the chosen people. *We accept the Bible terms as the definition of our Slavery, and its precepts as the guide of our conduct.* . . .

I think, then, I may safely conclude, and I firmly believe, that American Slavery is not only not a sin, but especially commanded by God through Moses, and approved by Christ through his apostles. And here I might close its defence; for what God ordains, and Christ sanctifies, should surely command the respect and toleration of man. . . .

I endorse without reserve the much abused sentiment . . . that "Slavery is the corner-stone of our republican edifice"; while I repudiate, as ridiculously absurd, that much lauded but nowhere accredited dogma of Mr. Jefferson, that "all men are born equal." No society has ever yet existed . . . without a natural variety of classes. The most marked of these must, in a country like ours, be the rich and the poor, the educated and the ignorant. It will scarcely be disputed that the very poor have less leisure to prepare themselves for the proper discharge of public duties than the rich; and that the ignorant are wholly unfit for them at all. In all countries save ours, these two classes, or the poor rather, who are presumed to be necessarily ignorant, are by law expressly excluded from all participation in the management of public affairs. In a Republican Government this cannot be done. Universal suffrage, though not essential in theory, seems to be in fact a necessary appendage to a republican system. Where universal suffrage obtains, it is obvious that the government is in the hands of a numerical majority; and it is hardly necessary to say that in every part of the world more than half the people are ignorant and poor. Though no one can look upon poverty as a crime, and we do not here generally regard it as any objection to a man in his individual capacity, still it must be admitted that it is a wretched and insecure government which is administered by its most ignorant citizens, and those who have the least at stake under it. Though intelligence and wealth have great influence here, as everywhere, in keeping in check reckless and unenlightened numbers, yet it is evident to close observers, if not to all, that these are rapidly usurping all power in the non-slaveholding States, and threaten a fearful crisis in republican institutions there at no remote period. In the slaveholding States, however, nearly one-half of the whole population, and those the poorest and most ignorant, have no political influence whatever, because they are slaves. Of the other half, a large proportion are both educated and independent in their circumstances, while those who unfortunately are not so, being still elevated far above the mass, are higher toned and more deeply interested in preserving a stable and well ordered government, than the same class in any other country. Hence, Slavery is truly the "corner-stone" and foundation of every well designed and durable "republican edifice.". . .

But the question is, whether free or slave labor is cheapest to us in this country, at this time, situated as we are. And it is decided at once by the fact that we cannot avail ourselves of any other than slave labor. We neither have, nor can we procure, other labor to any extent, or on anything like the terms mentioned. We must, therefore, content ourselves with our dear labor, under the consoling reflection that what is lost to us, is gained to humanity; and that, inasmuch as our slave costs us more than your free man costs you, by so much is he better off. . . . Slavery is rapidly filling up our country with a hardy and healthy race, peculiarly adapted to our climate and productions, and conferring signal political and social advantages on us as a people. . . .

Failing in all your attempts to prove that [slavery] is sinful in its nature, immoral in its effects, a political evil, and profitless to those who maintain it, you appeal to the sympathies of mankind, and attempt to arouse the world against us by the most shocking charges of tyranny and cruelty. You begin by a vehement denunciation of "the irresponsible power of one man over his fellow men." . . . I deny that the power of the slave-holder in America is "irresponsible." He is responsible to God. He is responsible to the world. . . . He is responsible to the community in which he lives, and to the laws under which he enjoys his civil rights. Those laws do not permit him to kill, to maim, or to punish beyond certain limits, or to overtask, or to refuse to feed and clothe his slave. In short, they forbid him to be tyrannical or cruel. . . . Still, though a slaveholder, I freely acknowledge my obligations as a man; and that I am bound to treat humanely the fellow-creatures whom God has entrusted to my charge. I feel, therefore, somewhat sensitive under the accusation of cruelty, and disposed to defend myself and fellow-slaveholders against it. It is certainly the interest of all, and I am convinced that it is also the desire of every one of us, to treat our slaves with proper kindness. It is necessary to our deriving the greatest amount of profit from them. Of this we are all satisfied. . . .

Slaveholders are no more perfect than other men. They have passions. Some of them, as you may suppose, do not at all times restrain them. Neither do husbands, parents and friends. And in each of these relations, as serious suffering as frequently arises from uncontrolled passions, as ever does in that of master and slave. . . . I have no hesitation in saying that our slaveholders are kind masters, as men usually are kind husbands, parents and friends — as a general rule, kinder. A bad master — he who overworks his slaves, provides ill for them, or treats them with undue severity — loses the esteem and respect of his fellow-citizens to as great an extent as he would for the violation of any of his social and most of his moral obligations. . . .

Of late years we have been not only annoyed, but greatly embarrassed in this matter, by the abolitionists. We have been compelled to curtail some privileges; we have been debarred from granting new ones. In the face of discussions which aim at loosening all ties between master and slave, we have in some measure to abandon our efforts to attach them to us, and control them through their affections and pride. We have to rely more and more on the power of fear. We must, in all our intercourse with them, assert and maintain strict mastery, and impress it on them that they are slaves. This is painful to us, and certainly no present advantage to them. But it is the direct consequence of the abolition agitation. We are determined to continue masters, and to do so we have to draw the rein tighter and tighter day by day to be assured that we hold them in complete check. How far this process will go on, depends wholly and solely on the abolitionists. When they desist, we can relax. We may not before. . . . I assure you that my sentiments, and feelings, and determinations, are those of every slaveholder in this country. . . .

Now I affirm, that in Great Britain the poor and laboring classes of your own race and color, not only your fellow-beings, but your *fellow-citizens*, are more miserable and degraded, morally and physically, than our slaves; to be elevated to the actual condition of whom, would be to these, your *fellow-citizens*, a most glorious act of *emancipation*. And I also affirm, that the poor and laboring classes of our older free States would not be in a much more enviable condition, but for our Slavery. . . . [Hammond then quotes from a British report giving examples of the terrible working conditions experienced by some free laborers in England.]

It is shocking beyond endurance to turn over your records, in which the condition of your laboring classes is but too faithfully depicted. Could our slaves but see it, they would join us in lynching the abolitionists, which, by the by, they would not now be loth to do. We never think of imposing on them such labor, either in amount or kind. We never put them to *any work*, under ten, more generally at twelve years of age, and then the very lightest. Destitution is absolutely unknown — never did a slave starve in America; while in moral sentiments and feelings, in religious information, and even in general intelligence, they are infinitely the superiors of your operatives. When you look around you, how dare you talk to us before the world of Slavery? For the condition of your wretched laborers, you, and every Briton who is not one of them, are responsible before God and man. If you are really humane, philanthropic, and charitable, here are objects for you. Relieve them. Emancipate them. Raise them from the condition of brutes, to the level of human beings — of American slaves, at least. . . .

The American slaveholders, collectively or individually, ask no favors of any man or race who tread the earth. In none of the attributes of men, mental or physical, do they acknowledge or fear superiority elsewhere. They stand in the broadest light of the knowledge, civilization and improvement of the age, as much favored of heaven as any of the *sons of* Adam. . . . They cannot be flattered, duped, nor bullied out of their rights or their propriety.

QUESTIONS FOR READING AND DISCUSSION

1. Why did Hammond oppose slavery in the abstract but defend it "as it is" in the South? Why did he refuse to try to end slavery?
2. What did Hammond mean by declaring that "slavery is the corner-stone of our republican edifice"? Why did he consider human equality "ridiculously absurd"?
3. How did abolitionists influence slaveholders? Why were opponents of slavery so misguided, according to Hammond?
4. Hammond argued that white laborers in Britain or the North were "more miserable and degraded" than slaves? Why? How might white laborers and slaves have replied to this assertion?

DOCUMENT 4

A Visit with a Poor White Farmer

The vast majority of white southerners did not own slaves. Even in plantation regions, many farmers worked small plots with the help of family members. Their attitudes about slaves and slavery were central tenets of southern politics and reinforced the leading position of slaveholders. Between 1852 and 1854, Frederick Law Olmsted, a northern journalist and free-labor proponent, made three trips to the South to report on the social and economic conditions in the slave states. One night in Mississippi, Olmsted stayed with a poor white farmer and his family, a visit he described in the following selection, first published in 1860.

Frederick Law Olmsted
The Cotton Kingdom, 1861

The next day, I passed a number of small Indian farms, very badly cultivated — the corn nearly concealed by weeds. The soil became poorer than before, and the cabins of poor people more frequent. I counted about ten plantations, or negro-cultivated farms, in twenty miles. A planter, at whose house I called after sunset, said it was not convenient for him to accommodate me, and I was obliged to ride until it was quite dark. The next house at which I arrived was one of the commonest sort of cabins. I had passed twenty like it during the day, and I thought I would take the opportunity to get an interior knowledge of them. The fact that a horse and waggon were kept, and that a considerable area of land in the rear of the cabin was planted with cotton, showed that the family were by no means of the lowest class, yet, as they were not able even to hire a

Fredrick Law Olmsted, *The Cotton Kingdom: A Traveller's Observations on Cotton and Slavery in the American Slave States* (New York: Mason Brothers, 1861).

slave, they may be considered to represent very favourably, I believe, the condition of the poor whites of the plantation districts. The whites of the county, I observe, by the census, are three to one of the slaves; in the nearest adjoining county, the proportion is reversed; and within a few miles the soil was richer, and large plantations occurred.

It was raining, and nearly nine o'clock. The door of the cabin was open, and I rode up and conversed with the occupant as he stood within. He said that he was not in the habit of taking in travellers, and his wife was about sick, but if I was a mind to put up with common fare, he didn't care. Grateful, I dismounted and took the seat he had vacated by the fire, while he led away my horse to an open shed in the rear. . . .

The house was all comprised in a single room, twenty-eight by twenty-five feet in area, and open to the roof above. There was a large fireplace at one end and a door on each side — no windows at all. Two bedsteads, a spinning-wheel, a packing-case, which served as a bureau, a cupboard, made of rough hewn slabs, two or three deer-skin seated chairs, a Connecticut clock, and a large poster of Jayne's patent medicines, constituted all the visible furniture, either useful or ornamental in purpose. A little girl, immediately, without having had any directions to do so, got a frying-pan and a chunk of bacon from the cupboard, and cutting slices from the latter, set it frying for my supper. The woman of the house sat sulkily in a chair tilted back and leaning against the logs, spitting occasionally at the fire, but took no notice of me, barely nodding when I saluted her. A baby lay crying on the floor. I quieted it and amused it with my watch till the little girl, having made "coffee" and put a piece of corn-bread on the table with the bacon, took charge of it. . . .

As soon as I had finished my supper . . . , the little girl put the fragments and the dishes in the cupboard, shoved the table into a corner, and dragged a quantity of quilts from one of the bedsteads, which she spread upon the floor, and presently crawled among them out of sight for the night. The woman picked up the child — which, though still a suckling, she said was twenty-two months old — and nursed it. . . . The man sat with me by the fire, his back towards her. The baby having fallen asleep was laid away somewhere, and the woman dragged off another lot of quilts from the beds, spreading them upon the floor. . . .

The woman suddenly dropped off her outer garment and stepped from the midst of its folds, in her petticoat; then, taking the baby from the place where she had deposited it, lay down and covered herself with the quilts upon the floor. The man told me that I could take the bed which remained on one of the bedsteads, and kicking off his shoes only, rolled himself into a blanket by the side of his wife. . . .

When, on rising in the morning, I said that I would like to wash my face, water was given me for the purpose in an earthen pie-dish. Just as breakfast, which was of exactly the same materials as my supper, was ready, rain began to fall, presently in such a smart shower as to put the fire out and compel us to move the table under the least leaky part of the roof.

At breakfast occured the following conversation:

"Are there many niggers in New York?"

"Very few."

"How do you get your work done?"

"There are many Irish and German people constantly coming there who are glad to get work to do."

"Oh, and you have them for slaves?"

"They want money and are willing to work for it. A great many American-born work for wages, too."

"What do you have to pay?"

"Ten or twelve dollars a month.". . . "What do they generally give the niggers on the plantations here?"

"A peck of meal and three pound of bacon is what they call 'lowance, in general, I believe. It takes a heap of meat on a big plantation. I was on one of William R. King's plantations over in Alabamy, where there was about fifty niggers, one Sunday last summer, and I see 'em weighin' outen the meat. Tell you, it took a powerful heap on it. . . . Ain't niggers all-fired sassy at the North?"

".No, not particularly."

"Ain't they all free, there? I hearn so."

"Yes."

"Well, how do they get along when they's free?"

"I never have seen a great many, to know their circumstances very well. Right about where I live they seem to me to live quite comfortably; more so than the niggers on these big plantations do, I should think."

"Oh, they have a mighty hard time on the big plantations. I'd ruther be dead than to be a nigger on one of these big plantations."

"Why, I thought they were pretty well taken care of on them."

The man and his wife both looked at me as if surprised, and smiled.

"Why, they are well fed, are they not?"

"Oh, but they work 'em so hard. My God, sir, in pickin' time on these plantations they start 'em to work 'fore light, and they don't give 'em time to eat."

"I supposed they generally gave them an hour or two at noon."

"No, sir; they just carry a piece of bread and meat in their pockets and they eat it when they can, standin' up. They have a hard life on't, that's a fact. I reckon you can get along about as well withouten slaves as with 'em, can't you, in New York?"

"In New York there is not nearly so large a proportion of very rich men as here. There are very few people who farm over three hundred acres, and the greater number — nineteen out of twenty, I suppose — work themselves with the hands they employ. Yes, I think it's better than it is here, for all concerned, a great deal. . . ."

"I no doubt that's so. I wish there warn't no niggers here. They are a great cuss to this country, I expect. But 'twouldn't do to free 'em; that wouldn't do nohow!"

"Are there many people here who think slavery a curse to the country?"

"Oh, yes, a great many. I reckon the majority would be right glad if we could get rid of the niggers. But it wouldn't never do to free 'em and leave 'em here. I don't know anybody, hardly, in favour of that. Make 'em free and leave 'em here and they'd steal everything we made. Nobody couldn't live here then."

These views of slavery seem to be universal among people of this class. They were repeated to me at least a dozen times.

"Where I used to live [Alabama], I remember when I was a boy — must ha' been about twenty years ago — folks was dreadful frightened about the niggers. I remember they built pens in the woods where they could hide, and Christmas time they went and got into the pens, 'fraid the niggers was risin'."

"I remember the same time where we was in South Carolina," said his wife; "we had all our things put up in bags, so we could tote 'em, if we heerd they was comin' our way."

They did not suppose the niggers ever thought of rising now, but could give no better reason for not supposing so than that "everybody said there warn't no danger on't now.". . .

He had lived here ten years. I could not make out why he had not accumulated wealth, so small a family and such an inexpensive style of living as he had. He generally planted twenty to thirty acres, he said; this year he had sixteen in cotton and about ten, he thought, in corn. Decently cultivated, this planting should have produced him five hundred dollars' worth of cotton, besides supplying him with bread and bacon—his chief expense, apparently. I suggested that this was a very large planting for his little family; he would need some help in picking time. He ought to have some now, he said; grass and bushes were all overgrowing him; he had to work just like a nigger; this durnation rain would just make the weeds jump, and he didn't expect he should have any cotton at all. There warn't much use in a man trying to get along by himself; everything seemed to set in agin him. He'd been trying to hire somebody, but he couldn't, and his wife was a sickly kind of a woman.

His wife reckoned he might hire some help if he'd look round sharp. . . .

When I asked what I should pay, the man hesitated and said he reckoned what I had had, wasn't worth much of anything; he was sorry he could not have accommodated me better. I offered him a dollar, for which he thanked me warmly. It is the first instance of hesitation in charging for a lodging which I have met with from a stranger at the South.

QUESTIONS FOR READING AND DISCUSSION

1. Why did Olmsted consider the family he visited "representative of the poor whites of the plantation districts"? How might their views have differed from "the lowest class" and from those of slaveholders?

2. Why did the farmer and his wife think slaves were "a great cuss to this country"? Did they hope to own slaves? Did they favor ending slavery? Why or why not?

3. If one imagines that Olmsted visited a poor white farm family in the North, is it likely that his observations would have been significantly different? How and why?

COMPARATIVE QUESTIONS

1. How did Bennet Barrow's plantation rules compare with the statements about slavery made by James Henry Hammond? Did they express similar views about slaves and their motivations?

2. What similarities and differences characterized slaves' experiences on Barrow's plantation and in Nat Turner's neighborhood?

3. In what ways did the attitudes toward slavery and blacks expressed by the poor white farmer and his wife visited by Frederick Law Olmsted differ, if at all, from those of Hammond and Barrow? Why?

4. Judging from the documents in this chapter, to what extent did the slave South embody values embraced throughout American society? To what extent were the values of black and white southerners distinctive? Why?

CHAPTER 13

THE HOUSE DIVIDED
1846–1861

Politicians defined the terms of the sectional crisis in speech after speech, grappling with the underlying question of what to do about slavery. Three of the most important answers to that question were presented by Abraham Lincoln, Frederick Douglass, and Jefferson Davis. Hearing and reading their speeches helped Americans decide what they believed and, ultimately, to choose sides. For some, like John Brown, actions spoke louder than words.

Document 1
The Kansas-Nebraska Act

The Kansas-Nebraska Act ruptured old political coalitions. For decades, the Whig and Democratic parties had been national parties, with leaders and voters in both free states and slave states. Kansas-Nebraska drove a sectional wedge into each party. The act alienated many northern Whigs and Democrats. Addressing an audience in Peoria, Illinois, in October 1854, Abraham Lincoln passionately denounced Kansas-Nebraska. In his speech, excerpted here, Lincoln explained the grave danger posed by the act.

Abraham Lincoln
Speech in Peoria, Illinois, October 16, 1854

Preceding the Presidential election of 1852, each of the great political parties, democrats and whigs, met in convention, and adopted resolutions endorsing the compromise of '50; as a "finality," a final settlement . . . of all slavery agitation. . . .

During this long period of time Nebraska had remained, substantially an uninhabited country, but now emigration to, and settlement within it began to take place. It is about one third as large as the present United States, and its importance so long overlooked, begins to come into view. . . . On January 4th, 1854, Judge [Stephen A.] Douglas introduces a new bill to give Nebraska territorial

Roy P. Basler, ed., *The Collected Works of Abraham Lincoln,* vol. 2 (New Brunswick, N.J.: Rutgers University Press, 1953) 247–82.

government. . . . [A]bout a month after the introduction of the bill, on the judge's own motion, it is so amended as to declare the Missouri Compromise inoperative and void; and, substantially, that the People who go and settle there may establish slavery, or exclude it, as they may see fit. In this shape the bill passed both branches of congress, and became a law.

This is the *repeal* of the Missouri Compromise. . . . I think, and shall try to show, that it is wrong; wrong in its direct effect, letting slavery into Kansas and Nebraska — and wrong in its prospective principle, allowing it to spread to every other part of the wide world, where men can be found inclined to take it.

This *declared* indifference, but as I must think, covert *real* zeal for the spread of slavery, I can not but hate. I hate it because of the monstrous injustice of slavery itself. I hate it because it deprives our republican example of its just influence in the world — enables the enemies of free institutions, with plausibility, to taunt us as hypocrites — causes the real friends of freedom to doubt our sincerity, and especially because it forces so many really good men amongst ourselves into an open war with the very fundamental principles of civil liberty — criticising the Declaration of Independence, and insisting that there is no right principle of action but *self-interest.*

Before proceeding, let me say I think I have no prejudice against the Southern people. They are just what we would be in their situation. If slavery did not now exist amongst them, they would not introduce it. If it did now exist amongst us, we should not instantly give it up. This I believe of the masses north and south. Doubtless there are individuals, on both sides, who would not hold slaves under any circumstances; and others who would gladly introduce slavery anew, if it were out of existence. We know that some southern men do free their slaves, go north, and become tip-top abolitionists; while some northern ones go south, and become most cruel slave-masters.

When southern people tell us they are no more responsible for the origin of slavery, than we; I acknowledge the fact. When it is said that the institution exists; and that it is very difficult to get rid of it, in any satisfactory way, I can understand and appreciate the saying. I surely will not blame them for not doing what I should not know how to do myself. If all earthly power were given to me, I should not know what to do, as to the existing institution. My first impulse would be to free all the slaves and send them to Liberia, — to their own native land. But a moment's reflection would convince me, that whatever of high hope, (as I think there is) there may be in this, in the long run, its sudden execution is impossible. If they were all landed there in a day, they would all perish in the next ten days; and there are not surplus shipping and surplus money enough in the world to carry them there in many times ten days. What then? Free them all, and keep them among us as underlings? Is it quite certain that this betters their condition? I think I would not hold one in slavery, at any rate; yet the point is not clear enough for me to denounce people upon. What next? Free them, and make them politically and socially, our equals? My own feelings will not admit of this; and if mine would, we well know that those of the great mass of white people will not. Whether this feeling accords with justice and sound judgment, is not the sole question, if indeed, it is any part of it. A universal feeling, whether well or ill-founded, can not be safely disregarded. We can not, then, make them equals. It does seem to me that systems of gradual emancipation might be adopted; but for their tardiness in this, I will not undertake to judge our brethren of the south.

When they remind us of their constitutional rights, I acknowledge them, not grudgingly, but fully, and fairly; and I would give them any legislation for the reclaiming of their fugitives, which should not, in its stringency, be more likely to carry a free man into slavery, than our ordinary criminal laws are to hang an innocent one.

But all this, to my judgment, furnishes no more excuse for permitting slavery to go into our own free territory, than it would for reviving the African slave trade by law. The law which forbids the bringing of slaves from Africa; and that which has so long forbid the taking them to Nebraska, can hardly be distinguished on any moral principle; and the repeal of the former could find quite as plausible excuses as that of the latter. . . .

Some men, mostly whigs, who condemn the repeal of the Missouri Compromise, nevertheless hesitate to go for its restoration, lest they be thrown in company with the abolitionist. Will they allow me as an old whig to tell them good humoredly, that I think this is very silly? Stand with anybody that stands RIGHT. Stand with him while he is right and PART with him when he goes wrong. Stand WITH the abolitionist in restoring the Missouri Compromise; and stand AGAINST him when he attempts to repeal the fugitive slave law. In the latter case you stand with the southern disunionist. What of that? you are still right. In both cases you are right. In both cases you oppose the dangerous extremes. In both you stand on middle ground and hold the ship level and steady. In both you are national and nothing less than national. This is good old whig ground. To desert such ground, because of any company, is to be less than a whig — less than a man — less than an American.

I particularly object to the NEW position which the avowed principle of this Nebraska law gives to slavery in the body politic. I object to it because it assumes that there CAN be MORAL RIGHT in the enslaving of one man by another. I object to it as a dangerous dalliance for a free people — a sad evidence that, feeling prosperity we forget right — that liberty, as a principle, we have ceased to revere. I object to it because the fathers of the republic eschewed, and rejected it. The argument of "Necessity" was the only argument they ever admitted in favor of slavery; and so far, and so far only as it carried them, did they ever go. They found the institution existing among us, which they could not help; and they cast blame upon the British King for having permitted its introduction. BEFORE the constitution, they prohibited its introduction into the north-western Territory — the only country we owned, then free from it. AT the framing and adoption of the constitution, they forbore to so much as mention the word "slave" or "slavery" in the whole instrument. . . . Thus, the thing is hid away, in the constitution, just as an afflicted man hides away a wen or a cancer. . . . Less than this our fathers COULD not do; and MORE they WOULD not do. Necessity drove them so far, and farther, they would not go. But this is not all. The earliest Congress, under the constitution, took the same view of slavery. They hedged and hemmed it in to the narrowest limits of necessity. . . .

Thus we see, the plain unmistakable spirit of that age, towards slavery, was hostility to the PRINCIPLE, and toleration, ONLY BY NECESSITY.

But NOW it is to be transformed into a "sacred right." Nebraska brings it forth, places it on the high road to extension and perpetuity; and, with a pat on its back, says to it, "Go, and God speed you." . . . Little by little, but steadily as man's march to the grave, we have been giving up the OLD for the NEW faith.

Near eighty years ago we began by declaring that all men are created equal; but now from that beginning we have run down to the other declaration, that for some men to enslave OTHERS is a "sacred right of self-government." These principles can not stand together. They are as opposite as God and mammon; and whoever holds to the one, must despise the other. . . .

Let no one be deceived. The spirit of seventy-six and the spirit of Nebraska, are utter antagonisms; and the former is being rapidly displaced by the latter. Fellow countrymen — Americans south, as well as north, shall we make no effort to arrest this? . . . In our greedy chase to make profit of the negro, let us beware, lest we "cancel and tear to pieces" even the white man's charter of freedom.

Our republican robe is soiled, and trailed in the dust. Let us repurify it. Let us turn and wash it white, in the spirit, if not the blood, of the Revolution. Let us turn slavery from its claims of "moral right," back upon its existing legal rights, and its arguments of "necessity." Let us return it to the position our fathers gave it; and there let it rest in peace. Let us re-adopt the Declaration of Independence, and with it, the practices, and policy, which harmonize with it. Let north and south — let all Americans — let all lovers of liberty everywhere — join in the great and good work. If we do this, we shall not only have saved the Union; but we shall have so saved it, as to make, and to keep it, forever worthy of the saving.

Questions for Reading and Discussion

1. In what way did the Kansas-Nebraska Act repeal the Missouri Compromise? Why did Lincoln consider the act the result of "covert *real* zeal for the spread of slavery"?

2. To what extent did Lincoln oppose slavery? Did he believe slaveholders should emancipate their slaves, and if so, what did he believe should happen to them? Would abolitionists have found his arguments convincing? What about slaveholders?

3. What did Lincoln mean by declaring, "I think I have no prejudice against the Southern people"? What strategies did he use to promote national unity?

4. Why did Lincoln believe "our republican robe is soiled, and trailed in the dust"? How did he use the historical legacy of the founders to support his arguments?

Document 2

The Antislavery Constitution

The political debate between North and South pivoted on the question of what the Constitution permitted — or required — the federal government to do about slavery. Abolitionist William Lloyd Garrison publicly burned the Constitution in 1854 because, he said, by permitting slavery it was "a covenant with death, an agreement with hell." Frederick Douglass, a former slave and prominent black abolitionist, declared that, on the contrary, the Constitution was opposed to slavery. In countless speeches to northern antislavery audiences, Douglass set forth his views of the Constitution, which he summarized in a pamphlet published in 1860, the source of the following excerpt.

Frederick Douglass

The Constitution of the United States: Is It Pro-Slavery or Anti-Slavery? 1860

I only ask you to look at the American Constitution . . . and you will see with me that no man is guaranteed a right of property in man, under the provisions of that instrument. If there are two ideas more distinct in their character and essence than another, those ideas are "persons" and "property," "men" and "things." Now, when it is proposed to transform persons into "property" and men into beasts of burden, I demand that the law that contemplates such a purpose shall be expressed with irresistible clearness. The thing must not be left to inference, but must be done in plain English. . . .

[Many Americans] are in the habit of treating the negro as an exception to general rules. When their own liberty is in question they will avail themselves of all rules of law which protect and defend their freedom; but when the black man's rights are in question they concede everything, admit everything for slavery, and put liberty to the proof. They reverse the common law usage, and presume the negro a slave unless he can prove himself free. I, on the other hand, presume him free unless he is proved to be otherwise. Let us look at the objects for which the Constitution was framed and adopted, and see if slavery is one of them. Here are its own objects as set forth by itself: "We, the people of these United States, in order to form a more perfect union, establish justice, ensure domestic tranquillity, provide for the common defence, promote the general welfare, and secure the blessings of liberty to ourselves and our prosperity, do ordain and establish this Constitution for the United States of America." . . . These are all good objects, and, slavery, so far from being among them, is a foe of them. But it has been said that negroes are not included within the benefits sought under this declaration. This is said by the slaveholders in America . . . but it is not said by the Constitution itself. Its language is "we the people"; not we the white people, not even we the citizens, not we the privileged class, not we the high, not we the low, but we the people; not we the horses, sheep, and swine, and wheel-barrows, but we the people, we the human inhabitants; and, if negroes are people, they are included in the benefits for which the Constitution of America was ordained and established. . . .

[T]he constitutionality of slavery can be made out only by disregarding the plain and common-sense reading of the Constitution itself; by discrediting and casting away as worthless the most beneficent rules of legal interpretation; by ruling the negro outside of these beneficent rules; by claiming everything for slavery; by denying everything for freedom; by assuming that the Constitution does not mean what it says, and that it says what it does not mean, by disregarding the written Constitution, and interpreting it in the light of a secret understanding. It is in this mean, contemptible, and underhand method that the American Constitution is pressed into the service of slavery. They go everywhere

Frederick Douglass, *The Constitution of the United States: Is It Pro-Slavery or Anti-Slavery?* (1860).

else for proof that the Constitution is pro-slavery but to the Constitution itself. The Constitution declares that no person shall be deprived of life, liberty, or property without due process of law; it secures to every man the right of trial by jury, the privilege of the writ of habeas corpus . . . [and] it secures to every State a republican form of government. Any one of these provisions, in the hands of abolition statesmen, and backed up by a right moral sentiment, would put an end to slavery in America. The Constitution forbids the passing of a bill of attainder: that is, a law entailing upon the child the disabilities and hardships imposed upon the parent. Every slave law in America might be repealed on this very ground. The slave is made a slave because his mother is a slave. But to all this it is said that the practice of the American people is against my view. I admit it. They have given the Constitution a slaveholding interpretation. I admit it. They have committed innumerable wrongs against the negro in the name of the Constitution. Yes, I admit it all; and I go with him who goes farthest in denouncing these wrongs. But it does not follow that the Constitution is in favour of these wrongs because the slaveholders have given it that interpretation. . . .

My argument against the dissolution of the American Union is this: It would place the slave system more exclusively under the control of the slaveholding States, and withdraw it from the power in the Northern States which is opposed to slavery. Slavery is essentially barbarous in its character. It, above all things else, dreads the presence of an advanced civilisation. It flourishes best where it meets no reproving frowns, and hears no condemning voices. While in the Union it will meet with both. Its hope of life, in the last resort, is to get out of the Union. I am, therefore, for drawing the bond of the Union more closely, and bringing the Slave States more completely under the power of the Free States. What they most dread, that I most desire. I have much confidence in the instincts of the slaveholders. They see that the Constitution will afford slavery no protection when it shall cease to be administered by slaveholders. They see, moreover, that if there is once a will in the people of America to abolish slavery, there is no word, no syllable in the Constitution to forbid that result. . . .

The American people in the Northern States have helped to enslave the black people. Their duty will not have been done till they give them back their plundered rights. . . . My position now is one of reform, not of revolution. I would act for the abolition of slavery through the Government. . . . If slaveholders have ruled the American Government for the last fifty years, let the anti-slavery men rule the nation for the next fifty years.

QUESTIONS FOR READING AND DISCUSSION

1. According to Douglass, what were the antislavery provisions of the Constitution? Was Douglass's interpretation a "plain and common-sense reading of the Constitution itself," as he claimed?
2. In his view, why did slavery exist? Why were Americans "in the habit of treating the negro as an exception to general rules"? Why was slavery "essentially barbarous"?
3. Why was Douglass "against the dissolution of the American Union"?
4. What needed to be done to put the antislavery powers of the Constitution into effect? Why did he advocate "reform, not revolution"?

DOCUMENT 3

The Pro-Slavery Constitution

Southern politicians argued that the Constitution required the federal government to protect owners of all forms of property, including slaves. The heated sectional debate about the scope of federal power and states' rights focused attention on the territories. Could settlers in a federal territory prohibit slavery or refuse to protect it? Or, regardless of territorial laws, did the Constitution mandate that slavery in federal territories be protected by federal laws? In a speech to the U.S. Senate in May 1860, excerpted here, Jefferson Davis made the case for federal protection. In less than a year, Senator Davis, a wealthy planter from Mississippi, became president of the Confederacy.

Jefferson Davis
Speech before the U.S. Senate, May 1860

Among the many blessings for which we are indebted to our ancestry, is that of transmitting to us a written Constitution; a fixed standard to which, in the progress of events, every case may be referred, and by which it may be measured. . . . With this . . . to check, to restrain, and to direct their posterity, they might reasonably hope the Government they founded should last forever; that it should secure the great purposes for which it was ordained and established; that it would be the shield of their posterity equally in every part of the country, and equally in all time to time. . . .

Our fathers were aware of the different interests of the navigating and planting States, as they were then regarded. They sought to compose those difficulties, and by compensating advantages given by one to the other, to form a Government equal and just in its operation; and which, like the gentle showers of heaven, should fall twice blessed, blessing him that gives and him that receives. This beneficial action and reaction between the different interests of the country constituted the bond of union and the motive of its formation. They constitute it to-day, if we are sufficiently wise to appreciate our interests, and sufficiently faithful to observe our trust. Indeed, with the extension of territory, with the multiplication of interests, with the varieties, increasing from time to time, of the products of this great country, the bonds which bind the Union together should have increased. . . .

The great principle which lay at the foundation of this fixed standard, the Constitution of the United States, was the equality of rights between the States. This was essential; it was necessary; it was a step which had to be taken first, before any progress could be made. It was the essential requisite of the very idea of sovereignty in the State; of a compact voluntarily entered into between sovereigns; and it is that equality of right under the Constitution on which we now insist. . . .

We claim protection [of slavery], first, because it is our right; secondly, because it is the duty of the General Government; and thirdly, because we have en-

Dunbar Rowland, ed., *Jefferson Davis, Constitutionalist: His Letters, Papers, and Speeches* (New York: AMS Press, 1923) 120–30.

tered into a compact together, which deprives each State of the power of using all the means which it might employ for its own defense. This is the general theory of the right of protection. . . . [I]f general protection be the general duty, I ask, in the name of reason and constitutional right—I ask you to point me to authority by which a discrimination is made between slave property and any other. Yet this is the question now fraught with evil to our country. It is this which has raised the hurricane threatening to sweep our political institutions before it. . . .

I have been the determined opponent of what is called squatter sovereignty. I never gave it countenance, and I am now least of all disposed to give it quarter. . . . What right had Congress then, or what right has it now, to abdicate any power conferred upon it as trustee of the States? . . . In 1850, following the promulgation of this notion of squatter sovereignty, we had the idea of non-intervention introduced into the Senate of the United States, and it is strange to me how that idea has expanded. . . . Non-intervention then meant, as the debates show, that Congress should neither prohibit nor establish slavery in the Territories. That I hold to now. Will any one suppose that Congress then meant by non-intervention that Congress should legislate in no regard in respect to property in slaves? Why, sir, the very acts which they passed at the time refute it. There is the fugitive slave law. . . .

By what species of legerdemain [sleight of hand, trickery] this doctrine of non-intervention has come to extend to a paralysis of the Government on the whole subject, to exclude the Congress from any kind of legislation whatever, I am at a loss to conceive. . . . I had no faith in it then; I considered it an evasion; I held that the duty of Congress ought to be performed, that the issue was before us, and ought to be met, the sooner the better; that truth would prevail if presented to the people. . . .

That is what we ask of Congress now. . . . I am not one of those who would willingly see this Congress enact a code to be applied to all Territories and for all time to come. I only ask that . . . when personal and property rights in the Territories are not protected, then the Congress, by existing laws and governmental machinery, shall intervene and provide such means as will secure in each case, as far as may be, an adequate remedy. I ask no slave code, nor horse code, nor machine code. I ask that the Territorial Legislature be made to understand beforehand that the Congress of the United States does not concede to them the power to interfere with the rights of person or property guaranteed by the Constitution, and that it will apply the remedy, if the Territorial Legislature should so far forget its duty, so far transcend its power, as to commit that violation of right. . . .

These are the general views which I entertain of our right of protection and the duty of the Government. They are those which are entertained by the constituency I have the honor to represent. . . . For weal or for woe, for prosperity or adversity, for the preservation of the great blessings which we enjoy, or the trial of a new and separate condition, I trust Mississippi never will surrender the smallest atom of the sovereignty, independence, and equality, to which she was born, to avoid any danger or any sacrifice to which she may thereby be exposed. . . .

We have made no war against [the North]. We have asked no discrimination in our favor. We claim to have but the Constitution fairly and equally administered. To consent to less than this, would be to sink in the scale of manhood; would be to make our posterity so degraded that they would curse this generation for robbing them of the rights their revolutionary fathers bequeathed them.

QUESTIONS FOR READING AND DISCUSSION

1. According to Davis, what constitutional principles guaranteed federal protection for slavery? To what extent were those principles enshrined in specific constitutional provisions?
2. How did "the great principle" of "the equality of rights between the States" serve to protect slavery?
3. Why did Davis oppose both "squatter sovereignty" and "non-intervention"?
4. How did he propose to resolve the disputes about slavery?
5. In what sense did Davis believe white southerners' "manhood" was at stake in the constitutional conflict?

DOCUMENT 4

John Brown: Pottawatomie and Harpers Ferry

Some Americans did not limit themselves to making speeches about slavery and the Constitution. John Brown, a militant abolitionist, decided to do something about slavery, to take matters into his own hands. Brown led a small group of supporters against pro-slavery men in Pottawatomie, Kansas, in 1856. Three years later, in October 1859, Brown directed an attack on the U.S. arsenal at Harpers Ferry, Virginia, which resulted in his arrest, trial, and conviction for murder and treason. The documents that follow offer two perspectives on Brown. The first is a confession by James Townsley in 1879; in this document he describes his participation in what became known as the Pottawatomie Massacre. The second document is John Brown's last speech, delivered shortly before he was executed.

Confession of James Townsley, December 6, 1879

I joined the Potawatomie rifle company at its re-organization in May, 1856, at which time John Brown, Jr., was elected captain. On the 21st of the same month information was received that the Georgians were marching on Lawrence, threatening its destruction. The company was immediately called together, and about four o'clock P.M. we started on a forced march to aid in its defense. About two miles south of Middle Creek we were joined by the Osawatomie company under Captain Dayton, and proceeded to Mount Vernon, where we waited about two hours, until the moon rose. We then marched all night, camping the next morning, the 22nd, for breakfast, near Ottawa Jones's. Before we arrived at this point news had been received that Lawrence had been destroyed, and a question was raised whether we should return or go on. During the forenoon, however, we proceeded up Ottawa Creek to within about five miles of Palmyra, and went into camp near the residence of Captain Shore. Here we remained undecided over night. About noon the next day, the 23rd, Old John Brown came to me and said he had just re-

Charles Robinson, *The Kansas Conflict* (New York: Harper & Brothers, 1892); F. B. Sanborn, *The Life and Letters of John Brown* (Boston: Roberts Brothers, 1891).

ceived information that trouble was expected on the Potawatomie, and wanted to know if I would take my team and take him and his boys back, so they could keep watch of what was going on. I told him I would do so. The party, consisting of Old John Brown, Watson Brown, Oliver Brown, Henry Thompson (John Brown's son-in-law), and Mr. Winer, were soon ready for the trip, and we started, as near as I can remember, about two o'clock P.M. All of the party except Winer, who rode a pony, rode with me in my wagon. When within two or three miles of the Potawatomie Creek, we turned off the main road to the right, drove down to the edge of the timber between two deep ravines, and camped about one mile above Dutch Henry's crossing.

After my team was fed and the party had taken supper, John Brown told me for the first time what he proposed to do. He said he wanted me to pilot the company up to the forks of the creek, some five or six miles above, into the neighborhood where I lived, and show them where all the pro-slavery men resided; that he proposed to sweep the creek as he came down of all the pro-slavery men living on it. I positively refused to do it. He insisted upon it, but when he found that I would not go, he decided to postpone the expedition until the following night. I then wanted to take my team and go home, but he would not let me do so, and said I should remain with them. We remained in camp that night and all the next day. Some time after dark we were ordered to march.

We started, the whole company, in a northerly direction, crossing Mosquito Creek above the residence of the Doyles. Soon after crossing the creek some one of the party knocked at the door of the cabin, but received no reply — I have forgotten whose cabin it was, if I knew at the time. The next place we came to was the residence of the Doyles. John Brown, three of his sons, and son-in-law went to the door, leaving Frederick Brown, Winer, and myself a short distance from the house. About this time a large dog attacked us. Frederick Brown struck the dog a blow with his short two-edged sword, after which I dealt him a blow with my sabre, and heard no more of him. The old man Doyle and two sons were called out and marched some distance from the house towards Dutch Henry's, in the road, where a halt was made. Old John Brown drew his revolver and shot the old man Doyle in the forehead; and Brown's two youngest sons immediately fell upon the younger Doyles with their short two-edged swords.

One of the young Doyles was stricken down in an instant, but the other attempted to escape, and was pursued a short distance by his assailant and cut down. The company then proceeded down Mosquito Creek, to the house of Allen Wilkinson. Here the old man Brown, three of his sons, and son-in-law, as at the Doyle residence, went to the door and ordered Wilkinson to come out, leaving Frederick Brown, Winer, and myself standing in the road east of the house. Wilkinson was taken and marched some distance south of his house and slain in the road, with a short sword, by one of the younger Browns. After he was killed his body was dragged out to one side and left.

We then crossed the Potawatomie and came to the house of Henry Sherman, generally known as Dutch Henry. Here John Brown and the party, excepting Frederick Brown, Winer, and myself, who were left outside a short distance from the door, went into the house and brought out one or two persons, talked with them some, and then took them in again. They afterwards brought out William Sherman, Dutch Henry's brother, marched him down into the Potawatomie Creek, where he was slain with swords by Brown's two youngest sons, and left lying in the creek.

It was the expressed intention of Brown to execute Dutch Henry also, but he was not found at home. He also hoped to find George Wilson, Probate Judge of Anderson County, there, and intended, if he did, to kill him too. Wilson had been notifying Free-State men to leave the Territory. I had received such a notice from him myself.

Brown wanted me to pilot the party into the neighborhood where I lived, and point out all the pro-slavery men in it, whom he proposed to put to death. I positively refused to do it, and on account of my refusal I remained in camp all of the night upon which the first attack was to be made, and the next day. I told him I was willing to go with him to Lecompton and attack the leaders, or fight the enemy in open field anywhere, but I did not want to engage in killing these men. That night and the acts then perpetrated are vividly fixed in my memory and I have thought of them many times since.

John Brown

Speech, November 2, 1859

I have, may it please the Court, a few words to say.

In the first place, I deny everything but what I have all along admitted, — the design on my part to free the slaves. I intended certainly to have made a clean thing of that matter, as I did last winter, when I went into Missouri and there took slaves without the snapping of a gun either side, moved them through the country, and finally left them in Canada. I designed to have done the same thing again, on a larger scale. That was all I intended. I never did intend murder, or treason, or the destruction of property, or to excite or incite slaves to rebellion, or to make insurrection.

I have another objection: and that is, it is unjust that I should suffer such a penalty. Had I interfered in the manner which I admit, and which I admit has been fairly proved (for I admire the truthfulness and candor of the greater portion of the witnesses who have testified in this case), — had I so interfered in behalf of the rich, the powerful, the intelligent, the so-called great, or in behalf of any of their friends, — either father, mother, brother, sister, wife, or children, or any of that class, — and suffered and sacrificed what I have in this interference, it would have been all right; and every man in this court would have deemed it an act worthy of reward rather than punishment.

This court acknowledges, as I suppose, the validity of the law of God. I see a book kissed here which I suppose to be the Bible, or at least the New Testament. That teaches me that all things whatsoever I would that men should do to me, I should do even so to them. It teaches me, further, to "remember them that are in bonds, as bound with them." I endeavored to act up to that instruction. I say, I am yet too young to understand that God is any respecter of persons. I believe that to have interfered as I have done — as I have always freely admitted I have done — in behalf of His despised poor, was not wrong, but right. Now, if it is deemed necessary that I should forfeit my life for the furtherance of the ends of justice, and mingle my blood further with the blood of my children and with the blood of millions in this slave country whose rights are disregarded by wicked, cruel, and unjust enactments, — I submit; so let it be done!

Let me say one word further.

I feel entirely satisfied with the treatment I have received on my trial. Considering all the circumstances, it has been more generous than I expected. But I feel no consciousness of guilt. I have stated from the first what was my intention, and what was not. I never had any design against the life of any person, nor any disposition to commit treason, or excite slaves to rebel, or make any general insurrection. I never encouraged any man to do so, but always discouraged any idea of that kind.

Let me say, also, a word in regard to the statements made by some of those connected with me. I hear it has been stated by some of them that I have induced them to join me. But the contrary is true. I do not say this to injure them but as regretting their weakness. There is not one of them but joined me of his own accord, and the greater part of them at their own expense. A number of them I never saw, and never had a word of conversation with, till the day they came to me; and that was for the purpose I have stated.

Now I have done.

QUESTIONS FOR READING AND DISCUSSION

1. Brown asserts that he never intended to "excite slaves to rebel, or make any general insurrection." What, then, was the purpose of the raid on Harpers Ferry?
2. Why did Brown believe he was "right"? Why did he "feel no consciousness of guilt"? Could he have used the same arguments to defend his actions at Pottawatomie?
3. How do you reconcile the John Brown who delivered this last speech with the ruthless killer at Pottawatomie? What did Townsley think about the Pottawatomie Massacre?
4. To what extent did the Constitution influence Brown's actions or attitudes? What did he believe were the principle consequences of his actions?

COMPARATIVE QUESTIONS

1. How did Abraham Lincoln's view of the Constitution's position on slavery differ from Frederick Douglass's? In what ways did Lincoln's and Douglass's views differ from Jefferson Davis's?
2. What might John Brown have thought about the constitutional interpretations of Lincoln, Douglass, and Davis? Judging from the documents in this chapter, how would Lincoln, Douglass, and Davis have reacted to Brown's actions?
3. How did each of these individuals define the political problem posed by slavery? What was at stake for these individuals and the people they represented in the debate over slavery?
4. To what extent were racial attitudes and assumptions important in these constitutional arguments?

CHAPTER 14

THE CRUCIBLE OF WAR
1861–1865

The American Civil War began with the dissolution of the Union. The Confederacy seceded from the Union and fought to maintain its independence. The North went to war to defeat the Confederacy and preserve the Union. Before long, the war confronted most Americans with unprecedented, unexpected, and often painful experiences. In the crucible of conflict, Union war aims shifted toward freedom, slaves fought in Yankee blue against their old masters, Union troops struck the hard hand of war against Confederate civilians, and hundreds of thousands of men became casualties, as the following documents illustrate.

DOCUMENT 1
President Lincoln's War Aims

Abraham Lincoln became president pledging to prohibit the extension of slavery to new territories and to do nothing about slavery in the states where it already existed. Within weeks, the nation plunged into war. Antislavery activists pressured Lincoln to make freedom a war aim. In 1862, when fellow Republican Horace Greeley, the editor of the New York Tribune, *criticized Lincoln's reluctance to embrace emancipation, Lincoln defended his policy in a public letter, the first selection that follows. Less than five months later, Lincoln issued the Emancipation Proclamation, the second selection. Later in 1863, after the ferocious battle at Gettysburg, Lincoln delivered his famous address at the dedication of the military cemetery. The Gettysburg Address, the third selection, infused the war to save the Union with universal significance.*

Letter to Horace Greeley, August 22, 1862

Executive Mansion,
Washington, August 22, 1862.
Hon. Horace Greely

Dear Sir

I have just read yours of the 19th. addressed to myself through the New-York Tribune. . . . If there be perceptable in it an impatient and dictatorial tone, I waive it in deference to an old friend, whose heart I have always supposed to be right.

As to the policy I "seem to be pursuing" as you say, I have not meant to leave any one in doubt.

I would save the Union. I would save it the shortest way under the Constitution. The sooner the national authority can be restored; the nearer the Union will be "the Union as it was." If there be those who would not save the Union, unless they could at the same time *save* slavery, I do not agree with them. If there be those who would not save the Union unless they could at the same time *destroy* slavery, I do not agree with them. My paramount object in this struggle *is* to save the Union, and is *not* either to save or to destroy slavery. If I could save the Union without freeing *any* slave I would do it, and if I could save it by freeing all the slaves I would do it; and if I could save it by freeing some and leaving others alone I would also do that. What I do about slavery, and the colored race, I do because I believe it helps to save the Union; and what I forbear, I forbear because I do not believe it would help to save the Union. I shall do *less* whenever I shall believe what I am doing hurts the cause, and I shall do *more* whenever I shall believe doing more will help the cause. I shall try to correct errors when shown to be errors; and I shall adopt new views so fast as they shall appear to be true views.

I have here stated my purpose according to my view of official duty; and I intend no modification of my oft-expressed personal wish that all men every where could be free.

The Emancipation Proclamation, January 1, 1863

I, Abraham Lincoln, President of the United States, by virtue of the power in me vested as Commander-in-Chief, of the Army and Navy of the United States in time of actual armed rebellion against authority and government of the United States, and as a fit and necessary war measure for suppressing said rebellion, do, on this first day of January, in the year of our Lord one thousand eight hundred and sixty three, and in accordance with my purpose so to do publicly proclaimed for the full period of one hundred days. . . order and designate as the States and parts of States wherein the people thereof respectively, are this day in rebellion against the United States, the following, to wit:

Arkansas, Texas, Louisiana, (except the Parishes of St. Bernard, Plaque-mines, Jefferson, St. Johns, St. Charles, St. James, Ascension, Assumption, Terre-

Roy P. Basler, ed., *The Collected Works of Abraham Lincoln* (New Brunswick, N.J.: Rutgers University Press, 1953) 5: 388–89; 6: 28–30; 7: 22–23.

bonne, Lafourche, St. Mary, St. Martin, and Orleans, including the City of New-Orleans) Mississippi, Alabama, Florida, Georgia, South-Carolina, North-Carolina, and Virginia, (except the fortyeight counties designated as West Virginia, and also the counties of Berkley, Accomac, Northampton, Elizabeth-City, York, Princess Ann, and Norfolk, including the cities of Norfolk & Portsmouth); and which excepted parts are, for the present, left precisely as if this proclamation were not issued.

And by virtue of the power, and for the purpose aforesaid, I do order and declare that all persons held as slaves within said designated States, and parts of States, are, and henceforward shall be free; and that the Executive government of the United States, including the military and naval authorities thereof, will recognize and maintain the freedom of said persons.

And I hereby enjoin upon the people so declared to be free to abstain from all violence, unless in necessary self-defence; and I recommend to them that, in all cases when allowed, they labor faithfully for reasonable wages.

And I further declare and make known, that such persons of suitable condition, will be received into the armed service of the United States to garrison forts, positions, stations, and other places, and to man vessels of all sorts in said service.

And upon this act, sincerely believed to be an act of justice, warranted by the Constitution, upon military necessity, I invoke the considerate judgment of mankind, and the gracious favor of Almighty God.

In witness whereof, I have hereunto set my hand and caused the seal of the United States to be affixed.

Done at the City of Washington, this first day of January, in the year of our Lord one thousand eight hundred and sixty three, and of the Independence of the United States of America the eighty-seventh.

The Gettysburg Address, November 19, 1863

Four score and seven years ago our fathers brought forth on this continent, a new nation, conceived in Liberty, and dedicated to the proposition that all men are created equal.

Now we are engaged in a great civil war, testing whether that nation, or any nation so conceived and so dedicated, can long endure. We are met on a great battle-field of that war. We have come to dedicate a portion of that field, as a final resting place for those who here gave their lives that that nation might live. It is altogether fitting and proper that we should do this.

But, in a larger sense, we can not dedicate — we can not consecrate — we can not hallow — this ground. The brave men, living and dead, who struggled here, have consecrated it, far above our poor power to add or detract. The world will little note, nor long remember what we say here, but it can never forget what they did here. It is for us the living, rather, to be dedicated here to the unfinished work which they who fought here have thus far so nobly advanced. It is rather for us to be here dedicated to the great task remaining before us — that from these honored dead we take increased devotion to that cause for which they gave the last full measure of devotion — that we here highly resolve that these dead shall not have died in vain—that this nation, under God, shall have a new birth of freedom — and that government of the people, by the people, for the people, shall not perish from the earth.

QUESTIONS FOR READING AND DISCUSSION

1. In his letter to Greeley, how far did Lincoln say he was willing to go to end slavery? What was his paramount goal? What was the significance of his distinction between his "*official* duty" and his "*personal* wish"?

2. To what extent were Lincoln's war aims altered by the Emancipation Proclamation? Why did he specify that the proclamation was "a fit and necessary war measure"? Why did he name specific states, counties, parishes, and cities?

3. In the Gettysburg Address, what did Lincoln say was at stake in the war? What meanings did the address associate with the Union? How might Lincoln's audience have shaped his message? Who was his audience, both locally and throughout the nation?

4. How did Lincoln's views toward slavery and the Union evolve during the war, judging from these documents?

DOCUMENT 2

A Former Slave's War Aims

Slaves and most free African Americans did not share Lincoln's constitutional reservations about emancipation. Many sought to fight in uniform to help obtain their freedom, as the following document reveals. This letter from a former slave was picked up by a policeman on a street in New Orleans in early September 1863 and turned over to military authorities, who preserved it. Both parts of the letter are in the same handwriting. (The spelling and punctuation have been faithfully reproduced from the original; if you find a passage puzzling, try reading it aloud. Note in particular that "the" should usually be read as "they.")

Statement from an Anonymous Former Slave, New Orleans, 1863

the president Shall be Commander in Chief of the Army and navy of the united States and of the militia of the Several States when called into the actual Service of the united States

Let See if Slavery was any value . . . the number of Slaves in the Southern States estimated 3,500,000 and the were worth $1200,000,000 in gold which would be a bout $1800,000,000 in Green Backs Eighteen hundred million Dollars the Collored population is not educated but what Great responciblity has been placeed on them the have been Steam boat pilots ingenears and Black Smiths Coopers Carpenters Shoe makers Drivers on plantations Sugar makers porters on Steam boats and at hotels Dineing Servant Porters in Commision houses Grocery Stores Public weighers Carrige Drivers preachers of the Gospel the best Soldiers the united States Can Raise but the tel lies Sometimes and So dos all negro traders the get

"Statements of a Colored Man [September 1863]," in *Freedom: A Documentary History of Emancipation, 1861–1867,* Series 2, *The Black Military Experience,* ed. Ira Berlin, Joseph Reidy, and Leslie S. Rowland (Cambridge: Cambridge University Press, 1982) 153–57.

Drunk and lawiers and merchants Generals and Governors and all Clases the black men has wives and Sweet harts jest like the white men Some white men has Collored wives and Sweet hearts god made all it is not a City rule for Collored people to ride in the white peoples cars but the bed togeather God mad all the must all Die

it is retten that a man can not Serve two master But it Seems that the Collored population has got two a rebel master and a union master the both want our Servises one wants us to make Cotton and Sugar And the Sell it and keep the money the union masters wants us to fight the battles under white officers and the injoy both money and the union black Soldiers And white officers will not play togeathe much longer the Constitution is if any man rebells against those united States his property Shall be confescated and Slaves declared and henceforth Set free forever when theire is a insurection or rebllion against these united States the Constitution gives the president of the united States full power to arm as many soldiers of African decent as he deems nescesisary to Surpress the Rebellion and officers Should be black or white According to their abillitys the Collored man Should guard Stations Garison forts and mand vessels according to his Compasitys

A well regulated militia being necessary to the cecurity of a free State the right of the people to keep and Bear arms Shall not be infringed

we are to Support the Constitution but no religious test Shall ever be required as a qualification to Any office or public trust under the united States the excitement of the wars is mostly keep up from the Churches the Say god is fighting the battle but it is the people But the will find that god fought our battle once the way to have peace is to distroy the enemy As long as theire is a Slave their will be rebles Against the Government of the united States So we must look out our white officers may be union men but Slave holders at heart the Are allways on hand when theire is money but Look out for them in the battle feild liberty is what we want and nothing Shorter

our Southern friend tells that the are fighting for negros and will have them our union friends Says the are not fighting to free the negroes we are fighting for the union and free navigation of the Mississippi river very well let the white fight for what the want and we negroes fight for what we want there are three things to fight for and two races of people divided into three Classes one wants negro Slaves the other the union the other Liberty So liberty must take the day nothing Shorter we are the Blackest and the bravest race the president Says there is a wide Difference Between the black Race and the white race But we Say that white corn and yellow will mix by the taussels but the black and white Race musc mix by the roots as the are so well mixed and has no tausels—freedom and liberty is the word with the Collered people

We the people of the united States in order to form a more perfect union Establish justice insure domestick tranquillity provide for the common defence promote the general wellfare and secure the blessings of liberty to ourselves and our posterity do ordain and establish this Constitution for the united States of America

My Dear union masters and reble masters or friends How are we Slave Population to take hold of a musket under white officers which a great part of them has been in the reble army and the meet to hold a war Consels all to them Selves Dear Sir I heard a federal officer Say after the fall of Port hudson to a Collored Soldier we will not want any more negro Soldiers go home to your master i my Self went to a union lawyer on Some Buiness the first question are you free or Slave Before the fall of porthudson the white Preachers told us we were all free as any white man and in Less time than a month after you weare taking us up and puting in the lockups and Cotton presses giving us nothing to eat nor nothing Sleep on And haveing negro traders for recruting officers Drawing his Sword over us like we were dogs By those means you will Soon have the union north if any union man can deny this i will write no more i am for the union and liberty to all men or nothing Shorter treason against the united States Shall consist only in Levying ware against them or in adhering to theire enemies giving them aid and Comfort no person Shall be convicted of treason unless on the testimoney of two witnesses to the Same overt Act or Confession in open Court the Congress Shall Have power to declare punishment of treason but no attainder of treason Shall work Corruption of blood or forfeiture Except during the life of the person attained

Now let us see whether the Colored population will be turn back in to Slavery and the union lost or not on the 4″ of last July it was Said to the colored population that the were all free and on the 4″ of August locked up in Cotton presses like Horses or hogs By reble watchmen and Saying to us Gen banks Says you are All free why do you not go to him and get passes And one half of the recruiting officers is rebles taken the oath to get a living and would Sink the Government into ashes the Scrptures says the enemy must Suffer death before we can Have peace the fall of porthudson and vicksburg is nothing the rebles must fall or the union must fall Sure the Southern men Says the are not fighting for money the are fighting for negros the northern men Say the did not com South to free the negroes but to Save the union very well for that much what is the colored men fighting for if the makes us free we are happy to hear it And when we are free men and a people we will fight for our rights and liberty we care nothing about the union we heave been in it Slaves over two hundred And fifty years we have made the contry and So far Saved the union and if we heave to fight for our rights let us fight under Colored officers for we are the men that will kill the Enemies of the Government pleas let me continue

Art 173 the Slave is entirely Subject to the will of his master Who may Correct and Chastise him though not with unusal Rigor nor So as to maim or mutilate him or to expose him to the danger of loss of life or to cause his death

Art 174 the Slave is incapable of making any kind of Contract Except those which relate to own emancipation

Art 175 All that a Slave possesses belongs to his master he Possesses nothing of his own excep his peculium that is to Say the Sum of money or movable estate which his master chooses He Should possess

Art 176 the can transmit nothing by Succession or otherwise but the Succession of free persons related to them which the would have Inherited had the been free may pass through them to such of their descendants as may have acquired their liberty before the Succession opened

A part of the Civil Code of louisiana the united States Shall guarantee to every State in this union a republican form of government and Shall protect each of them a gainst invaison and on Aplication of the legislature. or of the executive when the legislature. can not be convened against Domestic violence

now is the united States government and constitution free or a local Goverment if it is free let us colored population muster in to ams and garison forts guard Station and mand vessels and then we will know wheather we are free people or not then we will know wheather you want to make brest works of us or not or make us fools ornot I heard one of most Ables and distingush lawiers Say that the Colored population was all free and Had as much liberty in the union as he had in four or five days after I went to him to get him to atend Some buiness for me he Said to me Are you free or Slave Sir Said i am free By your own speeches was you born free no Sir Said i we have been made fools of from the time Butlers fleet landed hear but I have remained At my old Stand and will untill i See what i am dowing I know very well that the white union men cannot put down the rebeles for them that was not rebles Soon will be

i am Sory that I am not able to write good may the union forever Stand with peace and liberty to All good people

A Colored man

the president Shall be commander in chief of the Army and navy of the united States and of the miltia of the Several States when called Into actual Service of the united States

when the president ordered three hundred thousand Colored Soldiers to be mustered into the united States Army on the first Day of last April if So the rebles would have fell like the Surrender of vicksburg and porthudson

Declare freedom at onc and give us Somting to fight for Black Soldiers Black officers and all white rebles will Soon run them in or out of the union

the writer was born in 18.18 feb 16"

one of the union Colored friends

QUESTIONS FOR READING AND DISCUSSION

1. What did this man mean by writing that "the Collored population has got . . . a rebel master and a union master"? How did he view Union men? In what ways did they differ from rebels?

2. Why should black soldiers fight? Did this man believe the Constitution authorized Lincoln to arm African Americans and use them as soldiers? What was his view of the claim that "northern men Say the[y] did not com[e] South to free the negroes but to save the union"?

3. What was the significance of his statement that "there are three things to fight for and two races of people divided into three Classes"?

4. Why did this man write these things? Whom did he consider his audience? Do you think this document was forged or that it was an authentic statement by "A Colored man"? What evidence seems persuasive?

DOCUMENT 3

General William T. Sherman Explains the Hard Hand of War

During the Civil War, both Union and Confederate leaders targeted not only the armies of their enemies but also the will of the civilian populations to support their armies. General William T. Sherman's capture of Atlanta and subsequent March to the Sea in late 1864 epitomized the Union's policy of demoralizing Confederate civilians by demonstrating the inability of Confederate soldiers to defend southern citizens. After seizing At-

lanta, Sherman ordered the evacuation of the city's civilian population, for reasons he explained to his superior, General Henry W. Halleck. Sherman's evacuation order elicited protests from Confederate General John Bell Hood and from the mayor and city council of Atlanta, which Sherman answered with justifications of the war and its inherent cruelty. The following correspondence contrasts Sherman's views of the war with those of Hood and the city's white residents.

Correspondence, 1864

Atlanta, Georgia, September 20, 1864

Major-General Halleck, Chief of Staff, Washington, D.C.

GENERAL:

I have the honor herewith to submit copies of a correspondence between General Hood, of the Confederate Army, the Mayor of Atlanta, and myself, touching the removal of the inhabitants of Atlanta.

In explanation of the tone which marks some of these letters, I will only call your attention to the fact that, after I had announced my determination, General Hood took upon himself to question my motives. I could not tamely submit to such impertinence; and I have also seen that, in violation of all official usage, he has published in the Macon [Georgia] newspapers such parts of the correspondence as suited his purpose. This could have had no other object than to create a feeling on the part of the people; but if he expects to resort to such artifices, I think I can meet him there too.

It is sufficient for my Government to know that the removal of the inhabitants has been made with liberality and fairness, that it has been attended with no force, and that no women or children have suffered, unless for want of provisions by their natural protectors and friends.

My real reasons for this step were:

We want all the houses of Atlanta for military storage and occupation.

We want to contract the lines of defense, so as to diminish the garrison to the limit necessary to defend its narrow and vital parts, instead of embracing, as the lines now do, the vast suburbs. This . . . will make it necessary to destroy the very houses used by families as residences.

Atlanta is a fortified town, was stubbornly defended, and fairly captured. As captors, we have a right to it.

The residence here of a poor population would compel us, sooner or later, to feed them or to see them starve under our eyes.

The residence here of the families of our enemies would be a temptation and a means to keep up a correspondence dangerous and hurtful to our cause; a civil population calls for provost-guards, and absorbs the attention of officers in listening to everlasting complaints and special grievances that are not military.

William T. Sherman, *Memoirs of General William T. Sherman,* 2 vols. (New York: D. A. Appleton & Co., 1886).

These are my reasons; and, if satisfactory to the Government of the United States, it makes no difference whether it pleases General Hood and *his* people or not. I am, with respect, your obedient servant,

W. T. SHERMAN, Major-General commanding.

Atlanta, Georgia, September 7, 1864

General Hood, commanding Confederate Army.
GENERAL:
    I have deemed it to the interest of the United States that the citizens now residing in Atlanta should remove, those who prefer it to go south, and the rest north. For the latter I can provide food and transportation to points of their election in Tennessee, Kentucky, or farther north. For the former I can provide transportation by cars as far as Rough and Ready, and also wagons; but, that their removal may be made with as little discomfort as possible, it will be necessary for you to help the families from Rough and Ready to the [railroad] cars. . . . If you consent, I will undertake to remove all the families in Atlanta who prefer to go south to Rough and Ready, with all their movable effects, viz., clothing, trunks, reasonable furniture, bedding, etc., with their servants, white and black, with the proviso that no force shall be used toward the blacks, one way or the other. If they want to go with their masters or mistresses, they may do so; otherwise they will be sent away, unless they be men, when they may be employed by our quartermaster. Atlanta is no place for families or non-combatants, and I have no desire to send them north if you will assist in conveying them south. If this proposition meets your views, I will consent to a truce . . . stipulating that any wagons, horses, animals, or persons sent . . . for the purposes herein stated, shall in no manner be harmed or molested. . . .

W. T. SHERMAN, Major-General commanding.

September 9, 1864

Major-General W. T. Sherman, commanding United States Forces in Georgia.
GENERAL:
    . . . I do not consider that I have any alternative in this matter [of a truce]. I therefore accept your proposition to declare a truce of two days, or such time as may be necessary to accomplish the purpose mentioned, and shall render all assistance in my power to expedite the transportation of citizens in this direction. . . .

    And now, sir, permit me to say that the unprecedented measure you propose transcends, in studied and ingenious cruelty, all acts ever before brought to my attention in the dark history of war.

    In the name of God and humanity, I protest, believing that you will find that you are expelling from their homes and firesides the wives and children of a brave people. I am, general, very respectfully, your obedient servant,

J. B. HOOD, *General.*

Atlanta, Georgia, September 10, 1864

General J. B. Hood, commanding Army of Tennessee, Confederate Army.
GENERAL:
    . . . You style the measures proposed "unprecedented," and appeal to the dark history of war for a parallel, as an act of "studied and ingenious cruelty." It

is not unprecedented. . . . Nor is it necessary to appeal to the dark history of war, when recent and modern examples are so handy. You yourself burned dwelling-houses along your parapet, and I have seen to-day fifty houses that you have rendered uninhabitable because they stood in the way of your forts and men. You defended Atlanta on a line so close to town that every cannon-shot and many musket-shots from our line of investment, that overshot their mark, went into the habitations of women and children. . . . I have not accused you of heartless cruelty, but merely instance these cases of very recent occurrence, and could go on and enumerate hundreds of others, and challenge any fair man to judge which of us has the heart of pity for the families of a "brave people."

I say that it is kindness to these families of Atlanta to remove them now, at once, from scenes that women and children should not be exposed to, and the ."brave people" should scorn to commit their wives and children to the rude barbarians who thus, as you say, violate the laws of war, as illustrated in the pages of its dark history.

In the name of common-sense, I ask you not to appeal to a just God in such a sacrilegious manner. You who, in the midst of peace and prosperity, have plunged a nation into war — dark and cruel war — who dared and badgered us to battle, insulted our flag, seized our arsenals and forts that were left in the honorable custody of peaceful ordnance-sergeants, seized and made "prisoners of war" the very garrisons sent to protect your people against negroes and Indians, long before any overt act was committed by the (to you) hated Lincoln Government; tried to force Kentucky and Missouri into rebellion, [in] spite of themselves; falsified the vote of Louisiana; turned loose your privateers to plunder unarmed ships; expelled Union families by the thousands, burned their houses, and declared, by an act of your Congress, the confiscation of all debts due Northern men for goods had and received! Talk thus to the marines, but not to me, who have seen these things, and who will this day make as much sacrifice for the peace and honor of the South as the best-born Southerner among you! If we must be enemies, let us be men, and fight it out as we propose to do, and not deal in such hypocritical appeals to God and humanity. God will judge us in due time, and he will pronounce whether it be more humane to fight with a town full of women and the families of a brave people at our back, or to remove them in time to places of safety among their own friends and people. I am very respectfully, your obedient servant,

W. T. SHERMAN, Major-General commanding.

September 12, 1864

Major-General W. T. Sherman, commanding Military Division of the Mississippi
GENERAL:
I have the honor to acknowledge the receipt of your letter. . . .
I see nothing in your communication which induces me to modify the language of condemnation with which I characterized your order. It but strengthens me in the opinion that it stands "preëminent in the dark history of war for studied and ingenious cruelty." Your original order was stripped of all pretenses; you announced the edict for the sole reason that it was "to the interest of the United States." This alone you offered to us and the civilized world as an all sufficient reason for disregarding the laws of God and man. . . .

[Your letter] opens a wide field for the discussion of questions which I do not feel are committed to me. I am only a general of one of the armies of the Confederate States, charged with military operations in the field, under the direction of my superior officers, and I am not called upon to discuss with you the causes of the present war, or the political questions which led to or resulted from it. These grave and important questions have been committed to far abler hands than mine, and I shall only refer to them so far as to repel any unjust conclusion which might be drawn from my silence. You charge my country with "daring and badgering you to battle." The truth is, we sent commissioners to you, respectfully offering a peaceful separation, before the first gun was fired on either side. You say we insulted your flag. The truth is, we fired upon it, and those who fought under it, when you came to our doors upon the mission of subjugation. You say we seized upon your forts and arsenals, and made prisoners of the garrisons sent to protect us against negroes and Indians. The truth is, we, by force of arms, drove out insolent intruders and took possession of our own forts and arsenals, to resist your claims to dominion over masters, slaves, and Indians, all of whom are to this day, with a unanimity unexampled in the history of the world, warring against your attempts to become their masters. You say that we tried to force Missouri and Kentucky into rebellion in spite of themselves. The truth is, my Government, from the beginning of this struggle to this hour, has again and again offered, before the whole world, to leave it to the unbiased will of these States, and all others, to determine for themselves whether they will cast their destiny with your Government or ours; and your Government has resisted this fundamental principle of free institutions with the bayonet, and labors daily, by force and fraud, to fasten its hateful tyranny upon the unfortunate freemen of these States. You say we falsified the vote of Louisiana. The truth is, Louisiana not only separated herself from your Government by nearly a unanimous vote of her people, but has vindicated the act upon every battle-field from Gettysburg to the Sabine, and has exhibited an heroic devotion to her decision which challenges the admiration and respect of every man capable of feeling sympathy for the oppressed or admiration for heroic valor. You say that we turned loose pirates to plunder your unarmed ships. The truth is, when you robbed us of our part of the navy, we built and bought a few vessels, hoisted the flag of our country, and swept the seas, in defiance of your navy, around the whole circumference of the globe. You say we have expelled Union families by thousands. The truth is, not a single family has been expelled from the Confederate States, that I am aware of; but, on the contrary, the moderation of our Government toward traitors has been a fruitful theme of denunciation by its enemies and well-meaning friends of our cause. You say my Government, by acts of Congress, has confiscated "all debts due Northern men for goods sold and delivered." The truth is, our Congress gave due and ample time to your merchants and traders to depart from our shores with their ships, goods, and effects, and only sequestrated the property of our enemies in retaliation for their acts — declaring us traitors, and confiscating our property wherever their power extended, either in their country or our own. Such are your accusations, and such are the facts known of all men to be true.

You order into exile the whole population of a city; drive men, women, and children from their homes at the point of the bayonet, under the plea that it is to the interest of your Government, and on the claim that it is an act of "kindness to these families of Atlanta." . . . You issue a sweeping edict, covering all the inhabitants of a city, and add insult to the injury heaped upon the defenseless by assuming that you have done them a kindness. This you follow by the assertion that you will "make as much sacrifice for the peace and honor of the South as the best-born Southerner." And, because I characterize what you call a kindness as being real cruelty, you presume to sit in judgment between me and my God; and you decide that my earnest prayer to the Almighty Father to save our women and children from what you call kindness, is a "sacrilegious, hypocritical appeal."

You came into our country with your army, avowedly for the purpose of subjugating free white men, women, and children, and not only intend to rule over them, but you make negroes your allies, and desire to place over us an inferior race, which we have raised from barbarism to its present position, which is the highest ever attained by that race, in any country, in all time. I must, therefore, decline to accept your statements in reference to your kindness toward the people of Atlanta, and your willingness to sacrifice every thing for the peace and honor of the South, and refuse to be governed by your decision in regard to matters between myself, my country, and my God.

You say, "Let us it fight it out like men." To this my reply is — for myself, and I believe for all the true men, ay, and women and children, in my country — we will fight you to the death! Better die a thousand deaths than submit to live under you or your Government and your negro allies!

Having answered the points forced upon me by your letter . . . I close this correspondence with you; and, notwithstanding your comments upon my appeal to God in the cause of humanity, I again humbly and reverently invoke his almighty aid in defense of justice and right. Respectfully, your obedient servant,

J. B. HOOD, General.

Atlanta, Georgia, September 11, 1864

Major-General W. T. Sherman
SIR:

We the undersigned, Mayor and two of the Council for the city of Atlanta . . . ask leave most earnestly but respectfully to petition you to reconsider the order requiring them to leave Atlanta.

At first view, it struck us that the measure would involve extraordinary hardship and loss, but since we have seen the practical execution of it so far as it has progressed, and the individual condition of the people, and heard their statements as to the inconveniences, loss, and suffering attending it, we are satisfied that the amount of it will involve in the aggregate consequences appalling and heart-rending.

Many poor women are in advanced state of pregnancy, others now having young children, and whose husbands for the greater part are either in the army, prisoners, or dead. Some say: "I have such a one sick at my house; who will wait on them when I am gone?" Others say: "What are we to do? We have no house to go to, and no means to buy, build, or rent any; no parents, relatives, or friends, to go to." Another says: "I will try and take this or that article of property, but such and such things I must leave behind, though I need them much." . . .

[H]ow is it possible for the people still here (mostly women and children) to find any shelter? And how can they live through the winter in the woods — no shelter or subsistence, in the midst of strangers who know them not, and without the power to assist them much, if they were willing to do so?

This is but a feeble picture of the consequences of this measure. You know the woe, the horrors, and the suffering, cannot be described by words; imagination can only conceive of it, and we ask you to take these things into consideration. . . .

Respectfully submitted:
JAMES M. CALHOUN, Mayor.

Atlanta, Georgia, September 12, 1864

James M. Calhoun, Mayor . . . , representing City Council of Atlanta
GENTLEMEN:

I have your letter . . . in the nature of a petition to revoke my orders removing all the inhabitants from Atlanta. I have read it carefully, and give full credit to your statements of the distress that will be occasioned, and yet shall not revoke my orders, because they were not designed to meet the humanities of the case, but to prepare for the future struggles in which millions of good people outside of Atlanta have a deep interest. We must have peace, not only at Atlanta, but in all America. To secure this, we must stop the war that now desolates our once happy and favored country. To stop war, we must defeat the rebel armies which are arrayed against the laws and Constitution that all must respect and obey. To defeat those armies, we must prepare the way to reach them in their recesses, provided with the arms and instruments which enable us to accomplish our purpose. Now, I know the vindictive nature of our enemy, that we may have many years of military operations from this quarter; and, therefore, deem it wise and prudent to prepare in time. The use of Atlanta for warlike purposes is inconsistent with its character as a home for families. There will be no manufactures, commerce, or agriculture here, for the maintenance of families, and sooner or later want will compel the inhabitants to go. Why not go now, when all the arrangements are completed for the transfer, instead of waiting till the plunging shot of contending armies will renew the scenes of the past month? Of course, I do not apprehend any such thing at this moment, but you do not suppose this army will be here until the war is over. I cannot discuss this subject with you fairly, because I cannot impart to you what we propose to do, but I assert that our military plans make it necessary for the inhabitants to go away, and I can only renew my offer of services to make their exodus in any direction as easy and comfortable as possible.

You cannot qualify war in harsher terms than I will. War is cruelty, and you cannot refine it; and those who brought war into our country deserve all the curses and maledictions a people can pour out. I know I had no hand in making this war, and I know I will make more sacrifices to-day than any of you to secure peace. But you cannot have peace and a division of our country. If the United States submits to a division now, it will not stop, but will go on until we reap the fate of Mexico, which is eternal war. The United States does and must assert its authority, wherever it once had power; for, if it relaxes one bit to pressure, it is gone, and I believe that such is the national feeling. This feeling assumes various shapes, but always comes back to that of Union. Once admit the Union, once more acknowledge the authority of the national Government, and, instead of devoting your houses and streets and roads to the dread uses of war, I and this army become at once your protectors and supporters, shielding you from danger, let it come from what quarter it may. I know that a few individuals cannot resist a torrent of error and passion, such as swept the South into rebellion, but you can point out, so that we may know those who desire a government, and those who insist on war and its desolation.

You might as well appeal against the thunder-storm as against these terrible hardships of war. They are inevitable, and the only way the people of Atlanta can hope once more to live in peace and quiet at home, is to stop the war, which can only be done by admitting that it began in error and is perpetuated in pride.

We don't want your negroes, or your horses, or your houses, or your lands, or any thing you have, but we do want and will have a just obedience to the laws of the United States. That we will have, and, if it involves the destruction of your improvements, we cannot help it.

You have heretofore read public sentiment in your newspapers, that live by falsehood and excitement; and the quicker you seek for truth in other quarters, the better. I repeat then that, by the original compact of Government, the United States had certain rights in Georgia, which have never been relinquished and never will be; that the South began war by seizing forts, arsenals, mints, custom-houses, etc., etc., long before Mr. Lincoln was installed, and before the South had one jot or tittle of provocation. I myself have seen in Missouri, Kentucky, Tennessee, and Mississippi, hundreds and thousands of women and children fleeing from your armies and desperadoes, hungry and with bleeding feet. In Memphis, Vicksburg, and Mississippi, we fed thousands upon thousands of the families of rebel soldiers left on our hands, and whom we could not see starve. Now that war comes home to you, you feel very different. You deprecate its horrors, but did not feel them when you sent car-loads of soldiers and ammunition, and moulded shells and shot, to carry war into Kentucky and Tennessee, to desolate the homes of hundreds and thousands of good people who only asked to live in peace at their old homes, and under the Government of their inheritance. But these comparisons are idle. I want peace, and believe it can only be reached through union and war, and I will ever conduct war with a view to perfect and early success.

But, my dear sirs, when peace does come, you may call on me for any thing. Then will I share with you the last cracker, and watch with you to shield your homes and families against danger from every quarter.

Now you must go, and take with you the old and feeble, feed and nurse them, and build for them, in more quiet places, proper habitations to shield them against the weather until the mad passions of men cool down, and allow the Union and peace once more to settle over your old homes at Atlanta. Yours in haste,

W. T. SHERMAN, Major-General commanding.

QUESTIONS FOR READING AND DISCUSSION

1. How do Sherman's and Hood's justifications of war differ? What did Sherman consider Hood's "impertinence"? Why did Hood consider Sherman's order an act of "studied and ingenious cruelty"?

2. Why did Sherman believe it was "kindness" to expel Atlanta's residents? How did Atlanta citizens reply to his orders?

3. In what ways, according to Hood, did Sherman "make negroes your allies"? Did Sherman agree?

4. Did Sherman acknowledge any limits to his declaration that "war is cruelty"? Who was to blame for the horrors of war? According to Sherman, what did the Union want from Confederate civilians?

DOCUMENT 4

War Wounds

The human toll of the Civil War far exceeded that of any American war before or since. Behind the lines of each army, doctors and nurses attended to wounded men. Sometimes their efforts were aided by volunteers — both women and men — and by the soldiers' relatives. The celebrated poet Walt Whitman visited wounded soldiers near battlefields and in Washington, D.C., and, he wrote, made "impromptu jottings" in "blood-smutch'd little note-books." Passages from Whitman's notes, excerpted here, reveal the suffering that continued long after the smoke had cleared from the battlefield.

Walt Whitman
Specimen Days, 1862–1863

Falmouth, Va., opposite Fredericksburgh, December 21 [1862]. Begin my visits among the camp hospitals in the army of the Potomac. Spend a good part of the day in a large brick mansion on the banks of the Rappahannock, used as a hospital since the battle — seems to have receiv'd only the worst cases. Out doors, at the foot of a tree, within ten yards of the front of the house, I notice a heap of amputated feet, legs, arms, hands, &c., a full load for a one-horse cart. Several dead bodies lie near, each cover'd with its brown woolen blanket. In the door-yard, towards the river, are fresh graves, mostly of officers, their names on pieces of barrel-staves or broken boards, stuck in the dirt. (Most of these bodies were subsequently taken up and transported north to their friends.) The large mansion is quite crowded upstairs and down, everything impromptu, no system, all bad enough, but I have no doubt the best that can be done; all the wounds pretty bad, some frightful, the men in their old clothes, unclean and bloody. Some of the wounded are rebel soldiers and officers, prisoners. One, a Mississippian, a captain, hit badly in leg, I talk'd with some time; he ask'd me for papers, which I gave him. (I saw him three months afterward in Washington, with his leg amputated, doing well.) I went through the rooms, downstairs and up. Some of the men were dying. I had nothing to give at that visit, but wrote a few letters to folks home, mothers, &c. Also talk'd to three or four, who seem'd most susceptible to it, and needing it.

December 23 to 31 — The results of the late battle [Fredericksburg] are exhibited everywhere about here in thousands of cases, (hundreds die every day,) in the camp, brigade, and division hospitals. These are merely tents, and some-

Walt Whitman, *Specimen Days*, in *Complete Poetry and Collected Prose*, ed. J. E. Miller, Jr. (Boston: Houghton Mifflin, 1972) 712–27.

times very poor ones, the wounded lying on the ground, lucky if their blankets are spread on layers of pine or hemlock twigs, or small leaves. No cots; seldom even a mattress. It is pretty cold. The ground is frozen hard, and there is occasional snow. I go around from one case to another. I do not see that I do much good to these wounded and dying; but I cannot leave them. Once in a while some youngster holds on to me convulsively, and I do what I can for him; at any rate, stop with him and sit near him for hours, if he wishes it. . . .

January, 1863 . . . I am now remaining in and around Washington, daily visiting the hospitals. Am much in Patent-office, Eighth street, H street, Armory-square, and others. Am now able to do a little good, having money, (as almoner of others home,) and getting experience. To-day, Sunday afternoon and till nine in the evening, visited Campbell hospital; attended specially to one case in ward 1, very sick with pleurisy and typhoid fever, young man, farmer's son, D. F. Russell, company E, 60th New York, downhearted and feeble; a long time before he would take any interest; wrote a letter home to his mother, in Malone, Franklin county, N.Y., at his request; gave him some fruit and one or two other gifts; envelop'd and directed his letter, &c. Then went thoroughly through ward 6, observ'd every case in the ward, without, I think, missing one; gave perhaps from twenty to thirty persons, each one some little gift, such as oranges, apples, sweet crackers, figs, &c.

Thursday, Jan. 21. — Devoted the main part of the day to Armory-square hospital; went pretty thoroughly through wards F, G, H, and I; some fifty cases in each ward. In ward F supplied the men throughout with writing paper and stamp'd envelope each; distributed in small portions, to proper subjects, a large jar of first-rate preserv'd berries, which had been donated to me by a lady — her own cooking. Found several cases I thought good subjects for small sums of money, which I furnish'd. (The wounded men often come up broke, and it helps their spirits to have even the small sum I give them.) My paper and envelopes all gone, but distributed a good lot of amusing reading matter; also, as I thought judicious, tobacco, oranges, apples, &c. Interesting cases in ward 1; Charles Miller, bed 19, company D, 53d Pennsylvania, is only sixteen years of age, very bright, courageous boy, left leg amputated below the knee; next bed to him, another young lad very sick; gave each appropriate gifts. In the bed above, also, amputation of the left leg; gave him a little jar of raspberries; bed 1, this ward, gave a small sum; also to a soldier on crutches, sitting on his bed near. . . . (I am more and more surprised at the very great proportion of youngsters from fifteen to twenty-one in the army. I afterwards found a still greater proportion among the southerners.). . .

Wednesday, February 4th. —Visited Armory-square hospital, went pretty thoroughly through wards E and D. Supplied paper and envelopes to all who wish'd — as usual, found plenty of men who needed those articles. Wrote letters. Saw and talk'd with two or three members of the Brooklyn 14th regt. A poor fellow in ward D, with a fearful wound in a fearful condition, was having some loose splinters of bone taken from the neighborhood of the wound. The operation was long, and one of great pain — yet, after it was well commenced, the soldier bore it in silence. He sat up, propp'd — was much wasted — had lain a long time quiet in one position (not for days only but weeks,) a bloodless, brown-skinn'd face, with eyes full of determination — belong'd to a New York regiment. There was an unusual cluster of surgeons, medical cadets, nurses, &c., around his bed — I thought the whole thing was done with tenderness, and done well. In one case, the wife sat by the side of her husband, his sickness typhoid fever, pretty bad. In another, by the side of her son, a mother — she told me she had seven children, and this was the youngest. (A fine, kind, healthy, gentle mother, goodlooking, not very old, with a cap on her head, and dress'd like home — what a charm it gave to the whole ward.). . .

May, 1863. As I write this, the wounded have begun to arrive from Hooker's command from bloody Chancellorsville. I was down among the first arrivals. The men in charge told me the bad cases were yet to come. If that is so I pity them, for these are bad enough. You ought to see the scene of the wounded arriving at the landing here at the foot of Sixth street, at night. Two boat loads came about half-past seven last night. A little after eight it rain'd a long and violent shower. The pale, helpless soldiers had been debark'd, and lay around on the wharf and neighborhood anywhere. The rain was, probably, grateful to them; at any rate they were exposed to it. The few torches light up the spectacle. All around — on the wharf, on the ground, out on side places — the men are lying on blankets, old quilts, &c., with bloody rags bound round heads, arms, and legs. The attendants are few, and at night few outsiders also — only a few hard-work'd transportation men and drivers. (The wounded are getting to be common, and people grow callous.) The men, whatever their condition, lie there, and patiently wait till their turn comes to be taken up. Near by, the ambulances are now arriving in clusters, and one after another is call'd to back up and take its load. Extreme cases are sent off on stretchers. The men generally make little or no ado, whatever their sufferings. A few groans that cannot be suppress'd, and occasionally a scream of pain as they lift a man into the ambulance. To-day, as I write, hundreds more are expected, and to-morrow and the next day more, and so on for many days. Quite often they arrive at the rate of 1000 a day. . . .

June 18th. In my visits to the hospitals, I found it was in the simple matter of personal presence, and emanating ordinary cheer and magnetism, that I succeeded and help'd more than by medical nursing, or delicacies, or gifts of money, or anything else. During the war I possess'd the perfection of physical health. My habit, when practicable, was to prepare for starting out on one of those daily or nightly tours of from a couple to four or five hours, by fortifying myself with previous rest, the bath, clean clothes, a good meal, and as cheerful an appearance as possible.

June 25, Sundown. As I sit writing this paragraph I see a train of about thirty huge four-horse wagons, used as ambulances, fill'd with wounded, passing up Fourteenth street, on their way, probably, to Columbian, Carver, and mount Pleasant hospitals. This is the way the men come in now, seldom in small numbers, but almost always in these long, sad processions. Through the past winter, while our army lay opposite Fredericksburgh, the like strings of ambulances were of frequent occurrence along Seventh street, passing slowly up from the steamboat wharf, with loads from Aquia creek.

The soldiers are nearly all young men, and far more American than is generally supposed — I should say nine-tenths are native-born. Among the arrivals from Chancellorsville I find a large proportion of Ohio, Indiana, and Illinois men. As usual, there are all sorts of wounds. Some of the men fearfully burnt from the explosions of artillery caissons. One ward has a long row of officers, some with ugly hurts. Yesterday was perhaps worse than usual. Amputations are going on — the attendants are dressing wounds.

QUESTIONS FOR READING AND DISCUSSION

1. In what ways did Whitman help wounded men, and how did they respond to him? What did he mean by stating that he "found it was in the simple matter of personal presence, and emanating ordinary cheer and magnetism, that I succeeded"?
2. What did his distribution of paper, stamps, and envelopes suggest about the soldiers' own experiences and their distant friends and relatives?
3. Why did Whitman visit the hospitals? What did he learn there about the war?
4. Judging from Whitman's account, how did the hospital experiences of wounded men differ from their previous experiences in the army and in their homes, before they became soldiers?

COMPARATIVE QUESTIONS

1. How did Abraham Lincoln's war aims differ from those of the ex-slave in New Orleans?
2. To what extent were the views Lincoln expressed in the Gettysburg Address shared by the ex-slave in New Orleans, General William T. Sherman, and the wounded soldiers visited by Walt Whitman?
3. Given the war aims defined by Lincoln and the contrasting experiences of war illustrated by the other documents, what justified the immense sacrifices made by so many people?
4. War has been termed the continuation of politics by other means. Judging from the documents in this chapter, what key political conflicts shaped the course and outcome of the Civil War?

CHAPTER 15

RECONSTRUCTION
1863–1877

D uring the turbulent years of Reconstruction, the character of freedom for former slaves was the subject of intense debate within the South and across the nation. Most southern whites sought the most limited form of freedom for African Americans, as the black codes passed by several states suggested. Most former slaves sought to exercise their liberty to the full, as black conventions repeatedly declared. White vigilantes resorted to murder, lynching, and other acts of brutality to force blacks to limit their horizons. In the end, most northern white Republicans concluded that, once former slaves had the vote, the South — not the North or the federal government — should determine how best to define freedom and preserve order.

DOCUMENT 1
Black Codes Enacted in the South

After the Civil War, the legal status of former slaves was defined by state legislatures throughout the South. In the months following General Robert E. Lee's surrender at Appomattox, white legislators devised laws to regulate and control former slaves. Known as black codes, these laws defined freedom for African Americans in terms that resembled slavery in many respects, as revealed in the following provisions of the Mississippi Black Code, enacted in November 1865.

Mississippi Black Code, November 1865

AN ACT to confer Civil Rights on Freedmen, and for other purposes.

Be it enacted by the Legislature of the State of Mississippi. That all freedmen, free negroes and mulattoes may sue and be sued, . . . in all the courts of law and equity of this State, and may acquire personal property . . . by descent or purchase, and may dispose of the same, in the same manner. . . that white persons may: Provided that the provisions of this section shall not be so construed as to allow any freedman, free negro or mulatto, to rent or lease any lands or tenements,

---

W. L. Fleming, ed., *Laws of Mississippi Documentary History of Reconstruction*, 2 vols. (Cleveland: A. H. Clark, 1865) 281–90.

except in incorporated towns or cities in which places the corporate authorities shall control the same. . . .

That all freedmen, free negroes and mulattoes may intermarry with each other. . . . That all freedmen, free negroes and mulattoes, who do now and have heretofore lived and cohabited together as husband and wife shall be taken and held in law as legally married, and the issue shall be taken and held as legitimate for all purposes. That it shall not be lawful for any freedman, free negro or mulatto to inter-marry with any white person; nor for any white person to inter-marry with any freedman, free negro or mulatto; and any person who shall so intermarry shall be deemed guilty of felony, and on conviction thereof, shall be confined in the State penitentiary for life. . . .

That . . . freedmen, free negroes and mulattoes are now by law competent witnesses . . . in civil cases . . . and they shall also be competent witnesses in all criminal prosecutions where the crime charged is alleged to have been committed by a white person upon or against the person or property of a freedman, free negro or mulatto. . . .

That every freedman, free negro and mulatto, shall, on the second Monday of January, one thousand eight hundred and sixty-six, and annually thereafter, have a lawful home or employment, and shall have written evidence thereof; as follows, to wit: if living in any incorporated city, town or village, a license from the mayor thereof; and if living outside of any incorporated city, town or village, from the member of the board of police of his beat, authorizing him or her to do irregular and job work, or a written contract . . . which licenses may be revoked for cause, at any time, by the authority granting the same. . . .

That all contracts for labor made with freedmen, free negroes and mulattoes, for a longer period than one month shall be in writing and in duplicate, attested and read to said freedman, free negro or mulatto, by a beat, city or county officer, or two disinterested white persons of the county in which the labor is to be performed . . . and if the laborer shall quit the service of the employer, before expiration of his term of service, without good cause, he shall forfeit his wages for that year, up to the time of quitting. . . .

That every civil officer shall, and every person may arrest and carry back to his or her legal employer any freedman, free negro or mulatto, who shall have quit the service of his or her employer before the expiration of his or her term of service without good cause, and said officer and person, shall be entitled to receive for arresting and carrying back every deserting employee aforesaid, the sum of five dollars, and ten cents per mile from the place of arrest to the place of delivery, [to] be paid by the employer. . . .

An [A]ct to regulate the relation of Master and Apprentice, as related to Freedmen, Free Negroes, and Mulattoes.

Be it enacted by the Legislature of the State of Mississippi:

That it shall be the duty of all sheriffs, justices of the peace, and other civil officers of the several counties in this State, to report to the probate courts of their respective counties, semi-annually, at the January and July terms of said courts, all freedmen, free negroes and mulattoes, under the age of eighteen, within their respective counties, beats or districts, who are orphans, or whose parent or parents have not the means, or who refuse to provide for and support said minors, and thereupon it shall be the duty of said probate court, to order the clerk of said court to apprentice said minors to some competent and suitable person, on such terms as the court may direct. . . . Provided, that the former owner of said minors shall have the preference. . . .

That . . . the said court shall require the said master or mistress to execute bond and security, payable to the State of Mississippi, conditioned that he or she shall furnish said minor with sufficient food and clothing, to treat said minor humanely, furnish medical attention in case of sickness; [and to] teach or cause to be taught him or her to read and write, if under fifteen years old. . . . Provided, that said apprentice shall be bound by indenture, in case of males until they are twenty-one years old, and in case of females until they are eighteen years old. . . .

That in the management and control of said apprentices, said master or mistress shall have power to inflict such moderate corporeal chastisement as a father or guardian is allowed to inflict on his or her child or ward at common law. . . .

That if any apprentice shall leave the employment of his or her master or mistress, without his or her consent, said master or mistress may pursue and recapture said apprentice, and bring him or her before any justice of the peace of the county, whose duty it shall be to remand said apprentice to the service of his or her master or mistress; and in the event of a refusal on the part of said apprentice so to return, then said justice shall commit said apprentice to the jail of said county. . . .

That if any person entice away any apprentice from his or her master or mistress, or shall knowingly employ an apprentice, or furnish him or her food or clothing, without the written consent of his or her master or mistress, or shall sell or give said apprentice ardent spirits, without such consent, said person so offending shall be deemed guilty of a high misdemeanor, and shall, on conviction thereof before the county court, be punished as provided for the punishment of persons enticing from their employer hired freedmen, free Negroes or mulattoes. . . .

AN ACT to amend the Vagrant Laws of the State.

Be it further enacted,

That all freedmen, free negroes and mulattoes in this State, over the age of eighteen years, found on the second Monday in January, 1866, or thereafter, with no lawful employment or business, or found unlawfully assembling themselves together either in the day or night time, and all white persons so assembling with [them] on terms of equality, or living in adultery or fornication with a freedwoman, free negro, or mulatto, shall be deemed vagrants, and on conviction thereof, shall be fined in the sum of not exceeding, in the case of a freedman, free negro or mulatto, fifty dollars, and a white man two hundred dollars, and imprisoned at the discretion of the court, the free negro not exceeding ten days, and the white man not exceeding six months. . . .

That . . . in case any freedman, free negro or mulatto, shall fail for five days after the imposition of any fine or forfeiture upon him or her for violation of any of the provisions of this act, to pay the same, that it shall be, and is hereby made the duty of the sheriff of the proper county to hire out said freedman, free negro or mulatto, to any person who will, for the shortest period of service, pay said fine or forfeiture and all costs: Provided, a preference shall be given to the employer, if there be one, in which case the employer shall be entitled to deduct and retain the amount so paid from the wages of such freedman, free negro or mulatto, then due or to become due. . . .

AN ACT to punish certain offences. . . .

Be it enacted by the Legislature of the State of Mississippi:

That no freedman, free negro or mulatto . . . shall keep or carry fire-arms of any kind, or any ammunition, dirk or bowie knife, and on conviction thereof, in the county court, shall be punished by fine, not exceeding ten dollars, and pay the costs of such proceedings, and all such arms or ammunition shall be forfeited to the informer, and it shall be the duty of every civil and military officer to arrest any freedman, free negro or mulatto found with any such arms or ammunition, and cause him or her to be committed for trial in default of bail. . . .

That any freedman, free negro or mulatto, committing riots, routs, affrays, trespasses, malicious mischief, cruel treatment of animals, seditious speeches, insulting gestures, language or acts, or assaults on any person, disturbances of the peace, exercising the function of a minister of the Gospel, without a license from some regularly organized church, vending spirituous or intoxicating liquors, or committing any other misdemeanor . . . shall, upon conviction thereof, in the county court, be fined, not less than ten dollars, and not more than one hundred dollars, and may be imprisoned, at the discretion of the court, not exceeding thirty days. . . .

That if any white person shall sell, lend or give to any freedman, free negro or mulatto, any firearms, dirk or bowie-knife, or ammunition, or any spirituous or intoxicating liquors, such person or persons so offending, upon conviction thereof, in the county court of his or her county, shall be fined, not exceeding fifty dollars, and may be imprisoned, at the discretion of the court, not exceeding thirty days. . . .

That all the penal and criminal laws now in force in this State, defining offences and prescribing the mode of punishment for crimes and misdemeanors committed by slaves, free negroes or mulattoes, be and the same are hereby reenacted, and declared to be in full force and effect, against freedmen, free negroes and mulattoes, except so far as the mode and manner of trial and punishment have been changed or altered by law. . . .

That if any freedman, free negro or mulatto, convicted of any of the misdemeanors provided against in this act, shall fail or refuse, for the space of five days after conviction, to pay the fine and costs imposed, such person shall be hired out by the sheriff or other officer, at public outcry, to any white person who will pay said fine and all costs, and take such convict for the shortest time.

QUESTIONS FOR READING AND DISCUSSION

1. What civil rights, if any, did these laws confer on freed black men and women?
2. Why did the laws repeatedly refer to "freedmen, free negroes and mulattoes"?
3. In what ways did these laws limit the freedom of African Americans in Mississippi? Were these laws different from the laws governing slaves? If so, how and why?
4. Did former masters exercise any control over their former slaves? To what extent did these laws limit the freedom of white Mississippians?
5. What do these laws suggest about white southerners' anxieties and fears regarding the end of slavery? In what ways did the laws envision postemancipation society differing from antebellum slavery?

DOCUMENT 2

A Black Convention in Alabama

Beginning in 1867, state governments throughout the old Confederacy were reorganized under the auspices of Reconstruction legislation passed by Congress, which was controlled by northern Republicans. Congressional Reconstruction empowered former slaves by granting them the right to vote and permitting their views to be expressed through such traditional political processes as parties, conventions, campaigns, and elections. Across the South, African Americans assembled in conventions and hammered out resolutions that defined their own views of freedom, as revealed in the following address drawn up at a convention in Mobile, Alabama, and published in 1867.

"Address of the Colored Convention to the People of Alabama," 1867

As there seems to be considerable difference of opinion concerning the "legal rights of the colored man," it will not be amiss to say that we claim exactly *the same rights, privileges and immunities as are enjoyed by white men* — we ask nothing more and will be content with nothing less. *All legal* distinctions between the races are now abolished. The word white is stricken from our laws, and every privilege which white men were formerly permitted to enjoy, merely because they were white men, now that word is stricken out, we are entitled to on the ground that we are men. *Color can no longer be pleaded for the purpose of curtailing privileges, and every public right, privilege and immunity is enjoyable by every individual member of the public.* This is the touchstone that determines all these points. So long as a park or a street is a public park or street the entire public has the right to use it; so long as a car or a steamboat is a public conveyance, it must carry all who come to it, and serve all alike who pay alike. The law no longer knows white nor black, but simply men, and consequently we are entitled to ride in public conveyances, hold office, sit on juries and do everything else which we have in the past been prevented from doing solely on the ground of our color. . . .

We have said that we intend to claim all our rights, and we submit to our white friends that it is the height of folly on their part to withhold them any longer. One-half of the voters in Alabama are black men, and in a few months there is to be an entire reorganization of the State government. The new officers — legislative, executive and judicial — will owe their election largely, if not mainly to the colored people, and every one must see clearly that the voters will then be certain to require and the officers to compel a cessation of all illegal discriminations. The question which every man now illegally discriminating against us has to decide is whether it is politic to insist upon gratifying prejudices . . . with the certainty by so doing, of incurring the lasting displeasure of one-half of the voting population of the State. We can stand it if they can, but we assure them that they are being watched closely, and that their conduct will be remembered when we have power.

"Address of the Colored Convention to the People of Alabama," Montgomery *Daily State Sentinel*, May 21, 1867.

There are some good people who are always preaching patience and pro-crastination. They would have us wait a few months, years, or generations, until the whites voluntarily give us our rights, but we do not intend to wait one day longer than we are absolutely compelled to. Look at our demands, and then at theirs. We ask of them simply that they surrender unreasonable and unreasoning prejudice; . . . that they consent to allow others as well as themselves to prosper and be happy. But they would have us pay for what we do not get; tramp through the broiling sun or pelting rain, or stand upon a platform, while empty seats mockingly invite us to rest our wearied limbs; our sick must suffer or submit to indignity; we must put up with inconvenience of every kind; and the virtuous as-pirations of our children must be continually checked by the knowledge that no matter how upright their conduct, they will be looked on as less worthy of re-spect than the lowest wretch on earth who wears a white skin. We ask you — only while in public, however — to surrender your prejudices, — nothing but prejudices; and you ask us to sacrifice our personal comfort, health, pecuniary in-terests, self-respect, and the future prospects of our children. The men who make such requests must suppose us devoid of spirit and of brains, but find themselves mistaken. Solemnly and distinctly, we again say to you, men of Alabama, that we will not submit voluntarily to such infamous discrimination, and if you will in-sist upon tramping on the rights and outraging the feelings of those who are so soon to pass judgment upon you, then upon your own heads will rest the respon-sibility for the effect of your course.

All over the state of Alabama — all over the South indeed—the colored peo-ple have with singular unanimity, arrayed themselves under the Republican ban-ner, upon the Republican platform, and it is confidently predicted that nine-tenths of them will vote the Republican ticket. Do you ask, why is this? We answer, be-cause:

1. The Republican Party opposed and prohibited the extension of slavery.

2. It repealed the fugitive slave law.

3. It abolished slavery in the District of Columbia.

4. It abolished slavery in the rebellious states.

5. It abolished slavery throughout the rest of the Union.

6. It put down rebellion against the Union.

7. It passed the Freedmen's Bureau Bill and the Civil Rights Bill.

8. It enfranchised the colored people of the District of Columbia.

9. It enfranchised the colored people of the nine territories.

10. It enfranchised the colored people of the ten rebel states.

11. It provided for the formation of new constitutions and state governments in those ten states.

12. It passed new homestead laws, enabling the poor to obtain land.

In short, it has gone on, step by step, doing first one thing for us and then another, and it now proposes to enfranchise our people all over the Union. It is the only party which has ever attempted to extend our privileges, and as it has in the past always been trying to do this, it is but natural that we should trust it for the future.

While this has been the course of the Republican Party, the opposition has unitedly opposed every one of these measures, and it also now opposes the enfranchisement of our people in the North. Everywhere it has been against us in the past, and the great majority of its voters hate us as cordially now as ever before. It is sometimes alleged that the Republicans of the North have not been actuated by love for us in what they have done, and therefore that we should not join them; we answer that even if that were true they certainly never professed to hate us and the opposition "party has always been denouncing the "d——n nigger and abolitionist" with equal fervor. When we had no votes to give, the opposition placed us and the Republicans in the same boat, and now we reckon we'll stay in it. It may be and probably is true that some men acting with the Republican Party have cared nothing for the principles of that party; but it is also certainly true that ninety-nine-hundredths of all those who were conscientiously in favor of our rights were and are in the Republican Party, and that the great mass of those who hated, slandered and abused us were and are in the opposition party.

The memories of the opposition must be short indeed, to have forgotten their language of the past twenty years but we have *not* forgotten it.

But, say some of the members of the opposition party, "We intend to turn over a new leaf, and will hereafter give you all your rights." Perhaps they would, but we prefer not to put the new wine of political equality into the old bottles of "sectional animosity" and "caste feeling." We are somewhat fearful that those who have always opposed the extensions of rights are not sincere in their professions. . . .

Another fact should be borne in mind. While a few conservatives are making guarded promises to us the masses of that party are cursing us, and doing all they can to "make the d——d niggers stay in their place." If we were, therefore, to join that party, it would be simply as servants, and not as equals. Some leaders, who needed our votes might treat us decently, but the great majority would expect us to stay at home until election day, and then vote as our employers dictated. This we respectfully decline doing. It seems to us safest to have as little as possible to do with those members of the community who delight to abuse us, and they are nearly, if not quite, all to be found in the ranks of the opposition party. . . .

It cannot be disguised, however, that many men calling themselves conservatives are disposed to use unfair means to carry their points. The press . . . contain numerous threats that those colored people who do not vote as their employers command, will be discharged; that the property-holders will combine, import white laborers, and discharge their colored hands, etc. Numerous instances have come to our knowledge of persons who have already been discharged because they attended Republican meetings, and great numbers more have been threatened. "Vote as we command, or starve," is the argument these men propose to make [use] of, and with it they expect to succeed.

In this expectation they will be mistaken, and we warn them before it is prosecuted any further, that their game is a dangerous one for themselves. The property which they hold was nearly all earned by the sweat of our brows — not theirs. It has been forfeited to the Government by the treason of its owners, and is liable to be confiscated whenever the Republican Party demands it. The great majority of that party is now opposed to confiscation, but if the owners of property use the power which it gives them to make political slaves of the poor, a cry will go up to Congress which will make the party a unit for confiscation.

Conservatives of Alabama, do you propose to rush upon certain destruction? Are you mad, that you threaten to pursue a policy which could only result in causing thousands of men to cry out to their leaders, "Our wives and little ones are starving because we stood by you; because we would not be slaves!" When the nation abolished slavery, you used your local governments to neutralize and defeat its action, and the nation answered by abolishing your governments and enfranchising us. If you now use your property to neutralize or defeat this, its last act, it will answer by taking away the property you are only allowed to retain through its unparalleled mercy and which you have proved yourselves so unworthy of retaining. . . .

So complete, indeed, will be our victory, that our opponents will become disheartened unless they can divide us. This is the great danger which we have to guard against. . . . In nominations for office we expect that there will be no discriminations on account of color by either wing, but that the most capable and honest men will always be put in nomination. We understand full well that our people are too deficient in education to be generally qualified to fill the higher offices, but when qualified men are found, they must not be rejected for being black.

This lack of education, which is the consequence of our long servitude, and which so diminishes our powers for good, should not be allowed to characterize our children when they come upon the stage of action, and we therefore earnestly call upon every member of the Republican Party to demand the establishment of a thorough system of common schools throughout the State. It will benefit every citizen of the State, and, indeed, of the Union, for the well-being of each enures to the advantage of all. In a Republic, education is especially necessary, as the ignorant are always liable to be led astray by the arts of the demagogue.

With education secured to all; with the old and helpless properly cared for; with justice everywhere impartially administered, Alabama will commence a career of which she will have just cause to be proud. We shall all be prosperous and happy. The sad memories of the past will be forgotten amid the joys of the present and the prospect of the future.

Questions for Reading and Discussion

1. How did the Alabama Colored Convention define the "legal rights of the colored man"? Were they different from the legal rights of white men?

2. The convention favored the Republican party. Why were Republicans preferable to Democrats? What did the convention mean by stating, "we prefer not to put the new wine of political equality into the old bottles of 'sectional animosity' and 'caste feeling'"?

3. How did the convention propose to use political power to realize the opportunities presented by emancipation? To what extent did their address recommend punitive measures against former slaveholders and ex-Confederates? To what extent did they recommend policies specifically to aid freed men and women?

DOCUMENT 3

Klan Violence against Blacks

White vigilantes often terrorized African Americans after emancipation. The campaign of terror intensified with congressional Reconstruction and the mobilization of black voters in the Republican party. The violence attracted the attention of Congress, which held committee hearings throughout the South in 1871 to investigate the Ku Klux Klan. The following testimony of Elias Hill — a black preacher and teacher who lived in York County, South Carolina — illustrates the tactics and purposes of white vigilantes.

Elias Hill

Testimony before Congressional Committee Investigating the Ku Klux Klan, 1871

[The committee included a brief description of Hill.] Elias Hill is a remarkable character. He is crippled in both legs and arms, which are shriveled by rheumatism; he cannot walk, cannot help himself, has to be fed and cared for personally by others; was in early life a slave, whose freedom was purchased, his father buying his mother and getting Elias along with her, as a burden of which his master was glad to be rid. Stricken at seven years old with disease, he never was afterward able to walk, and he presents the appearance of a dwarf with the limbs of a child, the body of a man, and a finely developed intellectual head. He learned his letters and to read by calling the school children into the cabin as they passed, and also learned to write. He became a Baptist preacher, and after the war engaged in teaching colored children, and conducted the business correspondence of many of his colored neighbors. He is a man of blameless character, of unusual intelligence, speaks good English, and we put the story of his wrongs in his own language:

On the night of the 5th of last May, after I had heard a great deal of what they had done in that neighborhood, they came. It was between 12 and 1 o'clock at night when I was awakened and heard the dogs barking, and something walking, very much like horses. As I had often laid awake listening for such persons, for they had been all through the neighborhood, and disturbed all men and many women, I supposed that it was them. They came in a very rapid manner, and I could hardly tell whether it was the sound of horses or men. At last they came to my brother's door, which is in the same yard, and broke open the door and attacked his wife, and I heard her screaming and mourning. I could not understand what they said, for they were talking in an outlandish and unnatural tone, which I had heard they generally used at a negro's house. I heard them knocking around in her house. I was lying in my little cabin in the yard. At last I heard them have her in the yard. She was crying and the Ku-Klux were whipping her to make her tell where I lived. I heard her say, "Yon is his house." She has told me since that they first asked who had taken me out of her house. They said, "Where's Elias?" She said, "He doesn't stay here; yon is his house." They were then in the yard,

U. S. Congress, *Report of the Joint Select Committee to Inquire into the Condition of Affairs in the Late Insurrectionary States* (Washington, D.C., 1872) 1, 44–46.

and I had heard them strike her five or six licks when I heard her say this. Some one then hit my door. It flew open. One ran in the house, and stopping about the middle of the house, which is a small cabin, he turned around, as it seemed to me as I lay there awake, and said, "Who's here?" Then I knew they would take me, and I answered, "I am here." He shouted for joy, as it seemed, "Here he is! Here he is! We have found him!" and he threw the bedclothes off of me and caught me by one arm, while another man took me by the other and they carried me into the yard between the houses, my brother's and mine, and put me on the ground beside a boy. The first thing they asked me was, "Who did that burning? Who burned our houses?" — gin-houses, dwelling houses and such. Some had been burned in the neighborhood. I told them it was not me; I could not burn houses; it was unreasonable to ask me. Then they hit me with their fists, and said I did it, I ordered it. They went on asking me didn't I tell the black men to ravish all the white women. No, I answered them, They struck me again with their fists on my breast, and then they went on, "When did you hold a night-meeting of the Union League[1], and who were the officers? Who was the president?" I told them I had been the president, but that there had been no Union League meeting held at that place where they were formerly held since away in the fall. This was the 5th of May. They said that Jim Raney, that was hung, had been at my house since the time I had said the League was last held, and that he had made a speech. I told them that he had not, because I did not know the man. I said, "Upon honor." They said I had no honor, and hit me again. They went on asking me hadn't I been writing to Mr. A. S. Wallace, in Congress, to get letters from him. I told them I had. They asked what I had been writing about? I told them, "Only tidings." They said, with an oath, "I know the tidings were d——d good, and you were writing something about the Ku-Klux, and haven't you been preaching and praying about the Ku-Klux?" One asked, "Haven't you been preaching political sermons?" Generally, one asked me all the questions, but the rest were squatting over me — some six men I counted as I lay there, Said one, "Didn't you preach against the Ku-Klux," and wasn't that what Mr. Wallace was writing to me about? "Not at all," I said. "Let me see the letter," said he; "what was it about?" I said it was on the times. They wanted the letter. I told them if they would take me back into the house, and lay me in the bed, which was close adjoining my books and papers, I would try and get it. They said I would never go back to that bed, for they were going to kill me. "Never expect to go back; tell us where the letters are." I told them they were on the shelf somewhere, and I hoped they would not kill me. Two of them went into the house. . . . They staid in there a good while hunting about and then came out and asked me for a lamp. I told them there was a lamp somewhere. They said "Where?" I was so confused I said I could not tell exactly. They caught my leg — you see what it is — and pulled me over the yard, and then left me there, knowing I could not walk nor crawl, and all six went into the house. I was chilled with the cold lying in the yard at that time of night, for it was near 1 o'clock, and they had talked and beat me and so on until half an hour had passed since they first approached. After they had staid in the house for a considerable time, they came back to where I lay and asked if I wasn't afraid at

---

[1]**Union League:** Republican organization that helped mobilize African-American voters.

all. They pointed pistols at me all around my head once or twice, as if they were going to shoot me, telling me they were going to kill me; wasn't I ready to die, and willing to die? Didn't I preach? That they came to kill me — all the time pointing pistols at me. This second time they came out of the house, after plundering the house, searching for letters, they came at me with these pistols, and asked if I was ready to die. I told them that I was not exactly ready; that I would rather live; that I hoped they would not kill me that time. They said they would; I had better prepare. One caught me by the leg and hurt me, for my leg for forty years has been drawn each year, more and more year by year, and I made moan when it hurt so. One said "G——d d——n it, hush!" He had a horsewhip, and he told me to pull up my shirt, and he hit me. He told me at every lick, "Hold up your shirt." I made a moan every time he cut with the horsewhip. I reckon he struck me eight cuts right on the hip bone; it was almost the only place he could hit my body, my legs are so short — all my limbs drawn up and withered away with pain. I saw one of them standing over me or by me motion to them to quit. They all had disguises on. I then thought they would not kill me. One of them then took a strap, and buckled it around my neck and said, "Let's take him to the river and drown him.". . . After pulling the strap around my neck, he took it off and gave me a lick on my hip where he had struck me with the horsewhip. One of them said, "Now, you see, I've burned up the d——d letter of Wallace's and all," and he brought out a little book and says, "What's this for?" I told him I did not know; to let me see with a light and I could read it. They brought a lamp and I read it. It was a book in which I had keep an account of the school. I had been licensed to keep a school. I read them some of the names. He said that would do, and asked if I had been paid for those scholars I had put down. I said no. He said I would now have to die. I was somewhat afraid, but one said not to kill me. They said "Look here! Will you put a card in the paper next week like June Moore and Sol Hill?" They had been prevailed on to put a card in the paper to renounce all republicanism and never vote. I said, "If I had the money to pay the expense, I could." They said I could borrow, and gave me another lick. They asked me, "Will you quit preaching?" I told them I did not know. I said that to save my life. They said I must stop that republican paper that was coming to Clay Hill. It has been only a few weeks since it stopped. The republican weekly paper was then coming to me from Charleston. It came to my name. They said I must stop it, quit preaching, and put a card in the newspaper renouncing republicanism, and they would not kill me; but if I did not they would come back the next week and kill me. With that one of them went into the house where my brother and my sister-in-law lived, and brought her to pick me up. As she stooped down to pick me up one of them struck her, and as she was carrying me into the house another struck her with a strap. She carried me into the house and laid me on the bed. Then they gathered around and told me to pray for them. I tried to pray. They said, "Don't you pray against Ku-Klux, but pray that God may forgive Ku-Klux. Don't pray against us. Pray that God may bless and save us." I was so chilled with cold lying out of doors so long and in such pain I could not speak to pray, but I tried to, and they said that would do very well, and all went out of the house.

QUESTIONS FOR READING AND DISCUSSION

1. What did the Klan want from Hill? Why did they not kill him?
2. The Klan was concerned about Hill's preaching, teaching, and newspaper reading? Why?

3. Why did the Klan use such brutal violence against Hill and his relatives? According to Hill, how had others been treated by the Klan? Does it appear that the Klan randomly chose people to terrorize? Why or why not?

4. What significance, if any, should be attributed to the Klan's demand that Hill "pray that God may forgive the Ku-Klux"? For what did they seek forgiveness? Why?

DOCUMENT 4

A Northern Republican's Report on Reconstruction

By 1875, many Republican leaders in the North concluded that Reconstruction had done enough for former slaves. Concerned about the political consequences throughout the nation of federal support for southern, mostly black, Republicans, they decided that the best way to achieve order and stability in the South, as well as in the North, was to permit home rule in the former slave states. The disillusionment of many northern Republicans about Reconstruction and the conviction that southern blacks had to defend themselves with their own meager resources were illustrated in the observations — excerpted here — of Charles Nordhoff, a northern journalist, who spent five months traveling across the South in 1875.

Charles Nordhoff
The Cotton States, 1875

To make clear my point of view, it is proper to say that I am a Republican, and have never voted any other Federal ticket than the Republican; I have been opposed to slavery as long as I have had an opinion on any subject . . . ; and I am a thorough believer in the capacity of the people to rule themselves, even if they are very ignorant, better than any body else can rule them.

The following, then, are the conclusions I draw from my observations in the Cotton States:

There is not, in any of the States of which I speak, any desire for a new war; any hostility to the Union; any even remote wish to re-enslave the blacks; any hope or expectation of repealing any constitutional amendment, or in any way curtailing the rights of the blacks as citizens. The former slave-holders understand perfectly that the blacks can not be re-enslaved. . . .

That the Southern whites should rejoice over their defeat, now, is impossible. That their grandchildren will, I hope and believe. What we have a right to require is, that they shall accept the situation; and that they do. What they have a right to ask of us is, that we shall give them a fair chance under the new order of things; and that we have so far too greatly failed to do. . . .

The Southern Republicans seem to me unfair and unreasonable in another way. They complain constantly that the Southern whites still admire and are faith-

Charles Nordhoff, *The Cotton States in the Spring and Summer of 1875* (New York: D. A. Appleton & Co., 1876).

ful to their own leaders; and that they like to talk about the bravery of the South during the war, and about the great qualities of their leading men. There seems to me something childish, and even cowardly, in this complaint. . . .

In all the States I have seen, the Republican reconstructors did shamefully rob the people. In several of them they continue to do so. . . .

As to "intimidation," it is a serious mistake to imagine this exclusively a Democratic proceeding in the South. It has been practiced in the last three years quite as much, and even more rigorously, by the Republicans. The negroes are the most savage intimidators of all. In many localities which I visited, it was as much as a negro's life was worth to vote the Democratic ticket. . . . That there has also been Democratic intimidation is undeniable; but it does not belong to the Southern Republicans to complain of it.

Wherever one of these States has fallen under the control of Democrats, this has been followed by important financial reforms; economy of administration; and . . . by the restoration of peace and good-will. . . .

The misconduct of the Republican rulers in all these States has driven out of their party the great mass of the white people, the property-owners, tax-payers, and persons of intelligence and honesty. At first a considerable proportion of these were ranged on the Republican side. Now . . . the Republican party consists almost exclusively of the negroes and the Federal office-holders. . . .

Thus has been perpetuated what is called the "color-line" in politics, the Democratic party being composed of the great mass of the whites, including almost the entire body of those who own property, pay taxes, or have intelligence; while the Republican party is composed almost altogether of the negroes, who are, as a body, illiterate, without property, and easily misled by appeals to their fears, and to their gratitude to "General Grant," who is to them the embodiment of the Federal power.

This division of political parties on the race or color-line has been a great calamity to the Southern States.

It had its origin in the refusal of the Southern whites, after the war, to recognize the equal political rights of the blacks; and their attempts, in State legislatures, to pass laws hostile to them. This folly has been bitterly regretted by the wiser men in the South. . . .

The color-line is maintained mostly by Republican politicians, but they are helped by a part of the Democratic politicians, who see their advantage in having the white vote massed upon their side. . . .

Inevitably in such cases there must be a feeling of hostility by the whites toward the blacks, and it is an evidence of the good nature of the mass of whites that, in the main, they conduct themselves toward the blacks kindly and justly. They concentrate their dislike upon the men who have misled and now misuse the black vote, and this I can not call unjust. It is commonly said, "The negroes are not to blame; they do not know any better."

On the other hand, as the feeling is intense, it is often undiscriminating, and includes the just with the unjust among the Republicans. . . . [It] will last just as long as the color-line is maintained, and as long as Republicans maintain themselves in power by the help of the black vote, and by Federal influence. . . .

There was, in those Southern States which I have visited, for some years after the war and up to the year 1868, or in some cases 1870, much disorder, and a condition of lawlessness toward the blacks — a disposition . . . to trample them underfoot, to deny their equal rights, and to injure or kill them on slight or no provocations. The tremendous change in the social arrangements of the Southern States required time as well as laws and force to be accepted. The Southern whites had suffered a defeat which was sore to bear, and on top of this they saw their slaves — their most valuable and cherished property — taken away and made free, and not only free, but their political equals. One needs to go into the far South to know what this really meant, and what deep resentment and irritation it inevitably bred. . . .

I believe that there was, during some years, a necessity for the interference of the Federal power to repress disorders and crimes which would otherwise have spread, and inflicted, perhaps, irretrievable blows on society itself. But, after all, I am persuaded time was the great and real healer of disorders, as well as differences. We of the North do not always remember that even in the farthest South there were large property interests, important industries, many elements of civilization which can not bear long-continued disorders; and, moreover, that the men of the South are Americans, like ourselves, having, by nature or long training a love of order and permanence, and certain, therefore, to reconstitute society upon the new basis prescribed to them, and to do it by their own efforts, so soon as they were made to feel that the new order of things was inevitable. . . .

No thoughtful man can examine the history of the last ten years in the South, as he may hear it on the spot and from both parties, without being convinced that it was absolutely necessary to the security of the blacks, and the permanent peace of the Southern communities, to give the negro, ignorant, poor, and helpless as he was, every political right and privilege which any other citizen enjoys. That he should vote and that he should be capable of holding office was necessary, I am persuaded, to make him personally secure, and, what is of more importance, to convert him from a *freedman* into a *free man*.

That he has not always conducted himself well in the exercise of his political rights is perfectly and lamentably true; but this is less his fault than that of the bad white men who introduced him to political life. But, on the other hand, the vote has given him what nothing else could give — a substantive existence; it has made him a part of the State. . . .

General manhood suffrage is undoubtedly a danger to a community where, as in these States, the entire body of ignorance and poverty has been massed by adroit politicians upon one side. . . .

But the moment the color-line is broken, the conditions of the problem are essentially changed. Brains and honesty have once more a chance to come to the top. The negro, whose vote will be important to both parties, will find security in that fact. No politician will be so silly as to encroach upon his rights, or allow his opponents to do so; and the black man appears to me to have a sense of respectability which will prevent him, unencouraged by demagogues, from trying to force himself into positions for which he is unfit. He will have his fair chance, and he has no right to more.

Whenever the Federal interference in all its shapes ceases, it will be found, I believe, that the negroes will not at first cast a full vote; take away petty Federal "organizers," and the negro, left face to face with the white man, hearing both sides for the first time; knowing by experience, as he will presently, that the Democrat is not a monster, and that a Democratic victory does not mean his reenslavement, will lose much of his interest in elections. . . .

Of course, as soon as parties are re-arranged on a sound and natural basis, the negro vote will re-appear; for the leaders of each party, the Whig or Republican and the Democrat, will do their utmost to get his vote, and therein will be the absolute security of the black man. I believe, however, that for many years to come, until a new generation arrives at manhood perhaps, and, at any rate, until the black man becomes generally an independent farmer, he will be largely influenced in his political affiliations by the white. He will vote as his employer, or the planter from whom he rents land, or the white man whom he most trusts, and with whom, perhaps, he deposits his savings, tells him is best for his own interest. . . . But, at any rate, he will vote or not, as he pleases. And it is far better for him that he should act under such influences than that his vote should be massed against the property and intelligence of the white people to achieve the purposes of unscrupulous demagogues. . . .

These are my conclusions concerning those Southern States which I have seen. If they are unfavorable to the Republican rule there, I am sorry for it.

QUESTIONS FOR READING AND DISCUSSION

1. What did Nordhoff mean by observing that southern whites "accept the situation"? What "fair chance" did they "have a right to ask of" northerners, and why had northerners "greatly failed" to grant it?
2. Nordhoff criticized southern Republicans as "unfair and unreasonable." Why? To what standards had they failed to conform?
3. To what extent, according to Nordhoff, were "negroes . . . the most savage intimidators of all"? What were the consequences of Republican rule in the South? Did Nordhoff believe Reconstruction was necessary and justifiable? Why?
4. How did Nordhoff believe order could be established in the South? In his opinion, what would happen to black voters when home rule was established in the South?

COMPARATIVE QUESTIONS

1. How do the views of former slaves expressed by white Mississippians in their state's Black Code differ from those of the Black Convention in Alabama? To what extent do the two documents express contrasting conceptions of freedom?
2. To what extent do Nordhoff's observations justify the Klan's campaign of terror against black Republicans like Hill? To what extent do Nordhoff's conclusions endorse the activities of Hill and other Republicans?
3. In what ways do Nordhoff's conclusions about the South differ from those of black and white southerners in the other documents in this chapter? What explains the differences?
4. Documents in this chapter provide evidence that Reconstruction profoundly challenged fundamental assumptions among northerners and southerners, whites and blacks. Judging from these documents, what assumptions were challenged, and how, if at all, did those assumptions change during Reconstruction?

ACKNOWLEDGMENTS

Chapter 1   Document 2. Excerpt from *Diario of Christopher Columbus's First Voyage to America, 1492-1493*, translated and edited by Oliver C. Dunn and James E. Kelley, Jr. Published by the University of Oklahoma Press, 1989. Reprinted by permission.

Document 4. Excerpt from *We People Here: Nahuatl Accounts of the Conquest of Mexico, Repertorium Columbianum, vol. 1*, by James Lockhart. Copyright © 1994 The Regents of the University of California. Reprinted by permission.

Chapter 2   Excerpt from *Robert Cole's World: Agriculture and Society in Early Maryland* edited by Lois Green Carr, Russell R. Menard, and Lorena S. Walsh. Copyright © 1991 by the University of North Carolina Press. Published for the Omohundro Institute of Early American History and Culture. Used by permission of the publisher.

Excerpt from *The Old Dominion in the Seventeenth Century: A Documentary History of Virginia, 1606-1689* by Warren M. Billings. Published for the Omohundro Institute of Early American History and Culture. Copyright © 1974 by the University of North Carolina Press. Used by permission of the publisher.

Chapter 3   Excerpt from *A Key Into the Language of America* edited by John J. Teunissen and Evelyn J. Hinz. Published by Wayne State University Press, 1973.

Chapter 6   Excerpt from *Adams Family Correspondence,* Volumes 1-2, edited by L. H. Butterfield, 193-202. Copyright © 1963 by the Massachusetts Historical Society. Reprinted by permission of the publisher.

Document 2. Excerpt from *Valley of the Six Nations* edited by Charles M. Johnson. The Champlain Society, 1964: 38-41. Reprinted by permission of the publisher.

Document 3. Excerpt from *The Journals of the Lewis and Clark Expedition. July 28-November 1, 1805*, volume 5 edited by Gary E. Moulton. Copyright © 1988 by the University of Nebraska Press. Reprinted by permission of the University of Nebraska Press.

Abolition movement, 173
  Brown's activities and, 220–223
  mob action against, 176–179
  pro-slavery argument against,
    204, 207
Adam and Eve narrative, Bible, 4–7
Adams, Abigail, 97–98
  on equality of women after the
    American Revolution ("Re-
    member the Ladies"), 100–101
  on the fighting in Massachusetts,
    99–100
  on Paine's *Common Sense*, 98
Adams, John, 97–98
  on the fight for independence,
    101–104
  on Paine's *Common Sense*, 98, 100
Advertisement for runaway slaves,
    73–77
Afonso, king of the Congo, 9–13
Africa
  Portuguese colonization of, 9–13
  slave trade in, 214
African Americans. *See also* Free
    blacks; Slaves; Slave women
  free labor system and, 181
  Ku Klux Klan violence against,
    250–252
  poor white farmer on, 210–211
  rights of, 148. *See also* Civil rights
    movement
  Union League for voters and, 251
Agriculture. *See also* Farmers; Planta-
    tions; Tobacco farms
  free labor system and, 182–183
  Indians and, 50
Scottish immigrant's description of,
    71–72
  slavery in the South and, 196
Alabama, black convention in,
    246–249
Algonqian Indians, 1622 uprising by,
    27–30
Almanac, Franklin's, 66–71
America. *See* Ancient America; New
    World

American Indians. *See* Indians; In-
    dian women; *specific tribes*
American Revolution, 93–112
  Abigail Adams on the fighting in
    Massachusetts during, 99–100
  Brant's appeals to British allies
    during, 108–112
  Fourth of July address invoking
    ideals of, 148–151
  John Adams on the fight for inde-
    pendence in, 101–104
  Paine's case for independence in
    Common Sense and, 93–97
  soldier's memoir of service in,
    104–108
Ancient America, 1–10
Animals, Díaz del Castillo on Mexi-
    can use of, 19, 20
Anti-Federalists, 127
Apprentices, black codes on, 244
Arthur (thief and rapist in colonial
    New England), 60–64
Atlanta, Sherman's capture of,
    230–237
Aust, John, 37, 40

Bacon, Nathaniel, 39–41
Banking, Jackson on, 166–167
Bank of the United States, 166–167
Barrow, Bennet, 196–199
Bellows, Henry W., 181–184
Berkeley, William, 39
Bible, 205, 222
  Christian origin narrative in, 4–7
Bishop, Bridget, 56–59
Black codes, 242
  in Mississippi, 242–245
Black conventions, 242
  in Alabama, 246–249
Blacks. *See* African Americans; Free
    blacks
Boston
  massacre by the British in, 78–82
  Tea Party in, 82–85
  Washington on impending crisis
    and support for, 89, 90

Boudinot, Elias, 169, 170–172
Brant, Joseph, 108–112
Broadside, of a slave's confession of
    theft and rape, 60–64
Brown, John, 220
    speech before the court, 222–223
    Townsley on the Pottawatomie
        massacre of, 220–222

Calhoun, James M., 235–236
California gold rush, 181, 191–195
Cherokee Indians, removal of,
    168–172
Chesapeake Bay settlement, 27–42
    Opechancanough's 1622 uprising
        in, 27–30
    testimony on sex and race rela-
        tions in, 36–38
    tobacco planter's inventory in,
        31–36
Child-rearing, Manning on, 133
Children
    of Indians, 49, 50
    of poor white farmers, 209
    of Shoshone Indians, 156–157, 158
Christianity. See also Religion
    Columbus on converting Indians
        to, 14, 17
    Second Great Awakening in Ken-
        tucky and, 159–163
Civil rights movement
    black conventions and, 246–249
    Northern Republican's report on
        Reconstruction and, 253–256
Civil War, 224–241
    Emancipation Proclamation and,
        225–226
    former slave on the aims of,
        227–230
    Gettysburg Address and, 226
    Lincoln on his war aims, 224
    Sherman's views of war in,
        230–237
    Whitman on wounded soldiers in,
        238–241
Clark, William, 155
Clothing
    of American soldiers in the Revo-
        lutionary War, 106

Columbus on Indians' use of,
    16–17
Díaz del Castillo on Mexican use
    of, 18, 19, 20
Franklin's *Poor Richard's Almanac*
    on, 67–68
of Indians, 50–51, 157
tobacco planter's inventory of,
    33–34
Cocke, Thomas, 36, 38
Cole, Robert, 31–36
Colonies in Africa, and Portugal,
    9–13
Colonies in America, 27–92. *See also*
    specific colonies
advertisement for runaway slaves
    in, 73–77
Bacon's rebellion in, 39–41
Boston Massacre and reactions of
    colonists in, 78–82
Boston Tea Party protest and,
    82–85
broadside of a slave's confession
    of theft and rape in, 60–64
court records of crime in, 52–56
crowd actions against Tories in,
    86–89
in the eighteenth century, 60–77
Franklin's *Poor Richard's Almanac*
    on life in, 64–69
Opechancanough's 1622 uprising
    in, 27–30
Paine's case for independence in
    Common Sense and, 93–97
Scottish immigrant in, 69–73
in the seventeenth century, 27–59
testimony on sex and race rela-
    tions in, 36–38
tobacco planter's inventory in,
    31–36
Washington on impending crisis
    in, 89–92
Winthrop's Arbella sermon in,
    43–47
witch trials in, 56–59
Colton, Walter, 191–195
Columbus, Christopher, 14
    diary of, on first voyage, 14–17
Committees of public safety, 104

Common Sense (Paine), 93
  Abigail Adams on, 98
  excerpt from, 94–97
  John Adams on, 98, 100
Confessions of Nat Turner, The, 200–204
Congo, Portuguese colonization of,
    9–13
Congress, 218
  Hamilton's report on manufactur-
    ers to, 138–142
  hearings on Ku Klux Klan vio-
    lence held by, 250
  Jackson on power of, 165
  Warren on powers of, 129
Conservatives, and black conven-
    tions, 248
Constitution, 138, 228
  Davis's support for slavery and,
    218–219
  Douglass's opposition to slavery
    and, 215–217
  Fourth of July address invoking,
    150
  Jackson on federal power under,
    164–1666
  Lincoln's Civil War aims and, 225
  Madison on federal government
    and, 121–126
  Warren's opposition to, 126–130
"Constitution of the United States,
    The: Is It Pro-Slavery or Anti-
    Slavery?" (Douglass), 215–217
Continental Congress, 97
  John Adams on the work of,
    101–102
Cortés, Hernando, 17, 23–24
Cotton
  Columbus on Indians' use of, 15,
    16
  Díaz del Castillo on Mexican use
    of, 18, 20
  Hamilton's report on manufactur-
    ers and, 140
  poor white farmers and, 208–211
  slavery and, 196, 229
Courts
  crime records in, 52–56
  crowd actions against Tories and,
    86–89
  witch trial in, 56–59

Creation myths. *See* Origin narratives
Crime
  black codes on, 243, 246
  colonial court records of, 52–56
  crowd actions against Tories and,
    86–89
  Hewes's memoir of a British offi-
    cial and, 82–83
  slave's confession of theft and
    rape, 60–64
  witch trials and, 56–59
Crow Indians, 158
Curtin, Jeremiah, 1
Customs, Indian, 48–53

Davis, Jefferson, 218–219
Declaration of Independence, 98
  John Adams on, 102, 104–105
  Lincoln on slavery and, 213
"Declaration of Sentiments" (Stan-
    ton), 185–188
Democracy, Madison on, 125–126
Democratic party
  Kansas-Nebraska Act and, 212
  Northern Republican's report on
    Reconstruction and, 254,
    255–256
Díaz del Castillo, Bernal, 17–21
Discrimination. *See* Racial discrimi-
    nation
Disease
  among Mexicans, and Spanish ex-
    ploration, 25–26
  among Shoshone Indians, from
    Europeans, 157–158
Divorce, Seneca Falls Declaration on,
    186
Douglas, Stephen A., 212
Douglass, Frederick, 215–217

Economy
  Hamilton's report on manufactur-
    ers and, 138–142
  Jackson's farewell address on,
    165–168
Education
  black conventions on, 249
  Ku Klux Klan violence against
    blacks and, 252

Manning on free government and, 134

Rush on mode of, 113–116

of women, 135–138, 173–174

Emancipation Proclamation, 224, 225–226

Employment
black codes on, 243–244
Franklin's *Poor Richard's Almanac* on, 66–67
Hamilton's report on manufacturers and, 138–139, 140–141

England. *See* Great Britain

European settlers. *See also* New Spain
disease spread by, 157–158
in the New World, 1, 13–26

Eve, in creation narrative, 4–7

Faction, Madison on, 122–123

Family of poor white farmers, 209–211

Farewell addresses
of Jackson (1837), 164–168
of Washington (1796), 143–147

Farmers. *See also* Agriculture
farmer's view of his wife, 188–190
Indians lands used by, 148
inventory of possessions of, 31–36
poor white farmers in the South, 208–211

Farnham, Eliza, 188–190

Federal government
Hamilton's report on manufacturers and, 138–142
Indian removal and, 169
Jackson on power in, 164–168
John Adams on the formation of, 102–103
Madison on the Constitution and, 121–126
Manning on free government and, 132–135
Paine's arguments in *Common Sense* on, 96–97
Warren on form of, 127–128
Washington's Farewell Address on, 145–146

Federalist Papers, 121–126

Federalists, 138–139

Finance
Franklin's *Poor Richard's Almanac* on, 64–69
Jackson on federal power over, 166–167

Firearms, black codes on use of, 245

Florentine Codex, 21–26

Food
of American soldiers in the Revolutionary War, 106–107
Díaz del Castillo on Mexican, 18, 20
gold rush in California and, 193
of poor white farm family, 209
of Shoshone Indians, 155–156
tobacco planter's inventory of, 33, 35

Fourth of July address, 148–151

France, 150, 153

Franklin, Benjamin, 64–65
Poor Richard's Almanac of, 65–69

Free blacks
black codes and, 242–245
black conventions and, 246–249
Ku Klux Klan violence against, 250–252
Northern Republican's report on Reconstruction and, 255–256
Reconstruction and, 242

Freedmen. *See* Free blacks

Free government, Manning on, 132–135

Free labor system, 181
Bellows's criticism of, 181–184

Garrison, William Lloyd, 215

Gender relations
farmer's view of his wife, 188–190
Grimké on women's rights and, 174–175
race relations in seventeenth-century Virginia and, 36–38
seventeenth-century court records of crime involving, 53, 54–56

Genesis, 4–7

Georgia, Indian removal in, 168–172

Germain, Lord, Brant's appeal to, 108, 109–110

Gettysburg Address (Lincoln), 224, 226

Gold
  Columbus on Indians' use of, 15, 17
  Díaz del Castillo on Mexican, 19, 20
  Mexican description of Spanish taking of, 24, 26
Gold rush, California, 181, 191–195
Government. *See* Federal government; State government
Great Britain, 149–150, 153
  Boston Massacre and colonists' feelings about, 78–82
  Boston Tea Party protest and, 82–85
  Brant's appeals to, 108–112
  crowd actions against loyalists to, 86–89
  Hewes's memoir of arrogance of officers of, 82–85
  Paine's case for independence in *Common Sense* and, 93–97
  poor and laboring classes in, 207 *
  Washington on impending crisis with, 89–92
Greeley, Horace, 224, 225
Grimké, Sarah, 173–175
Guns
  black codes on use of, 245
  Indians' use of, 50
  tobacco planter's inventory of, 33, 35

Haldimand, Frederick, 110–112
Halleck, Henry W., 21–232
Hamilton, Alexander, 138–142
Hammond, James Henry, 204–208
Harpers Ferry, Virginia, attack, 220
Harrison, William H., 151
Hewes, George R. T., 82–85
Hill, Elias, 250–252
Hood, J. B., 232–235
Hospitals, Whitman on wounded soldiers in, 238–241
Houses, of poor white farmers, 209
Huitzilopochtli, 24
Human sacrifice, Mexican, 18, 19
Hutchinson, Thomas, 83, 86

Immigration
  Hamilton's report on manufacturers and, 141
  Scottish immigrant's life in Pennsylvania, 69–73
Indians. *See also specific tribes*
  appeals to British allies from, 108–112
  Bacon's statement on, 40–41
  before 1492, 1
  Columbus on, during his first voyage, 13–17
  court records of crime involving, 55
  Jefferson on abilities of, 119
  Jefferson's policy toward, 148, 151–154
  Lewis's description of, 155–158
  loss of lands and removal of, 168–172
  origin narratives of, 1–4
  slave's confession of theft and rape and, 60–64
  Washington on relations with, 90
  William's observations on, 48–52
Indian women
  Díaz del Castillo on Mexican, 19
  Mexican description of Spanish conquest of Mexico and, 26
  in Seneca origin narrative, 1–4
  William's observations on, 49, 50
"Influence of the Trading Spirit upon the Social and Moral Life of America, The" (Bellows), 181–184
Insurrections, slave, 200–204
Inventory of a tobacco planter, 31–36

Jackson, Andrew, 164
  on the Cherokee Nation, 168–172
  farewell address (1837) of, 164–168
  on power in the federal government, 164–168
Jamestown, Virginia, 27, 29
João III, king of Portugal, 9–13
Jefferson, Thomas, 117, 148, 205
  address to Mandan Indians by, 151, 153–154

on attitudes toward slaves,
117–120
Fourth of July address invoking,
150
Indian policy of, 148, 151–154
on the influence of slavery,
120–121
Louisiana Purchase and, 152–153
Jobs. *See* Employment; Workers

Kansas-Nebraska Act, Lincoln on,
212–215
Kentucky, Second Great Awakening
in, 159–163
Kentucky Revival, The (McNemar),
159–163
King James Bible, 4–7
Ku Klux Klan, 250–252

Labor. *See* Workers
Land policy, and Indian removal,
168–172
Language, Indian, 48–53
Laws and legislation
black codes in the South and,
242–245
Paine's arguments in *Common
Sense* on, 96–97
Rush on education and, 116
Washington's Farewell Address
on, 145
Winthrop's Arbella sermon on,
44–47
Legends. *See* Origin narratives
"Letter to an English Abolitionist"
(Hammond), 204–208
Letters on the Equality of the Sexes
(Grimké), 173–175
Lewis, Meriwether, 155–158
Liberia, 213
Lincoln, Abraham, 181
Civil War aims of, 225
Emancipation Proclamation of,
225–226
Gettysburg Address of, 226
on the Kansas-Nebraska Act,
212–215
Long, John ("Jack"), 36–37
Louisiana, 229
Louisiana Purchase, 152–153

Lovejoy, Elijah, 176–179
Loyalists, crowd actions against,
86–89
Lynching of African Americans, during Reconstruction, 24, 252

McNemar, Richard, 159–163
Madison, James, 121
on government and the Constitution, 121–126
Magna Carta, 96
Malcolm, John, 82–83
Mandan Indians, 156
Jefferson's address to, 151,
153–154
Manning, William, 132–135
Manufacturing, Hamilton's report
on, 138–142
Markets
Díaz del Castillo on Mexican,
20–21
gold rush in California and, 193
Marriage
black codes on, 243
farmer's view of his wife,
188–190
Grimké on women's rights and,
174–175
Seneca Falls Declaration on, 186
seventeenth-century court records
of crime involving, 54, 55
among Shoshone Indians,
156–157
between slaves, 198
Martin, Joseph Plumb, 104–108
Maryland. *See* Chesapeake Bay settlement
Mason, Priscilla, 135, 137–138
Massachusetts, 129
Abigail Adams on the fighting in,
99–100
Boston Massacre in, 78–82
Boston Tea Party protest in,
82–85
crowd actions against Tories in,
86–89
debate in, about ratification of the
Constitution, 126
Franklin's *Poor Richard's Almanac*
in, 64–69

Massachusetts *(continued)*
  Hewes's memoir of British arrogance in, 82–85
  slave's confession of theft and rape in, 60–64
Mather, Cotton, 56
Men. *See also* Gender relations
  education of, 137
  Seneca Falls Declaration on history of, 186–187
Metcalfe, Deborah, 61, 63
Mexico
  Díaz del Castillo on the conquest of, 17–21
  Mexican description of the conquest of, 21–26
Military, Warren on need for, 128–129
Mining, and gold rush, 181, 191–195
Minorities. *See also* African Americans; Indians; Indian women
  gold rush in California and, 194
Missionaries, in Africa, 9
Mississippi
  black codes in, 242–245
  poor white farmers in, 208–211
Missouri Compromise, 213, 214
Mobs
  anti-abolitionist, 176–179
  against Tories, 86–89
"Model of Christian Charity, A" (Winthrop), 44–47
Mohawk Indians, 108–112
Monarchy, Paine's arguments against, 96–97
Money management, Franklin's *Poor Richard's Almanac* on, 65
Montezuma, 18, 19, 20, 23–24
Mulattos
  black codes and, 242–245
  testimony on sex and race relations between a white woman and, 36–38
Myths. *See* Origin narratives

Nahuatl language, 21, 23
Native Americans. *See* Indians; *specific tribes*
New England, 43
  court records of crime in, 52–56

slave's confession of theft and rape in, 60–64
William's observations on Indians of, 48–52
Winthrop's Arbella sermon in, 43–47
witch trials in, 56–59
New Spain, 14, 158
  Díaz del Castillo on the conquest of, 17–21
  Mexican description of Spaniards in, 21–26
Newspapers, advertisement for runaway slaves in, 73–77
New World, 9–17. *See also* New Spain
  Columbus on, during his first voyage, 13–17
  European settlers in, 1, 9
Nordhoff, Charles, 253–256
North. *See also* New England
  African Americans in, 210–211
  colonies in, 43–59
  Reconstruction and, 242
  Republican view of Reconstruction and, 253–256
  slavery and, 117, 218
  William's observations on Indians in, 48–52
North America. *See* New World
Notes on the State of Virginia (Jefferson), 117–121

Observations on the New Constitution (Warren), 127–130
Ohio, 106
Oliver, Peter, 86–89
Oliver, Thomas, 87
Olmsted, Frederick Law, 208–211
Opechancanough, 27–30
Origin narratives, 1
  Christian, 4–7
  Seneca Indian, 1–4

Paine, Thomas, 93
  Common Sense by, 93, 94–97
  reactions to writings of, 98, 100
Pennsylvania
  Rush on mode of education in, 113–116
  Scottish immigrant's life in, 69–73

Philadelphia, women's education in, 135–138

Plantations. *See also* Tobacco farms
  inventory of possessions on, 31–36
  rules for slaves on, 196–199
  Scottish immigrant's life on, 69–73

Political parties. *See also specific parties*
  Northern Republican's report on Reconstruction and, 254–255

Politics, and black conventions, 246–249

Poor Richard's Almanac (Franklin), 64–69

Portugal, Congo colony of, 9–13

Pottawatomie, Kansas, massacre, 220–222

Poverty
  laboring classes in Great Britain and, 207
  white farmers in the South and, 208–211

Prejudice. *See also* Racial discrimination
  black convention on, 247
  Jefferson on, 118
  Rush on mode of education and, 114

Property ownership
  black codes on, 242–243
  Boston Massacre and, 79–80
  Indian removal and, 169–170
  Madison on, 122–123
  tobacco planter's inventory of, 31–36

Puritans, 43
  court records of crime and, 52–56
  Winthrop's Arbella sermon and, 43–47
  William's observations on Indians and, 48
  witch trials and, 56–59

Race
  Jefferson on, 117–121
  Northern Republican's report on Reconstruction and, 254, 255
  sex relations in seventeenth-century Virginia and, 36–38

Racial discrimination
  black conventions on, 249
  Northern Republican's report on Reconstruction and, 255, 257

Raney, Jim, 251

Rape, slave's confession of, 60–64

Rebellions
  Boston Tea Party, 82–85
  colonists' support for, 93
  crowd actions against Tories and, 86–89
  in seventeenth-century Virginia, 39–41
  slave insurrections and, 163–167

Reconstruction, 242–256
  black codes during, 242–245
  black conventions during, 246–249
  Ku Klux Klan violence during, 250–252
  Northern Republican's report on, 253–256

Religion. *See also* Christianity; Puritans
  Columbus on Indians and, 14–15, 17
  court records of crime regarding, 52–53, 54, 55
  Indian beliefs and, 51
  Mexican, 20, 24
  Rush on mode of education and, 114–115
  Scottish immigrant's letter on, 72
  slave's confession of theft and rape and, 64
  slave insurrection and, 200–204
  Washington's Farewell Address on, 146
  Winthrop's Arbella sermon on, 43–47
  witch trials and, 56–59
  women's education and, 137–138

Report on the Subject of Manufacturers (Hamilton), 138

Republic, Madison on the form of, 125–126

Republican party
  black conventions and, 246, 247–248
  black voters in, 250
  ideals of the Revolution and, 148

Republican party *(continued)*
  Northern Republican's report on
    Reconstruction and, 253–256
  Union League for the black vote
    and, 251
Revival, religious, in Kentucky,
  159–163
Revolts. *See also* Rebellions
  by slaves, 200–204
Revolutionary War. *See* American
  Revolution
Rights
  of African Americans, 148,
    246–249. *See also* Civil rights
    movement
  Fourth of July address invoking,
    149–150
  of Indians, 148
  Madison on, 122–125
  of slaves, 214
  of women. *See* Women's rights
Runaway slaves, advertisement for,
  73–77
Ross, 168, 169–170
Rush, Benjamin, 113–116

Sacajawea, 156
Sahagún, Bernardino de, 21–26
Salem, witch trials in, 56–59
Schools. *See* Education
Scotland, immigration from, 69–73
Second Great Awakening, 159–163
Seneca Falls Declaration, 185–188
Seneca Indian origin narrative,
  1–4
Senate. *See* Congress
Sermon, Puritan, 43–47
Servants on a tobacco plantation, 31
Sexual relations, in seventeenth-cen-
  tury Virginia, 36–38
Sherman, William Tecumseh, 230–237
Shoshone Indians, Lewis's descrip-
  tion of, 155–158
Sioux Indians, 157
Slavery
  abolition movement and, 173,
    176–179, 204, 207, 220–223
  Davis's arguments for, 218–219
  Douglass's arguments against,
    215–217

Emancipation Proclamation and,
  224, 225–226
gold rush in California and,
  194–195
Hammond's arguments for,
  204–206
Jefferson on the influence of,
  117–121
Lincoln on the Kansas-Nebraska
  Act and, 212–215
similarity of black codes to, 242
in the South, 117, 196–199,
  213–214, 218, 227
Slaves
  aims of the Civil War and, 227–230
  confession of theft and rape by,
    60–64
  Díaz del Castillo on Mexican, 20
  emancipation of, 224, 225–226, 227
  freed. *See* Free blacks
  Jefferson on attitudes toward,
    117–121
  marriage among, 198
  monetary value of, 227
  plantation rules for, 196–199
  poor white southern farmers on,
    209–210
  insurrections by, 200–204
  rights of, 214
  runaway, advertisement for, 73–77
  testimony on sex and race rela-
    tions between a white woman
    and, 36–38
Slave trade, Lincoln on, 214
Slave women
  Grimké on, 175
  white women and impact of, 175
Smallpox, 25, 157
Social conditions
  Franklin's *Poor Richard's Almanac*
    on, 64–69
  free labor system and, 181–184
  gold rush in California and,
    192–194
  seventeenth-century court records
    of crime and, 52–56
  sex and race relations in seven-
    teenth-century Virginia and,
    36–38
  witch trials and, 56–59

South
    Bacon's rebellion in, 39–41
    black codes in, 242–245
    black conventions in, 246–249
    colonies in, 27–42
    Ku Klux Klan violence against
        blacks in, 250–252
    Northern Republican's report Re-
        construction in, 253–256
    Opechancanough's 1622 uprising
        in, 27–30
    poor white farmers in, 208–211
    Reconstruction and, 242
    sex and race relations in the sev-
        enteenth century in, 36–38
    slave insurrections in, 200–204
    slavery in, 117, 196–199, 213–214,
        218, 227
    tobacco planter's inventory in,
        31–36
South Carolina, 210
    advertisement for runaway slaves
        in, 73–77
    Continental Congress and,
        102–103
    Ku Klux Klan in, 250–252
Spain, conquest of the New World
        by, 153. *See also* New Spain
"Specimen Days" (Whitman),
        238–241
Sproat, Reverend, 135–136
Stanton, Elizabeth Cady, 185
    "Declaration of Sentiments" of,
        185–188
State government
    black codes enacted by, 242
    black conventions and,
        246–247
    Franklin's *Poor Richard's Almanac*
        on, 65–66, 68
    Madison on, 125–126
Suffolk County court records, 52–56
Suffrage. *See* Voting rights

Taxation
    Boston Massacre and, 79–80
    Boston Tea Party protest against,
        82–85
    Franklin's *Poor Richard's Almanac*
        on, 65–66, 68

Washington on impending crisis
        involving, 89–90
Tenochtitlán, 18–21
Theft
    broadside of a slave's confession
        of, 60–64
    court records, 53
    slave's confession of, 60–64
Thomson, Alexander, 69–73
*Thoughts upon the Mode of Education
        Proper in a Republic* (Rush),
        113–116
Tobacco farm, planter's inventory
        on, 31–36
Tories, 93
    crowd actions against, 86–89
    tea trade and, 85
Townsley, James, 220–222
Trade
    gold rush in California and, 193
    Indians and, 28, 52, 152
    in slaves, 214
    tea importing and, 83–85
Turner, Nat, 200–204

Union League, 251

Van Buren, Martin, 164
Violence
    anti-abolitionist mob and,
        176–179
    Ku Klux Klan violence and,
        250–252
    Northern Republican's report on
        Reconstruction and, 255
Virginia
    advertisement for runaway slaves
        in, 73–77
    American Revolution and, 100,
        101
    Bacon's rebellion in, 39–41
    Jefferson on racial attitudes in,
        117–121
    Opechancanough's 1622 uprising
        in, 27–30
    slave insurrection in, 200–204
    Washington on impending crisis
        and support from, 89–92
Voting rights
    black conventions and, 246–249

Voting rights *(continued)*
  for free blacks, and Reconstruction, 242, 250
  Ku Klux Klan violence against blacks and, 250, 252
  Northern Republican's report on Reconstruction and, 255–256
  pro-slavery argument and, 206
  Seneca Falls Declaration on, 187–188
  Union League for the black vote and, 251

Wallace, Mary, 135, 136–137
Wallace, S. A., 251
War, Sherman's views of, 230–237
Warren, Joseph, 78, 83
  oration on the Boston Massacre by, 78–82
Warren, Mercy Otis, 126–130
Washington, George, 89–90, 138
  on the crisis in the colonies before the Revolution (1774), 90–92
  farewell address (1796) of, 143–147
  John Adams on, 102
Waterhouse, Edward, 27–30
Watkins, Katherine, 36–38
Weapons
  black codes on use of, 245
  Columbus on Indians' use of, 14, 16
  Díaz del Castillo on Mexican use of, 19
  Mexican description of Spanish use of, 21–22, 25
  of Shoshone Indians, 157
  tobacco planter's inventory of, 33, 35
Wendover, Peter, 148–151
Whately, Phyllis (Phillis Wheatly), 119
Whig party, 181, 212, 255
White Americans
  black codes and, 242, 246, 246
  black conventions on suffrage and, 246–249
  Jefferson on racial attitudes of, 117–121

Ku Klux Klan violence against blacks and, 250–252
Northern Republican's report Reconstruction and, 253–256
poor white farmers in the South, 208–211
Reconstruction and, 242
slave insurrections and, 200
women slaves and, 175
Whitman, Walt, 238–241
Williams, Roger, 48–52
Winthrop, John, 43
  Arbella sermon of, 44–47
Witch trials, 56–59
Women. *See also* Gender relations; Indian women; Slave women
  Abigail Adams and status of, 101
  crowd actions against Tories organized by, 88–89
  education of, 135–138, 173–174
  free labor system and, 181
  gold rush in California and, 192
  Rush on mode of education of, 116
  seventeenth-century court records of crime involving, 53, 54–56
  among Shoshone Indians, 156–157, 158
  as slaves, 175
  slave's confession of rape, 60–64
  witch trials and, 56–59
Women's rights
  "Declaration of Sentiments" on, 185–188
  Grimké on, 173–175
Workers
  black codes on, 243–244
  Díaz del Castillo on Mexican, 19, 20
  Hamilton's report on manufacturers and, 138–139
  pro-slavery argument on slaves as, 206
  Winthrop's Arbella sermon on, 46

Yeomen, 31
Young Ladies Academy of Philadelphia, 135–138